Sufism – The Living Tradition

Sufism

The Living Tradition

Sufi Epistemology Encounters Modernity in the *Tariqa* of Shaykh 'Abd al-Qadir al-Sufi

Riyad Asvat

Sufism, the Living Tradition

First Edition: Madinah Press 2015

Madinah Press is an imprint of Madinah Media

Author:	Riyad Asvat
Editor:	Shaykh Abdalhaqq Bewley
Typeset by:	Abdassamad Clarke
Cover design by:	Abdassamad Clarke

The photo on the cover is of Shaykh Dr. 'Abd al-Qādir al-Sufi

A catalogue record of this book is available from the British Library.

ISBN-13	hardback:	978 0 646 92624-7
	paperback:	978-0-9953884-0-6

Printed and bound by Art Printing Works Sdn Bhd, Kuala Lumpur, Malaysia
And by Lightning Source

Contents

DEFINITIONS OF TERMS IN THE TITLES ix

INTRODUCTION 1

CHAPTER 1: THE CHAIN OF MASTERS 6
1. THE PROPHET MUḤAMMAD ﷺ (571-632) 8
2. ʿALĪ IBN ABĪ ṬĀLIB (600-661) 12
3. ḤASAN AL-BAṢRĪ (642-728) 13
4. ḤABĪB IBN MUḤAMMAD AL-ʿAJAMĪ (D. 737) 15
5. DĀWŪD AL-ṬĀʾĪ (D. 783) 16
6. MAʿRŪF AL-KARKHĪ (D. 815) 17
7. SARĪ AL-SAQAṬĪ (D. 837) 18
8. ABŪ AL-QĀSIM AL-JUNAYD (D. 908 OR 909 OR 910) 19
9. ABŪ BAKR AL-SHIBLĪ (861-946) 23
42. ʿABD AL-QĀDIR AL-SUFI 24
BIRR AT THE LEVEL OF *FUTUWWA* – THE INDIVIDUAL 26
BIRR AT THE LEVEL OF *JAMĀʿA* – THE COMMUNITY 28
BIRR AT THE LEVEL OF THE *UMMA* – HUMANITY 30

CHAPTER 2: SUFI EPISTEMOLOGY: THE SOURCES OF SUFI KNOWLEDGE 35
NAFS, *MULK* AND *ʿILM AL-ʿAQL* 42
RŪḤ, *MALAKŪT* AND *ʿILM AL-AḤWĀL* 44
SIRR, THE *JABARŪT* AND *ʿILM AL-ASRĀR* 45
FANĀʾ 46
BAQĀʾ 50

CHAPTER 3: SUFI EPISTEMOLOGY AND COSMOLOGY 53
COSMOGONY AND COSMOLOGY 54
TANZĪH AND *TASHBĪH* 60

Al-Nafas al-Raḥmānī 63
Waḥdat al-wujūd 64

Chapter 4: Sufi Epistemology and the Science of Unveiling 67
A New Paradigm for the 21st Century 67
The Rules of al-Junayd 68
1. Conformity with the *sharī'a* as revealed by God and practised by the Prophet ﷺ 68
2. Taking a shaykh of instruction (*tarbiya*) 72
3. Engaging in *dhikr* (invocation and remembrance of Allah) 76
4. Transformation of states (*aḥwāl*) into stations (*maqamāt*) 77
5. *Khalwa* – Withdrawal from the world through the invocation of the *al-ism al-a'ẓam* (the Supreme Name – Allah) under the supervision of a Sufi master 80
Sufism within its social and historical context 81
Sufi encounters with modernity 88
The colonial period 88
The neo-colonial period 90
Secularism 91
The influence of the *Murābiṭūn* on the *ṭarīqa* of Shaykh 'Abd al-Qādir 93

Chapter 5: The Sufi Deconstruction of Modern Science 102
Pre-Modern Worldview in Muslim Society 102
The Pre-Modern Worldview Giving Way to Modernism in European Society 107
The Epistemological Foundations of the Modern Worldview 112
The Philosophy of Social Science 116
Shaykh 'Abd al-Qādir's Views on Social Science and Social Theory 120

Chapter 6: Sufi Deconstruction of Modern Philosophy 126
Knowledge and Metaphysics 130
Ontology 135
Heideggerian Ontology 139
The Heideggerian Need 144
(a) The End of Metaphysics 144
(b) A philosophical history of Being 148

(c) Religion 155
Why Heidegger's Need Remained Unfulfilled 157

Chapter 7: From Islamic Philosophy to Sufism: Intellect to Presence 166
Knowledge by Presence 168
The ontological foundations for epistemology in Islamic Philosophy 170
Al-'ilm al-ḥuḍūrī: The Science of Presence 186
Philosophical reflections on *fanā'* 189
Praxis, *Himma* and *Maḥabba* 196

Chapter 8: The Sufi Path of Social Cohesion: Calling Things by Their Names 202
Secularism 204
Critique of Political Economy 207
Democracy and oligarchy 217
The New Nomos 221

Postface 230
Sufi Epistemology 230
Epistemologies of Modernity 233
The Search for New Epistemologies 236
Shaykh 'Abd al-Qādir's Contributions to Epistemology 237

Notes 241

Glossary 275

Bibliography 289

Index 303

DIAGRAMS

Diagram 1 – the Chain of Masters 7

Diagram 2 43

Diagram 3 109

Definitions of Terms in the Titles

EPISTEMOLOGY

Epistemology is the branch of philosophy dealing with theories of knowledge. This book is particularly focused on those aspects of epistemology which give an indication of what knowledge is and further how it is acquired in order to understand and interpret the meaning of reality.

MODERNITY

Modernity refers to the post-medieval period when modes of thought and practices were supported by rational methods in all fields of inquiry. Modernist epistemology took the form of mechanism, materialism and structuralism. The assumptions that underpinned modernization were secularism, individualism and a commitment to progress through science and technology. Development was defined as the control of nature for the benefit of human beings, according to the principle of liberal market forces. Modernity in turn led to the establishment of nationalism, capitalism and democracy and the end of the age of faith and the supremacy of the Catholic Church.

SUFISM

Sufism (known as *tasawwuf* in Arabic) is defined as "the science of the journey to the King [God]. ... It is taking the ancient way, the primordial path of direct experience of the Real [God]." This statement outlines the theory and practice of Sufism, that is, the goal of Sufism and the methodology by which that goal is reached. The goal is direct experience of the presence of God (through *dhawq* – which literally means taste). The methodology is the actual undertaking of the Sufi journey (*sulūk*) itself. In his classical review of Sufism, Abu Bakr al-Kalabādhī (d. 990) wrote that they "were only named Sufis because of their habit of wearing wool (*ṣūf*)." He added: "... they did not put on raiment soft to touch or beautiful to behold, to give delight to the soul, they only clothed themselves to hide their nakedness, contenting themselves with rough haircloth and coarse wool." The act of wearing wool signifies the act of having embarked on the journey (*sulūk*) towards direct experience of God and moreover, having made that the priority of one's life. This definition indicates that action is essential for achieving the goal of Sufism. Further, this direct knowledge, that is the experience of the Divine Presence, cannot be attained through transmission or mere book-learning.

ṬARĪQA

Ṭarīqa (lit. 'road') is the path of transformation of the self outlined by a Sufi master, or shaykh in Arabic. The shaykh guides the disciple on the journey (*sulūk*) of his or her spiritual development and experiences. The term is also synonymous with the English word "order", as in "religious order." It is therefore used to describe the various different mystical orders that exist under the broad umbrella of Sufism such as the Shādhilī, the Naqshabandī, the Mevlevi, the Chishti and the Tījānī to name but a few.

Introduction

This book aims to demonstrate that the modern idea defining epistemology as a branch of philosophy with only two sources for knowledge – reason and sense perception or, in other words, rationalism and empiricism – is wholly insufficient as a complete description of the true nature of knowledge. It will do this by focusing on the contrasting epistemological positions of modernity and Sufism and, in particular, on those aspects of knowledge which are required for the understanding and interpretation of the meaning of reality.

It is also clear that beliefs, and the knowledge employed in justifying and explaining them, lead to certain values and these values lead, in turn, to the institutionalization of specific types of behaviour. The institutions that develop around these values go on to form the core of the cultures and civilizations that grow up based on those beliefs. In this way, the beliefs inherent in Sufism, and the areas of Sufi knowledge that elucidate them, may well be able to contribute to social cohesion and harmony in the modern world.

The Sufi model we will be looking at, with regard to both theory and practice, is that of the contemporary Sufi Master, Shaykh 'Abd al-Qādir al-Sufi, and the conceptual framework adopted in order to examine these issues is existentialist, by which we mean that evidence for the validity of particular epistemic truths can only truly be ascertained from the actual results produced by the values and institutions that are born out of those truths. The community we will focus on is the one established in Cape Town by Shaykh 'Abd al-Qādir. The main institutions around which it functions are the market, the mosque, the college and the Murābiṭūn movement. Shaykh 'Abd al-Qādir's *zāwiya*, the place where he lives and holds his meetings, is a hive of constant activity and, based on this, our aim is to highlight the contemporary practical implications of the Sufi epistemology which underlies his work.

Shaykh 'Abd al-Qādir's family name is Dallas. He was born in Scotland on 7th October 1930. After attending school in Ayr, he went on to study at the Royal Academy of Dramatic Arts and the University of London. Following that, he worked as a contract writer and adapter for the BBC. He embraced Islam in Fes, Morocco in 1967 and then joined the Qādirī-Shādhilī-Darqāwī *ṭarīqa* as a student of Shaykh Muḥammad ibn al-Ḥabīb, who conferred on him the honorific title of al-Sufi and made him his representative (*muqaddam*) in Britain. After the death of Shaykh Muḥammad ibn al-Ḥabīb he went to his second master Shaykh Muḥammad al-Faytūrī Ḥamūda of Benghazi in Libya who put him into seclusion (*khalwa*). He emerged after having experienced *fanā'* (annihilation in God) and was given authorization (*idhn*) to guide others as a shaykh of *tarbiya* (Sufi Master of Instruction).

His authorization to lead the Qādirī-Shādhilī-Darqāwī *ṭarīqa* came from both his masters and he now has disciples throughout the world. Shaykh 'Abd al-Qādir is a playwright, novelist, author and essayist and, in 2001, the Universiti Sains Malaysia conferred on him an Honorary Doctorate of Literature for his literary output. Following the tradition of his predecessors, he has established mosques, schools, colleges, and taken care of the poor and needy. He also organizes regular conferences dealing with current issues of importance. The teachings of Shaykh 'Abd al-Qādir relate to: (i) Muslim minorities in non-Muslim countries; (ii) Western culture; (iii) Muslims in Muslim countries; and (iv) Sufism.

In Sufism knowledge is classified into five categories:[1] *'ilm al-'aql* (science of the intellect), *'ilm al-aḥwāl* (science of states), *'ilm al-asrār* (science of the innnermost consciousness), *fanā'* (annihilation of the self in God) and *baqā'* (subsistence in God, when the Sufi returns to mankind after annihilation in God). These five levels of knowledge correspond to the Prophetic tripartite classification of Islam into three branches: *islām* (outward practice), *īmān* (creed) and *iḥsān* (Sufism).[2] These, in turn, correspond with the three stages of the Sufi journey to God: *sharī'a*, *ṭarīqa* and *ḥaqīqa*. *Sharī'a* literally means "road" but in this usage refers to the legal parameters of Islam, the science of the outward. It implies the recognition of biological laws that function at different levels of existence. *Ṭarīqa* means "path" or "way" and refers to travelling on the Path to God under the guidance of a Sufi master. *Ḥaqīqa* means "reality" and refers to the inward illuminations of knowledge which flood the heart of the seeker on the Path. The highest levels of *ḥaqīqa* are *fanā'* and *baqā'*.

At this juncture it is necessary to acknowledge that, from the point of view of rationalism and empiricism, religious beliefs and experiences are unverifiable. Intellectual arguments in philosophy and science have not resolved the issue of the epistemic status of religious belief, nor can they. However, from the Sufi point of view, rationalism and empiricism only hold sway in the realm of the first category of knowledge, the science of the intellect (*'ilm al-'aql*), and only cover the physical dimensions of existence or, in Sufic terminology, the *mulk* (the domain of solid forms). For the

Sufi there are, however, other cosmological dimensions of human existence: the *malakūt* (the domain of unseen forms) and the *jabarūt* (the domain of Divine power). The human being is able to perceive the *malakūt* (the domain of unseen forms) by means of *ʿilm al-aḥwāl* (the science of states) and the *jabarūt* (kingdom of Divine power) by means of *ʿilm al-asrār* (the science of the innermost consciousness).

In order to overcome the circularity of the philosophical – rationalist and empiricist – argument, religionists have sought entry at various points into this closed circle. This is to be expected because, although religion and science are now considered mutually exclusive, it has to be borne in mind that pioneers of modern science, such as Copernicus, Galileo, Kepler, Newton and Boyle were deeply committed Christians.[3] Scientists have argued, for example, that modern physics leads to considerations of metaphysics and biology leads to considerations of teleology.[4] Ibn Rushd (1126-1198) argued in the twelfth century that there is harmony between philosophy and religion. Religion and philosophy (and by extension science) may be mutually exclusive but they are not antagonistic and Ibn Rushd saw religion and science as supplementing one another.[5] Similar arguments by later theologians such as Thomas Aquinas (1225-1274) and John Calvin (1509-1564) held that religion and faith have a rational validity that is independent of inductive reasoning and science.[6] Similarly Sufis have maintained that communicating spiritual truths acquired through *dhawq* (taste) is not empirically feasible, a little like the incommunicability of the taste of a strawberry. It is not possible to communicate to someone else exactly what a strawberry tastes like even though it is undeniable that strawberries have a very specific and identifiable taste.

In this book we will compare the quality of life produced by modern civilization and that produced by Islamic civilizations in which Sufism has played a key role, concentrating on the existential reality, in terms of values, institutions, culture and civilization, of those who adhere to the particular variety of epistemic truths that underpin both the former – modern civilization – and the latter – Islamic civilization. On the Islamic side this will be firmly grounded in the primary sources of Sufism: the Qur'ān, the *sunna* (normative practice of the Prophet Muḥammad) and the *ʿamal ahl al-Madīna* (the practice of the first three generations of Muslims in Madīna, the city in which Islam was first established).

In its encounter with modernity, Sufism has come under sustained attack, both physically and intellectually, from three groups: the colonizers of Muslim countries such as the British, French and Italians; neo-colonial regimes such as those of Egypt, Saudi Arabia and Turkey and; Muslim modernists.[7] In the book we will investigate the underlying causes of this conflict.

My hypothesis is, firstly, that the modernist worldview is based on epistemological foundations that are essentially different from those of Sufism and, secondly, that the limitations of modernist epistemology have been fully exploited in the modern world for political and economic reasons. We will examine the nature of the conflict between the epistemologies of modernity and Sufism and the possible limitations of the former and the potential transcendence of the latter. Then we will look at Shaykh ʿAbd al-Qādir's contribution to this matter: his criticism of modernist epistemology, his contribution towards the creation of a new epistemology, and the practical implications that this has for the world we live in.

Chapter 1

The Chain of Masters

There are three key characteristics that underpin Shaykh 'Abd al-Qādir's vision of Sufism: firstly that Sufism originated entirely from Islam; secondly, that the *sharīʿa* – the legal parameters of Islam – and Sufism are inextricably connected; and, thirdly, that politics constitutes an essential element of the *sharīʿa* and, therefore, that political activism is absolutely germane to Sufism. In order to ascertain whether these characteristics are truly representative of Sufism we will start by looking at the *silsila* (chain of transmission) of the branches of the Qādirī-Shādhilī-Darqāwī *ṭarīqa* of which he is the present shaykh. The term *silsila* refers to the chain of authoritative spiritual transmission from one master to another, going back to and originating with the Prophet ﷺ. There are two separate chains in the *silsila* of Shaykh 'Abd al-Qādir with a common thread linking the two. (See diagram 1 below.) Between the Prophet ﷺ and Shaykh 'Abd al-Qādir on the al-Fayṭūrī side of the *silsila* there are forty-two masters and, on the Ibn al-Ḥabīb side, forty-one.

We will look briefly at the first nine masters of the Ibn al-Ḥabīb side of the *silsila*. They represent the formative period of Sufism, extending from the time of the Prophet ﷺ (571-632) to the death of

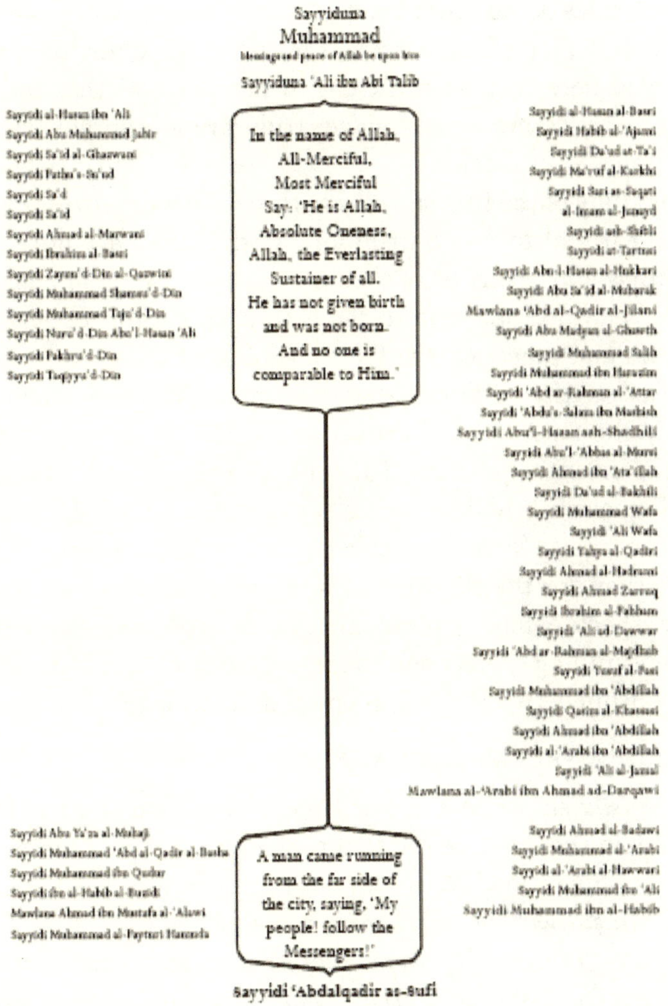

Sayyiduna
Muhammad
blessings and peace of Allah be upon him

Sayyiduna 'Ali ibn Abi Talib

In the name of Allah,
All-Merciful,
Most Merciful
Say: 'He is Allah,
Absolute Oneness,
Allah, the Everlasting
Sustainer of all.
He has not given birth
and was not born.
And no one is
comparable to Him.'

Sayyidi al-Hasan ibn 'Ali
Sayyidi Abu Muhammad Jabir
Sayyidi Sa'id al-Ghazwani
Sayyidi Fathu's-Su'ud
Sayyidi Sa'd
Sayyidi Sa'id
Sayyidi Ahmad al-Marwani
Sayyidi Ibrahim al-Basri
Sayyidi Zaynu'd-Din al-Qazwini
Sayyidi Muhammad Shamsu'd-Din
Sayyidi Muhammad Taju'd-Din
Sayyidi Nuru'd-Din Abu'l-Hasan 'Ali
Sayyidi Fakhru'd-Din
Sayyidi Taqiyyu'd-Din

Sayyidi al-Hasan al-Basri
Sayyidi Habib al-'Ajami
Sayyidi Da'ud at-Ta'i
Sayyidi Ma'ruf al-Karkhi
Sayyidi Sari as-Saqati
al-Imam al-Junayd
Sayyidi ash-Shibli
Sayyidi at-Tartusi
Sayyidi Abu-l-Hasan al-Hakkari
Sayyidi Abu Sa'id al-Mubarak
Mawlana 'Abd al-Qadir al-Jilani
Sayyidi Abu Madyan al-Ghawth
Sayyidi Muhammad Salih
Sayyidi Muhammad ibn Harazim
Sayyidi 'Abd ar-Rahman al-'Attar
Sayyidi 'Abdu's-Salam ibn Mashish
Sayyidi Abu'l-Hasan ash-Shadhili
Sayyidi Abu'l-'Abbas al-Mursi
Sayyidi Ahmad ibn 'Ata'illah
Sayyidi Da'ud al-Bakhili
Sayyidi Muhammad Wafa
Sayyidi 'Ali Wafa
Sayyidi Yahya al-Qadiri
Sayyidi Ahmad al-Hadrami
Sayyidi Ahmad Zarruq
Sayyidi Ibrahim al-Fahham
Sayyidi 'Ali ad-Dawwar
Sayyidi 'Abd ar-Rahman al-Majdhub
Sayyidi Yusuf al-Fasi
Sayyidi Muhammad ibn 'Abdillah
Sayyidi Qasim al-Khassasi
Sayyidi Ahmad ibn 'Abdillah
Sayyidi al-'Arabi ibn 'Abdillah
Sayyidi 'Ali al-Jamal
Mawlana al-'Arabi ibn Ahmad ad-Darqawi

Sayyidi Abu Ya'za al-Muhaji
Sayyidi Muhammad 'Abd al-Qadir al-Basha
Sayyidi Muhammad ibn Qaddur
Sayyidi ibn al-Habib al-Buzidi
Mawlana Ahmad ibn Mustafa al-'Alawi
Sayyidi Muhammad al-Faytouri Hamuda

A man came running
from the far side of
the city, saying, 'My
people! follow the
Messengers!'

Sayyidi Ahmad al-Badawi
Sayyidi Muhammad al-'Arabi
Sayyidi al-'Arabi al-Hawwari
Sayyidi Muhammad ibn 'Ali
Sayyidi Muhammad ibn al-Habib

Sayyidi 'Abdalqadir as-Sufi

Diagram 1[1]

al-Shiblī in 946, a period of 375 years. The tenth review will outline the teachings and methodology of the forty-second and latest master on the Ibn al-Ḥabīb side of the *silsila* who is Shaykh ʿAbd al-Qādir himself. Ideally it would be better to survey all the masters on both sides of the *silsila* but even a brief overview of them would be much too long for our present purpose. Hopefully the masters reviewed here will be sufficient to demonstrate that the three characteristics mentioned above truly are a common factor in traditional Sufic teaching.

This study of the first shaykhs of the *silsila* will provide a survey of the early history of Sufism and a brief summary of the lives, teachings and practices of the Sufi masters comprising it. It will also give an introduction to the following features of Sufism: its theories and practices, the five categories of the classification of knowledge, the different stages of spiritual development, and finally the Sufi's goal of arrival at the Divine Presence and the correspondent acquisition of direct knowledge of God. Through the above analysis it will become clear how this knowledge pervades the three major themes which characterize Shaykh ʿAbd al-Qādir's work. They are: the elimination of the split between the inner and outer aspects of human personality, knowledge of the methodology for determining correct behaviour (*uṣūl al-fiqh*), and affirming the relationship between political power and ideology.

1. The Prophet Muḥammad ﷺ (571-632)

The *silsila* shows that the originator of Sufism and the first in the link in the chain of the Qādirī-Shādhilī-Darqāwī *ṭarīqa* is the Prophet Muḥammad ﷺ himself. He did not, however, use the terms Sufism (*taṣawwuf*) or Sufi. The terms he did use instead were *iḥsān* and *muḥsinīn* from the Arabic root *ḥasana*, as exemplified in the following Qur'ānic verse: "*Those who do good* (*aḥsan*) *will have the best* (*al-ḥusnā*) *and more.*"[2] (10:26) *Iḥsān* is one of the three branches of Islam as indicated by the Prophet in the famous Ḥadīth Jibrīl,[3] the others being *īmān* (belief) and *islām* (outward practice). The Prophet's Companion 'Umar said that in reply to the Angel Gabriel's question "tell me about *iḥsān*" the Prophet ﷺ said: "It is to worship God as though you are seeing Him and even if you do not see Him, He sees you."[4]

A whole science developed around the term *iḥsān*, which came to be called *taṣawwuf*. The same is true of *īmān* and the science for understanding it came to be called *'aqīda* and *'ilm al-kalām*. The science for the application of the outward practices of Islam – the *sharī'a* – became known as *fiqh*. In Shaykh 'Abd al-Qādir's view, success in establishing the *sharī'a* depends on having correct beliefs (*'aqīda*) and spiritual development in *taṣawwuf* depends on the establishment of the *sharī'a*. The renowned jurist Mālik ibn Anas (711-795) stated that: "Anyone who practices *taṣawwuf* without applying the *fiqh* is a heretic, while anyone who applies the *fiqh* without practicing *taṣawwuf* is a deviant. Whoever combines the two achieves realization."[5] The Mālikī scholar, jurist and Sufi, Aḥmad Zarrūq (1442-1493) stated that the position of *taṣawwuf* in respect to the *dīn* (religion) is like that of the spirit in respect to the body. He also said that about two thousand aspects of Sufism have been defined, delineated and explained but all of them are facets of one thing, that is, a person's sincerity in turning to God.

In Abū Bakr al-Kalābādhī's (d. 990s) survey of Sufis and Sufism, *The Doctrine of the Sufis* (*Kitab al-ta'arruf li-madhhab ahl al-taṣawwuf*), he discusses the meaning of the words 'to worship God as though you are seeing Him'. The discussion centers on the following Qur'ānic passage:

> *When Mūsā [Moses] came to Our appointed time and his Lord spoke to him, he said, 'My Lord, show me Yourself so that I may look at You!' He said, 'You will not see Me but look at the mountain. If it remains firm in its place then you will see Me.' But when his Lord manifested Himself to the mountain, He*

crushed it flat and Mūsā fell unconscious to the ground. When he regained consciousness he said, 'Glory be to You! I turn in repentance to You and I am the first of the believers.' (7:143)[6]

Al-Kalābādhī explained that the Sufis are agreed that:

> Vision (of God) is possible through the intellect, and obligatory through the hearing.[7] As for its being intellectually possible, this is because God exists and everything which exists may [logically speaking] be seen. For God has implanted in us vision. And if this vision of God had not been possible, then the petition of Moses, *'O Lord, show Thyself to me, that I may look upon Thee'*, would have been (evidence of) ignorance and unbelief. Moreover, when God made the vision dependent on the condition that the mountain should abide firm – for He says, *'And if it abide firm in its place, then shalt thou see Me'* – and seeing also that its abiding firm would have been intellectually possible, if God had made it firm – it necessarily follows that the vision that was dependent on this was intellectually permissible and possible.[8]

Al-Kalābādhī then produces evidence from the hadiths[9] (sayings of the Prophet ﷺ) asserting that vision of the Divine is a reality and that it is necessary to believe that it is true.[10] In his examination of this issue al-Kalābādhī states that whilst vision of God is an established fact, it is conditional upon the annihilation (*fanā'*) of the experiencing locus of the subject. This is necessary because, as the Qur'ān says: "*Eyesight cannot perceive Him but He perceives eyesight. He is the All-Penetrating, the All-Aware.*"[11] Shaykh ʿAbd al-Qādir says that God took Moses to the station of *maʿrifa* by stating, "*You will not see Me but look at the mountain*". *Maʿrifa* is gnosis, the direct awareness of the Divine Reality in the heart, the organ in the human being with the capacity to perceive spiritual realities that the intellect cannot grasp. When the mountain disintegrated Moses fell unconscious. This is understood by the teachers of Sufism to be a description of what the Sufis call *fanā' fi'llāh.*[12] *Fanā' fi'llāh* means annihilation in God, the cessation of personal actions, attributes and essence.

The knowledge that Moses attained during *fanā'* is in the vision or, to use Ibn al-'Arabī's expression, Divine Self-disclosure. Moses' return to consciousness is described by the Sufis as *baqā' bi'llāh.*[13] *Baqa bi'llāh* refers to subsistence in God after the Sufi has returned from his state of annihilation. The Prophet Muḥammad's own experience of *ma'rifa, fanā'* and *baqā'* are described in the accounts of the *Isrā'* (Night-journey) and *Mi'rāj* (Ascension) and referred to in the first verse of Surat al-Isra in the Qur'ān:

> *Glory be to Him Who took His slave on a journey by night from the Masjid al-Haram (Sacred Mosque in Makka) to the Masjid al-Aqsa (the Distant Mosque in Jerusalem) whose surroundings We have blessed, in order to show him some of Our Signs. He is the All-Hearing, the All-Seeing.*[14]

The Night-journey was a bestowal of *ma'rifa* upon the Prophet ﷺ. Accompanied by the Archangel Gabriel, he travelled between the two mosques on a celestial being called Burāq, described by the Prophet ﷺ as a white animal taller than a donkey but smaller than a mule and whose step covered a distance equal to the range of its vision.[15] During this journey he was witness to the *malakūt* (the kingdom of unseen forms) and the *jabarūt* (kingdom of power or lights), which were some of the Signs of God. Another verse of the Qur'ān describes what happened at the end of the Prophet's ascent through the seven heavens:

> *He was two bow-lengths away or even closer. Then He revealed to His slave what He revealed. His heart did not lie about what he saw. What! Do you dispute with him about what he saw?*[16]

Shaykh 'Abd al-Qādir explains that two bow-lengths is the closest it is possible to come to God because, in the language of the Arabs, two bow-lengths is the nearest that a person is allowed to approach a king. He says, "In other words, it was an intimacy of the most extreme limit of what is permitted."[17] For Shaykh 'Abd al-Qādir these verses of Qur'ān refer to the *fanā'* of the Prophet and the Prophet's return designated his *baqā'*.

Ma'rifa (*'ilm al-aḥwāl* and *'ilm al-asrār*), *fanā'* and *baqā'*, epistemic sources of Sufism, are, therefore, firmly grounded in the Prophetic *sunna*. The Prophet ﷺ did not, however, envisage a society made up of individuals whose inner selves were disconnected from their outer selves. Madīna al-Munawwara – the Illuminated City – was established by the Prophet ﷺ and set up as a model community for future generations and its socio/spiritual fabric was based on an ethos in which the inward and outward sciences were unified. This Madinan phenomenon was recorded by Mālik ibn Anas in his book *al-Muwaṭṭa'* and shows that Madinan society was a nomocracy (law governed society). Islamic governance was administered by the Prophet ﷺ who, in delivering legal judgments covering all areas of life, directed every aspect of the society he had brought into being. The legal judgements of the Prophet found their basis in the Qur'ānic revelations and came to constitute Islamic law.

From the above we have clear evidence that Shaykh 'Abd al-Qādir's interpretation of Sufism accords with the Prophetic example, since it is clear from the Prophetic example that Sufism originated from Islam, that the *sharī'a* and Sufism are inextricably connected, and that politics constitutes an essential element of the *sharī'a*.

2. 'Alī ibn Abī Ṭālib (600-661)

'Alī ibn Abī Ṭālib was the son of 'Abd Manāf (otherwise known as Abū Ṭālib) and a first cousin of the Prophet Muḥammad ﷺ. After the death of 'Abd al-Muṭṭalib, the grandfather of the Prophet ﷺ and leader of the Qurayshī clan of Hāshim, 'Abd Manāf, the Prophet's uncle, became the clan leader and cared for the Prophet ﷺ. 'Alī was brought up by the Prophet ﷺ after 'Abd Manāf got into financial difficulties. At the age of ten he became Muslim and lived with the Prophet ﷺ for thirteen years. He married Fāṭima, the daughter of the Prophet ﷺ, and they had five children, one of whom died in childhood. He was an accomplished warrior, caliph, jurist and scholar. The Prophet ﷺ is reported to have said: "I am the city of knowledge and ʿAlī is its gate."[18] Ḍirār al-Asadī, a companion of ʿAlī, outlined his qualities in the following words:

> He was a man of strong willpower and determination. His speech was full of wisdom. ... He was nearest to the poor. He never allowed a powerful man to take advantage of his power. The weak were never disappointed of his justice. I bear witness that in many battles he woke up during the night and took hold of his beard and started to cry as though he was in a state of commotion and exclaimed, 'Oh world! Do not try to betray me for I have left you long ago. Do not have any desire for me for I hate you. Your age is short and your end is despised. Oh! the provision is very little, the journey is too long and the way is full of danger.'[19]

In the above statement ʿAlī is describing a station (*maqām*) on the Sufi's journey called *faqr* (poverty). The Sufi historian and master Al-Hujwīrī explained *faqr* as having both a form (*rasm*) and an essence (*ḥaqīqa*). The form is destitution and the essence is fortune and free choice. The one who has found the essence averts his gaze from all created things and, in a state of complete annihilation, sees only God. The poor man (*faqīr*) has nothing and so can suffer no loss. He does not become rich by having things nor indigent by having nothing. Both these conditions are the same for him because, "Worldly wealth holds them [Sufis] back from the path of contentment (*riḍā*)."[20] This station is attained only by the most spiritually developed Sufis, the masters.

The characteristics underpinning Shaykh ʿAbd al-Qādir's view of Sufism are found in the example of ʿAlī ibn Abī Ṭālib.

3. Ḥasan al-Baṣrī (642-728)

Ḥasan al-Baṣrī lived during the generation that followed the

Prophet ﷺ and his Companions. He was born in Madīna during the caliphate of ʿUmar ibn al-Khaṭṭāb and attended the Friday sermons of the third caliph, ʿUthmān ibn ʿAffān, where he met ʿAlī ibn Abī Ṭālib who initiated him into Sufism. Al-Baṣrī was a scholar who had memorized the Qurʾān and learnt reading, writing, and mathematics early in life. When he was fifteen-years-old he moved to Basra in Iraq where he studied *fiqh* (jurisprudence), *ḥadīth* and Arabic from the Companions of the Prophet who were living there at the time. He taught at the main mosque in Basra and was later appointed as a judge there in 720.

As a Sufi master he held special gatherings in his home for his disciples. Al-Hujwīrī tells us that al-Baṣrī wore a patched woollen robe and is quoted as saying: "I saw seventy Companions who fought at Badr and they all wore woollen garments; and the greatest Ṣiddīq [the first caliph Abū Bakr] wore a garment of wool in his detachment from the world (*tajrīd*)."[21] Shaykh ʿAbd al-Qādir explains that this means that the Sufi "has 'put on the wool'. This is distinct from those who confirm the way of Islam with the tongue and by book learning. It is taking the ancient way, the primordial path of direct experience of the Real [God]."[22] Shaykh ʿAbd al-Qādir is indicating here that action is essential for achieving the goals of Sufism. Further, this direct knowledge, that is immediate experience of the Divine Presence, cannot be attained through transmission or mere book-learning. The act of wearing wool signifies the act of having embarked on the journey towards direct experience of God and, moreover, of having made that the priority of one's life.

Al-Baṣrī was fearlessly critical of the rulers of his time. He opposed al-Ḥajjāj, the Umayyad caliph ʿAbd al-Malik's (r. 685-705) governor in Iraq. He nevertheless disapproved of removing evil governors through rebellion. When the followers of the rebel leader

Ibn Ash'ath (d. 704) ordered him to join them, he explained that the violent actions of tyrants were a punishment sent by God and must be endured with patience.[23] Muslim jurists were averse to anarchy because they regarded it to be even worse than oppression. When the Umayyad caliph 'Umar ibn 'Abd al-'Azīz (r. 717-720) requested his advice, al-Baṣrī told him that the just ruler must educate his subjects, reform the corrupt, strengthen the weak, ensure justice for the oppressed, and be a refuge for all who are in need of compassion. The just ruler should be the guardian of the orphan, the provider of the poor, the young and the old. When the ruler is just, the society is healthy and when he is corrupt, the society is corrupt.[24]

Ḥasan al-Baṣrī was, therefore, both a Sufi and, at the same time, an Islamic scholar and jurist who was politically active. These characteristics accord with Shaykh 'Abd al-Qādir's understanding of Sufism.

4. Ḥabīb ibn Muḥammad al-'Ajamī (d. 737)

Ḥabīb al-'Ajamī, was a Persian who had settled in Basra. Al-'Ajamī began his career as a usurer and property owner. His life-experience led him to repent and his conversion was aided by Ḥasan al-Baṣrī, from whom he acquired knowledge of the theory and practice of religion. He became a noted authority of Prophetic *ḥadīth* and transmitted from al-Ḥasan al-Baṣrī, Ibn Sīrīn, and others. He frequently attended the gatherings of Ḥasan al-Baṣrī and became his disciple and one of his closest associates.

After his conversion, al-'Ajamī gave away all his possessions until he was left penniless.[25] He subsequently spent his daytime hours at a *zāwiya*[26] on the banks of the Euphrates. The respected author and scholar, Abū Nu'aym al-Isfahānī (d.1038), reported that on his tenth day at the *zāwiya* he became concerned about the upkeep of his wife. At exactly the same time a delivery of flour, a skinned sheep, oil, honey, herbs and seasonings was made to his house. The porters then handed his wife a purse containing three hundred silver dirhams (coins) and said, "Say to Ḥabīb: 'You increase your output, and we will increase your wages'."[27] After that al-ʿAjamī dedicated his entire time to the service of God. This is reminiscent of the teaching of the earlier master ʿAlī ibn Abī Ṭālib, who said: "Do not let your wife and children be your chief cares; for if they be friends of God, God will look after His friends, and if they are enemies of God, why should you take care of God's enemies?"[28] Al-ʿAjamī taught his disciples that God is pleased with a heart which is not sullied by hypocrisy because there is no connection between hypocrisy and love. Love exists when one is pleased with whatever is decreed by God.[29]

Ḥabīb al-ʿAjamī was an Islamic scholar and, as we have seen, his Sufism was firmly grounded in the *sharīʿa*. These again are key characteristics in Shaykh ʿAbd al-Qādir's vision of Sufism.

5. Dāwūd al-Ṭāʾī (d. 783)

Dāwūd al-Ṭāʾī narrated hadiths from a number of the *Tābiʿīn*[30] and studied *fiqh* with Abū Ḥanīfa, the founder of the Ḥanafī school of law. He was well-versed in all the sciences and unrivalled in jurisprudence.[31] Abū al-Faraj ibn al-Jawzī (d. 1200) the famous Ḥanbalī scholar reported:

> "Abū Ḥanīfa said to Dāwūd, 'Abū Sulayman! As for the instrument [meaning legal methodology] we have mastered it.' Dāwūd said, 'What is left?' Abū Ḥanīfa said: 'What is left is to put it into practice!' Dāwūd said: 'When I heard this, my soul stirred me to seclusion and solitariness, but I told it: Sit with them for a year and do not raise a peep during that time.' During that year, he said, 'A question would come up which made me crave to answer more than someone parched craves water, but I would not answer.' After one year, he went into seclusion."[32]

When Sufyān al-Thawrī, the great jurist, visited Dāwūd al-Ṭāʾī with Abū Khālid al-Aḥmar, the latter was annoyed that al-Ṭā'ī did not look at al-Thawrī during the visit. After they departed al-Aḥmar made his displeasure known to al-Thawrī. Al-Thawrī turned to al-Aḥmar and said: "He is unconcerned with affection. Did you not see his eyes? They see other than what we fiddle with."[33] Ma'rūf al-Karkhī described him as one who held no desire for worldly goods and the world and its people had no allure for him. He used to regard dervishes (*fuqarā'*) as perfect although they displayed many faults.[34]

Dāwūd al-Ṭā'ī was also an accomplished Islamic scholar and his Sufism was firmly grounded in the *sharī'a*. These are foundational characteristics of Shaykh 'Abd al-Qādir's understanding of Sufism.

6. Ma'rūf al-Karkhī (d. 815)

Al-Karkhī was of Persian descent, the client (*mawlā*) of 'Alī ibn Mūsā al-Riḍā, through whom he accepted Islam. Al-Karkhī was a *murīd* (disciple) of Dāwūd al-Ṭā'ī and the advice he received from him was to obey God continually and to serve and advise people.[35] The following statement by him summarizes the source of his motivation for action and service. "When God chooses good for a person He opens the door to action for him and closes the door to argumentation; and when God chooses evil for a person he opens the door of argumentation and closes the door to action."[36] His actions certainly confounded his uncle the governor, who, on passing some wasteland, observed al-Karkhī sitting there eating bread. In front of him there was a dog and al-Karkhī was putting one morsel in his own mouth and then another in the dog's. "Are you not ashamed to eat bread with a dog?" cried his uncle. "It is out of shame that I am giving bread to the poor,"[37] replied Ma'rūf." It was his way of chiding the governor for neglecting the poor.

The deep significance of the Sufi teaching of patience (*ṣabr*) is clear from the following account given by the scholar, jurist and

Sufi Abū Ṭālib al-Makkī (d. 996).

> It was reported that whenever food was presented to Ma'rūf as a gift he always accepted and ate it. Someone said to him, 'Your brother Bishr ibn al-Ḥārith always refuses such food,' and Ma'rūf replied, 'Abstaining causes my brother's hands to be tied, whilst gnosis causes my hands to be stretched forth. I am only a guest in the house of my Lord ... when He feeds me I eat; when He does not, I have to be patient. I have neither objection nor choice.'[38]

It was neither death, nor paradise nor hell that impelled al-Karkhī to action but it was love of God that prompted him to act. He taught that God has power over death, paradise and hell and, when you love Him, He will protect you from all these things.[39]

Ma'rūf al-Karkhī's political acumen is evident from his lesson to the governor and his teachings came from a profound knowledge of the *sharī'a*. Here again we see similarities between the earlier masters and Shaykh 'Abd al-Qādir.

7. Sarī al-Saqaṭī (d. 837)

Al-Saqaṭī traded in spices in the market in Baghdad. He was renowned for his learning in the Islamic sciences. During his lifetime of ninety-eight years he saw the reign of seven or eight caliphs. Al-Saqaṭī was highly esteemed amongst people in general but also amongst influential members of society in politics, scholarship and the military.

His turning to Sufism was precipitated by a fire in the market which housed his shop. When told that his shop was saved from the fire, he exclaimed, "God be praised". This sentiment shocked him and he later said, "Instantly I was brought to my senses with the realization that, granted that my shop was unharmed, should I not have been thinking about others."[40] He subsequently devoted himself to Sufism, becoming famous for his scrupulousness (*wara'*). He was the first to outline the "arrangement of 'stations' (*maqamāt*) and the explanation of spiritual 'states' (*aḥwāl*)."[41] He is regarded as the founder of the Sufi school of Baghdad, or the Iraqi school, whose members were renowned for being the masters of unification (*arbāb al-tawḥīd*). Al-Saqaṭī was the maternal uncle and Sufi master of Abū al-Qāsim al-Junayd, the famed theoretician of Sufism. Al-Saqaṭī has been likened to Socrates for the way he transmitted his knowledge to his disciples through questioning them. Al-Junayd related:

> I came to al-Sarī one day and found him different from usual and I asked him, 'What is the matter?' He replied, 'A young man came to me and asked about repentance. I answered 'repentance is not to forget your sin.' The young man objected and said, 'On the contrary, repentance is to forget your sin.'

When al-Junayd said that he was of the same view as the young man, al-Saqaṭī asked him for his reasons. Al-Junayd replied that if a person had been on bad terms with God and afterwards came to be on good terms, to think of the former state was bad.[42] Like Socrates, al-Saqaṭī left behind no writings; it is through al-Junayd that his teachings have survived.

Sarī al-Saqaṭī was a great renowned scholar respected by politicians, generals of the army and other scholars. His Sufism was based on the *sharīʿa*, a key element in the *ṭarīqa* of Shaykh 'Abd al-Qādir.

8. Abū al-Qāsim al-Junayd (d. 908 or 909 or 910)

Al-Junayd was born and raised in Baghdad, the Abbasid capital. His father died while he was still a boy and he was brought up by his maternal uncle, the above-mentioned Sufi master, Sarī al-Saqaṭī. In his youth he studied *ḥadīth* and *sharīʿa* under the eminent jurist Abū Thawr (d. 855). He also studied theology and ethics and, according to al-Hujwīrī, he was "perfect in every branch of science."[43] It has been stated that he followed the legal school of Sufyān al-Thawrī. On completion of his studies he attended the gatherings of the Sufi Master al-Ḥārith al-Muḥāsibī (d. 857). He insisted that the Sufi's knowledge must always relate back to the Qur'ān and the *sunna*. He said, "Whoever has not learned the Qur'ān by heart, and has not learned law, before embarking on Sufism, is a man who has no right to lead."[44] Al-Junayd was the most important theoretician of Sufism and is acknowledged by the Sufis as their *imām* (leading spokesman in this usage). His teachings cover such subjects as *ma'rifa*, *tawḥīd* (unification), *mīthāq* (the Primordial Covenant), *fanā'* and *baqā'*.

Ma'rifa is the direct awareness of spiritual realities in the heart through the science of states (*'ilm al-aḥwāl*) and the science of the innermost consciousness (*'ilm al-asrār*). Al-Hujwīrī recorded the following incident depicting one of al-Junayd's capabilities by virtue of his knowledge of these sciences. He related that one of al-Junayd's disciples, who bore him a grudge, returned one day with the intention of testing him. Al-Junayd asked him if he wanted a formal or a spiritual answer. The disciple wanted both. Al-Junayd said that the formal answer was that if he had tested himself he would not have needed to test him. Al-Junayd's spiritual answer was that he deposed the disciple of *wilāya* (saintship). The disciple's face immediately changed colour and he shouted that the light of certainty (*yaqīn*) had gone from his heart. He then earnestly begged to be forgiven and abandoned his foolish self-conceit. Al-Junayd said to him, "Did you not know God's saints possess mysterious powers? You cannot endure their blows." He cast a breath at the disciple, who forthwith resumed his former purpose and repented for criticizing the Shaykhs [Masters].[45]

Al-Junayd described *tawḥīd* as the "isolation of the Eternal from that which was created."[46] He indicated that the understanding of *tawḥīd* is contingent on the annihilation of the self. He said a person is veiled from God by his or her own self and that one cannot reach God through oneself; it is by God alone that one reaches Him.

Mīthāq is described in the following passage from the Qur'ān:

> *"When your Lord took out all their descendents from the loins of the children of Adam and made them testify against themselves, 'Am I not your Lord?' They said, 'We testify that indeed You are!'"*[47]

Al-Junayd explains:

> In this verse God tells us that He spoke to them when they did not exist, except so far as they existed in Him. This existence is not the same type of existence as is usually attributed to God's creatures; it is a type of existence which only God knows and only he is aware of. God knows their existence. Embracing them, He sees them in the beginning when they were non-existent and unaware of their future existence in this world. The existence of these is timeless.[48]

To know about the kind of existence referred to here requires that one experience *fanā'*, annihilation in God, the cessation of personal actions, attributes and essence.[49] The knowledge that the Sufi attains during *fanā'* is, as we saw earlier, in the vision or, to use Ibn al-'Arabī's expression, in Divine Self-disclosure. Al-Junayd outlined the tenets of Sufism, which, if followed, could lead to the experience of *fanā'*. Briefly, these tenets are:

- Conformity with the *sharī'a* as revealed by God in the Qur'ān and practised by the Prophet ﷺ.
- Taking on a shaykh (master) of instruction.
- Engaging in *nawāfil 'ibāda*, that is worship over and above what is obligatory, for example *dhikr* (invocation and remembrance of God).
- Rejecting stray thoughts, especially those coming from Satan, through *wara'* (scrupulousness), *taqwā* (being aware and in awe

of God) and *ṣidq* (truthfulness).

- *Khalwa*, meaning withdrawal from the world in the concentration of invocation of the *al-ism al-aʿẓam* (the Supreme Name – i.e. Allah) under the supervision of an authorized master.

Al-Junayd explains that after *fanā'*, God restores the personal attributes and actions to the Sufi. He or she is then in the station of *baqā'*, that is subsistence in God. Al-Junayd said that when the Sufi returns to this world after having "reached the zenith of spiritual achievement vouchsafed by God, he becomes a pattern for his fellow men."[50] Those who have achieved the stage of *baqā'* are the elect of the élite of mankind. From the epistemological perspective, mankind is divided into three groups: the common, the élite and the elect of the élite. Al-Junayd refers to the elect of the élite as the most excellent of the believers (*ṣafwa min al-ʿibād*) and the pure ones (*khulāṣa min al-khalq*).[51] He goes on to say that God has made them "leaders in the right path" and refers to them as "unfurled flags" and "lighthouses erected for guidance" for humanity.[52] Al-Junayd wrote that they:

> "are those who guide in the crises of religion and theirs is the light, which leads in the darkness of ignorance, the brilliance of their knowledge shining through darkness. God has made them the symbol of His mercy for His creatures and a blessing for those of humanity who so choose. They are the instruments whereby He instructs the ignorant, reminds the negligent, guides the seeker aright ..."[53]

Individuals of this group are fearless defenders of justice standing up against whoever deviates from the law whether they are rulers, scholars, judges or even Sufis. They are able to do this because they look "on this world fully conscious of its transience and aware of its imminent disintegration."[54] They see the world from the perspective of God and are content with His decree. Al-Junayd was, however, opposed to writing about Sufism for public distribution or from speaking publicly about Sufism. His teaching of Sufism was done privately and his writings on it were in the form of correspondence with fellow Sufis and not intended for the general public.[55]

Al-Junayd displayed all the characteristics that are so highly regarded by Shaykh ʿAbd al-Qādir in his *ṭarīqa*. It can be rightly said that Shaykh ʿAbd al-Qādir's Sufism is modeled on that of al-Junayd.

9. Abū Bakr al-Shiblī (861-946)

Al-Shiblī grew up in Baghdad, where his father had been the chamberlain of the Abbasid Caliph al-Muwaffaq (r. 870-891), and he himself became the governor of Nihawand. His uncle was the governor in Alexandria. He was a scholar and jurist (*faqīh*) in the school of Mālik. He transmitted *ḥadīth* with *isnād* (chains of authority) and memorized the *Muwaṭṭa'* of Mālik. He was unique in his age for both outward knowledge and spiritual states. When al-Shiblī attended a class of the scholar Abū ʿImrān, he (Abū ʿImrān) rose for him and sat him at his side. One of the companions of Abū ʿImrān wanted to embarrass al-Shiblī by showing him up as ignorant. He asked him: "Abū Bakr [al-Shiblī], when a woman's menstrual blood resembles the blood of false menstruation, what does she do?" He gave him eighteen answers. Abū ʿImrān went to him and kissed his hand. He said, "Abū Bakr, I know twelve, and six I have never heard before!"[56] Aḥmad ibn ʿAṭā' is reported to have said, "I heard al-Shiblī say, 'I wrote *ḥadīth* for twenty years and I sat with the *fuqahā'* [jurists] for twenty years.'"[57]

His conversion to Sufism began when he attended an assembly of the Sufi Master Khayr al-Nassāj (d. 934). Out of respect for al-Junayd's status al-Nassāj sent al-Shiblī to him for his *sulūk*. Al-Shiblī entered the Sufi path by giving away all he possessed and throwing into the Tigris River seventy satchels of books in his own handwriting. He also gave away sixty thousand dinars (gold coins), country estates and urban real estate that his father had left him. He then became a disciple of al-Junayd. The spiritual state of Al-Shiblī surpassed that of all the Sufis of his time, as acknowledged by his master al-Junayd who said of him, "Do not look at al-Shiblī with the eye by which you look at others… Every people has a crown and the crown of these people [i.e. the Sufis] is al-Shiblī."[58] Al-Shiblī is renowned for his contemplation of God (*mushāhada*). Al-Hujwīrī says of contemplation:

> By contemplation the Sufis mean spiritual vision of God in public and private, without asking how or in what manner… There are really two kinds of contemplation. The former is the result of perfect faith, the latter of rapturous love, for in the rapture of love a man attains to such a degree that his whole being is absorbed in the thought of his beloved and he sees nothing else. Muḥammad b. Wāsiʿ says: 'I never saw anything without seeing God therein,' i.e. through perfect faith. The vision is from God to His creatures. Shiblī says: 'I never saw anything except God,' i.e. in the rapture of love and the fervour of contemplation. One sees the act with his bodily eye and, as he looks, beholds the Agent with his spiritual eye; another is rapt by love of the Agent from all things else, so that he sees only the Agent.[59]

Al-Shiblī is recorded as being in a state of rapturous love for God at most times, except when it was time for prayer and when he was questioned, as at the time when he attended the scholar Abū 'Imrān's class. It also appears that there were times that those fellow Sufis who cared for his welfare would confine him to a mental asylum whilst he was in a state of rapture. Al-Shiblī is reported to have said that he and al-Ḥallāj were of one belief but his "madness" saved him and al-Ḥallāj's sanity destroyed him.[60]

Al-Shiblī was an Islamic scholar and jurist. His Sufism displayed all the characteristics on which Shaykh 'Abd al-Qādir has grounded his own Sufic teaching.

42. ʿABD AL-QĀDIR AL-SUFI

This brief survey of the first nine masters of Shaykh ʿAbd al-Qādir's *ṭarīqa* has shown that their teachings were firmly grounded on the same premises on which Shaykh ʿAbd al-Qādir has established his *ṭarīqa*. The three key characteristics,[61] which underpin Shaykh ʿAbd al-Qādir's vision of Sufism and which we have seen confirmed in the teachings of the early masters, are all integrated in the one who properly establishes the *ʿamal ahl al-Madīna* (the practice of the first three generations of Muslims in Madīna). We will see how the *ʿamal ahl al-Madīna* animates the three major strands which characterize Shaykh ʿAbd al-Qādir's work: that of eliminating the split between the inner and outer aspects of the human personality; that of possessing the methodology for determining correct behaviour (*uṣūl al-fiqh*); and that of affirming the relationship between political power and precept, which in this context means belief.

In his *Book of ʿAmal*, a collection of transcripts of discourses given between 27 October 2007 and 12 January 2008 at the Nizamia Mosque in Cape Town, Shaykh ʿAbd al-Qādir explained that the foundational element of Sufism is *birr* – action which is just. The command to act justly comes from Divine Revelation and, in carrying out that command, an individual demonstrates that he or she does not associate any other power with God's power.[62] Shaykh ʿAbd al-Qādir said, "We began our journey into the matter of *ʿamal* (behaviour/action) with a deliberate turning-upside-down of Imam al-Ghazālī's famous definition: *ʿilm al-muʿāmala* (the science of behaviour) precedes *ʿilm al-mukāshafa* (the science of unveiling). The purpose of this reversal lay in the claim that the process and procedure of right action was itself dependent on a prior *rūḥānī* (spiritual) illumination."[63]

We may infer from this that for Shaykh ʿAbd al-Qādir just action in obedience to the Divine command leads to *fanā'* and Divine unveiling (*mukāshafa*). It is a process that begins with revelation (*waḥy*) and ends with unveiling. The ontological significance of this view is that the nature of the universe and matter is essentially spiritual. This view inhibits the bifurcation of reality into inner and outer domains, making secularism and structuralism untenable. Shaykh 'Abd al-Qādir's teaching shows that *birr* functions at three different levels, namely: *futuwwa* (the individual functioning at the level of community), *jamā'a* (the community functioning within the context of broader society), and *umma* (the whole Muslim community as one entity functioning within the world).

BIRR AT THE LEVEL OF *FUTUWWA* – THE INDIVIDUAL

Futuwwa, which connotes high morality, fraternity, chivalry, altruism, honour and virtue is, according to Shaykh 'Abd al-Qādir, a fundamental characteristic of the Prophet Muḥammad ﷺ. God says of the Prophet ﷺ: "*A Messenger has come to you from among yourselves. Your suffering is distressing to him; he is deeply concerned for you; he is gentle and merciful to the believers.*" (9:128-9) The Prophet ﷺ advised people to want for their brother or sister what they want for themselves, to remove injurious obstacles from the road, to treat neighbours with kindness, to show hospitality to guests, to avoid suspicion, not to be inquisitive about others, not to spy on others, not to envy others, not to maintain hostility against another, not to bid against another, not to oppress others, not to humiliate others, not to look down upon others and finally to respect the blood, wealth and the honour of others.[65]

Shaykh 'Abd al-Qādir says that the Sufi master Abū Ḥafṣ al-Nishaburi defined *futuwwa* as teaching by action not word.[66] And Dhū al-Nūn al-Miṣrī said concerning it: "The one who looks into the imperfections of others is prevented from seeing his own imperfections. The one who keeps sight of his own faults no longer sees the faults of others."[67] Such nobility of character is attained by accomplished Sufis who have traversed the difficult Sufi path. Interestingly, in the past, the name *futuwwa* was used interchangeably for professional and artisanal guilds and Sufi *ṭarīqas*. In this context, the Sufi master al-Kalābādhī's advice to his disciples was: "Do not be concerned with your subsistence, it is guaranteed for you. But rather be concerned with the work that has been assigned to you."[68] The work assigned to human beings, the purpose of human life, is to serve God.[69]

Spiritual illumination manifests outwardly as *futuwwa* and, in this way, the inner and outer aspects of the human personality become integrated so that there is no split between them. However, historically "there is no escaping that ... a polarization took place between formal scholarship and *bāṭinī* [inner] knowledge."[70] Shaykh 'Abd al-Qādir's teaching aims at eliminating this split. The outer sciences of Islam are the *sharī'a*, including the Qur'ān, the *sunna*, incorporating *ḥadīth*, and *'ilm al-'aql*, that is all the sciences related to the intellect. The inner sciences are *ma'rifa* (*'ilm al-aḥwāl* and *'ilm al-asrār*), *fanā'*, and *baqā'*. The inner and outer sciences supplement one another other and this relationship was, in the Prophetic model, not subject to separation. Outward (physical) actions impact on a person's inner spirituality and vice versa.

Islam teaches that humans cannot be seen as separate objects in a material world; a human being's individual reality and the social environment in which that human being lives form one unified reality. The human being's individual and social reality are inseparable. They are the same phenomenon viewed from different perspectives. The overall renewal of society depends on the renewal of the individual and the renewal of the individual depends on the renewal of society. In other words, the renewal of society correlates directly to the renewal of the individual. *"Allah never changes a people's state until they change what is in themselves.*"[71]

So it is clear that when *birr* is practised at the individual level the split between the inner and outer aspects of human personality is eliminated. This is a key goal that Shaykh 'Abd al-Qādir has focused on in his *ṭarīqa*.

Birr at the Level of *Jamā'a* – The Community

Whilst emphasizing that the inner sciences are of great importance, Shaykh 'Abd al-Qādir pointed out, in a series of talks in 1980 in San Antonio, USA, that inner spiritual development has no worth if the *sharī'a* of Islam is abandoned. It is not only correct moral behaviour at an individual level that is required by the *sharī'a* but such behaviour at the social level as well. If people's socio-economic and political duties are fulfilled, the society will be transformed. Harmony and social stability depends on the methodology (*uṣūl al-fiqh*) used to determine just behaviour (*birr*). With the aim of harmonizing the inner and outer dimensions of human existence, Shaykh 'Abd al-Qādir proposes the re-establishment of *'amal ahl al-Madīna* (the practice of the first three generations of Muslims in Madīna). In his seminal work, *Root Islamic Education*, based on these talks in San Antonio, he argues that the prime example of a society in which the inward and outward sciences had been unified was that of Madīna in the first days of Islam, the city in which the human social contract was "at its healthiest and most balanced".[72] This phenomenon was recorded by Mālik ibn Anas in his book *Al-Muwaṭṭà*. Madīna was a nomocracy (law-governed society) governed by the Prophet Muḥammad ﷺ, God's caliph (representative) on earth, in accordance with His revelation, the Qur'ān.

In the *Muwaṭṭa'*, Mālik ibn Anas provides a composite picture of life in Madīna, including the judgments of the caliphs, governors and scholars up until the time of its compilation in the middle of the second century AH (Islamic dating). The *Muwaṭṭa'* is a book primarily about action (*'amal*). For Mālik the actions of human beings are the text. As Yasin Dutton points out, this view "allows us a fundamentally different perspective on Islamic legal history where the true expression of the law is seen as being preserved not in a corpus of texts but in the actions, or *'amal*, of men."[73] A similar assessment is made by Abdalhaqq Bewley who says that for the Madinans the Qur'ān and *Sunna* were a matter of direct transmission. They had been conscientiously and scrupulously preserved and passed down as a lived reality through the two generations after the Prophet and his Companions. "The textual sources were, for them, sounding boards or yardsticks against which their ongoing practice should be measured to make sure that there was no deviation and the road remained clearly delineated."[74]

Shaykh 'Abd al-Qādir points out that correct outward behaviour should not cause one to wither inwardly. He has repeatedly brought to attention Mālik ibn Anas' statement about combining the practice of Sufism and obedience to the law.[75] In *Root Islamic Education* Shaykh 'Abd al-Qādir describes three jurists who followed the *'amal ahl al-Madīna*. Being jurists, they were knowledgeable of the outer sciences and of how their legal decisions impacted on society and governance. Yet their *'amal* (actions) elevated them spiritually and precipitated for them the opening of inner knowledge. One of these jurists was Abū Sa'īd Ṣaḥnūn.

Shaykh 'Abd al-Qādir describes Ṣaḥnūn as a man of the highest integrity and reliability. He was *ḥāfiẓ* (expert) in knowledge and a thoroughly accomplished *faqīh* (jurisprudent). He was scrupulous and utterly uncompromising in his defence of the truth. He was ascetic (*zāhid*) with regards to things of this world. He wore rough garments and ate coarse food but was generous in times of hardship as well as at times of ease. He never accepted gifts from the sultans but would give his companions large sums of money. Along with these outward qualities Ṣaḥnūn was, at the same time, a man with a very soft heart. He cried very much out of his fear of God. He was modest and humble, noble in his conduct, and had excellent manners. "His heart was sound. It did not have the least enmity toward other people. ... When Ṣaḥnūn remained silent it was for the sake of Allah. And when he spoke it was for the sake of Allah. When he had the desire to speak he would remain silent and when he had the desire to remain silent he would speak."[76] The behaviour and character of Abū Saʿīd Ṣaḥnūn is the same as that of the Sufis reviewed in this chapter except that in Shaykh ʿAbd al-Qādir's words:

> This is a protected *taṣawwuf* because it is not accessible, touchable, visible or speakable. It is buried in the hearts of great men of knowledge of *kitab wa sunna* [Qur'ān and the normative practice of the Prophet ﷺ]. And if we take this path, there is no need for anything visible on the face of the earth that you can call Sufism ...[77]

Shaykh ʿAbd al-Qādir describes this as "the pure *salafī* phenomenon"[78] meaning that it was the behaviour of the Prophet, his Companions, the generation after them (*tābiʿīn*) and the generation after them (*tābiʿī at-tābiʿīn*) in Madīna. This is the *ʿamal ahl al-Madīna* and Mālik ibn Anas lived it and recorded it. This brief discussion of the Madinan phenomenon shows that the people of Madīna possessed the methodology for determining correct behaviour which enabled them to practice *birr* at the social level. According to Shaykh ʿAbd al-Qādir the implementation of *ʿamal ahl al-Madīna* is an urgent necessity for the betterment of society in the world today.

BIRR AT THE LEVEL OF THE *UMMA* – HUMANITY

Shaykh ʿAbd al-Qādir quotes the following Qur'ānic verse which summarizes very succinctly how he views the world. *"It is He who made the earth a stable home for you and the sky a dome, and formed you, giving you the best of forms, and provided you with good and wholesome things. That is God your Lord. Blessed be God, the Lord of the worlds."*[79] Shaykh 'Abd al-Qādir explains that "*the best of forms*" means that human beings are imbued with *fiṭra* which is defined as an inborn natural predisposition and which exists at birth in all human beings. The destinies of all things in the universe, including human beings, are predetermined by their life-form.[80]

Shaykh 'Abd al-Qādir comments that Johann Wolfgang von Goethe (1749-1832) tried to move the modern imagination towards seeing biological phenomena as entities moving through time and "thus taking their meaning from their full realization in nature, from seed to decay".[81] This way of defining a human being incorporates everything about us, our life-cycle, our habitat, our familial and social relations, our livelihood and our capacity for language. Whilst forms in the mineral, vegetal and animal kingdoms submit to their destinies unconsciously and involuntarily, human beings are consciously able to play their part in preserving the natural order and balance of the universe.

This ability is made possible by the human capacity for language.[82] Language makes it possible for human beings to think and reflect on themselves and the part they play in maintaining the balance and order in the universe. Via this capacity for language, God speaks to human beings. His speech comes in the form of *waḥy* (revelation/inspiration) and the recipients of *waḥy* are called Prophets. The poet and philosopher Muḥammad Iqbal regarded *waḥy* as "a universal property of life" affecting plants, animals and human beings, "varying in character according to the needs of the recipient, or the needs of the species to which the recipient belongs".[83]

God's *waḥy* or revelation to the Prophet Muḥammad ﷺ took the form of the Qur'ān and it outlined what humans need to do in order to attain direct knowledge of Him. The term *fiṭra*, for Shaykh 'Abd al-Qādir, also incorporates the inborn natural predisposition in the human to know God. To know God requires that you first be in harmony with the destiny of your life-form. In Qur'ānic terminology this harmonization is called service or worship (*'ubūdiyya*). In this schema, action, in other words behaviour, precedes knowledge of God. This means that a particular way of behaving is a prerequisite for reaching God. As the Prophet Muḥammad said, "Religion is behaviour (*al-dīn al-mu'āmala*)."

The Prophet Muḥammad ﷺ lived by the Qur'ānic laws and established a society that was based on them. Everything that he did was in accordance with the guidance of the Qur'ān, making him, as the Qur'ān tells us, an exemplar worthy of imitation: "*You have an excellent model* (*uswatun ḥasana*) *in the Messenger of God.*"[84] The *umma* of Islam is the whole worldwide body of Muslims as one distinct community, about whom God says in the Qur'ān, "*In this way We have made you a middlemost community* (*umma*), *so that you may act as witnesses against mankind and the Messenger as a witness against you.*"[85] This verse can be interpreted as meaning that the Muslim *umma* is a justly balanced society setting the standard for mankind. This, of course, is made possible through the Prophet ﷺ being the exemplary standard for society as a whole.

But humankind, Shaykh 'Abd al-Qādir asserts, has rejected the guidance of the Qur'ān and adopted humanism as an alternative doctrine.[86] The human being is now considered the centre of reality and the measure of all things, and reality itself is interpreted exclusively in terms of human experiences and values. Empiricism and rationalism have become the primary sources for the acquisition of knowledge. For Shaykh 'Abd al-Qādir humanism "is nothing more than the stoic and useless philosophy of loss."[87] He says:

> Men cannot arrive at knowledge and wisdom, let alone understanding, by thinking a way out of the human situation. Philosophy, a man-made construct, by its nature becomes more dark, more inaccessible, and more metaphoric. The philosopher, his life continuing, is forced to metaphors of hope: the light at the end of the tunnel; the bright clearing in the dark forest.[88]

Shaykh ʿAbd al-Qādir says that humanism should be replaced by the establishment of Qurʾānic teachings and Prophetic practice. He explains that God has set up "Ascending Steps" of *birr* (just behaviour) that lead to the highest *maʿrifa* (gnosis). These are the Ascending Steps – a reference to Qurʾān 70 – that the Sufis ascend on their *sulūk* (travelling on the Path) taking them to the highest spiritual stations. The Ascending Steps are actions, examples of which are contained in the following verses of the Qurʾān: "*What will convey to you what the steep ascent is? It is freeing a slave or feeding on a day of hunger an orphaned relative or a poor man in the dust; then to be one of those who believe and urge each other to steadfastness and urge each other to compassion. They are the Companions of the Right.*"[89] The "Companions of the Right," are those Muslims, whose precepts, which in this case means beliefs, propel them to just actions (*birr*). The establishment of justice at the level of *umma* has been a recurring theme in Shaykh ʿAbd al-Qādir's teachings.

What has been made apparent by this overview of Prophetic practice and the first nine masters of the *silsila* of the Qādirī-Shādhilī-Darqāwī *ṭarīqa* is that: (i) Sufism originated from Islam; (ii) the *sharīʿa* and Sufism are inextricably connected; and (iii) politics constitutes an essential element of the *sharīʿa* and, therefore, political activism is germane to Sufism. These three characteristics also define Shaykh 'Abd al-Qādir's vision of Sufism. He further shows how all three are integrated in the one who establishes the *'amal ahl al-Madīna* (the practice of the People of Madīna in the first three generations of Islam). The methodology of *'amal ahl al-Madīna* animates the three major strands which characterize Shaykh 'Abd al-Qādir's work, which are: (i) eliminating the split between the inner and outer aspects of human personality; (ii) possessing the methodology for determining correct behaviour (*uṣūl al-fiqh*); and (iii) affirming the relationship between precepts and political power.

Chapter 2

SUFI EPISTEMOLOGY: THE SOURCES OF SUFI KNOWLEDGE

For Muslims, the acquisition of knowledge is a religious duty and the Qur'ān tells us that *"he who has been given wisdom has been given great good."*[1] This Divine guidance and the injunction of the Prophet Muḥammad ﷺ that "seeking knowledge is an obligation for every Muslim"[2] has inspired Muslim society, not only in its scientific and rational pursuits but also in its quest for knowledge of God. Knowledge in Islam relates all things to God. As well as providing information for overcoming the varied exigencies of life, knowledge has the higher goal of leading its possessor to eternal happiness in paradise.[3] In this context, what a human being needs is knowledge of what is pleasing to God, and the doing of what is pleasing God is the key to attaining direct knowledge of God. In other words, actions precede knowledge of God. Or, to put it another way, there is a unity of knowledge and practice, as we see in the previously quoted words of the Prophet Muḥammad ﷺ, "Religion is behaviour (*al-dīn al-mu'āmala*)."[4]

This behavioural knowledge is referred to often in the Qur'ān, as in the words: *"We have sent down the Book to you making all things clear and as guidance and mercy and good news for the Muslims.*"[5] The text of the Qur'ān, and the way that it was implemented in practice by the Prophet ﷺ and his Companions, form the primary sources of knowledge for all epistemological endeavours in Islam. The Qur'ānic text and Prophetic practice have been approached in different ways by jurists, exegetes, linguists, grammarians, theologians, philosophers, theosophers and Sufis throughout the history of Islam. These different disciplines provide a framework within which Islamic epistemology can be investigated and the reality is that there is often a considerable overlap between these different branches of learning.

The jurists developed the skills needed to extrapolate from the primary sources of Islamic law when making legal judgments. Analogical extrapolation (*qiyās*) and personal judgements in legal matters (*ijtihād*) became necessary when applying the law to new situations in all schools of Islamic law. Muslim jurists such as Ibn Rushd (1126-1198) also found logic and demonstrative reasoning, deriving from Greek philosophy, useful when applying Qur'ānic law to unfolding events. The Greek philosophical tradition had passed into the possession of Muslims in the ninth and tenth centuries, "without break or diminution".[6]

Philosophy, however, "never flourished except amongst its own practitioners, and it was generally marginal to mainstream Islamic society."[7] Nevertheless, logic played an important role in Islam, especially the idea that logic represents a basic set of techniques which lie behind much human thinking and behaviour. In theology and law, for example, deduction was appropriate, since it worked logically from generally accepted propositions to conclusions that were accepted as valid. For instance, in Islamic theology certain conclusions follow if the basic principles of theology are applied.

Islamic theologians go even further than the jurists with regards to engaging with other intellectual traditions. Islamic theology is a defensive theology and a polemical art designed to defend Islamic belief and practice against agnostics and the theologians of other religions. Whilst the fixed frame of reference in Islamic theology is the Qur'ān and Sunna, its primary focus is on questions originating in a variety of different philosophies and theologies.

In contrast to theology, which is knowledge of God obtained through revelation, and philosophy, which is knowledge of the Divine acquired through reasoning, theosophy is about knowledge of God obtained by direct intuition of the Divine Essence. In Islam it is called *ḥikmat al-ishrāq* (Philosophy of Illumination). The idea of *ishrāq* was introduced by Ibn Sīnā (980-1037), also known as Avicenna, and later developed into a philosophical system by Shihāb al-Dīn Suhrawardī (1153-1191). He adopted the name "Philosophy of Illumination" for it in order to distinguish it from the philosophical positions and methods of the Peripatetics, that is, of Aristotle and his followers.

Suhrawardī indicated that knowledge is acquired from two sources: rational demonstration and intuition. The "latter has logical and epistemological priority over the former [rational demonstration]. However, this pre-eminence of direct intuition over philosophical reasoning is, to a great extent, ontological in nature."[8] The basic principle of *ḥikmat al-ishrāq* is that to know something it is necessary to have experience of it.[9] The epistemology of theosophy transcends that of law, theology and philosophy. Theosophy acknowledges the existence of realities that go beyond rationalism and empiricism and are experienced by the inner self.

It is within the context of Sufism that it becomes possible to investigate the experiences of the inner self. In Knysh's survey of Sufi history he found that:

> ... at the center of Sufi epistemology lies the notion of a supersensory,

revealed knowledge that is confined to the select few. In Sufi manuals, this kind of knowledge is variously described as "direct vision" (*mushāhada*), "flashes" (*lawāqiḥ*), "gnosis" (*ma'rifa*), illumination (*ishrāq*), "direct tasting" (*dhawq*), verification (*taḥqīq*), etc.[10]

The Qur'ānic term referring to this type of knowledge is *kashf* (stripping away, unveiling).[11] It refers to the unveiling of the different dimensions of space and time as well as the unveiling of what lies beyond phenomenal reality and empirical existence. A Qur'ānic verse referring to this unveiling is: "*We have stripped you of your covering* (*kashafnā*) *and today your sight is sharp.*"[12] *Kashf* results in knowledge whose proof lies in the actual experience of the direct perception of the realities unveiled.[13] The *Risāla* of Abū al-Qāsim al-Qushayrī (986-1076), one of the foundational texts of Sufism, identifies three stages that the Sufi has to pass through as he progresses towards his Creator: *muḥāḍara, mukāshafa* and *mushāhada.*[14]

Muḥāḍara is the positioning of the Sufi in his relation to God. At this stage, while he is still veiled, he aligns himself to God through demonstrative reasoning (*burhān*) and the workings of the intellect (*'aql*). *Mukāshafa* is when the veil is partly lifted. At this stage the Sufi transcends discursive reasoning; that is to say, he sees beyond God's signs (*āyāt*) and observes His attributes (*ṣifāt*). In the last stage of *mushāhada*, the Sufi experiences the Presence of the Reality (*al-ḥaqīqa*). Abū Ḥāmid al-Ghazālī (1058-1111) says that by *'ilm al-mukāshafa* (the science of unveiling) "we mean the drawing aside of the veil so that the Real One would show Himself in all His splendor; and this is effected with a clarity which sets the object present right before the eyes, without any possible grounds for doubt."[15]

The advanced stages in the spiritual journey of Sufism transcend rationalism and empiricism and take the Sufi ever closer to the unveiling of realities that are only accessible through the heart.

According to Louis Gardet, the heart (*qalb*), in Sufi terminology, does not denote the emotionalization of religious values. Rather it relates to the Sufi idea of *maʿrifa*, the direct awareness of the spiritual dimensions of existence.[16] Muḥammad Waziri speaks of the meta-rational nature of *sulūk*, pointing out that progression in *sulūk* begins with reason but that reason can create confusion because it is confined to the realm of Possible Being with no access to Necessary Being. Only when *sulūk* is undertaken by means of the Light of God and Divine grace, with no recourse to reason or passions (*nafs*), will one attain complete unveiling.[17]

Ibn al-ʿArabī emphasized the necessary connection between the law and *kashf*. This had become necessary due to discussion about the meta-rational and super-sensory stages of *sulūk* and the confusion arising out of it, which had led to heated debates within Muslim society about the relationship of Sufism to the *sharīʿa*. Ibn al-ʿArabī gives a clear understanding of "the men of God", in terms of who they are and the ranks amongst them. There are three types of such men and they are all obedient to the law of God. The first of them are the worshippers (*ʿubbād*), who occupy themselves with renunciation, constant devotion and outwardly praiseworthy acts. The second group are the Sufis, who see all acts as belonging to God and who possess earnestness, piety, renunciation, trust in God and other virtues. They have knowledge of states, stations and unveilings. Their behaviour is characterized by high morals (*akhlāq*) and chivalry (*futuwwa*). The third level is made up of people who follow in the footsteps of Abū Bakr.[18] Such people perform the obligatory five prayers each day and the supererogatory practices, they visit the markets and speak as common people do "but they are alone with God in their hearts and they do not diverge from servanthood at all."[19] The following passage of the *Futūḥāt al-Makkiyya* explains the people of the third level further:

> The perfect one among men is he who has combined the call to God with the curtain of the station (*sitr al-maqām* – the specific realities of his own time and place); for he calls to God by his recital of the books of *ḥadīth* and those on the subtle affinities (*raqā'iq*), and by stories of the shaykhs; so that the people recognize them as the model. ... Thus the perfect saint (*al-walī al-kāmil*) must embrace behaviour (in accordance with) the law so that God opens up in his heart an eye to understanding Him and inspiration into the meaning of the Qur'ān.[20]

The men of God can therefore be ranked, with the Prophet Muḥammad ﷺ being the highest, followed by the Companions, the Sufis and ordinary worshippers in that order. This accords with Shaykh 'Abd al-Qādir's position on Sufism which is, as noted earlier, that *'amal* (actions) elevates people spiritually and furthermore initiates unveiling (*mukāshafa*) for them.[21]

As we have said, knowledge in Sufism is classified into five categories: *'ilm al-'aql* (science of the intellect), *'ilm al-aḥwāl* (science of states), *'ilm al-asrār* (science of the innermost consciousness), *fanā'* (annihilation) and *baqā'* (subsistence). These five categories of knowledge correspond to the Prophetic terminology for the three branches of Islam namely, *islām* (*sharī'a* – law), *īmān* (creed) and *iḥsān* (Sufism), which in turn correspond with the three stages of the Sufi's journey (*sulūk*) to God: *sharī'a*, *ṭarīqa* and *ḥaqīqa*. Ibn 'Ajība states that the

> ... *ṭarīqa* is the result of the *sharī'a*. The *sharī'a* is for the correction of the outward limbs, and that leads to the *ṭarīqa*, which is the correction of the inward secret. This, in turn, leads to the *ḥaqīqa*, which is the removal of the veil and the witnessing of the beloved ones on the other side of the veil. Let us say that *sharī'a* (law) is to worship Him, and *ṭarīqa* (the path) is to travel to Him, and *ḥaqīqa* (reality) is to witness Him.[22]

Shaykh 'Abd al-Qādir defines these four terms – *sulūk*, *sharī'a*, *ṭarīqa* and *ḥaqīqa* – as follows. *Sulūk* is the Sufi's journey on the path towards God and the science of all the inward elements of wayfaring.[23] The *sālik* (wayfarer) has to be grounded in the necessary wisdom to prevent insanity, that is to prevent them becoming mad-in-God (*majdhūb*), when love of God awakens in the heart. This wisdom is contained in the *sharīʿa*. When the world and everything in it becomes a trial for the wayfarer he or she needs to hold on to this wisdom so that withdrawal (seclusion) is avoided. The science of *sulūk* makes the benefits of *jadhb* (attraction to God) possible without one becoming *majdhūb*.

Shaykh ʿAbd al-Qādir says that his way is to be *sālik/majdhūb*: outwardly sober and inwardly drunk.[24] He explains that accepting the *sharīʿa* shows one's deep cognition that the human creature is limited and, like all bodies in the physical world, has to obey given laws.[25] *Ṭarīqa* is the path of transformation of the self, outlined by a Sufi master. He describes it as the interiorisation of the cosmic landscape through spiritual vision.[26] *Ḥaqīqa* – reality – is the science of the inward. It is the inward illuminations of knowledge which flood the heart of the seeker.[27] Acquiring the knowledge of reality is by taste (*dhawq*) and state (*ḥāl*).[28] Shaykh ʿAbd al-Qādir defines *dhawq* as the first of the Divine manifestations (*tajalliyāt*).

> The first *dhawq* will come in the company of the Shaykh by intense concentration on Allah in his presence. *Dhawq* will come upon the *faqīr* [the Sufi] in the *samāʿ*, the singing of the Diwan[29] and the dance. ... By *dhawq* the heart comes into being as a live organ of spiritual awareness and knowledges. *Dhawq* is life itself, for the first time breaking in. Or, if you like, it is the first impulse of wakefulness after a long night of sleep. The sleeper awakes. Sleeps again. Stirs. The stirring precedes rising and full daylight experience after the night of ignorance.[30]

There are three realms in Sufi cosmology – *mulk*, *malakūt* and *jabarūt* – and three corresponding dimensions of human personality – *nafs*, *rūḥ* and *sirr* – and the sciences appropriate to each dimension are, respectively: *ʿilm al-ʿaql*, *ʿilm al-aḥwāl* and *ʿilm al-asrār*. The *nafs* (the body and psyche of the human being) inhabits the *mulk* (the kingdom of physical forms) and the means by which it perceives its realm of existence is through *ʿilm al-ʿaql* (the science of the intellect). The *rūḥ* (soul/spirit) inhabits the *malakūt* (the kingdom of unseen forms) and the means of perceiving its realm is *ʿilm al-aḥwāl* (science of states). The *sirr* (innermost consciousness) inhabits the *jabarūt* (kingdom of power or lights) and perceives its realm by means of *ʿilm al-asrār* (the science of the innermost consciousness). The science of the intellect relates to rationalism and empiricism but the sciences of states and innermost consciousness are inaccessible to most modern people due to their rigid adherence to rationalist and empiricist methodologies.

Nafs, Mulk and ʿIlm al-ʿaql

Mulk is the visible kingdom. It is what is experienced in the sensory (*ḥiss*) and in illusion (*wahm*). "Of its nature *mulk* is both solid, sensory, and pure-space, illusory."[31] Shaykh ʿAbd al-Qādir says that this dual view of matter is now confirmed by modern science. Fritjof Capra notes that in sub-atomic physics and quantum mechanics:

> ... the solid material objects of classical physics dissolve into wave-like patterns of probabilities. But this again seems paradoxical. How can the physical world consist of mere probabilities? Well, it turns out that the patterns, ultimately, do not represent probabilities of things, but rather probabilities of correlations.[32]

Shaykh ʿAbd al-Qādir says that the apparent substantiality of *mulk* veils most people from the fact that it does not really have the solidity it appears to have. In the language of the Qur'ān, the physical universe is made with the Real. In order to understand its true nature one must penetrate its seeming solidity. However, since human beings are part of the physical universe, breaking the *mulk* façade will explode the experiencing locus of the self, that

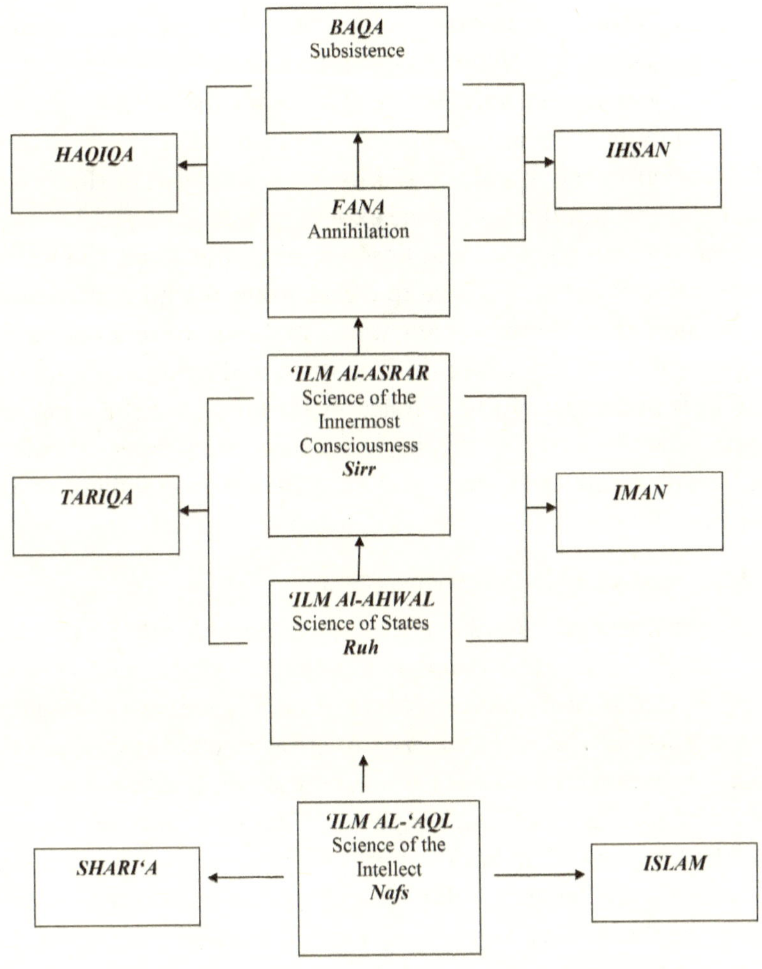
The Five Sources of Sufi Knowledge
BAQA
Subsistence
HAQIQA
IHSAN
FANA
Annihilation
'ILM Al-ASRAR
Science of the
Innermost
Consciousness
Sirr
TARIQA
IMAN
'ILM Al-AHWAL
Science of States
Ruh
'ILM AL-'AQL
Science of the
Intellect
Nafs
SHARI'A
ISLAM

Diagram 2

is, take one to a state of *fanā'*. *Fanā'*, however, is the penultimate stage of *sulūk* and, for embarking on *sulūk*, awareness of one's selfhood is the basic necessary condition. Without self-awareness a human being is *majnūn* (mad) and, as such, cannot embark on the Sufi journey. Shaykh 'Abd al-Qādir says that unless "there is a functioning locus of experience it is not possible to arrive at its dislocation in the act of self-discovery. ... The goal of the People [Sufis] is the annihilation of the experiencing self (*nafs*)."[33]

Through processes we will describe at a later stage, the *nafs* is subdued and the Sufi is able to discern that the human creature is far more than the solid body in the material world it outwardly appears to be.[34] *'Ilm al-'aql* – rationalism and empiricism –allows the *nafs* to navigate in its physical environment of the *mulk* and to survive in it. Law, theology, exegesis, linguistics, theology, philosophy and theosophy are all different expressions of the science of the intellect and have developed from it.

Rūḥ, Malakūt and 'Ilm al-Aḥwāl

Rūḥ means soul or spirit and it inhabits the *malakūt*, the kingdom of unseen forms. The *malakūt* is what is experienced through *dhawq*, that is taste. Shaykh 'Abd al-Qādir says that the organ of experience for the *rūḥ* and *sirr* (innermost consciousness) is the heart. What was the arena of action for the *nafs* becomes the arena of vision for the *rūḥ*.[35] Shaykh 'Abd al-Qādir describes the *malakūt* as "the kingdom of the source-forms of the creational realities, the Lote-tree,[36] the Balance,[37] the Throne[38] and so on. It is the realm of vision as the *mulk* is the realm of event."[39] He also tells us that the vision of the Garden is houris,[40] youths, rivers and gardens.

'Abd al-'Azīz al-Dabbāgh gives us a rare insight into the nature of the *dhawq* experienced by the *rūḥ* and *sirr*: He said:

> Three days after the death of Sayyidī 'Umar I experienced

> illumination – praise be to God. ... Things began to reveal themselves to me and they appeared as if they were right in front of me. I saw all the towns and cities and small villages. I saw everything that is on the land. ... I saw all the seas and I saw all the seven earths and all the beasts of burden and the creatures found on them. I saw the sky and it was as if I was above it looking at what it contains. Then behold there was a great light like sudden lightning that came from every direction. The light appeared above me and below me, on my right and on my left and from behind. ... And when I lay down I perceived that my body was all eyes. My eye saw, my head saw, my leg saw, and all my limbs saw. I looked at the clothes I had on and found that they didn't hinder the sight which was spread throughout my body. I realized that lying face down or standing up made no difference.[41]

The science that allows the traveler on the Path to navigate this realm is *'ilm al-aḥwāl*, the science of states. Shaykh 'Abd al-Qādir advises that once the *malakūt* opens its treasures to the seeker, he or she must beware of becoming fascinated by its wonders. The seeker must never be content with phenomena. Arrival at God is the Sufi's goal and they should never let anything divert them from that goal. The science of states is an epistemological source that transcends modernist epistemology but that does not put the two into conflict with each other. They can supplement one another in the task of development of the human personality, when it is recognized that human beings have dimensions of personality other than just the physical.

Sirr, the Jabarūt and 'Ilm al-asrār

Sirr literally means secret but the Sufis have described it as the innermost consciousness. There are, according to Shaykh 'Abd al-Qādir, three zones of *sirr* experience. The first zone of the *sirr* is active and involves the capacity to grasp what is seen and to hold to *himma*[42] for God alone. The second zone is passive and this knowledge is arrived at in the depths of *murāqaba* – watching.

The third zone is so subtle that it cannot be talked about except in the coded language of poetry, such as that used by the Sultan of the Lovers, Shaykh Ibn al-Fāriḍ (1181-1235). It is active and passive and holds the unitary discovery. Ibn al-ʿArabī says that in this zone there is a clear distinction between God and His creation.[43] Shaykh ʿAbd al-Qādir explains that, by the *sirr*, Sufis become immersed in the natural study of themselves, in a way similar to that which a biologist employs when examining an organism in its environment. What they discover is that their capacity for acquiring knowledge is deepened and they are able to taste the finer meanings of "the self/cosmos locus."[44]

Shaykh ʿAbd al-Qādir defines *jabarūt* as the kingdom of power and the kingdom of lights. These lights are the *barzakh* – the inter-space – between the visible and the invisible. The barriers separating the kingdoms are not realities in themselves but without them nothing would be defined. In fact that "which sets up the barriers, and is the barriers, is none other than the One Reality in its sublime perfection unrelated to any form."[45] This understanding is verified by many verses of the Qur'ān.[46] The science of the innermost consciousness is an epistemic source that transcends modernist epistemology but that again does not put the two into conflict with each other. They can supplement one another in the *sulūk*.

Fanā'

According to Shaykh ʿAbd al-Qādir, beyond these three worlds of *mulk*, *malakūt* and *jabarūt*, in other words beyond space, time and phenomena, is God. The Sufi's goal is to reach God. His or her access to knowledge of God is dependent on the annihilation (*fanā'*) of the *nafs*, *rūḥ* and *sirr* and their capacities. The methodology by which this goal can be attained will be discussed later. After annihilation of the *nafs*, *rūḥ* and *sirr* all that remains is God consciousness.

Fanā' means 'annihilation' and, in the context of Sufism, it is understood to be annihilation in God, the cessation of individual actions, attributes and essence. Al-Junayd explained that belief in God implies obedience to His commands and obedience leads to ascent toward Him and ultimately to reaching Him. When God is attained, His manifestation is so overwhelming that the elect worshipper is unable to describe Him and he discovers the meaning of his existence. From this comes the vision of God and the loss of his individual identity.[47]

As Ibn 'Ajība points out, *fanā'* can only be grasped by the people of taste and penetrating inner sight; it is beyond the grasp of the intellect and the written records of it.[48] The taste of *fanā'* is not anything like the taste that is experienced by the *rūḥ* and the *sirr.* Whilst taste is the same term applied to the experiences of the *rūḥ* and *sirr,* the taste of the experience of *fanā'* is fundamentally different. The goal of the Sufis is to reach God and their access to knowing Him is dependent on the annihilation of the self and its capacities. The knowledge that the Sufi attains during *fanā'* is in the vision or, using Ibn al-'Arabī's expression, in Divine Self-disclosure. Shaykh 'Abd al-Qādir says that *fanā'* is arrived at by a process of withdrawal from the sensory by the means of the Supreme Name (Allah) until even the Name disappears. He says that from the depth of the Original Void the secrets and the lights emerge. The Sufi "will pass through the heavens, each with its own colour and meanings. Light upon light. Until the great *tajallī*[49] which unveils the secret and indicates Allah."[50]

The unique defining elements of Sufism are the experiences of *fanā'* and *baqā'*, the state that follows *fanā'*. The ultimate goal of the Sufi, the direct experience of the Divine Presence, is attained when the individual self is annihilated and becomes the locus for the Self-disclosure of Being (God). An example of poetic expression of *fanā'* is Muḥammad ibn al-Ḥabīb's (1876-1972) *qaṣīda, Withdrawal into the Perception of the Essence.* He was Shaykh 'Abd al-Qādir's first shaykh. In this poem he says:

> The Face of the Beloved appeared and shone in the early dawn.
> His light pervaded my heart so I prostrated myself in awe.
> He said to me, 'Rise – ask of Me! You will have whatever you desire.'
> I replied, 'You, You are enough for me! Away from You I cannot live!'
> He said, 'My slave, there is good news for you, so enjoy the vision.
> ...
> The one who is veiled from Us has not tasted the sweetness of life.'[51]

Another example is his *qaṣīda, Fanā' in Allah*, where he says in guidance to his disciples:

> O seeker of *fanā'* in Allah, say constantly, 'Allah, Allah!'
> And withdraw into Him from other-than-Him, and with your heart – see Allah.
> Gather your concerns in Him and He will be enough in place of other-than-Allah.
> Be a pure slave to Him and you will be free from other-than-Allah.[52]

Sufi theoreticians like al-Junayd and Shaykh 'Abd al-Qādir have noted that the ecstatic statements made by such Sufis as Bāyazīd al-Bisṭāmī (804-874) and Manṣūr al-Ḥallāj (858-922) with regard to the state of *fanā'* should not be understood to mean a fusion of the Divine and human essences, attributes and actions. Al-Ḥallāj is regarded by many scholars as a pantheist on the basis of his famous statement *ana'l-ḥaqq* (I am the Truth). The verse in his book, *Ṭawāsīn*, in which these words appear are:

> And I said: 'If you do not know Him, then know His signs, I am His sign (*tajallī*) and I am the Truth! And this is because I have not ceased to realize the Truth!'[53]

Yet, in another verse in the *Ṭawāsīn*, al-Ḥallāj makes a statement diametrically opposed to this:

> Oh you who are uncertain, do not identify 'I am' with the Divine I – not now, nor in the future, not in the past. Even if the 'I am' was a consummated gnostic, and if this was my state, it was not the perfection. Even though I am His I am not He.[54]

Shaykh 'Abd al-Qādir explains that most of the *Ṭawāsīn* cannot be understood by means of the intellect. The linguistic definition of *fanā'* as a state of annihilation does not give one an understanding of its meaning. Its meaning can only be understood through taste; it cannot be understood through linguistic analysis or reasoning. Shaykh 'Abd al-Qādir, in his introduction to the translation of the *Ṭawāsīn*, says that to grasp anything of the *Ṭawāsīn* one must follow the instruction of an authorized shaykh of instruction. What is required is an existential transformation, which comes from invocation whilst fasting and being in a state of ritual purity. When these conditions are fulfilled, the foundations are laid for an understanding of the ecstasy of Manṣūr al-Ḥallāj with its "sublime paradoxes and mind-stopping clashes of contradiction."[55]

Ibn al-'Arabī explains that God, without altering His Individuality, manifests Himself through His attribute of light in the forms of phenomenal objects. The self-manifestation of God does not alter His immutability in any way. He is not subject to change, multiplicity, incarnation (*ḥulūl*), union (*ittiḥād*) or division. "Between the Essence (*dhāt*) of the Creator and the essences of His creatures, the Essence of the Knower and the essences of the known, the relation of 'otherness' is clearly seen!"[56] God is absolutely transcendent (*tanzīh muṭlaq*) but despite His Absolute Transcendence, the Qur'ān and *ḥadīth* talk of His Immanence (*tashbīh*). God says of Himself in the Qur'ān that: "*He is the First and the Last, the Outward and the Inward.*"[57] As such, He is immanent at the stage of manifestation of phenomena. Ibn al-'Arabī warns the believer that "if you assert only transcendence you limit God and if you assert only immanence you define Him. But if you assert both things you follow the right course and you are a leader and master in *ma'rifa* (gnosis)."[58]

Shaykh 'Abd al-Qādir has described four categories of human beings, depending on how they perceive creation: *mahjūb*, *maghzūb*, *majdhūb* and *maḥbūb*. A person who acknowledges only phenomena is veiled and called *mahjūb*. One who identifies the phenomenal with God or regards the phenomenal as real is *maghzūb*, an illusionist. Someone who is enraptured and bewildered by the effect of Divine attraction is *majdhūb*. The one who can clearly distinguish between the phenomenal and the Real and lives his life in accordance with that knowledge is *maḥbūb*, one favoured and loved by God. Al-Ḥallāj was *majdhūb* and his inability to conceal this state led to his tragic end. According to Shaykh 'Abd al-Qādir, al-Ḥallāj has a high place of honour amongst Sufis but never attained the goal of *baqā'* (see below) and therefore could not transmit his Light with *idhn* (authorization) from al-Junayd the master he had left.

Baqā'

The term *baqā'* is used for the state of subsistence in God that occurs after the Sufi has returned, so to speak, from the experience of *fanā'*. Al-Junayd explains that after *fanā'* God restores personal attributes and actions to the Sufi. When the Sufi returns to this world after having "reached the zenith of spiritual achievement vouchsafed by God, he becomes a pattern for his fellow men."[59] Al-Kalābādhī said that *baqā'* "is the station of the Prophets."[60] Ibn al-'Arabī said that like the Prophets, the friends of God (*awliyā-Allāh*, commonly translated in English as "saints") also take great benefit from the Divine Presence. He said that the friend of God (*walī-Allāh*), before Divine Self-disclosure, did not dare to describe God except in terms of the words of the Revealed Books and the reports related by God's Messengers. After *fanā'* the Sufi speaks about God with the firm knowledge that has been granted to them through Divine Self-disclosure.[61] Shaykh 'Abd al-Qādir summarizes the matter very succinctly by describing the man of *baqā'* as:

> ... outwardly slave, inwardly free, outwardly dark, inwardly illuminated, outwardly sober, inwardly drunk. He is the *barzakh* (interspace) of the two oceans – the *sharī'a* and the *ḥaqīqa*. Separation does not veil him from gatheredness and gatheredness does not veil him from separation.[62]

When expressed this way sobriety is not viewed in contradistinction to ecstasy. The way of ecstasy is the way of sobriety and the ecstatic Sufi is fully aware of his or her inner ecstasy and can conceal it. *Fanā'* must proceed to *baqā'* if the Sufi's light is to be shared and transmitted to illuminate other people.

From all this it can be seen that Sufi epistemology is based on the Qur'ān in exactly the same way that the Qur'ān also forms the primary basis of knowledge for the jurisprudents, linguists, philosophers and theosophers. The three realms in Sufi cosmology are *mulk*, *malakūt* and *jabarūt* and the three corresponding dimensions of human personality are *nafs*, *rūḥ* and *sirr*, the sciences appropriate to each of these dimensions being *'ilm al-'aql*, *'ilm al-aḥwāl* and *'ilm al-asrār*. The *nafs* inhabits the *mulk* and the means by which it perceives its realm of existence is through *'ilm al-'aql*. The *rūḥ* inhabits the *malakūt* and the means of perceiving its realm is *'ilm al-aḥwāl*. The *sirr* inhabits the *jabarūt* and perceives its domain by means of *'ilm al-asrār*.

Knowledge in Sufism is classified into five categories: *'ilm al-'aql*; *'ilm al-aḥwāl*, *'ilm al-asrār*, *fanā'* and *baqā'*. These five categories of knowledge correspond to the Prophetic terminology for the three branches of Islam: *islām*, *īmān* and *iḥsān*, which in turn correspond with the three stages of the Sufi *sulūk*: *sharī'a*, *ṭarīqa* and *ḥaqīqa*.

From the Sufi perspective, rationalism and empiricism, the sources of modernist epistemology, also constitute epistemic sources in Sufism, being subsumed under *'ilm al-'aql*. The science of states and the science of the innermost consciousness are epistemological sources that transcend modernist epistemology but that does not put them into conflict with it. They can supplement one another in the development of the human personality, provided it is recognized that human beings have dimensions of personality that transcend the merely physical.

Chapter 3

Sufi Epistemology and Cosmology

This chapter sets out to examine cosmogony – the origin of the universe – and cosmology – the structure and order of the universe – from the Sufi perspective, a cosmogony and cosmology constructed out of knowledge attained from the five epistemic sources discussed in the last chapter. As a fundamental issue in cosmogony and cosmology, time will also be a focus here. There is no greater authority on these subjects than Ibn al-ʿArabī, also known as the Greatest Master (Shaykh al-Akbar) of Sufism, famous for his "breathtaking insights into the mysteries of the cosmos, the Islamic Scripture, and religious faith."[1] From the thirteenth century onwards "practically every Muslim thinker of note took it upon himself to define his position vis-a-vis"[2] the great master. The vast corpus of texts left by Ibn al-ʿArabī has been the subject of differing interpretations by generations of scholars and here we will present an overview of Shaykh ʿAbd al-Qādir's commentaries on various aspects of these texts.

Cosmogony and cosmology

Shaykh ʿAbd al-Qādir's understanding of cosmogony and cosmology, which is in agreement with that of Ibn al-ʿArabī, is based on the Qur'ān and the *ḥadīth* of the Prophet Muḥammad ﷺ. Ibn al-ʿArabī relates the planets and stars and their motion to the Divine Names and uses a cosmological framework to explain the Divine creative process. Seven centuries before it became scientifically known in the West, Ibn al-ʿArabī stated that the stars were not fixed and went on to explain why their motion is not ordinarily visible. Another of his remarkable achievements was that he provided the average velocities for the motion of stars, which are consistent with those made in recent times. He observed the retrograde motion of celestial spheres and also explained the formation of planets in the solar system in ways that are widely accepted today. He also wrote about heliocentrism over five centuries before Copernicus did and acknowledged that the earth was spherical, rotating about its axis and revolving around the sun.

In Ibn al-ʿArabī's cosmology God's purpose for creating the universe was *ḥubb* (love), based on the famous *ḥadīth qudsī*,[3] "I was a hidden treasure and I loved to be known. So I created the Universe in order to be known."[4] From this love, according to Ibn al-ʿArabī, was formed *al-ʿamā'*, the Great Mist or Cloud, which has been described elsewhere as "the primordial non-spatiality in non-time"[5] or abstract space. From *al-ʿamā'* emerged the Universal Intellect (*al-ʿaql al-kullī*) or, in Qur'ānic terminology, the Highest Pen (*al-qalam al-aʿlā*). The Universal Intellect is aware of its ontic 'shadow' which is called the Universal Soul (*al-nafs al-kulliyya*) or the Qur'ānic Preserved Tablet (*al-lawḥ al-maḥfūẓ*), on which is written, by the Highest Pen, all that happens until the end of cosmic time. The universe is composed of the letters and words of God that are continuously being written. The Universal Soul produced the

Level of Nature (*martaba al-ṭabīʿa*) and Prime Matter (*al-hayūlā al-ūlā*).

The Level of Nature does not refer to nature in a physical sense but to the four foundational elements of heat, coldness, wetness and dryness. These two – the Level of Nature and Prime Matter – then generated the Universal Body (*al-jism al-kull*). The first thing formed in the Universal Body was the Throne (*al-ʿarsh*) on which God established His authority. The entire creation appeared in the Throne and all creatures beneath it are considered to be covered with Mercy from God. Inside the Throne appeared the Pedestal (*al-kursī*), whose dimensions, compared to the Throne, are described by Ibn al-ʿArabī as a tiny ring in a vast desert. Within the Pedestal is the Isotropic Orb (*al-falak al-aṭlas*), which is so described because it has no distinguishing features and is homogeneous in all directions. Within this Isotropic Orb were created the stars (*al-falak al-mukawkab*), galaxies (*al-falak al-burūj*), the Seven Gardens (*al-jinān*) and our solar system. The solar system, in turn, contains the sun, the planets, the perfect man (*al-insān al-kāmil*), human beings, animals, plants and minerals. The size of the solar system in relation to the Pedestal is again compared by Ibn al-ʿArabī to a tiny ring in the vast desert.[6]

Ibn al-ʿArabī distinguished between the apparent perspective of someone viewing the sun and planets from the earth and the actual motion of the planets and stars themselves. According to him, day and night are caused by the rotation of the earth and not the movement of the sun. Another central feature of Ibn al-ʿArabī's cosmology is that the material universe – the Pedestal – emerged from the immaterial spiritual Throne. This key feature is intimately related to his overall vision of the oneness of existence, something scholars have named *waḥdat al-wujūd*, a term which, as noted before, does not appear in his writings.[7] Oneness of existence, in turn, can only be understood through Ibn al-ʿArabī's concept of time.

Broadly speaking, there are two opposing views in the philosophy of time: the rational view, based on a physical understanding of time, and the idealistic view, based on metaphysics. The rationalists believe that time, and everything else in the world, can be understood by the human mind. The idealists believe that time does not have a separate existence; it is a construct of the mind. Time for Ibn al-ʿArabī is a projection of the human imagination (*wahm*) and, like space and motion, it does not have physical existence. It is an illusion that is nevertheless encountered in everyday experience. Ibn al-ʿArabī uses the words time and space as synonyms because time has no absolute meaning but is used relative to something to describe the state (*ḥāl*) of that thing. In other words, it is used by the human mind to chronologically classify events and the motion of objects. Time has no extension or duration because the future and past are imaginary and, therefore, the real meaning of time is the existence of an object in the present moment. Once this is understood, it is acceptable to adopt definitions of time when comparing one event in relation to another or the motion of one object in relation to another.

Having first defined time in this way, Ibn al-ʿArabī then explains his understanding of time as it appears in the Qurʾān and the *ḥadīth* of the Prophet Muḥammad ﷺ. The word *zamān* (time) does not appear in the Qurʾān but *yawm* (day), *nahār* (daytime) and *layl* (night) do. Ibn al-ʿArabī points out that time is the fourth fundamental constituent of existence in the space-time continuum. The four constituents are: the formable essence (*al-jawhar al-ṣuwarī*), the accidental form (*al-aʿrāḍ*), time (*al-zamān*), and place (*al-makān*). He said that these – and six others which are derived from them – were enough to describe the state of all things in the world. These fundamental constituents, in turn, are nothing but imaginary reflections of the unique non-divisible Single Essence (*al-jawhar al-fard*).

Just as Ibn al-ʿArabī's cosmology distinguishes the material universe – the Pedestal – from the spiritual – the Throne – it also distinguishes between physical and spiritual time. *Zamān ṭabīʿī* (natural or physical time) compares the motion of physical bodies and *zamān fawq ṭabīʿī* (para-natural time)[8] compares spiritual states, that is, different states of consciousness. The latter precede the former. Examples from the Qur'ān, given by Ibn al-ʿArabī, of the latter are the Night Journey (*isrā*) and Ascension (*miʿrāj* of the Prophet ﷺ)[9] and the story of the Companions of the Cave.[10] These experiences occurred in para-natural time and are related to the consciousness of the *rūḥ* and *sirr*. Others who experience similar spiritual states are the *awliyā'* (saints), who are "the people of attention, those who never overlook Allah's rule in things".[11] Ibn al-ʿArabī describes the *quṭb* – the 'Axis' of the spiritual universe – who is at the apex of the hierarchy of the *awliyā'*, as *ṣāḥib al-waqt* (the master of time). The *ṣāḥib al-waqt* witnesses space and time in their totality. The *aqṭāb* – the Axes – are able to do this because their perception is described by the Sufis as in fact being 'out of time'.

There has been much debate in philosophy and science as to whether time is discrete or continuous. Ibn al-ʿArabī was in agreement with the Ashʿarite[12] theologians who believe that time and space are discrete, that is, they are composed of indivisible particles. Furthermore, he believed that the entire world is annihilated and recreated in each particle of time. The basic unit or quantum of time for Ibn al-ʿArabī is the 'day'. This is based on the Qur'ānic verse: "*Every day* (*yawm*) *He is engaged in some affair* (*sha'n*)."[13] Other meanings of *sha'n* are: matter, concern, business, situation and event. Having said that, we must bear in mind that he regarded space, time and motion to be illusory and, as such, time can, in reality, be neither discrete nor continuous. This paradoxical conclusion is the result of Ibn al-ʿArabī's theory of the oneness of existence.

For Ibn al-ʿArabī, the apparent discrete parts of existence are in reality manifestations of a single One and Unique Real Existence that is neither multiple nor divisible. From a physicist's point of view, more specifically that of Mohamed Haj Yousef, we are told:

> The notion of either discreteness or continuousness is indispensable when we imagine multitudes, but with absolute Unity there would be no meaning to such conceptions. Therefore, Ibn ʿArabī's concept of time is that it would be discrete, if we approached it on the (ultimately imaginary) plane of apparent multiplicity, but in reality there is no such reality as 'time' at all. The same perspective can be applied to space.[14]

Ibn al-ʿArabī also refers to each 'day' as *yawm al-shản* (the day of the event) because in it God creates the totality of all events. Since God is One, and His command (*amr*) is one, God re-creates the world in a new image each 'day', similar to the previous one, but with slight changes. However, this single act will affect each entity and creature in the world differently, depending on their individual characteristics. If one looked to the past, in one direction, from the present, and looked to the future in the opposite direction, a circle would be created with no beginning and no end. This is what Ibn al-ʿArabī calls the circle of time. The present moment is like a point on a circle, which defines the future and the past, but time does not have a beginning or an end. The circle of existence, *al-dahr* (the age or time/space), is infinite. Sufis, consider *al-dahr* to be one of the names of God based on the statements of the Prophet Muḥammad ﷺ: "Do not curse *al-dahr* because Allah is *al-dahr*" and the *ḥadīth qudsī*, in which God says: "The son of Adam hurts me, he curses *al-dahr* and I am *al-dahr*, the command is in My Hand, I circulate the daytime and the night."[15]

As well as seeing time as circular, Ibn al-'Arabī also regards time as cyclical or periodic (*dawrī*), that is, periods of time in which the same kinds of event happen in repeated cycles, such as a daily, weekly, monthly and yearly. Each cycle is a 'day', which as we have noted, is, for Ibn al-'Arabī, the basic unit or quantum of time. The 'day' of the earth is from sunrise to sunset, the 'day' of the moon is 28 days, the 'day' of the sun is 360 days (not 365.25 days), the 'day' of Mercury is 30 years, the 'day' of the Zodiac is 12,000 years, the longest planet 'day' is 36,000 years etc. For Ibn al-'Arabī, the days of the earthly week are infused with cosmic significance and, just like the earthly week, the cosmic week is made up of seven cosmic days. The cosmic Saturday (*al-sabt*) is considered to be the 'day of eternity' (*yawm al-abad*) and all the cosmic days of the cosmic week are actually occurring on the cosmic Saturday.

God has seven basic Divine Attributes and each of the seven cosmic days are based on these Attributes: Life, Will, Power, Knowledge, Hearing, Sight, and Speech. Ibn al-'Arabī points out that all these together form a circle beginning with Divine Speech – the Divine Command: '*Be*'.[16] Ibn al-'Arabī then points out that, paradoxically, it is God Who is both the Speaker and the Hearer. Here again from a physicist's point of view Yousef says:

> So this brings us back to the initial receptive state of 'Hearing', because everything in the world is at the end perceived through vibrations, even the visible and other things. Therefore, the creation takes place always, at every moment in time and in every point of space. In terms of the same divine creative cycle of the seven [cosmic] Days ... the world is re-created every moment in six Days (from Sunday to Friday) and displayed on the seventh Day (Saturday). Indeed in terms of Ibn 'Arabī's famous theory of the oneness of being, the speaker is in fact Allah and the hearer is nothing other than Allah.[17]

Since the time human beings live in is 'Saturday' – the 'day of eternity' – the other six cosmic days account for space, thereby creating a unit of space-time. Space, with its six directions, is created in the six cosmic days before 'Saturday', and then it comes into existence in time on 'Saturday'.

Tanzīh and tashbīh

The two perspectives of God signified by the terms *tanzīh* and *tashbīh* are very important in gaining an understanding of Shaykh 'Abd al-Qādir's cosmology. *Tanzīh* means transcendence, incomparability, disconnecting God from creation, or declaring that God transcends all human attributes and qualities. *Tashbīh* means similar, comparable, immanent, acknowledging God's participation in the world of forms, affirming that certain similarities exist between God and His creation. The Qur'ān and the *ḥadīth* are replete with verses and sayings that illustrate aspects of *tanzīh* and *tashbīh*. *Tanzīh* could not be more clear than in the verse "*Glory to your Lord, the Lord of Might, beyond anything that they describe* [*ascribe to Him*]."[18] We see *tashbīh* in the verse, "*Both East and West belong to God, so wherever you turn, the Face of God is there.*"[19] Ibn al-'Arabī says that the theologians, such as the Ash'arites and Mu'tazilites, and philosophers, such as Ibn Sīnā, overemphasized *tanzīh* because the rational faculty is not capable of grasping anything but God's Oneness and transcendence.

It is only through the capacity of *khayāl* that one can perceive *tashbīh* and combine the two perspectives. Ibn al-'Arabī states that anyone "who does not know the status of *khayāl* is totally devoid of knowledge."[20] *Khayāl* is seen by the Sufis "as the creative source of manifestation, the very cause of our existence, and the powerful intermediary that enables us to remain in constant contact with the Infinite and the Absolute."[21] The four levels of *khayāl*, according to Shaykh 'Abd al-Qādir, are *al-khayāl al-muṭlaq*, *al-khayāl al-*

muḥaqqaq, *al-khayāl al-munfaṣil* and *al-khayāl al-muttaṣil*. *Al-khayāl al-muṭlaq* is the first manifestation of the universe; it is the *'amā'* (the great mist), the energy that contains all the forms but is as yet undifferentiated. The distinction here is between Absolute Being (God) and Absolute non-Being (the *'amā'*). *Al-khayāl al-muḥaqqaq* is the level which contains the knowledge that there are two ways of perceiving reality: that of *sharī'a* and that of *ḥaqīqa*. *Sharī'a* relates to the manifestations of forms whilst *ḥaqīqa* relates to unity (*tawḥīd*). The term *al-khayāl al-munfaṣil* pertains to the way by which the universe is ordered into different forms and kingdoms, such as the mineral kingdom, animal kingdom, jinn etc. *Al-khayāl al-muttaṣil* is the *khayāl* that enables one to create pictures in the mind. It separates reality from fantasy and things as they are from things as they can be.

Knowledge of *khayāl* comes through unveiling or direct-tasting, a state bestowed by God upon 'His servants who are God-fearing (possessing *taqwā*)'.[22] With regard to combining *tanzīh* and *tashbīh*, Ibn al-'Arabī pointed out that the "common people stand in the station of declaring similarity (*tashbīh*) [through faith], the People of Unveiling declare both similarity and incomparability (*tanzīh* and *tashbīh*), and the rational thinkers declare incomparability (*tanzīh*) alone. Hence God combines the two sides in His elect."[23] In his explanation of the apparently contradictory statements of the Qur'ān, such as "*There is nothing like Him, and He is the All-Hearing, the All-Seeing*,"[24] Shaykh 'Abd al-Qādir notes that in the first part of the statement God declares Himself to be beyond any association with forms and is thus disconnected, whereas in the second part God affirms that He participates in the form-world through seeing and hearing and thus connects. In the view of Shaykh 'Abd al-Qādir, then, to practice disconnection alone is to limit and restrict God and also to defy the Prophetic teaching method of metaphoric-wisdom.[25]

The types of paradoxes and contradictions we have seen above are not unknown in Western philosophy and science. We find them, for example, in Martin Heidegger's (1889-1976) paradox of Being about which he wrote: "Being is most universal, encountered in every being, and is therefore most common... At the same time, Being is most singular, whose uniqueness cannot be attained by any being whatsoever."[26] Bertrand Russell (1872-1970), the mathematician turned philosopher, discovered that even reasoning that seems to be sound leads to paradox and contradictions.[27] Kurt Gödel (1906-1978) demonstrated "that mathematics is necessarily incomplete, containing true statements that cannot be formally proved."[28] Alan Turing (1912-1954), widely considered the father of computer science and artificial intelligence, showed that no formal axiomatic system can be complete.[29] Contrary to modern science's distinct separation of mind and matter, the neuroscientist Antonio Damasio (b. 1944), says that there is a connection between reason, feelings and the body in anatomical and functional terms. In his book *Descartes' Error* he states:

> The comprehensive understanding of the human mind requires an organismic perspective: that not only must the mind move from non-physical *cogitum* to the realm of biological tissue, but it must also be related to the whole organism possessed of integrated body proper and the brain and fully interactive with a physical and social environment.[30]

From the beginning of the twentieth century physicists have been dealing with the paradoxical nature of matter. The physicist Fritjof Capra, for example, explains that sub-atomic units of matter appear sometimes as particles and sometimes as waves depending on how they are observed. This dual, paradoxical aspect of matter led to the formulation of quantum mechanics.[31]

Based upon the above-mentioned findings of mathematicians

and scientists, an outline of what is known as the 'Complexity Theory' or 'nonlinear dynamics' is becoming apparent. The Complexity Theory analyses living systems in terms of four interconnected perspectives – form, matter, process and meaning – thereby making it possible to "apply a unified understanding of life to phenomena in the realm of matter, as well as to phenomena in the realm of meaning."[32] Whereas science and mathematics are only now beginning to develop a unified approach to overcome the paradoxes that they have encountered, Shaykh 'Abd al-Qādir, and Ibn al-'Arabī before him, saw the need to join the two "paradoxically opposing" perspectives of *tanzīh* and *tashbīh*. In whatever manner you approach the subject, the existence of matter has no 'proof' – it has to be experienced.

Al-Nafas al-Raḥmānī

The doctrine that completes the creational view of Ibn al-'Arabī is known as *al-Nafas al-Raḥmānī*, the Breath of the Merciful.[33] The creation of the universe is likened to a held breath which bursts out, bringing into existence the multiple forms. The Qur'ānic teaching with regards to creation is based on the following verse: *"His command when He desires a thing is just to say to it, 'Be!' – and it is."*[34] Shaykh 'Abd al-Qādir says that this is not some magical act from some exterior Being. The breathing-out of the command is the coming into being of phenomenal reality from the Hidden to the Manifest. The Breath of the Merciful is Nature. Shaykh 'Abd al-Qādir comments that:

> The coming into existence of the Universe from non-existence into existence is an action, through the Divine Command there is a movement from repose into the activity of creation. This movement, this outflowing we call love.[35]

In scientific terms this action and movement, or Divine Love, can be seen in the uncertainty principle of quantum theory.[36] In subatomic physics matter is always in a state of motion. The particles – the electrons, protons and neutrons inside the atomic nucleus – are all moving, some at enormous velocities. Modern physics depicts matter not as inert but as continuously moving at the molecular, atomic and nuclear levels.[37] Yousef points out the similarities of Ibn al-ʿArabī's views on *al-Nafas al-Raḥmānī* and String Theory in subatomic physics. He says that around 1985:

> ... the new String Theory suggested that all elementary particles can be represented by fundamental building blocks called 'strings' that can be closed, like loops, or open, like a hair. The different vibrational modes (of 'notes') of the string represent the different particle types, since different modes are seen as different masses or spins. One mode of variation makes the string appear as an electron, another as a photon.[38]

For Shaykh ʿAbd al-Qādir the cosmos is a manifestation of the words of God, composed of the sounds – the vibrational modes of the notes of the string represented by the different particle types – produced by the Breath of the Merciful out of Divine Love.

Waḥdat al-wujūd

In his work, *Fuṣūṣ al-Ḥikam*, Ibn al-ʿArabī states: "Every particle of the world is from the whole of the world. That is: every single particle is capable of receiving into itself all the realities of all the single particles of the world."[39] The universe is one organism and all its parts are interrelated and interdependent; the cosmos is consistent, structured and hierarchical. Extrapolating from this, Ibn al-ʿArabī suggested that, just as there are elements of outward power that dominate over others, there are also inward components that direct others. Just as the heart dominates the body, it is the perfect man (*al-insān al-kāmil*) who is the raison d'être (the purpose of existence) of the whole universe. Commenting on this theme Shaykh ʿAbd al-Qādir says that the

> ... focal point of this universal reality, which is nothing else than an endless fulgurating display of light upon light, is man, not just the species man, but man at his apogee, the Perfect Man, himself Light and knowing himself to be Light, *al-insān al-kāmil*.[40]

The perfect man is the eye of the universe through which God contemplates His creation. In him is gathered together all the forms in the universe. He personifies the whole creational process, containing the matrices,[41] the elements, plants, animals and angels. He is a small universe and likewise the universe is the 'big man' (*al-insān al-kabīr*). The perfect man is permeated by all the Divine Names and Divine Attributes. Shaykh 'Abd al-Qādir says that the scientific theory of matter called the 'Hadron Bootstrap Model' corresponds to this conception of the human being and the universe. To sum it up briefly, this model shows that every particle consists of all other particles. At present, this model relates only to certain kinds of particles called hadrons. Fritjof Capra says:

> In the bootstrap model, then, all hadrons are composite structures whose components are again hadrons. The essential feature of the model is the picture of the binding forces holding these structures together. The forces between the constituent particles are pictured as the exchange of other particles.[42]

This is a general feature of sub-atomic physics, in which the forces that hold the particles together are also particles. The concept is extremely hard to visualise because it is a consequence of the four-dimensional space/time character of the sub-atomic world. Our intellects and our language cannot deal with the image it presents because the distinction between the constituent particles and the particles representing the binding forces are blurred, causing the notion of objects consisting of discrete constituent parts to break down.

So the Sufis have been able to attain profound knowledge of

cosmogony and cosmology using other epistemological means in addition to rationalism and empiricism. Shaykh ʿAbd al-Qādir has provided extensive commentaries on Ibn al-ʿArabī's writings about these matters. In the thirteenth century Ibn al-ʿArabī explained the formation of planets in the solar system in ways that are widely accepted today, espousing heliocentrism and acknowledging that the earth was spherical, rotating about its axis and revolving around the sun. He anticipated String Theory and the Hadron Bootstrap Model in physics as well. Shaykh ʿAbd al-Qādir is in agreement with Ibn al-ʿArabī on the need to join the two paradoxically opposing perspectives of *tanzīh* and *tashbīh.* These types of paradoxes and contradictions are not unknown in Western philosophy and science. They are to be found in Heidegger's and Russell's philosophy, Gödel's mathematics, Turing's artificial intelligence, Damasio's neuroscience and famously, from the beginning of the twentieth century, atomic physicists have been conclusively demonstrating the paradoxical nature of matter.

Chapter 4

Sufi Epistemology and the Science of Unveiling

A New Paradigm for the 21st Century

In Shaykh ʿAbd al-Qādir's view, Sufi epistemology, with the exception of *ʿilm al-ʿaql*, is derived from suprasensory knowledge that also goes by the names of *mushāhada*, *maʿrifa* and *dhawq*. As we have seen, the term used in the Qur'ān for this kind of knowledge is *kashf* and it refers to the unveiling of the different dimensions of space and time as well as the unveiling of what lies beyond phenomenal reality and existence. Such knowledge is ontological and is acquired as one becomes aware of the different levels of being that comprise the human being. These levels of being are the *nafs*, *rūḥ* and *sirr*. After these levels another more profound level of being and knowledge is attained through *fanā'* followed by *baqā'*. We will now discuss the methods whereby unveiling (*kashf*) is attained in classical Sufism, as outlined by its leading theoretician Abū al-Qāsim al-Junayd. This is also the methodology that is used by Shaykh ʿAbd al-Qādir in his *ṭarīqa*. The following are al-Junayd's rules[1] of Sufism, the practical steps by which Sufis acquire unveiling (*mukāshafa*):

- Conformity to the *sharīʿa* (legal parameters of Islam) as revealed by God in the Qur'ān and as practised by the Prophet Muḥammad ﷺ.
- Taking a shaykh (master) of instruction (*tarbiya*).
- Engaging in *dhikr* (invocation and remembrance of God).
- The transformation of states (*aḥwāl*) into stations (*maqamāt*).
- *Khalwa* i.e. withdrawal from the world in the concentration of invocation of the *al-ism al-aʿẓam* (the Supreme Name – Allah) under the supervision of an authorized master.

By taking a detailed look at these rules it will become evident how al-Junayd's methodology has been absorbed by Shaykh ʿAbd al-Qādir and how the essence of the teaching is transmitted by him in different forms. Through the lens of this survey the discussion will also focus on Sufism in general, and the teachings of Shaykh ʿAbd al-Qādir in particular, within the appropriate social and historical contexts.

The Rules of al-Junayd

1. Conformity with the sharīʿa as revealed by God and practised by the Prophet ﷺ

The Prophet ﷺ is regarded by the Sufis as *al-Qawtham* – the complete, perfect man. The significance of following him, Shaykh ʿAbd al-Qādir says, relates to identity and character. He points out that an identity cannot be formed in a psychological vacuum but rather it is developed through a person's transactions within the social nexus they inhabit. These social transactions should be in accordance with the commands of God and his Messenger.[2] The Prophet ﷺ should not be worshipped, says Shaykh ʿAbd al-Qādir, or deified, or made into a symbol. He is merely being accepted as a witness of Reality, knowing it inwardly and outwardly and being in harmony with it.[3]

The Prophet ﷺ said, "I was only sent to perfect noble qualities of character."[4] The word the Prophet ﷺ used for character is *akhlāq*, a word derived from *khalq* meaning created form. Shaykh 'Abd al-Qādir paraphrases the above *ḥadīth* in the words, "I was only sent to ennoble the human form" and adds:

> The human form, like that of the animal, is not like in a snapshot. To understand the form of the lion, for example, you have to understand how it lives with the other lions, how it breeds, how it hunts, its habitat – you have to know its whole life-cycle to know what the form of the lion is. ... This is very important because the Sufis have always insisted that this difference is where many of the *fuqahā'* [jurists] have failed to understand the true nature of the *dīn* [religion], because it cannot be fixed in principles of law. It always goes back to *akhlāq*, this living form of the character of the human creature.[5]

This ennobling of character is accomplished through the process of transmission from someone who is completely at peace, functioning in the quotidian social reality of the community. Shaykh 'Abd al-Qādir says that these qualities are to be found in the Prophet Muḥammad[6] ﷺ. With this in mind he had Qāḍī 'Iyāḍ's *Kitāb al-shifā bi ta'rīf ḥuqūq al-muṣṭafā* translated and published in 1991. In it are recorded many of the personal characteristics of the Prophet Muḥammad ﷺ. A particular quality of the Prophet ﷺ that Sufis emphasize is that he was cheerful and joyful in the midst of extreme trial and tribulation. The Prophetic teaching is that faith in God means that one can rest in the knowledge that one's provision and protection are from God. An example of the Prophet's ﷺ belief that God is the Provider is that once 90,000 dirhams (silver coins) came into the treasury. He ﷺ placed them on a mat, called the people to him and distributed all of them. His Companion Anas said, "The Messenger of God did not store up anything for the next day."[7]

A famous example of the Prophet's complete faith in God's protection is that on one occasion a man called Ghawrath ibn al-

Ḥārith went to assassinate him while he was sitting under a tree. He quietly approached the Prophet ﷺ from behind, pulled out his sword and, standing over the Prophet, said, "Who will protect you from me?" The Prophet ﷺ replied, "God". The sword fell from his hand and the Prophet ﷺ grabbed it and said, "Who will protect you from me?" The man said, "Punish me but in a good manner." The Prophet ﷺ pardoned him and let him go.[8]

Learning within one's daily experience that God is the Protector and Provider is seen by the Sufis as the quickest way to knowing oneself. Shaykh 'Abd al-Qādir says:

> You are the whole man, but not as you are. Muḥammad is the measure of man. He is *al-Qawtham*, the completely perfect man, or, as the Sufis call him, *al-insān al-kāmil* [the complete human being]. This is the station of the one who has achieved the goal, who knows himself.[9]

Knowing oneself entails being aware of one's inner reality. If someone denies their inner reality, they effectively dismantle the Prophetic behaviour pattern which gives substance to that inner reality. Shaykh 'Abd al-Qādir says that Sufism insists on the holistic picture of men and women being in a state of transformation both outwardly and inwardly, socially and individually. There can, therefore, be no Sufi tradition without the social reality of Islam, which extols simplicity in behaviour and moderation in possessions, which promotes kindness and courtesy between people, which demands respect for every one regardless of gender, and which insists on care for the young and old.

> It is Sufism, as guardian of the Islam of the Companions, that demands a radiant city as the setting for the man of knowledge to experience his gnosis. The Sufi's place is in the community.[10]

The creation of such a community was the great social achievement of the Prophet ﷺ. In a remarkably short time, beginning with a small group of people, he built up a highly educated, enlightened society. Guided by Divine Revelation, he instructed them and purified their practices. In Mecca they remained non-violent in spite of being savagely persecuted, humiliated and tortured. The Prophet ﷺ delivered the Qur'ānic Message of God, which contained laws enabling human society to function harmoniously and peacefully. These laws also enabled humans to coexist with their environment. The Prophet ﷺ taught that the aim of leadership was to preserve social order and assure prosperity. He said that wealth belonged to God and human beings possessed it as a trust from Him. It was to be used as a means to an end, the end being Paradise.

Strict parameters were laid out for the acquisition of wealth, under which usury, hoarding, gambling and unjust trading practices were prohibited. The law guaranteed the movement of wealth among all sections of society, implying the end of the oligarchic order that prevailed in pre-Islamic Mecca. Socially, all human beings were regarded as equals in the sight of God. The Revelation called for women to be treated with honour, for non-Muslims to be respected and for the freeing of slaves to be regarded as a meritorious act. The Revelation also called for changes in moral behaviour. It encouraged self-sacrifice for the benefit of others and called for abstinence from alcohol, fornication, adultery, homosexuality and female infanticide.

What was being introduced by the Prophet ﷺ was his *ḥikma*, his wisdom, which he later defined through the use of the two opposite terms, *ḥilm* and *jāhiliyya*.[11] Shaykh 'Abd al-Qādir defines *ḥilm* as a state of calm serenity, which is not overcome by anger from within or threats of violence from without. *Ḥilm* implies that the *nafs* (ego) has been tamed and is under one's control.[12] Its opposite is another Qur'ānic term *jāhiliyya*[13] which is:

> ... the energy force of the unbridled *nafs*, utterly flamboyant and expressed, ruthless in its infantile determination to experience

> gratification whether of appetite or violence. This was the natural flow of destructive energy that came from the *nafs* which saw itself as separate from existence and in conflict with reality.[14]

The Path of Sufism requires that, to be complete, a human being should be in a continuous state of transformation, both outwardly and inwardly, and so Sufism promotes the creation of a polity conforming to the *sharīʿa*, which is conducive to this process taking place and in which men and women of knowledge are, therefore, enabled to experience *maʿrifa* – direct knowledge of the Divine Reality.

2. Taking a shaykh of instruction (*tarbiya*)[15]

The *sulūk* of the Sufi entails travelling from the station of *islām* to the station of *īmān* and then on to the station of *iḥsān*. It can also be said to be a journey from *mulk* to *malakūt* and then on to *jabarūt*. It is to move from the sensory to the meaning, from witnessing the cosmos to witnessing the Creator of the cosmos, from the manifest world to the unseen world, from the unification of actions to the unification of Attributes and on to the unification of the Essence. This travel requires struggle against the *nafs* and its habits and this is only possible under the guidance of a master. The shaykh's sole intention in this is to set the disciple on the path of realising his own capacities and this is only possible if the shaykh is "himself a completely radiant and surrendered slave of Reality."[16]

Obedience and following the master are essential because the journey is difficult and dangerous. The slightest deviation has the possibility of severing one from the path, resulting in the destination not being reached. The disciple should take on the discipline and counsel of the realised master who shows him or her the frivolity of the self and the faults of its actions. Obedience to the rules as laid down by the shaykh of instruction helps dismantle the thickly veiled and highly associative self. The self is prone to assign power to entities other than God and this is its greatest and unpardonable fault known in Arabic as *shirk*.

One of the qualities of the master is that he understands the different stages of travelling the path. This enables him to help people according to their strengths and possibilities. With regards to strengths and possibilities there are disciples at various stages who can be described as follows: those who are in denial of super-sensory experience, the reluctant who are hesitant but are not like those who deny, the truthful who engage in struggle and invocation, and those who embrace turbulence and carry extremely difficult burdens. The master is able to identify the stage reached by each disciple because he has completed the journey, become annihilated in God and returned to guide others. He has travelled the path of the Sufis until he has tasted its bitterness and sweetness, its benefits and its harm, its highs and its lows. Its lows are obscurity and diminishment in society, isolation and difficulty. Its highs are independence and influence amongst people.

Having had these experiences himself, the master is able to know when to tell a disciple who loves obscurity and isolation to mix with society. This is better for the annihilation of the self of that disciple because annihilation comes through what is difficult and heavy for the self. In a similar way, a disciple who has become addicted to independence and influence has to be directed to obscurity and isolation. Abandoning the attractions of reputation requires one to forsake attachment to wealth. On the Sufi path, the abandoning of reputation is obligatory as it is a deadly poison to spiritual development. In place of wealth and reputation the disciple must strengthen his attachment to God, the Owner of the treasures of the heavens and the earth. The master is well acquainted with the difficulties and ease of the journey and will, therefore, take the strong disciple on the difficult path, to shorten the distance for him, and take the weak disciple along an easier path. Ibn ʿAjība says, "There is no doubt that, if the path is short and near, it must be difficult and steep, whereas if it is easy and often travelled, then the distance is much greater."[17]

The master is also familiar with both the dangerous and safe places along the path so that he can guide the disciple with regards to them. He sees danger for the disciple who keeps company with ignorant people or with scholars of the *sharīʿa* who think that what they know constitutes knowledge of what the *sunna* is. The master is also aware that safety lies in keeping distant from people and what they possess. As the Prophet ﷺ said, "Be one who does without in this world and Allah will love you. Be one who does without what is in the hands of people and they will love you."[18] Doing without material possessions and relying on God to fulfil one's needs increases the Sufi in the certainty that God is the Provider. The master is also aware of everything that may obstruct the Sufi on his journey, particularly self-complacence at being able to perform miracles and other things beyond normal human possibility. When this happens, the disciple is reminded that the goal lies ahead and that frivolities and the desires of the self are merely distractions on the path.

The master is acquainted with the outward as well as the inward aspects of knowledge, in other words those pertaining to the *sharīʿa* as well as those pertaining to *ṭarīqa* and *ḥaqīqa*. The condition of friendship with God (*wilāya* – sainthood) is that the master must have knowledge of the *sharīʿa* and act according to it. It is the consensus of the Sufi masters that a certain amount of outward knowledge is necessary, with the strict minimum being the maintenance of the rules of purification, prayer, *zakāt*, fasting, pilgrimage, etc. He should have enough knowledge of the Qur'ān and the *sunna* to fulfil the obligations of the *sharīʿa* and upon which to base the actions of his *sulūk*. The master also teaches the disciple about the intrigues of the self and shows him or her the path of realisation of states, stations and ecstasy. The guidance of the master is not restricted to formal teaching. An important master in Shaykh ʿAbd al-Qādir's *ṭarīqa*, Abū al-Ḥasan al-Shādhilī, said that the master also helps his disciple from behind the veil, meaning even when there is a physical distance between them. Al-Shādhilī is reported to have said, "By Allah, I take a man to Allah in one single breath."[19] Al-Mursī said, "What is between me and a man is that I glance at him and he becomes independent."[20]

The master cures the disciple of his inner sicknesses, the greatest of which are anxiety about provision, fear of creation, management and choice, anger and impatience. He focuses the hearts of the disciples on God by guiding them to complete annihilation in Him so that their hearts are completely dedicated to Him. When cured, the hearts become filled with the light of certainty and the disciples become independent of everything else. They rely on God alone and are thereby relieved of management and choice. The one who attains this has tasted the sweetness of faith (*īmān*) and is pleased with God in every state and time. When the disciple finds everything that God decrees for him or her to be sweet, whether it is good or bad, because it is all from the Beloved, he or she is ready to enter into the Presence of the Lord of the Universe. In a *ḥadīth qudsī* God says of the accomplished Sufi:

> If the main occupation of My slave is to be occupied with Me, I make his yearning and his sweetness in remembering Me. If I make him find his sweetness and his yearning in My remembrance, he loves Me passionately and I love him passionately. I remove the veil between Me and him. He does not forget when people forget. The speech of such people is the speech of the Prophets, and they are the real heroes.[21]

Then the disciple sees the advantages of purification of the self and the benefits of taking the shaykh of instruction.

3. Engaging in dhikr (invocation and remembrance of Allah)

Reference to the practice of *dhikr* is found repeatedly in the Qur'ān. A few examples are: "*Remember* (*udhkur*) *your Lord when you forget*,"[22] "*You who believe! Remember* (*udhkurū*) *Allah much and glorify Him in the morning and the evening*."[23] and: "*Only in the remembrance of Allah* (*dhikrillāh*) *can the heart find peace*."[24] God can be remembered anywhere and at any time and this remembrance can be done out loud or silently, privately or in a gathering (*majlis al-dhikr*). There are three different levels of *dhikr*. The first is *dhikr* of the tongue with intention in the heart. At this stage the subject (*dhākir*) is conscious of his experience, what he is saying and the One whose Name he is repeating. The second stage is *dhikr* of the heart. Awareness of the heart should accompany the remembrance of the tongue. The third stage, in which everything but God is absent, is called *dhikr* of the *sirr*. The first stage is reached by the common people, the second by the élite and the third by the elect of the élite.

Shaykh 'Abd al-Qādir says that the goal of the Sufi is the wiping out of his illusory experiencing self. The daily prayers, fasting and *zakāt*

> ... shudder and move this seeming solidity until we recognize that the *nafs* is in constant movement, constant flux, it is cloud-form and not mountain. ... The means by which we set in motion the mountain solidity of forms in experience, in order to open ourselves to the transparent cloud-nature of stuff, is the great science that the Prophets transmit to their people. It is called in the language of the desert Messenger, *dhikrullah*.[25]

The repository of *dhikr* is the Qur'ān and it is the storehouse of all the *dhikr* practised. Most Orders have a *wird* or *waẓīfa* which the disciples recite regularly. A *wird* is a collection of Qur'ānic verses, prayers from the *ḥadīth* and the writings of the great masters.

4. Transformation of States (*Aḥwāl*) into Stations (*Maqamāt*)

Commenting on an Ibn al-'Arabī statement, "the Qur'ān is laden with quality," Shaykh 'Abd al-Qādir says that what the Master means is that the Qur'ān is not just a Book but a dynamic thing "laden with quality". The Qur'ān is a record of the ontological experiences of the Prophet and as such these records indicate states (*aḥwāl*). The Qur'ān is therefore a source-book of guidance with relation to all the states that the human being might experience. So the *dhikr* is a key that opens the self to these states. Al-Qushayrī noted that, "The states (*aḥwāl*) are gifts, the stations (*maqamāt*) are earnings."[26] A *ḥāl* (state) is transient and fleeting by nature and a *maqām* (station) denotes fixity and stability. The state is bestowed on the Sufi by God and the fixing of the state into a station requires self-exertion on the part of the Sufi. Shaykh 'Abd al-Qādir says that before approaching the matter of states we should remember that the self has no solidity but is a dynamic energy source like a radio station sending out signals from an identifiable point. He says that if states

> ... are imagined to be something happening to someone then the true perspective is lost. That, from the experiential point of view, there is a radio station and there is a programme, signals are coming and going, is never in question, otherwise it would not matter what happened to us. What is important is that we begin to think about these matters with a more fluid and less definitive imagery, the 'fuzzy mathematics' of the biologist trying to describe dynamic organisms rather than the fixed and rigid arithmetic that measures solid forms.[27]

The idea that the self has any constancy is merely an illusion propped up by habit patterns which give it the illusion of solidity.

The Sufi in his or her development recognizes that there is a constant transition from one state to another.[28] The Sufi has to learn to adjust to these changes in a similar way to that of a sailor changing the sail according to the prevailing winds.

In *The Hundred Steps*, Shaykh 'Abd al-Qādir lists the following states and stations that a Sufi has to go through on the journey to God: *faqr* (poverty), *tawba* (turning away from wrong actions), *wara'* (scrupulousness), *zuhd* (doing-without), *tawakkul* (reliance on God), *ṣabr* (patience), *shukr* (thankfulness), *taqwā* (fearful awareness of God), *ikhlāṣ* (pure, unadulterated sincerity), *ṣidq* (truthfulness), *irāda* (stripping away of self will and accepting what God wills), *'ubūdiyya* (obedience, service and devotion to God), *khawf* (fear of God), *rajā'* (hope in God), *riḍā* (contentment), *futuwwa* (nobility), *qabḍ* (constriction), *basṭ* (expansion), *wajd* (the first degree of ecstasy, finding oneself), *wijdān* (the second degree of ecstasy, when the sweetness of witnessing lasts), *wujūd* (presence and awareness), *jadhb* (Divine attraction which takes one to *ma'rifa*), *lawā'iḥ* (first flashes of awareness of lights), *lawāmi'* (gleams of genuine lights that come to the longing heart), *ṭawāli'* (Shaykh 'Abd al-Qādir explains that the *lawā'iḥ* lights are like meteors, the *lawāmi'* lights are like the Milky Way through clouds and the *ṭawāli'* lights are like the full view of the Northern Lights that fill the whole night sky), *shawq* (desire, the hearts longing to meet the Beloved), *dhawq* (tasting), *sukr* (drunkenness), *ṣaḥwa* (sobriety), *farq* (separation), *jam'* (gatheredness), *jam' al-jam'* (gatheredness of gatheredness), *tawḥīd* (the affirmation of unity), *tafrīd* (isolation), *af'āl* (one's acts being the actions of God), *ṣifāt* (one's attributes being the attributes of God), *dhāt* (one's essence being the Essence of God), *ma'rifa* (gnosis), *ghurba* (exile), *'uzla* (retirement in order to fix in the heart the meanings and secrets attained in the *khalwa*), *simsima* (gnosis that is too fine to express), *tajallī* (God's unveiling of visions to His slave); *takhallī* (revelation of the treasure-chests of one's inwardness), *murāqaba* (watching), *mushāhada* (witnessing), *wilāya* (friendship with God), *fanā'* (annihilation in God), *balā'* (trials which purify the Sufi in his or her new situation and adjust the lens of his or her new vision), *baqā'* (going on in Allah), *saḥq* (the disappearance of your structure under the force of God), *maḥq* (annihilation in His source), *ṣā'iqa* (annihilation in the Divine manifestation), *nāsūt* (man/womanhood), *lāhūt* (this is when the God's Lordship over existence in its inward aspect is defined), *raḥamūt* (when the gnosis of the Real replaces the concept of essence), *maḥabba* (love), *qurb* (nearness), *taraqqī* (rising), *talaqqī* (receiving), *lisān* (audition), *tamkīn* (fixity), *talwīn* (change), *tajrīd* (stripping away) and *kamāl* (perfection).

Stations manifest fleetingly at first as states and they then become fixed in the disciple. This process is likened to dyeing cloth, which is dipped in the same colour and dried repeatedly until the colour becomes fixed. Once the dye is fixed the station is established. As the disciple moves from one station to the next he or she increases in knowledge and gnosis. Shaykh 'Abd al-Qādir says that everything that is on the earth moves from state to state indicating that there are degrees of existence.[29] For example there are in existence forms that are devoid of organic life, then higher up there are living organisms and then even higher up there are human beings who have unveiling from the unseen. Furthermore, a human being's life on earth is only one phase of his or her existence that was preceded by a phase in the world of spirits before birth and will be followed by an after death state in the grave and so on as the journey to God continues. The science of Sufism is designed to take the Sufi through all the states mentioned above whilst one is still alive in this world. After reaching *fanā'* and *baqā'* the Sufi does not cease in his or her journey but now the journey is in God by the gifts of God.[30]

5. *Khalwa* – Withdrawal from the world through the invocation of the *al-ism al-aʿẓam* (the Supreme Name – Allah) under the supervision of a Sufi master

Khalwa means retreat or seclusion and specifically denotes solitary isolation. In al-Junayd's explanation it refers to seclusion from the distractions of the phenomenal world and being in the Divine Presence. Shaykh ʿAbd al-Qādir explains that in *khalwa* the Supreme Name, Allah, is repeated in a way designated in the Darqāwī *ṭarīqa*.[31] It entails the elongation of the Name whilst visualising the letters of the Name in the heart. This leads to stillness of the mind and suspension of thought. The invocation of the Name leads the Sufi to the Named. Shaykh ʿAbd al-Qādir says:

> In the first *maqamāt* [stations] the *murīd* [disciple] is guided by the Shaykh, but when he reaches a certain point he must go on alone and from that moment the Shaykh follows after the *murīd* as it were, making plain after the matter is complete, and it is direct witnessing of the Lord of creation. *ʿIlm al-ladunī* – face to face knowledge.[32]

This method of invoking the *al-ism al-aʿẓam* has been passed down in the *ṭarīqa* of Shaykh ʿAbd al-Qādir from the time of the great master Abū al-Ḥasan al-Shādhilī (1196-1258). It took the Master Muḥammad al-ʿArabī al-Darqāwī (1760-1823) "just a month and a few days"[33] of using this technique to be annihilated in God. He indicated that if one uses this technique, paying close attention to its conditions, the veil between the disciple and God will be lifted in three weeks or less. Al-Darqāwī says that if this *dhikr* is done for longer than seven weeks and the veil has not lifted the disciple "has no intention, no true sincerity, no love, no resolution, and no certainty. Allah is the authority for what we say."[34] Whilst in *khalwa* it is important that the disciple informs the master, with honesty and care, of everything that happens because the master's guidance is indispensable during this experience.

Shaykh ʿAbd al-Qādir has incorporated these rules of al-Junayd into the practices of his *ṭarīqa*. An appreciation of how he has done this will become clear once it is viewed within the contemporary social and historical context.

Sufism within its social and historical context

The important social functions performed by the Sufis have been noted by various studies covering almost the entire Islamic historical period and spanning various Muslim societies worldwide. The actual characteristics of Sufis and Sufism have been obscured partly by an overemphasis on texts, both poetic and doctrinal, without reference to their wider social and historical contexts. This model of Sufism primarily focuses on the erudite hermit's pursuit of Divine union. Anything linking Sufism with less elevated goals has been regarded as peripheral and inauthentic. As an example, Nile Green has argued that until the 1990s "the scholarly marginalization of Sufi shrines and the variety of activities surrounding them continued, phenomena which traditional scholarship regarded as related only tenuously to Sufism if related to it at all."[35] Green's survey covered Indian Sufism in the seventeenth century.

It has been the custom for Sufi masters to be buried in their *zāwiyas* but the *zāwiyas* did not cease performing their functions with the death of the master. The succeeding master often continued the role of the previous master. The scene of pilgrims begging at the shrines of Sufi saints does seem far removed from the image of the Sufi saint which was adopted from the "intellectualist European milieu, and in more recent times from an Anglo-American neglect of social theory."[36] This view neglects the fact that the Sufi saint spent as much time administering to the worldly needs of his disciples as with the lofty goal of Divine Self-unveiling. Sufis played an active role in the social, political and economic lives of the societies in which they lived.[37]

Green's study focused on the Sufi masters Shah Nur, Shah Palangposh, Shah Musafir and Niẓām al-Dīn of Aurangabad, the Mughal capital during and just after the reign of Sultan Awrangzeb (1618-1707). Green found that Sufis of late Mughal Aurangabad used their powers to cure the sick, to retrieve property for those from whom it was stolen and to protect their disciples during periods of socio-political unrest. Sufi masters used their ability to do miracles (*karāmāt*) as part of their social function of assisting people in times of sickness, drought and other natural phenomena. These miraculous aspects of Sufism were closely related to gnostic knowledge (*maʿrifa*). With regards to miracles Green has argued that:

> While some modern commentators may prefer a Sufism of certain knowledge to one also comprising the working of wonders, the fact remains that the roots of Sufism lie as far beyond the historical limits of modernity as they do beyond the philosophical boundaries of modernism. This conflict between the modern and pre-modern mentalities was manifested in twentieth-century Muslim representations of Sufi history no less than in Western scholarly accounts from the same period.[38]

In his book, *Sufis as Warriors*, Richard Eaton has shown that fourteenth century Sufis were engaged in military expeditions for the expansion of territory by Muslims in the Bijapur plateau in India.[39] He also notes that Turkoman Sufis had participated in battles on the Anatolian frontier in the thirteenth century and draws attention to similar militant participation by Sufis in south-western Iran during the late fifteenth century. In his study of eighteenth century Mughal India, Mohammad Umar looks at the Sufi master Shāh Waliyullāh's (1703-1762) gallant efforts to stop the decline of the empire.[40] Shāh Waliyullāh observed the decline of the social order and addressed all sections of the community with his concerns. Among those whom he counselled were the *sulṭān*, the *wazīrs* (the ministers of the *sulṭān*), the *amīrs* (governors), the generals of the army, the *'ulamā'* (scholars), descendants of the Sufi masters, artisans, craftsmen and the community in general.

His writings included discussions on the social and economic abuses that preceded the downfall of the Roman and Sassanid empires. In a ten-point letter to the *sulṭān, wazīrs* and *amīrs*, he suggested that various measures be taken to stem the decline of the empire. These included a concerted effort to re-take land forcibly occupied by the Jats,[41] increasing crown territories to stop the treasury from sliding into bankruptcy, better organization of the armies, that only such persons be appointed as judges (*qāḍīs*) and city administrators (*muḥtasibs*) against whom no charges of corruption and bribery had been levelled. He insisted that the appointed imams of mosques must be adequately paid and should be required to efficiently carry out their duties, and that the ruler and others in authority should not indulge in prohibited pastimes. All these suggestions emanated from his knowledge of the *sharī'a.*

Since Shaykh 'Abd al-Qādir entered his *ṭarīqa* in Morocco, the focus of this discussion will now turn to the Maghrib, literally the West, referring to the coastal plain of North Africa. In his study of Moroccan Sufism, *Realm of the Saint: Power and Authority in Moroccan Sufism,* Vincent Cornell argued that in order to understand sainthood, a way had to be found to assess extraordinary individuals without taking recourse to "inadequate and impressionistic concepts such as charisma or resorting to reductionist theoretical models."[42] Of particular significance to us here is the relationship between charisma and institution building in sociological and anthropological studies of Sufism. Max Weber (1864-1920) introduced the term charisma into sociological writings and he regarded charismatic authority as one of three forms of authority, the others being traditional or feudal and legal or rational forms of authority. Weber defined charisma as:

> ... a certain quality of an individual personality, by virtue of which one is "set apart" from ordinary people and treated as endowed with supernatural, superhuman, or at least specifically exceptional powers or qualities. These as such are not accessible to the ordinary person, but are regarded as divine in origin or as exemplary, and on the basis of them the individual concerned is treated as a leader.[43]

Studies of the charismatic dimension of human action, in Shmuel Noah Eisenstadt's view, are attempts to come close to the essence of being, that is attempts at creating a cosmological vision of social order.[44] These studies impinge on the epistemological and ontological standing of sociological concepts such as culture and social structure.[45] Eisenstadt points out that studies analysing the correlation between charisma and institution building in social theory have oscillated "between seeing the relationship between culture and social structure in any given society as either static and homogeneous – or as entirely open, almost endlessly malleable and continuously changing."[46] In the first view, cultural orientations or rules are seen as uniform and static throughout the history of the societies in which they are institutionalized. The other view holds that culture is the result of patterns of behaviour, of structure and of power which can be activated in different social situations.[47] The first view constitutes the dominant paradigm that has been used in the examination of Moroccan Sufism by social scientists.

In *Realm of the Saint*, Cornell shows that social scientists, in their study of Moroccan Sufism, base their discussions on the writings of the French historian Alfred Bel. According to Bel, Moroccan religiosity is a syncretic fusion of pre-Islamic Berber superstition, Arab Islam and Sufism which, after gaining approval of a section of the scholarly élite, "evolved into an intolerant form of popular Sufism and a self-satisfied fatalism that contributed to the overall decline of Islamic civilization."[48] Cornell goes on to say that, despite Bel's lack of objectivity, his model is accepted by prominent, anthropologists, social historians and political scientists as definitive. Cornell argues that, whilst dealing with the paranormal is difficult from the scientific point of view, it is necessary for understanding major facets in Islamic Studies. Neither simply locating a saint in a particular social structure nor explaining the phenomenon of sainthood according to the principles of mysticism are adequate tools when conceptualizing sainthood. Such a study of sainthood must unite both social and doctrinal perspectives. It must acknowledge that sainthood is a social phenomenon because, in any case, the extraordinary is recognized in practice before it is defined in theory. As Cornell says:

> To restate the point in the terms used by Moroccan Sufis: if the nature of a person's knowledge (*'ilm*) is revealed through one's actions (*'amal*), then the nature of a person's sainthood (*walāya*) will also be revealed through the actions of the saint experienced by others (*wilāya*). An example of this understanding can be found in Aḥmad Zarrūq's statement, 'The inner essence of the slave is known through his outward state,' or in Aḥmad ibn 'Āshir's 'Knowledge without practice is like a tree without fruit'.[49]

What we see in this definition is a clear distinction between the terms *wilāya* and *walāya*. They have been used interchangeably both in Islamic Studies and informal Arabic. In Cornell's view *walāya* refers to the internal visage (*bāṭin*) of sainthood and as such it is the product of a mystical epistemology that relies on its own educational apparatus and training. This epistemology contextualizes the theoretical and practical factors that enter into the Sufi definition of sainthood. The concept of *wilāya* is the outward visage (*ẓāhir*) of sainthood, that is, the actions of the saint were seen directly by the people which they understood in terms of power.[50] The Sufi was empowered by his gnostic knowledge to influence the destiny of his society by helping the poor and confronting those who oppressed the weak.[51]

Despite Cornell's efforts, the status of Sufi epistemology remains unresolved in sociological and anthropological studies of Sufism. For example, Ernest Gellner in *Postmodernism, Reason and Religion,*[52] implies that Sufis, due to being Muslims, hold the same position on truth as do Muslim fundamentalists. He says that there are three basic positions in the contemporary world, which are: religious fundamentalism, relativism and Enlightenment rationalism. When explaining these positions he says that fundamentalists believe they are the possessors of the unique truth. Relativism, as exemplified by "postmodernism" in a variety of formulations, denies the idea of a unique truth and lastly, referring to Enlightenment rationalism, "a position of which I am more or less an adherent, which retains the faith in the uniqueness of truth, but does not believe we ever possess it definitely, and which uses, as the foundation for practical conduct and inquiry, not any substantive conviction, but only a loyalty to certain procedural rules."[53]

The first position described by Gellner may well be the position of Muslim fundamentalists and modernists but it is contrary to Islam. (Refer to al-Rasheed,[54] Crecelius,[55] Keddie,[56] Kedourie,[57] Ayubi,[58] Tibi,[59] and Layish[60]) In contrast to Gellner's thesis, Islam does not claim a monopoly on truth because, basic to *ʿaqīda* (belief) in Islam, is the postulate that God is the Truth (*al-Ḥaqq*) and no one and nothing can encompass Him. What is at issue here, however, is knowledge of the Truth, and the process of acquiring that knowledge has been described in the techniques of Sufism as outlined by al-Junayd. The goal of Sufism is to create a society that has within it people who have direct knowledge of the Truth, because without these gnostics (*ʿārifīn*) social coherence is unattainable. As noted in the biography of al-Junayd,[61] from the epistemological perspective mankind is divided into three groups: the common, the élite and the elect of the élite. Also, as noted before, Shaykh 'Abd al-Qādir says that just as the heart dominates the body, the perfect human being (*al-insān al-kāmil*) is the purpose for the existence of the universe.

During his life, the Prophet Muḥammad ﷺ was at the top of the hierarchy of the elect amongst humankind. Since his death there has always remained on the earth the embodiment of the Light of Muḥammad (*nūri-muḥammadiyya*) – the *quṭb* (the pivot of existence), the perfected friend of God. Sufism is the transmission of this Light, which cascades down through a series of perfected human beings who are to the earth as the respiratory-system is to the purification of the blood in the body. The disappearance of these saints would mean the death of the planet and Shaykh 'Abd al-Qādir adds that what man is to the earth, the earth is to the universe, with size having nothing to do with these matters. From among these saints there are three hundred who make up the elect. They are perfect in their humility, poverty, love and awe. From among them there are forty who are most complete in knowledge and stations. From these there are the twelve *nuqabā'* (Chieftains) and from these are the seven *abdāl* (Substitutes) who are the highest of the human species. From the *abdāl* come the four *awtād* (Pillars) and from them are the two Imams and one of these is the *quṭb*.[62] In Sufi cosmology the three hundred saints referred to here are the indispensable supports of human society.

It is clear from the examples cited above that the Sufi masters have also performed an important social function. Whilst determined to guide their disciples towards direct knowledge of God and closeness to Him they administered to their worldly needs as well. They fought in wars, counselled their political leaders, administered justice in courts of law as judges, provided food, cured the sick, retrieved stolen property, provided relief from drought, educated people and refined their characters. There are two aspects to Sufism, the inward and the outward, the spiritual and the material, the personal and the social, and clearly the Sufis are engaged in keeping them in balance.

Sufi encounters with modernity

Whilst some Sufis have preferred a reclusive lifestyle most have been part of the Muslim mainstream. Sufis are engaged in inviting people to Islam, teaching them the tenets of the faith, demonstrating how to implement them, and defending the Muslim community and territories when that is necessary. Large scale encounters between Sufis and modernists can be divided into three periods: (i) colonial; (ii) neo-colonial; and (iii) secularism. As stated before, beliefs and their justification in relation to knowledge, lead to certain values and these values lead to the institutionalization of specific types of behaviour. The economic and political institutions that result form the core of the culture and civilization that develops around them. The legal, educational, and health-care systems and modes of recreation of a society are also based on these epistemological foundations. All the encounters that Sufis have had with modernity can be seen as a clash of differing epistemologies and institutions. Abdelwahhab Elmesseri describes this process as the forceful imposition of "Western cultural and epistemological paradigms" onto the people of the world through colonialism.[63]

The colonial period

In many parts of the world Sufis resisted the colonization of their societies, the political and military oppression of their countries and the economic exploitation of their people. The life and teaching of the Algerian Sufi master Amīr 'Abd al-Qādir al-Jazā'irī (1808-83) provides a clear illustration of the role of Sufism in activities such as inviting people to Islam, teaching and implementing the tenets of the faith and defending Muslim communities and territories. He was a scholar, warrior and Sufi whose *Kitāb al-Mawāqif* is an important commentary on the writings of Ibn al-ʿArabī. With regards to the Qur'ān being a source of knowledge for him, he said:

> Whenever [God] wishes to communicate to me a command or give me good news, warn me, communicate a piece of knowledge, or give me advice I have sought touching on some matter, He informs me of what He wishes by means of an *ishāra*[64] through a noble verse of the Qur'ān.[65]

ʿAbd al-Qādir al-Jazā'irī of the Qādiriyya *ṭarīqa* fought against French colonialists in Algeria from 1832 to 1847. Investigating all the anti-colonial revolts that were led by Sufis is a major research project by itself and is outside the scope of this book but some other examples of Sufi masters who actively resisted the forces of colonization are: ʿUmar al-Mukhtār (1858-1931) of the Sanūsī *ṭarīqa* who fought against the Italians in Libya; Mā' al-ʿAynayn al-Qalqamī of the Qādiriyya *ṭarīqa* who fought the French in northern Mauritania and southern Morocco from 1905 to 1909; al-Hajj ʿUmar Tāl of the Tījānī *ṭarīqa* who fought the French in Guinea, Senegal and Mali from 1852 to 1864; Muḥammad ʿAbdallāh al-Ṣūmālī who led one of the longest resistance movements in Africa against both the British and the Italians from 1899 to 1920; the Mahdī of Sudan who led his followers against the British between 1881 and 1885; the Naqshabandī Sufi master Imam Shāmil (1797-1871) who fought the Tsarist Russians for thirty-five years in the Caucasus; it was the Sufi *ṭarīqas* who helped belief in Islam to survive during the communist era of the USSR; and Ma Hualong of the Naqshabandī *ṭarīqa* who led the Hui Muslims against the Chinese authorities between 1862 and 1876 (it is estimated that even today 125,000 Hui Muslims follow the Naqshabandī *ṭarīqa* in north-western China[66]).

It was also Sufi masters such as Abadin Tadia Tjoessoep (1626-1699) who resisted Dutch colonialism in Indonesia and were deported with many of their followers to prison camps in South Africa where their descendants remain as Muslims to the present day.[67] What we observe in all these cases is that Sufis actively opposed the intolerance, injustices, exploitation, and violent suppression of their societies in the modern period.

The Neo-Colonial Period

Turkey, Egypt and Saudi Arabia are exemplars of neo-colonial societies and we will look at them later in more detail. The development of these modern states was clearly inspired by Europe and later on by the United States of America and the political and economic institutions that emerged in these countries were in keeping with the goals of global capitalism, such as those of the United Nations Organization, the World Trade Organization, the International Monetary Fund and the World Bank. Furthermore their legal, educational and health-care systems were born out of visions of reality belonging to Western civilization.

The creation of the Republic of Turkey in 1923 and the abolition there, in 1925, of the *ṭarīqas* (Sufi orders) led to the closing of the *tekkes* (centres for Sufi gathering). In order to survive, Sufism bypassed the formal structures of the *ṭarīqas* and effectively went underground. In late 19th century Egypt, under British occupation, governmental authority was imposed on the Sufi orders, the *takiyas* (another name for *tekkes*) and the tombs of saints and two sets of legislation – the Internal Regulations for the Sufi Orders of 1903 and 1905 – formed the basis for governing the Sufi orders until 1976. The regulations prohibited and regulated certain aspects of ritual and belief. The principal challenge to the orders however came from the reformist movement particularly from the 1920s onwards.

With the incorporation of the Kingdom of Saudi Arabia into the global capitalist economy in 1932 the Saudis promoted Wahhabism as a means to eradicate the only real threat to their power. That threat would have come from the Sufis who upheld traditional Islam and were outspoken critics of modernist institutions. With this in mind and armed with vast amounts of petro-dollars the Wahhabis suppressed Sufism in Saudi Arabia and set out to do the same in Muslim communities throughout the world.

Secularism

Modernity and secularism are closely related to each other. Modernity refers to the post-medieval period when modes of thought and practices were supported by rational methods in all fields of inquiry. Modernist epistemology took the form of mechanism, materialism and structuralism, and the assumptions that underpinned modernization were secularism, individualism and a commitment to progress through science and technology. Modernity in turn led to the establishment of nationalism, capitalism and democracy. Muslims in the modern period have succumbed to the secularization of their religion due to the encroaching influence of modernity. Religion for them, as in the rest of the world, has been relegated to merely personal matters, whilst their socio-economic and political affairs are now determined by non-Islamic systems such as capitalism (both laissez-faire and state), liberal democracy, dictatorships and one-party totalitarianism.

Secularization has affected most modern Muslims inclined to Sufism by means of what 'Umar Vadillo calls "the esotericisation of *taṣawwuf*." He explains that the esotericists maintain that Sufism is the esoteric part of Islam, by which they mean that Sufism is the interior or inward part of Islam and the *sharīʿa* is the quite separate exterior or outward part of Islam.[68] René Guénon (1886-1951), also known as 'Abd al-Wāḥid Yaḥyā, was the foremost proponent for this split in Islam in modern times. The problem with this understanding of Islam, according to Vadillo, is that the Prophetic methodology does not countenance such a split and, in fact, the Prophet Muḥammad ﷺ had taught people to develop a balance between the inner and outer dimensions of personality. One of the giants of Moroccan Sufism, ʿAlī al-Jamal (d. 1780), insisted that one's outward (*sharīʿa*) and inward spiritual reality (*ḥaqīqa*) are inseparable. He wrote that the

> ...*faqīr* (Sufi) will not obtain the fruit of knowledge until his *sharīʿa* and his *ḥaqīqa* are one thing. It is like the first Predecessors, may Allah be pleased with them! Gatheredness did not veil them from separation and separation did not veil them to gatheredness.[69]

The Amman Declaration, which was unanimously adopted by the "Islamic World's political and temporal leaderships" at the Organization of the Islamic Conference summit in Mecca in December 2005, falls squarely within the terms of this secularization of Islam. Based on *fatwās* (authoritative legal statements) provided by scholars such as the Shaykh al-Azhar, Muḥammad Sayyid Ṭanṭāwī, Ayatollah Sistānī and Shaykh Yūsuf al-Qarḍāwī, King Abdullah II of Jordan convened an international Islamic conference of two hundred of the "world's leading Islamic scholars" from fifty countries in July 2005 in Amman. The scholars unanimously approved a ruling on three fundamental issues, which became known as the "Three Points of the Amman Message" and it was then adopted by the Organization of the Islamic Conference. The summary of the Message states:

> It [the Amman Message] thus assures balanced Islamic solutions for essential issues like human rights; women's rights; freedom of religion; legitimate jihad; good citizenship of Muslims in non-Muslim countries, and just and democratic government.[71]

It seems that this whole exercise was an overt attempt to make the world Muslim community accept the secularization of Islam and Muslim societies through the process of democratization.

Religion is to be relegated to personal and esoteric matters whilst socio-economic and political matters are to come under the aegis of capitalism and the democratic ethos of the United Nations Organization. Included among those who endorsed the Amman Message were many Sufi shaykhs and authorities on Sufism and Islam[71] and, given their high status on the world stage, it is an indication of how successful the secularization of Muslim societies has been. The Sufis of the *ṭarīqa* of Shaykh ʿAbd al-Qādir, on the other hand, have taught that Islam certainly produces a healthy and balanced society but only when the inner and outer aspects of the human personality are inextricably united.

The influence of the *Murābiṭūn* on the *ṭarīqa* of Shaykh ʿAbd al-Qādir

As mentioned in the introduction, Shaykh ʿAbd al-Qādir embraced Islam in 1967 in Fes, Morocco, after which he joined the Qādirī-Shādhilī-Darqāwī *ṭarīqa* as a student of Muḥammad ibn al-Ḥabīb in Meknes, Morocco. His *idhn* (authorization) to lead the Qādirī-Shādhilī-Darqāwī *ṭarīqa* came from Ibn al-Ḥabīb and his second master Muḥammad al-Faytūrī Ḥamūda of Benghazi, Libya. His attachment to the Mālikī school of law and Junaydī Sufism grew firstly out of this Maghribī milieu and later from his own deep research into what constituted the purest sources of Islamic knowledge. This research and study led Shaykh ʿAbd al-Qādir to draw inspiration for some of his work and teachings from the Murābiṭūn (Almoravid) dynasty, which ruled North Africa and the Iberian Peninsula from 1040 to 1147. The word *murābiṭūn* means the people of the *ribāṭ* and the dynasty took it as their name because of the West African movement, centred on *ribāṭs*, from which it emerged.

In North and West Africa a *ribāṭ* was a fortress where soldiers were garrisoned for the purpose of defending the territory of the Muslims and repelling enemy attacks but it was also a place of learning and intensive worship, which had its roots in the Qur'ān[72] and the *ḥadīth*[73] and the example of the early Muslims. These *ribāṭs* were known for their spreading of knowledge through the combating of illiteracy and the study of the religious sciences. They were places of worship, from which corruption and injustice were fought. With the establishment of stability through governmental authority some *ribāṭs* evolved into great cities such as Marrakesh, while others became *zāwiyas* in which Sufism was taught and where the poor and those who wished to escape from sedition sought refuge. A saint is referred to in Morocco and Algeria by several terms, one of which, reflecting this, is *murābiṭ*.

Another aspect of Murābiṭūn history that Shaykh ʿAbd al-Qādir focuses on is the relationship of the rulers to the scholars. The close collaboration between the ruler and those who taught Mālikī law was a feature that lasted till the end of Murābiṭūn rule in 1147. Amongst these scholars were the famous Andalusian[75] jurist Qāḍī Abū Bakr ibn al-ʿArabī (d. 1148) and the noted jurist and *ḥadīth* specialist Qāḍī ʿIyāḍ ibn Mūsā al-Yaḥṣubī (d. 1149-50). Abū Bakr ibn al-ʿArabī was appointed *qāḍī* (judge) of Seville in 1134. In many respects the government of al-Andalus was a partnership between the Murābiṭ governor and the *qāḍī*. For the administration of his post the *qāḍī* headed his own body of officials which included junior judges and the *muḥtasib*, the official who oversaw the markets and matters of public order.

It was the *qāḍī*, rather than the governor, who delivered the Friday sermon (*khuṭba*) at the main mosque. He also controlled the treasury (*bayt al-māl*) where the money from the annual *zakāt* collection was kept, thereby enabling him to stipulate to the governor the specific purposes for which it could be used. The governor's chief minister (*wazīr*) had to consult with the *qāḍī* daily before presenting his proposals to the governor. The *qāḍī* exercised substantial power through the decision-making processes that he was engaged in. As a consequence, when Abū Bakr ibn al-ʿArabī became *qāḍī* he became one of the most powerful men in al-Andalus.[76]

While travelling in the East, Abū Bakr ibn al-ʿArabī had met Abū Ḥāmid al-Ghazālī, the famous Sufi and author of *Iḥyāʾ ʿUlūm al-Dīn*, which is interesting because of the subsequent antagonism towards al-Ghazālī on the part of the Muslims of al-Andalus and the light that that shines on the nature of Sufism and one of the central themes of this book. Qāḍī Abū Bakr respected al-Ghazālī and did not reject him personally nor did he reject his teachings. However, it was decided that al-Ghazālī's approach was so inappropriate for the Muslims of Spain that copies of his great work were publicly burnt.[77]

Al-Ghazālī had reacted to the rigid orthodoxy of the Islam practised in Iraq and his aim, as a Sufi, was to restore the inward reality of practices which had become lifeless outward rituals. The situation in al-Andalus and the Maghrib was entirely different. There the *sharīʿa* had become eroded and was in danger of being lost completely. What was needed was its revival as a whole and the Murābiṭūn were doing just that by introducing into their domains a Madinan Islam in which the inward and outward were, as in the case of the early Muslims, undifferentiated. Aisha Bewley, describing this phenomenon, says:

> This strong fresh breeze, redolent with direct contact with the very sources of the *sharīʿa* and *sunna*, swept through the Maghrib with the Murābiṭūn, purifying everything it touched, driving out the decadence and corruption that had eaten away at the deen. In such circumstances there was no need, indeed no room, for the teachings of Imam al-Ghazālī. To introduce them would in fact hinder rather than help in the task of re-establishing the basic Madinan paradigm ... This is what forced the *amīr* to take the action he took.[78]

This historical example importantly illustrates two aspects of Sufism. Firstly, that it is the task of the Sufis to establish the true reality of Islam in the place and time they are situated. And secondly, that what is needed to do this, as we also saw earlier with those Sufis who fought colonialism, can vary considerably according to the specific needs of the particular place and time they find themselves living in. It also goes a long way towards explaining the approach that Shaykh 'Abd al-Qādir has taken in the course of his life and teaching over the past four decades at the end of the 20th and the beginning of the 21st Centuries.

The other great scholar of the Murābiṭūn was Qāḍī 'Iyāḍ ibn Mūsā al-Yaḥṣubī of Ceuta, on the African north coast, the most celebrated Mālikī scholar in the Muslim West of his time. He was the leading scholar of his time in *ḥadīth* and the sciences associated with it, as well as a scholar of Qur'ānic commentary (*tafsīr*) and related sciences. He was also an exemplary Mālikī *faqīh*, a grammarian, a linguist, a poet, an historian and an orator. He was known to be steadfast, forbearing and generous and gave away a lot in charity. He was in constant action and firm with regards to the truth.[79] Qāḍī 'Iyāḍ travelled to al-Andalus where he studied under a hundred teachers including Ibn Ḥamdīn, Abū Bakr ibn al-'Arabī and Abū 'Alī al-Ṣadafī.

On his return to Ceuta he was raised to the rank of *shūrā* (the ruler's consultative body) and in 1121-2 he was appointed *qāḍī* of the city. In 1136 he was made the *qāḍī* of Granada. Qāḍī 'Iyāḍ was endowed with literary talent and wrote more than twenty works, some of which have survived. His best known published works are *al-Shifā' bi-ta'rīf ḥuqūq al-Muṣṭafā* – an authoritative study of the Prophet Muḥammad ﷺ which continues to enjoy widespread popularity today, partly due to the fact that Shaykh 'Abd al-Qādir has overseen a very widely distributed English translation of it – *Mashāriq al-anwār ʿalā ṣiḥāḥ al-athār* and *Tartīb al-Madārik wa taqrīb al-masālik bi-maʿrifat aʿlām madhhab Mālik* which constitutes the best testimonial for the Mālikī school.[80]

In his seminal text, *Root Islamic Education*, Shaykh ʿAbd al-Qādir makes commentary on excerpts from Qāḍī ʿIyāḍ's *Tartīb al-Madārik*. We have already looked at his commentary on aspects of the book relating to the balance between the inner and outer aspects of the human personality. Here we will concentrate on aspects of the *Tartīb al-Madārik* relating to power relationships within society. Governance in Islamic society, according to Shaykh ʿAbd al-Qādir, is characterized by the ruler exercising political authority over the people and by the "*fuqahā*ʾ (jurists) ruling the *amīr* (ruler) by defining *sharīʿa* limits, not by cult of personality."[81] Shaykh ʿAbd al-Qādir argues that the injunction to follow the Qurʾān and *Sunna* necessarily involves governance and that the model for this governance is to be found in the first Muslim community in Madīna. He insists that the socio-economic, political, economic and spiritual goals of Islam are not unattainable. On the contrary, he stresses that these goals were attained and implemented by the Prophet ﷺ and subsequent generations in Madīna. This is the *ʿamal ahl al-Madīna* (practice of the People of Madīna) and Mālik ibn Anas lived it and recorded it in his *Muwaṭṭá* for posterity.

During Murābiṭūn rule governance (*amr*) took place when the ruler appointed jurists to the consultative body (*shūrā*) who then, as was usually the case in al-Andalus, went on to become judges. *Mushāwarūn* (counsellors or advisors) such as Yaḥyā ibn Yaḥyā (d. 848) and ʿAbd al-Malik ibn Ḥabīb (d 852) went on to become eminent jurists. Shaykh ʿAbd al-Qādir says that the history of Islam is a series of repeated manifestations of Islamic governance in which the ruler is answerable to a body of jurists whose judgements were made according to the Qur'ān and *Sunna*. He says:

> We can show you a line that goes from Madīna al-Munawwara at the time of the Messenger, may Allah bless him and give him peace, through to Imam Mālik, and from Imam Mālik continues for five hundred years – in the Middle East, to the gates of China, to the gates of India and to the gates of Russia, right across North Africa, right into Europe. For five hundred years, you find that the leadership was in the hands of slaves who were *fuqahā'* and before whom *amīrs* bowed their heads.[82]

Shaykh 'Abd al-Qādir explains that in order for someone to be a jurist he has to embody three elements. Firstly, he must know the Qur'ān and *Sunna* within the context of the *'amal ahl al-Madīna*. In other words he must know how people lived in Madīna, that is, he must be aware of their day-to-day lives. The second necessary element for the jurist is his ability to make judgements in cases that are brought before him. He must also have an acceptable moral character. The third element is that he must pass sentences and rulings in the knowledge that the total superstructure of the Islamic society guarantees that the sentence will be executed. It is by that token that governance is accomplished.

Three jurists descended from Mālik ibn Anas, who followed the *'amal ahl al-Madīna*, are discussed by Shaykh 'Abd al-Qādir in *Root Islamic Education* namely, 'Abd al-Malik ibn Ḥabīb, Abū 'Amr al-Ḥārith ibn Miskīn Muḥammad ibn Yūsuf and Abū Sa'īd Ṣaḥnūn. After noting their characteristics, Shaykh 'Abd al-Qādir goes on to state that these jurists practised a protected Sufism that was "not accessible, touchable, visible or speakable"[83] because it was buried in their hearts.

Let us take Abū Sa'īd Ṣaḥnūn as an example. His full name was Ṣaḥnūn Abū Sa'īd 'Abd al-Salam al-Tanūkhī and he was born in 776-7 in Qayrawān, a major metropolis of the time, in what is now Tunisia. He is credited with converting al-Andalus and the Maghrib to the way of Mālik. Some of his teachers, such as Ibn al-Qāsim, Asad ibn al-Furāt, al-Buhlūl ibn Rāshid and 'Alī ibn Ziyād, had been students of Mālik ibn Anas himself. He was a master of law and his personal ethics were rigorous and demanding. These are the qualities which explain his success and the veneration in which he was held by people and the rulers of the time. Due to his prestige the city of Qayrawān became a major centre for the study of Mālikī law.

Although he possessed 12,000 olive-trees, he lived a life that was austere to the point of asceticism. He chose to live in poverty and distributed his considerable income in the form of alms. He frequently sought seclusion in the *ribāṭ* of Qaṣr Ziyād.[84] He was compassionate and easily moved to tears but was meticulous in the application of justice and refused to accept gifts, payments or favours from the rulers. He was appointed *qāḍī* in 849 after the Aghlabid ruler Abū al-'Abbās Muḥammad (r. 841-856) promised to give him a free hand in matters of justice. He wrote, in sixteen volumes, the *Mudawwana*, a compendium of the legal modality of the school of Madīna as formulated by Mālik ibn Anas. The widespread adoption of the Mālikī school in North Africa and Spain can be attributed to Abū Sa'īd Ṣaḥnūn's transmission of the *Mudawwana*.

Shaykh 'Abd al-Qādir describes the character and behaviour of Abū Sa'īd Ṣaḥnūn as a protected form of Sufism. Abū Sa'īd Ṣaḥnūn himself said:

> Whoever does not act by his knowledge, knowledge does not benefit him. Knowledge is a light that Allah places in the hearts. When someone acts by it Allah illuminates his heart. If he does not act by it and loves this world, the love of this world blinds his heart and knowledge does not illuminate him.[85]

The *sulūk* of the Sufi transcends the intellect and leads to unveiling (*kashf*) of the realities that are accessible only through the heart. This perception of the heart emerges from an existential mode of behaviour and leads inexorably to greater awareness of God. For Shaykh ʿAbd al-Qādir this existential mode of behaviour takes its purest form in the *ʿamal ahl al-Madīna* (the practice of the people of Madīna). Murābiṭūn society re-activated this teaching and this is why he has seen in them an inspiring example for the people of this time. The unification of the inward, or spiritual, and the outward, integral to Mālik ibn Anas' teaching of the *ʿamal ahl al-Madīna*, is embedded in Mālik's statement that whoever practices Sufism without learning *fiqh* corrupts his faith and whoever learns *fiqh* without practicing Sufism corrupts himself. Only he who combines the two will succeed.

So a balance between the *sharīʿa* and the *ḥaqīqa*, between the outer law and the inner reality is integral to the way of Mālik. By this understanding, practice or behaviour is evidence of knowledge, making theory and practice inseparable. Although the institutions of classical Sufism – the *zāwiya* and swearing allegiance (*bayʿa*) to the master – have certainly played their part in his work, Shaykh ʿAbd al-Qādir has established mosques, colleges, markets and the Murābiṭūn Daʿwa Movement, and he has made political leadership an integral element in all the communities he has established throughout the world. For Shaykh ʿAbd al-Qādir this has simply been the natural response of the Sufi master in his task of implementing the measures needed for the restoration of Islam in the face of the social and historical changes of the time in which he lives. It should be noted here, however, that although the external forms of the institutions may be different from those of al-Junayd, the essential goal of Sufism within the *ṭarīqa* of Shaykh ʿAbd al-Qādir nevertheless remains the same, namely *maʿrifa, fanāʾ* and *baqāʾ*. He has simply taken al-Junayd's rules and applied them within the contemporary social and historical context.

Chapter 5

The Sufi Deconstruction of Modern Science

Pre-Modern Worldview in Muslim Society

Unlike the modern world, in which the epistemological foundations for understanding and interpreting the meaning of reality are rationalism and empiricism alone, in Islam there are, as we have seen, in addition to these, other what might be called "religious" epistemic sources. In pre-modern Muslim society, people's lived experience was within, to use Charles Taylor's expression, a "context of understanding". Taylor states:

> By 'context of understanding' here, I mean both matters that will probably have been explicitly formulated by almost everyone, such as the plurality of options [such as other religions or even atheism], and some which form the implicit, largely unfocussed background of this experience and search, its 'pre-ontology', to use a Heideggerian term.[1]

All beliefs and behaviour exist within a context, or framework, of understanding, which is taken-for-granted, which remains implicit, and may even be unacknowledged by the people concerned because it was never formulated. Philosophers such as Wittgenstein,

Heidegger or Polanyi have called this the "background".[2] In pre-modern Islamic society this "background" understanding allowed the believers to function in a way in which there was no distinction between experience and its construed meaning. The presence of God was seemingly undeniable. The natural world displayed order, design, divine purpose and action. The fertility of the earth, the abundance of sustenance and fresh water, shelter from the elements, as well as floods, earthquakes and forest-fires, all these things were seen as acts of God. Rulers ruled in the name of God and society was ordered in ways that involved revealed guidance and worship.

It was taken for granted that the mercy and compassion of God would repel the forces of evil. Atheism was almost inconceivable in a world that had these features as its background understanding. The existence of God, and His direct involvement in the cosmos, was apparent. Religion was something that was related to action rather than thought. It was action/behaviour that enabled people to deepen the capacities of their hearts. This, it was understood, could not be acquired through reason. Knowledge of God and reality came only through dedicated practice and lay beyond thoughts and concepts. Knowing about God was different from knowing God. Knowing about God was the subject of *'ilm al-kalām* or *'aqīda*, that is, theology, whereas knowing God was the subject of Sufism because experience of God cannot be contained within the dogmas of theologians or the hypotheses of scientists or the speculation of philosophers. God is beyond space and time and human speculation.

Very soon after the beginning of the revelation of the Qur'ān, the process began whereby these revelations were recorded in a written codex. The textual codex, whilst having many benefits, was the first stage in what we might call Islamic materialism[3] and reductionism.[4] The Prophet Muḥammad ﷺ was unlettered and retained the Qur'ān in his memory as it was revealed to him. He in turn recited it to his Companions who memorized it in part or in full. Although the Qur'ān was transmitted and preserved orally in the time of the Prophet ﷺ, he also dictated it to scribes, who wrote it down on paper, papyrus, leather, shoulder blades of animals and leaf stalks of date palms. One single copy of the Qur'ān was compiled from all these materials, and also from oral reports, by the first caliph Abū Bakr. This copy was later kept by the second caliph 'Umar and then passed to his daughter Ḥafṣa. 'Uthmān, the third caliph, using this initial copy, had a number of further copies made and sent them to various places around the Muslim world. It is this version, known as the *Muṣḥaf 'Uthmānī*, that has become the standard Qur'ānic text today.

The second major area of codification to affect Islam was that of the *ḥadīth*. From the perspective of Mālik ibn Anas, a *ḥadīth* is a report of what the Prophet ﷺ said, although in its early usage it also included reports of what he did. Studies of *ḥadīth* were aimed at determining the normative practice, the *Sunna*, of the Prophet ﷺ, which is the second primary source of Islamic law. The *ḥadīth* literature that emerged has been classified in eleven categories. The *Ṣaḥīfa* is a collection of *ḥadīth* written by a Companion or Follower of the next generation, such as the one written by Abū Hurayra and handed down to his student Hammām ibn Munabbih. A *Juz'* is a collection of *ḥadīth* compiled by a Companion or Follower on a particular subject, such as 'intention' for example. A *Risāla* (pl. *Rasā'il*) is a collection of *ḥadīth* that deals with one of the eight topics of the *Jāmi'* collections, such as those of al-Bukhārī and al-Tirmidhī. The *Muṣannaf* is a large collection of *ḥadīth* in which various topics are divided into various books or chapters. Examples of this category are the *Muwaṭṭa'* of Mālik ibn Anas and *Ṣaḥīḥ Muslim*. The other categories of *ḥadīth* literature are *Musnad, Muʿjam, Sunan, Mustadrak, Mustakhraj* and *Arbaʿīniyyat* (collections of forty *ḥadīth*).

Shaykh ʿAbd al-Qādir tells us that after the time of Mālik ibn Anas there "began the ossification, complexification, [and] structuralisation of the method by which *ḥadīth* were collected, by which *ḥadīth* were narrated [and] by which *ḥadīth* were transmitted."[5] Amongst Muslims there are two views with regards to the origins of Islamic law, that of Mālik and that of post-Shāfiʿī scholars. For post-Shāfiʿī scholars, knowledge of Islam and Islamic law is restricted to the knowledge of texts: firstly the text of Qur'ān and secondly those of *ḥadīth*, particularly the collections of al-Bukhārī and Muslim and to a lesser degree the collections of al-Tirmidhī, Abū Dāwūd, al-Nasā'ī and Ibn Mājah.[6]

The Mālikī view, as expressed in the *Muwaṭṭa'*,[7] also sees Islamic law as based on Qur'ān and *sunna* but it differs from the post-Shāfiʿī definition of *sunna*. *Sunna* for the post-Shāfiʿī scholars refers almost invariably to *ḥadīth*, whilst in its *Muwaṭṭan* sense it is not coterminous with *ḥadīth* but is, rather, intimately linked with the idea of *ʿamal*, or 'practice'. *Ḥadīth*, in its *Muwaṭṭan* connotation therefore, refers to texts, while *sunna* refers to actions. However, not only must *sunna* be distinguished from *ḥadīth*, but *sunna* must also be distinguished from *ʿamal*. Dutton explains that:

> ... *sunna* in the *Muwaṭṭan* sense refers to a practice originating in the practice, or *sunna*, of the Prophet, *ʿamal* is a broader concept which includes not only the *sunna* established by the Prophet but also the *ijtihād* [independent reasoning] of later authorities. Thus all *sunna* is *ʿamal*, but not all *ʿamal* is *sunna*; indeed, as we shall see, Mālik typically differentiates those parts of *ʿamal* that contain elements of later *ijtihād* in addition to a base in Qur'ān and/or *sunna* by using the word *amr* rather than *sunna*.[8]

Mālik regarded the Qur'ān, *sunna* and *ijtihād* as bound together in one whole, namely the *'amal ahl al-Madīna* (practice of the people of Madīna). The *Muwaṭṭa'* provides a composite picture of this, including the judgements of the caliphs, governors and scholars up until the time of its compilation in the middle of the second century AH. Although Mālik presents the *Muwaṭṭa'* in the textual form of a book it is, in fact, all about action (*'amal*) and, as Dutton says, it "allows us a fundamentally different perspective on Islamic legal history where the true expression of the law is seen as being preserved not in a corpus of texts but in the actions, or *'amal*, of men."[9]

Mālik was aware of the problems associated with the codification of *ḥadīth*. It was with this in mind that he provided, in the *Muwaṭṭa'*, a particular methodology by which the *fiqh* could be extrapolated from the Qur'ān and the *sunna*. This methodology of Islamic law, which we can call the *madhhab* (legal school) of Madīna, is the "*umm al-madhāhib*" or "mother of the *madhhabs*" due to the fact that all *madhhabs*, in a certain sense, derive from it. Once the Islamic socio-political and economic order are in place, all the *madhāhib* (plural of *madhhab*) work well in the implementation of the Qur'ān and the *sunna*. The crucial point is that the *madhāhib* (Ḥanafī, Shāfi'ī, Mālikī[10] and Ḥanbalī) were not what established the Islamic socio-political and economic order in the first place. They were only developed in the second and third centuries after the Hijra (the Prophet's migration to Madīna) when the Islamic socio-political and economic order was already in place. The methodology of codification upon which the *madhāhib* are based was not present in the original *madhhab* of Madīna, which is also known as *'amal ahl al-Madīna*.

The original *madhhab* of Madīna was based on the actions of men and women, and the *madhhabs* that developed out of it were based on texts with, as in the case of the Ḥanafīs, the added application of the use of reason. The methodology of Mālik ibn Anas is based on *fiṭra*,[11] which is unstructured, natural and organic. The destinies of all things in the universe, including human beings, are predetermined by their natural pre-disposition and life-form. Mālik ibn Anas was aware that it was the methodology outlined by him that would have to be resorted to if the integrity of the Muslim world community was ever shattered and thus in need of restoration. This sentiment is reflected in his statement: "the last of this community will not be put right except by what put it right in the first place." Elaborating on this statement, Shaykh 'Abd al-Qādir argues that it is only through Mālik ibn Anas that one can have access to the very source of Islam in order to be able to restore it again to its primal form.

After Islamic rule in all parts of the world was defeated and undermined by colonialism, the basic institutions of Islamic governance disappeared or became atrophied through the encroachment of global capitalism. In both these cases it was empiricist and rationalist epistemologies with their attendant scientific and technological methodologies that made these processes possible. Shaykh 'Abd al-Qādir is of the opinion that the re-establishment of Islamic institutions will be the natural consequence of the adoption of the unstructured and *fiṭra* based Mālikī methodology.

The Pre-Modern Worldview Giving Way to Modernism in European Society

It was in Europe that the dominant worldview that now pervades the entire world, including Muslim society, developed. Prior to the modern age, the worldview in Europe was that of scholasticism, which was a harmonization of Christian theological thinking and the classical philosophical tradition of the Ancient World. In pre-modern Europe, people's lived experience was within a

Christian context of understanding, in which the presence of God was undeniable. The natural world was interpreted as displaying order, design, divine purpose and action, and kings ruled in the name of God. Society was ordered in ways that implemented what was understood as Divinely revealed guidance and worship. The Catholic philosopher Charles Taylor says that, with regard to institutions and practices, the pre-modern European state

> ... was in some way connected to, based on, guaranteed by, some faith in, or adherence to, God, or some notion of ultimate reality. ... If we go back a few centuries in our civilization, we see that God was present in the above sense in a whole host of social practices – not just the political – and at all levels of society ...[12]

The functioning mode of local government was the parish, and guilds also played a major role in the economic life of society. The modes of celebration were religious and every kind of public activity involved God in some way.

Europe went through various phases on its way to its present modern worldview. The transformation of pre-modern Christian society involved the eclipse of God's control of individual and social action. It also involved the rise of the belief in the power of the individual to morally organise society. This is the basis of Humanism which eventually resulted in the secularisation of society. According to Charles Taylor,[13] the intermediary stages in this development towards secularism saw the rise of Deism, Unitarianism and Reason. Deism, Unitarianism and Reason were in turn aided by three essential foundational building blocks: an "instrumental stance towards the world, secularization of time, and Reform". The process is illustrated in diagram 3 overleaf.

By "an instrumental stance towards the world" Taylor means Utilitarianism, which can be defined as a theory that regards the maximization of utility, happiness, welfare and well-being as being

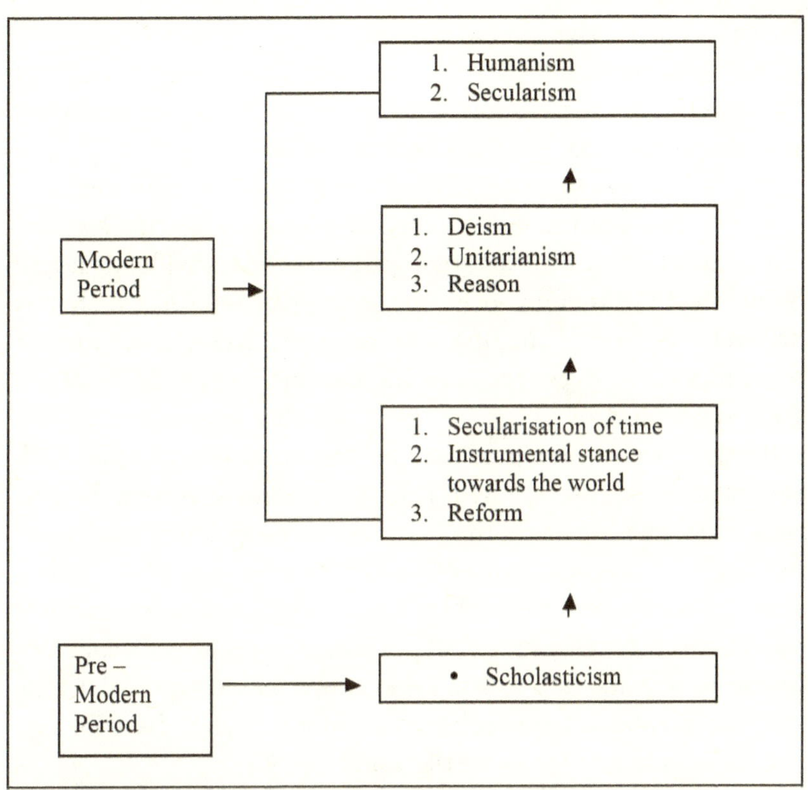

Diagram 3

the greatest good that can be acquired. In this process people should remain neutral as to their own welfare and that of other people. Utilitarianism as a social theory came to be split on the issue of whether this good can be achieved individually, as John Locke (1632-1704) and Jeremy Bentham (1748-1832) believed, or whether it should be a communal achievement as Jean-Jaques Rousseau (1712-1778), Georg Wilhelm Friedrich Hegel (1770-1831), Karl Marx (1818-1883) and Friedrich Wilhelm von Humboldt (1767-1835) suggested. The greatest good however, was to be achieved through constructive human action.

This demand for constructive action and the "secularization of time" went together. Contact with cosmic time became tenuous and emphasis was now on secular time, which is merely a resource that has to be used wisely to extract the maximization of good. The Puritan Reformers inculcated Utilitarianism and the secularization of time amongst believers. Individualism and discipline were reinforced by the process of reform, which was driven by the aim of creating new forms of religious life. Through this process of reform religious life became more individualistic and centred less on collective ritual worship and action. In fact collective ritual worship and action had atrophied together with earlier ideas of cosmic order, such as those which underlay the traditional monarchies of the past. Cosmic order brought into play teleology in nature and purposive forces underlying social reality. These in turn were inseparable from higher time and maintained themselves through a matrix of purposive forces already apparent in nature. The modern order, however, was based on secular time and was meant to be established by human action based on an instrumental stance towards the world.

So an instrumental stance towards the world, secularization of time and reform were the essential building blocks for the intermediary stages of Deism, Unitarianism and Reason. Deism is the belief that, although God created the world, He exercises no providential control of what goes on in it. A Deist affirms a Divine Creator but denies Divine Revelation, holding that human reason alone is capable of providing everything necessary for living a good moral and religious life. As a consequence the relationship between God and human beings is to be mediated by an impersonal, immanent moral order. Taylor describes it in this way:

> On one level, we have the natural order, the universe, purged of

> enchantment, and freed from miraculous interventions and special providences from God, operating by universal, unrespondent causal laws. On another level, we have a social order, designed for us, which we have to come to discern by reason, and establish by constructive activity and discipline.[14]

The Law defining this order, whether as constitutional law or as ethical norms, can be expressed in rational terms quite independently of God. Human relationships are then subsumed under codes such as Natural Law, the Utilitarian principle, and the Categorical Imperative. Nature or Reason is taken to be the way in which God reveals Himself to His Creation. A religion such as this, which requires rational scrutiny, does not require revelation. It becomes inconceivable that God would resort to such shortcuts when human reason suffices to provide all the guidance that is needed. Religion, then, is a matter of right belief, with theology providing the correct description of matters relating to faith. Personal fidelity, prayer and devotion will not result in any intimate relationship with God or mystic experience, something unacceptable to dispassionate reason. Unitarianism "can be seen as an attempt to hold on to the central figure of Jesus, while cutting loose from the main soteriological doctrines of historical Christianity."[15] In this view, what is important about Jesus is that he introduced rational principles of conduct in law and ethics. His role is that of a teacher and "as an inspiring trailblazer of what we will later call Enlightenment."[16]

Taylor's argument, then, is that once an instrumental stance towards the world, secularization of time and Reform are established as the essential building blocks of the intermediary stages of Deism, Unitarianism and Nature or Reason, then Humanism and secularism become triumphant. Within this scheme there is no room for a transcendent God or the supernatural. From this point of view we can say that the secular age is one in which human flourishing is the goal not only for individuals but also for society as a whole. Having identified these foundational principles we are better placed to look at the methodology of social science because these foundational principles became the new context for the understanding of modern society.

The Epistemological Foundations of the Modern Worldview

It is claimed that the inspiration for the modernist paradigm came, firstly, from a desire to escape the tyranny and irrationality of the Catholic Church and, secondly, from the desire to overcome the squalor, disease, poverty, starvation and brute labour of the European Middle Ages.[17] The transition from medieval to modern modes of thought and practices was supported by rational methods in all fields of inquiry. Galileo Galilei's (1564-1642) heliocentrism (*Dialogue Concerning the Two World Systems*, 1632) and Isaac Newton's mechanics (*Principia Mathematica*, 1667) set the agenda in physics, and René Descartes' (1596-1650) '*cogito ergo sum* – I think therefore I am' (*Principles of Philosophy*, 1644) and Immanuel Kant's (1724–1804) theory that objective experience is constructed by the functioning of the human mind (*Critique of Pure Reason*, 1781) in philosophy.

The foundations for other aspects of modernist thought and practice were laid by Charles Darwin's (1809-1882) evolutionary theory (*On the Origin of Species*, 1859), Sigmund Freud's (1856-1939) psychological building blocks (*The Ego and the Id*, 1923), Adam Smith's (1723-1790) economic free market (*The Wealth of Nations*, 1776) and Thomas Hobbes' (1588-1679) theory of the social contract in political theory (*Leviathan*, 1651). It is on the epistemological foundations of sciences based on these texts, together with others in a similar vein, that the new model of humanity took shape. The French Revolution (1789) with its accompanying "Reign of Terror", and the Napoleonic state that followed it, determined the future course of modernity. Developments in science and technology in Europe led to the Industrial Revolution, and the Voyages of Discovery to the colonization of Africa, the Americas and Asia.

The social sciences adopted the paradigm of mechanical science, with its belief in the objectivity and universality of scientific knowledge and method, as the model for morality, law and government.[18] A study of the philosophy of social science is an essential prerequisite for understanding social theory since social theory "is made in the context of ideas and the construction of intellectual histories."[19] As a generic term "social science" is the academic study of society and covers the fields of knowledge other than the natural sciences. The conceptualization of the social sciences differs radically from the pre-modern period to the modern period.

Although the exact chronology of what happened is disputed by historians, the pre-modern traditional worldview was supplanted by the modern worldview beginning from around the fifteenth century. Within a comparatively short period, empiricism and rationalism became the primary sources for the acquisition of knowledge. The Age of Enlightenment had arrived and was "frequently portrayed as a campaign on behalf of freedom and reason as against dogmatic faith and its sectarian and barbarous consequences in the history of Western civilization."[20] Anthropocentrism continued to be the dominant paradigm of modern society, that is, the human being was considered the centre of reality and the measure of all things. From then on, however, it required that reality be interpreted exclusively in terms of human experience and values.

In Hicham Djait's analysis, the new modernist paradigm opened the way for industry, technology, and industrialized labour.[21] Reacting to the injustices of capitalism, Karl Marx (1818-

1883) proposed the new system of communism (*The Communist Manifesto*, 1848). Marx intended to free humankind from religion, considering it as, in his phrase, "the opium of the masses". Friedrich Nietzsche (1822-1900), who was not the standard bearer of atheism he is commonly thought to be, saw it coming anyway and declared that "God is dead"[22] because the scientific method of Francis Bacon (1561-1626), amongst others, meant that the "real world" was now limited to the world of sense perception and all else was fantasy. Renaissance and Enlightenment Man now acquired the godlike attributes of unfettered power and will. Without divine and moral imperatives and restrictions people were free to do whatever they desired. The superstitions of the European Middle Ages were supposedly replaced by the clarity of rationalism. Humanism's drive to conquer and dominate the other, inherent in this worldview, is what has been been at the core of all modern methodologies.

Liberal democracy, with its capitalist economic system, and totalitarianism, with its communist economy (state capitalism), formed the core of the culture and institutions of their respective systems. The legal, educational, and health-care systems, as well as the modes of recreation, of these societies were born out of these visions of reality. It was envisaged that these institutions would then lead to globalization. According to John Ralston Saul, the multitude of benefits that were to result from globalization was proclaimed by politicians, academics, business leaders and think tanks alike. These benefits were that: the nation state would wither away, power would lie with global markets, economics and not politics would shape human events, global markets would establish international economic balances, the cycles of boom-and-bust would end, waves of trade would generate economic prosperity all over the world, dictatorships would turn into democracies and governments would become debt-free.[23] With the fall of the USSR

Francis Fukuyama declared that the end of history had already arrived. He stated that what

> ... we may be witnessing is not just the end of the Cold War, or the passing of a particular period of post-war history, but the end of history as such: that is, the end point of mankind's ideological evolution and the universalization of Western liberal democracy as the final form of human government.[24]

The institutions that developed to facilitate the goals of global capitalism were the United Nations Organization, the World Trade Organization, the International Monetary Fund and the World Bank. Finally humankind had achieved one global world state, one world government (UNO) and one currency, the US dollar.[25]

This is, of course, the meta-narrative of modernity. The classical social theorists, such as Georg Wilhelm Friedrich Hegel (1770-1831), Karl Marx (1818-1883), Herbert Spencer (1820-1903), Émile Durkheim (1858-1917) and Max Weber (1864-1920) developed such meta- or master narratives, which were clearly Eurocentric. The theories outlined in these meta-narratives are linear, evolutionary explanations of human history, showing European and North American cultures as the most advanced and the rest of the human species as undeveloped. The world is divided in a variety of dualisms such as East/West, traditional/modern, organic/mechanical, sacred/secular, irrational/rational and savage/civilized. Within these paradigms the great achievements of modernity were seen to be overwhelmingly capitalism and democracy. Even Karl Marx saw capitalism as a stage in the development of socialism. Later sociologists argued for multiple modernities, stating that modernity was not a single phenomenon but, rather, that it had taken multiple forms and produced different institutional arrangements in different countries. Masoud Kamali says:

> Although many of their institutions are broadly similar, there are also

> many differences between the modernization patterns and models of different Western countries. Furthermore in one particular country, for example Egypt, Iran or Turkey, many different modernization projects are carried out and managed by different sociopolitical agents; this forms the institutional and structural basis of multiple modernities."[26]

Despite the more balanced assessments made by exponents of the multiple modernities approach, the global financial crisis of 2008 onwards has amply shown that the meta-narrative of modernity is the dominant paradigm globally. It is both the mythology and existential reality of this age. A mythology need not be true; its importance lies in the acceptance of it by its adherents. There are multiple modernities but hierarchically the global capitalist paradigm is dominant. In the analysis of Shaykh 'Abd al-Qādir, which is supported by that of Niall Ferguson,[27] Peter T. White[28] and Mike Whitney,[29] capitalism is today's dominant "religion", and Enlightenment, Rationalism and Humanism are its mythology and all-encompassing meta-narrative. Before looking at Shaykh 'Abd al-Qādir's critique of modernist science, one key aspect of social science theory that needs to be investigated is the unresolved intellectual dilemma between rationalism and subjectivism.

The Philosophy of Social Science

There are two broad approaches in the natural sciences: empiricist and rationalist. These approaches are mirrored in the two approaches of the social sciences: positivist and interpretive. The invention of positivism has been credited to Auguste Comte (1798-1857) and its main features in the social sciences are the acceptance of the empiricist account of the natural sciences and the notion that science is the highest form of knowledge. For positivism the empirical scientific method must be applied to the study of human mental and social life. With these features it was assumed that the social sciences would be accepted as scientific disciplines and that social problems and conflicts would be resolved once reliable social scientific knowledge had been established, in the same way that natural scientific knowledge solves the problems of engineering and technology.

The rationalist (and interpretive) approach, on the other hand, proceeds from the premise that, irrespective of the advantages and drawbacks of positivism as an adequate philosophy of the natural sciences, the social sciences are qualitatively different from the natural sciences. Human beings and human societies differ from the objects studied by the natural sciences because they are self-conscious. Max Weber and Alfred Schutz (1899-1959) exemplified this approach. At that time, during the development of the social sciences, it was still believed by social theorists that philosophers were there purely to support their work. Philosophy, it was believed, played a role in exposing the prejudices, superstitions and unquestioned assumptions that were obstacles to the progress of science. This view was subsequently contested among others by Peter Winch (1926-1997), Alisdair McIntyre (b. 1929) and Hans-Georg Gadamer (1900-2002). They held the view that the individual and individual action are framed by the wider culture "in the same way perhaps as the sentences that I speak as an individual are framed by the rules of the language in which I speak."[30]

In time, philosophy's role was scrutinized even further with reference to domination and ideology. The major figures in this area of analysis belonged to the Frankfurt School of critical theory, among whom were Max Horkheimer (1895-1973), Herbert Marcuse (1898-1979), Theodor Adorno (1903-1969) and Jurgen Habermas (b. 1929). Further considerations of the interpretive approach led to post-modernism, post-structuralism and the philosophy of meta-Reality in the social sciences. Post-modernism denies the possibility and usefulness of meta-narratives such as those of Herbert Spencer,

Georg Wilhelm Friedrich Hegel, Max Weber, Karl Marx and Émile Durkheim. Instead of grand, large-scale theories and philosophies of the world, post-modernism prefers to emphasize difference, change and fragmentation. Two important philosophical theorists of post-modernism were Jean-Franciose Lyotard (1924-1998) and Jean Baudrillard (1929-2007).

Post-structuralism, whilst emphasizing difference, change and fragmentation, does so from a critique of Western philosophy and therefore shares its concerns. For a philosophical exposition of post-structuralism it is necessary to look at the work of Michel Foucault (1926-1984) and Jacques Derrida (1930-2004). Foucault's work illustrates how philosophy can be used to understand domination and shows how to build social structures in order to minimize the risks of domination. In his search for firm foundations of knowledge Derrida condemned logocentrism, that is, the reliance of Western philosophy on Logos, logic and rationality. Derrida was also critical of the photocentricism of Western philosophy, that is, the priority given to the spoken word rather than the written text. The term deconstruction is mostly associated with Derrida. It is a post-structuralist concept referring "to the systematic analysis of texts to show how they 'construct' their object and give the impression that they refer to some definite 'presence' – an external reality, or an unquestionable foundation of knowledge."[31]

Finally, we come to the philosophy of meta-Reality in social science. It is ironic that it is advocated by Roy Bhaskar (b. 1944), the initiator of Critical Realism. Critical Realism is closely related to the empiricist tradition and promotes the idea that the more compelling the knowledge of the external world the stronger the moral and political arguments that can be developed from it. Critical realism sees a close link between knowledge of self and society and focuses on emancipation and freedom from domination. Bhaskar explains his move from Critical Realism to meta-Reality as a deepening of the understanding of being. Bashkar notes that there are seven levels of being, saying:

> Each of these seven levels presupposes the earlier ones; so that the seventh level, which is distinctive of the philosophy of meta-Reality, does not involve the denial of any of the previous levels. It follows from this that the kind of unity and identity involved at this level is very different from the atomistic, punctualist or blockist identities and unities thought by conventional philosophy.[32]

At the first level, being is thought of as structured and differentiated and at the seventh level being is thought of as incorporating non-duality and unity.

To sum up, it can be said that there has been a dichotomy in the modern social sciences, since the Enlightenment, between objective social scientific knowledge and the influence that subjective historical and cultural factors have on that knowledge, that is, between the positivist and interpretive approaches. However the paradigm of mechanical science associated with Galileo and Newton was generally adopted as the model for all aspects of social organization. As Benton and Crabb observed:

> Although the advocates of rival epistemologies – empiricists, rationalists and Kantians – differed from each other on many issues they still shared many thematic commitments, most especially their belief in the objectivity and universality of scientific knowledge and method."[33]

The principles governing this paradigm are the universal applicability of the concepts of science across space and time, objectivity, the irrelevance of the personal characteristics of the investigators to the knowledge claims that they make, and that reason, observation and experiments should be the criteria by which those knowledge-claims are tested.

Shaykh 'Abd al-Qādir's Views on Social Science and Social Theory

The abiding conundrum faced by the social sciences is to find a way of resolving the dichotomy between rationalism and subjectivism. Whilst classical social theories dealt with macro-level issues such as capitalism, the national state, globalism, order, inequality, freedom, and change, they have not been able to resolve the dualities between reason and emotion and between the objective and the subjective. Anthony Thomson argues that:

> In the first decade of the twenty-first century, a feeling of déjà vu permeates social thought. ... It is an exciting if confusing period for sociology and social theory, characterized by multiple competing paradigms. ... The contemporary struggle is over the nature, direction and ultimate ends of the global transformation that is underway.[34]

The duality between the rational and the emotional, the objective and the subjective, the inward and the outward, which characterizes modernity has been addressed by Shaykh 'Abd al-Qādir. In his words, modernist ideology is what has "separated the man from his idea and the political and economic from the elements of personality."[35] Shaykh 'Abd al-Qādir has shown that the means for resolving the key questions of social science philosophy and theory can be found in the writings of Mālik ibn Anas. Mālik's central teaching relates to the instruction of the Prophet Muḥammad ﷺ: "I have left two matters with you. As long as you hold to them, you will not go the wrong way. They are the Book of Allah [Qur'ān] and the *sunna* of His Prophet."[36] In *Root Islamic Education* Shaykh 'Abd al-Qādir shows how the unification of the inward, or spiritual, and outward was integral to Mālik's teaching of the *'amal ahl al-Madīna*.

This relationship of inwardness to outwardness was clarified by Mālik's statement that the practice of Sufism without following the *sharīʿa* corrupts one's faith and following the *sharīʿa* without practising Sufism corrupts oneself. Only someone who combines the two is successful. What can be understood from this is that, in the teaching of Mālik, there is a balance between the *sharīʿa* – the (outwardly practised) law – and *ḥaqīqa* – the (inwardly perceived) reality, between the outer law and the inner state. For Mālik, practice or behaviour is, in itself, evidence of knowledge, or to put it differently, the *ʿamal ahl al-Madīna* guarantees that theory and practice are inseparable. Religion, in Mālik's view, was not something people thought but something they did, and religious truth was only acquired through practical action, which in turn led to the discovery of deeper levels of being.

Shaykh ʿAbd al-Qādir explains that God "has set up creation through a dynamic interplay of opposites. ... For everything, Allah, the Exalted, has said, there has been created an opposite. Everything is paired."[37] He says that in the realm of the learning process, knowledge is also dominated by two great opposites: the *sharīʿa*, the law of the outward, and *ḥaqīqa*, the inner reality. Human beings are the *barzakh*, that is the interspace, between the two. The science of *ḥaqīqa* is derived from the Divine Name al-Ḥaqq, the Real, which is both the Essence of God and that from which the whole phenomenal world is made manifest, because God is one in His acts, attributes and essence. *Ḥaqīqa*, then, is the non-spatial reality from which the time/space zone of duality emerges. Thus "Man has access in outwardness to the universal realities of the cosmos. In inwardness he has access to his own reality in the unseen worlds."[38]

The science of *ḥaqīqa*, which deals with knowledge about the nature of consciousness, is guarded by the *sharīʿa*. In other words, there is no way for a human being to gain access to the deeper levels of being and God except on the path of the *sharīʿa*. Shaykh ʿAbd al-

Qādir says that if you follow the *sharīʿa* it will confront you with the Reality and expose the illusory nature of phenomenal existence.[39] A society grounded on a balance between the *sharīʿa* and *ḥaqīqa*, in which the individuals strive to reach unitary experience, not just unitary information, is one that can truly live in harmony. Shaykh ʿAbd al-Qādir notes:

> No legal system, no social order, no socio-economic schema, however far reaching or even scientific ... can bring man a human society unless it functions in a manner which gives him access to his own inwardness and in which the ultimate project of the society is not simply its continuity or expansion, but rather the meaning of the man in it while he is still alive. The only social pattern which makes this its central thesis is Islam...[40]

Shaykh ʿAbd al-Qādir is of the opinion that in Islam, social and political matters are part of a cosmology and not part of sociology. He gives the example that the social act of lengthening the prayer to show off one's piety to people is a means of bringing the end of the world closer, thereby making wrong action a cosmological act. Thus it is necessary to understand the *sharīʿa* not as a social blueprint or a political manifesto or a legal paradigm, but rather as a biological and cosmological possibility for society.

Shaykh ʿAbd al-Qādir argues that the institutions of the modern state are instruments of tyranny based on stasis and paralysis and says that, in Qurʾānic terms, this model can be defined as Pharaonic.[41] It is non-dual and thus not in dynamic movement and change. It is totalitarian and its people are unarmed and helpless. Everyone is committed to the same unified projects, which are: the gross national product, development, and social evolution. The 'religion' of the modern state is basically the production process. Development is defined in terms of the building of roads, bridges and dams, power stations, factories, etc. There is no concept of use value. The process of mineral exploitation, building etc. are ends in themselves not merely the means to an end. "It is a kind of desperate goalless activity – a social version of the insane man desperately re-arranging an already tidy room."[42]

The most important and necessary element of this Pharaonic model is that there should be no inwardly directed personal project whose end result would inevitably be the rejection of the ruling mystical doctrine of Pharaonic power. The danger to the system is that others would also be attracted to reject the model. In other words if a man or woman was able to find their own meaning within themselves then the desperate and obsessive character of the social activity of development, growth, gross national product, etc., would be called into question. It would then become apparent that the goals of a totally outwardly-directed society were, in fact, just as insane and unbalanced, as those of a group totally engrossed in an obsessively inwardly-directed existence.[43]

Opposite to this modern social system is the model of the Qur'ānic prophets, amongst whom are Moses, Noah, Jonah and Muḥammad. Shaykh 'Abd al-Qādir says that no human culture survives forever, however greatly human beings may desire it to do so. He describes the Islamic model as being biological, like that of a green plant. It grows up a tender shoot and if it survives it becomes a strong plant and provides nourishment. The plant of Islam, says Shaykh 'Abd al-Qādir, is like the gourd tree, besides which the Prophet Yūnus (Jonah) lived. The gourd tree is trunkless and supple and its tenacity and power lie in its clinging to the earth. Just like the gourd plant, Islam is a non-permanent and non-solid social reality. Its strength is in its apparent weakness, that is, its strength is in slavehood to God (*'ubūdiyya*). Shaykh 'Abd al-Qādir points out that when human beings abandon slavehood to God and start to believe that the source of their power is other than God, they then enter into a fantasy and endanger their frail mortal condition. He says that human beings may reach the ends of the universe and construct great towers but when anyone

> ... abrogates power from Allah he enters into a fantasy of permanence and his downfall is inevitable. It is this deep underlying principle which informs every aspect of the Islamic *sharīʿa* – and this is nothing less than knowledge of *tawḥīd*, Divine Unity – *ḥaqīqa*.[44]

In conclusion, the epistemological poverty of the modern social sciences can be traced back to the paradigm of the mechanical sciences, which was generally adopted as the model for all aspects of modern social organization. Shaykh ʿAbd al-Qādir recognizes that all people, including Muslims, through the codification of previously oral and aural traditions and, subsequently, secularization, have taken on a materialistic, technological way of thinking, devoid of inwardness and spirituality – a way of thinking that has its underpinnings in Kantian and Cartesian philosophy, Newtonian physics, Darwinian biology, Freudian psychology, Smith's capitalist free market economics and Hobbes' political theories, amongst many others in a similar vein. It is upon these epistemological building blocks that the whole edifice of modern civilization has been constructed. Modern politics, law, education, economics, medicine, and psychology were all founded on these philosophical and scientific foundations.

Shaykh ʿAbd al-Qādir points out that Sufism insists on the total picture of a human being who is, both outwardly and inwardly, in a state of continual transformation. In Shaykh ʿAbd al-Qādir's view, the inner and outer aspects of life are inextricably and dynamically connected. The renewal of the individual and the renewal of society are one and the same process. This connection came to an end with the birth of the modern period and its scientific epistemologies. He believes that it is necessary for humankind to adopt the non-permanent and non-solid social reality offered by Islam, whose strength lies, paradoxically, in slavehood to God. Human beings, he recommends, should not abandon slavehood to God and start to believe that the source of their power is from other than God. In doing this he is advocating the path of the recognition of Divine Unity, which underlies all aspects of the Islamic *sharīʿa*.

Chapter 6

Sufi Deconstruction of Modern Philosophy

It is, evidently, clear that Shaykh 'Abd al-Qādir holds the view that all people, including Muslims, have taken on a materialistic, technological way of thinking, devoid of inwardness and spirituality, on a socio-economic and political level. We have also seen that he is of the opinion that the inner and outer aspects of life are inextricably and dynamically connected. This vital connection was, however, severed at the advent of the modern period with its emphasis on empirical scientific knowledge. We will now look at the part played by philosophy in the process of the denial of the inner self and all that this has entailed.

An unbroken line can be traced in European philosophical discourse running from René Descartes (1596-1690) to Friedrich Nietzsche (1844-1900). Nietzsche, like Georg Wilhelm Friedrich Hegel (1770-1831) before him, had seen that the greatest event to affect Western civilization had been the "death of God" in the Judeo/Christian tradition and the consequent prevalence of nihilism in European thinking. With Martin Heidegger (1889-1976) the chain is broken because he wanted to establish an ontological basis for the European philosophical discourse and move away from the metaphysics that had been dominating it up till then. Shaykh 'Abd al-Qādir points out that Martin Heidegger's writings provide...

> ... a crucial ground-plan for examining the nature of man's being in an emergent technological total process – he was not only the first to apprehend this issue but also the only one to realise that the 'mechanising' of man, or his reduction to one element inside the technological process, stemmed from an ongoing split in Western thinking that ran through philosophy from Kant[1] to Descartes.[2]

The issues raised by Shaykh 'Abd al-Qādir in this passage can only be understood if they are dealt with in an historical context. In this case the implication is that modernity and its roots should be analyzed within the context of the Western philosophical tradition.

Modern philosophy began in Europe in the seventeenth century and has now permeated all societies throughout the world. Modernity is associated with the far-reaching changes that appeared in Western society, particularly the growth of industrialism and the rapid growth of cities during the nineteenth and twentieth centuries. These comprehensive changes transformed traditional social practices, religious beliefs and institutions, even literature, art and architecture. The two major intellectual trends that underpinned modernity were rationalism and empiricism.

The beginning of modern philosophy is often attributed to Descartes who is famous for his dictum 'cogito ergo sum' – 'I think, therefore I am.'[3] On this narrow foundation Descartes was convinced that he himself existed, that he had certain ideas, and that God existed. Whilst the concept in fact goes back to Aristotle and Plato, Descartes is recognized as the first person to have formulated the body/mind dichotomy as we know it today. He regarded the body and the mind to be as distinct from one another as two separate substances. He regarded the body as material and its essential property as having spatial existence. And he held that the mind was an immaterial substance that thinks. Descartes was unable to resolve the dichotomy resulting from this view, which later came to be known as the body-mind problem. Along with Descartes, Benedict Spinoza (1632-1677) and Gottfried Wilhelm Leibniz (1646-1716) are known as rationalists.

From the point of view of epistemology, rationalism emphasizes the role of reason in the acquisition of knowledge, whilst at the same time downplaying the role of observation and experience. Spinoza identified three levels of knowledge: that which is received through sense perception, that which is acquired through reason, and that which is gained through intuition, which allows one to logically deduce the essence of things. The other great rationalist philosopher, Leibniz, did not have a systematic view on epistemology. In his dispute with John Locke (1632-1704) Leibniz, like Descartes, held that there are innate concepts and principles in logic, metaphysics, pure mathematics and ethics. These innate concepts are necessary truths, which are all knowable *a priori*, that is, they are necessarily true and cannot be falsified by perceptual experience and contingent facts. It is through the senses that these truths are brought to one's attention.

In opposition to rationalism another system of thought appeared called empiricism. Key to empiricism is the notion that experience is the primary source of knowledge. The only knowledge acceptable to empiricists is that which is obtained through sense perception, stressing the importance of observation and experiment. Locke provided empiricist arguments against the epistemological claims of the rationalists. For Locke, the mind at birth is a 'tabula rasa', or 'blank tablet', and it is only through experience and perception that it acquires its mental content. This implies that the mind has no innate ideas. Although Locke rejected the idea that the mind had innate ideas, he believed that it had innate faculties by which it remembers, perceives, synthesizes ideas, and wills. George Berkeley (1685-1783), another empiricist philosopher, accepted Locke's assertion that knowledge comes from sense perception and experience.

According to Berkeley, Locke's overall theory leads to scepticism about physical objects.[4] In order to avoid this problem, Locke suggested that we discard the stipulation that our current ideas of objects correspond to or represent these objects. However in Berkeley's view this step still does not resolve the issue of the relationship between ideas and physical objects because Locke's theory still requires inductive inferences from ideas to physical objects. In order to refute skepticism with regards to the external world, Berkeley argued that objects exist if and when they are perceived, thereby defending the thesis that physical objects are identical to collections of ideas. Objects, which are collections of ideas, are perceivable as long as one perceives their constituent members. Berkeley argued further that our ideas have a Divine origin.

Although many famous philosophers such as David Hume (1711-1776), Immanuel Kant (1724-1804), Hegel (1770-1831), John Stuart Mill (1806-1873), Bertrand Russell (1872-1970), Alfred Jules Ayer (1910-1989), and a host of others, have made contributions to the philosophical study of epistemology, there are still numerous burning questions that need to be answered. These questions relate to the nature of reason, the nature of truth, the justification of induction and deduction, observation, perception, experiment and evidence. In dealing with these problems the two branches of philosophy that have profoundly influenced epistemology are ontology and metaphysics.

Knowledge and Metaphysics

The word metaphysics is derived from the Greek words *meta*, which means 'beyond' and *physica*, which means 'physics'. The etymological implication is that metaphysics is the study of matters that are beyond the physical but this is not necessarily the case. Many subjects considered as sub-branches of metaphysics by the ancient Greeks have now become branches of philosophy in their own right, such as the philosophies of science, mind, religion, language and perception. Some subjects, which the medieval philosophers would have considered to be part of physics, are now classified as metaphysics, for example, identity across time, freedom of will/determinism and the relation between body and mind.

Metaphysics also aims to understand the features of the material universe and how they exist in relation to each other. Some of these features include matter, mind, orderliness, structure, events, states, change, necessity, causation and values. The wide range of topics covered by metaphysics sets out to answer questions dealing with: existence, objects with properties, abstract objects, cosmology, cosmogony, determinism, free will, interpretations of quantum theory in physics (for example, metaphysicians may reformulate Einstein's statement[5] and ask, 'Does God play dice?'), identity, change, mind, matter, necessity, probability, possibility, space, time, spirituality and religion.

Metaphysics has always been influenced by the prevailing intellectual climate. Before the Enlightenment the tenor of metaphysics was theological, holding that the universal order was created by God, who had a complete understanding of that order, and that human beings could get glimpses of that order through natural science, mathematics and logic. This view was vehemently opposed by David Hume (1711-1776) and other empiricist and rationalist philosophers. After the Enlightenment a new set of familiar facts came into existence called the 'Galilean worldview.'[6] The scientific revolution replaced the theological worldview with one that was based on physical science, empiricism and rationalism.

This, however, did not mean that metaphysical speculation came to an end, rather it now centred on idealism, a group of philosophies that assert that reality is mentally constructed. In idealism, mentally constructed facts about reality are the familiar class of facts whilst facts relating to the physical world are exotic and need to be qualified. The problem of qualifying the exotic class of facts, whatever the priority given to them – theological, scientific, idealist, etc. – has dominated philosophy from the time of Descartes till today. Attempts to harmonize the religious worldview with idealism have been attributed to Immanuel Kant. As the motto inscribed on his tombstone suggests, the two areas of great interest to Kant were understanding the universe and the laws of ethics.[7]

For Kant the world was made up of objects that occupy space, have properties, exist in time, participate in events, are subject to causality, obey the laws of physics, geometry, arithmetic and logic. Our understanding of the world, on the other hand, is subject related, that is, it is based on perception, observation, thoughts, concepts, inferences and judgements. The overarching metaphysical problem of philosophy, according to Kant, was the correlation of the object related aspects of the world to the subject related aspects. He concluded that both these aspects are mutually dependent and inseparable from each other. In other words the nature of reality, as we know it, is inseparable from the nature of the mind that knows it. Kant said:

> Hitherto it has been assumed that all our knowledge must conform to objects. But all attempts have, on this assumption, ended in failure.

> We must therefore make trial whether we may not have more success, in the tasks of metaphysics, if we suppose that objects conform to our knowledge.[8]

It was previously assumed that objects in space and time exist independently of us but Kant replaced this realism with the theory that the objective world is the product of our minds, that is, our perception, conception and judgement. Kant believed that there are certain necessary principles that form the foundations for our understanding of the universe. These are: the truths of arithmetic, physics, and geometry, causation, the idea that objects do not come into existence ex-nihilo and they do not go out of existence into nowhere and nothingness. These claims, according to Kant, are *a priori* and synthetic. That is, they are truths not by logic or definition and are essential for understanding reality. Kant called this knowledge 'synthetic *a priori* knowledge' without which no other knowledge would be possible. Synthetic *a priori* knowledge cannot be received from sources external to us and without it we would be unable to make sense of the world.

All *a priori* elements for Kant were determined by our subjective constitutions, that is, the ways in which we perceive, conceptualise and think. The world is experienced by us as a spatial, temporal and causal reality, not because it is such, but because the essential nature and structure of our minds are spatial, temporal and causal. The three fundamental powers of our minds are: the capacity to receive sensory data, the ability to conceptualise, think and judge, that is intellectually process the data and understand it, and lastly the ability to draw valid conclusions, to reason. Kant denies the possibility of having knowledge that is purely sensory and, alternatively, knowledge that is purely conceptual. In other words, thoughts without sensory data are empty and conversely sensory data without thoughts are blind.

Kant divided the organisation of his *Critique of Pure Reason* into two sections: Transcendental Aesthetic and Transcendental Logic. The word aesthetic in the term Transcendental Aesthetic is not used in its contemporary sense, it refers instead to the original Greek word *aesthesis*, meaning sensation or perception. The section entitled Transcendental Aesthetic deals with the *a priori* fundamentals of sensory and perceptual experience. Here, Kant aims to demonstrate that sensations and perceptions, or 'intuitions' as he calls them, have *a priori* spatial and temporal forms. Further, he maintains that the empirical objects that make up the external world are spatio-temporal. It is due to the truth of his first proposition that the latter proposition is true and not vice versa. The logic in Transcendental Logic is derived from the Greek word *logos*, which means proposition or meaning and deals with the *a priori* elements that constitute the conceptual and intellectual make-up of human beings. Kant divides Transcendental Logic into Transcendental Analytic and Transcendental Dialectic. Transcendental Analytic is concerned with the nature of understanding, that is, the features upon which our ability to conceptualise and form judgements rest.

Kant's argument states that, in the absence of certain *a priori* concepts he calls categories, no thinking and understanding would be possible. Transcendental Dialectic is concerned with the capacity to use the powers of reasoning. The aim of Transcendental Dialectic is to illustrate that, when detached from sensory experience, pure reason can provide no genuine knowledge. This is essentially Kant's critique of pure reason, that is the deduction of facts about the mind or the self on purely rational foundations with no reference to sensory experience is not possible and ends in failure. This leads to his criticism of metaphysics and arguments for the existence of God.

The core of Kant's metaphysics is in his Transcendental

Analytic. It analyses how the mind works to make understanding and knowledge possible. At the same time he explains how the properties that the world has enables them to be known. The senses present the mind with a multiplicity of intuitions and sensations. Whilst these intuitions may have properties of space and time, their natures do not give them determinacy, permanence or objectivity. For one to be able to perceive objects in an intelligible, stable and predictable way that persists in time and space, one has to be capable of unifying and interpreting the multiplicity of intuitions. Kant calls this ability 'synthesis'. Synthesis allows one to unify sensations and understand them as representations of objects and properties in the external world.

In Kant's view, then, we would have no awareness of the external world nor would we be able to make sense of any of our experiences in the absence of synthesis. The rules of synthesis, as asserted by Kant, are *a priori* rules. The most fundamental of all *a priori* rules enable a number of sensations to be attributed to the same object. For Kant concepts or categories are the *a priori* rules for synthesis. These categories enable human understanding to perceive sensations as representing objects in the external world. Kant identifies the following twelve categories: Unity, Plurality, Totality, Reality, Negation, Limitation, Substance, Causality, Community, Possibility, Existence and Necessity.

Another aspect of Kant's thinking is that the mind must possess self-consciousness. The plurality or multiplicity of sensations and conceptions must belong to a single unified consciousness. He wrote:

> It must be possible for the 'I think' to accompany all my representations... for the manifold of representations ... would not be one and all my representations if they did not all belong to one self-consciousness.[9]

Kant held the view that the unity of consciousness necessitated self-consciousness and self-consciousness needed the ability for one to ascribe one's sensations and conceptions to oneself. Kant clearly summarised his metaphysical system when he wrote:

> The consciousness of my existence is at the same time an immediate consciousness of the existence of other things outside me.[10]

Kant believed that knowledge, intelligible experience and unity of consciousness, which give us the experience of an objective, external world, depend on sense perception and the possession and application of *a priori* categories. It was Descartes who claimed that the essential quality of being human was thinking and it was Kant who went on to explain how the process of thinking works. The post-Kantian German idealist philosopher Hegel, however, was dissatisfied with Kant's view that 'things-in-themselves' cannot be known. He believed that Kant's metaphysical system was deficient due to his failure to examine the categories and their interconnections more adequately. Hegel's philosophy sets out to identify reality in its multifarious forms as a manifestation of 'reason' and this has connotations for both epistemology and ontology.

Ontology

Ontology is the philosophical investigation of existence and sets out to answer such questions as: what exists, what are things made out of, what does being mean? Ontology also includes the investigation of problems about the general features and relationships of extant things. There are, therefore, two philosophical projects which ontology deals with. Firstly, what exists (extant things/beings/objects) and what is it made of and, secondly, what are the general features and relationships of the things that do exist. These two projects of ontology in turn create two sets of problems. The first set of problems relate to finding a way of answering the questions of what exists and what it is made of. This leads to issues of ontological commitment. In this context, the opinion, attributed to Willard van Orman Quine (1908-2000), that the best guide to what exists can be derived from our current scientific theories, is generally accepted as correct.[11] The second set of problems relates to endeavours to establish what ontological questions really are.

This is known as meta-ontology and sets out to do three things: firstly, to define the tasks that ontology aims to accomplish, secondly, to clarify how ontological questions should be understood and, thirdly, to outline the methodology by which they are best answered. In the last few decades there has been little interest in meta-ontology, partly because the meta-ontological opinion of Quine has again been accepted as the best one.[12] However, the importance of the contributions made by Hegel to the modern study of ontology cannot be overstated because his arguments signify an epistemological turn from metaphysics to ontology in the quest for knowledge of reality.

Hegel believed that Kant's philosophy did not signify the finality of the philosophical discourse because it did not lead to a unified theory of reality. Such a theory should be able to systematically explain all aspects of reality emanating from one principle or subject. Hegel believed that the essential task of philosophy was the systematic explanation of the physical universe and all life-forms, including human beings, their social and political systems, culture, religion, art and philosophy, in a single unified theory of reality. Such a theory would replace faith with knowledge because, for Hegel, the principle that explained all of reality was reason. Reason, for him, was not a quality belonging to human beings but rather the sum total of reality. Reason and reality are identical in his system, making reason real and reality reasonable. The goal of reason is to recognize itself through itself. It is then the role of philosophy to give a coherent account of this self-knowledge.

Hegel's conception of reason has both ontological and epistemological connotations. Reason is not simply a human faculty for acquiring knowledge, it is also that which represents or describes reality. The ontological connotation inherent in this position is aimed at eradicating the sharp distinction between knower and the object of knowledge. Hegel challenged the dominant epistemological tradition with its internal differentiation of subject and object and the consequent relatedness of the subject to the object. There are three different principles supporting Hegel's basic notion of the ontological integrity of reason. Firstly, everything which is real must be considered as the partial realization of a primary structure which is the basis of reality. Without this primary structure which Hegel called 'the absolute' and 'reason' one cannot comprehend the concepts of object and objectivity. Hegel's second principle relates to the internal constitution of the structure of reason which, for him, is made up of a complex unity of thinking and being. The implication of this is that thinking and being are one and the same and that only the faculty of thinking possesses being. This position has been described as 'ontological monism' or the 'monism of reason'. The third principle is that there can be no adequate theory of reality without a dynamic or process oriented ontology. Hegel calls this process the 'self-knowledge of cognition'.

In the early years of his intellectual career, Hegel showed a keen interest in public education and enlightenment. Hegel criticized the transformation of Christianity into what he called "positive religion", that is, religion, whose content and principles are incomprehensible to human reason, thereby making them appear unnatural. Hegel conceived of what he called "natural religion", a religion which was consistent with human nature. Such a religion would bring about harmony between people, their needs and convictions and, at the same time, circumvent alienation between people. This process, in which there is a dynamic generation and reconciliation of oppositions, Hegel calls 'Life' (*Leben*) and 'Being' (*Sein*).

In 1807 Hegel wrote a book entitled *The Phenomenology of Spirit*. As an introduction to his system of philosophy, Hegel proposed what he called the 'Science of the Experience of Consciousness' or 'Phenomenology of Spirit'. According to Hegel, for comprehension of the real composition of the world and of objects and objectivity, it must be assumed that there is a structural unity between the world and human beings. This structural unity has the attribute or capacity of self-consciousness. The core of Hegel's philosophical system is the discipline he called "Logic". His most comprehensive work, *Science of Logic* (1812-16), is dedicated to it. In *Science of Logic*, Hegel contends that all true knowledge is self-knowledge and the subject that knows about itself is reason. In his *Encyclopedia of the Philosophical Sciences* Hegel discusses his philosophy of nature and how it is possible to recognize nature in its entirety as integrated under a single set of laws.

Hegel was both a controversial and also influential philosopher who made a significant impact on the development of modern Western thought.[13] Hegel's work led to the establishment of Hegelianism[14] in northern Europe, Italy, France, Eastern Europe, America and Britain. In the twentieth century many anti-Hegelian movements such as Neo-Kantianism, Marxism, existentialism, pragmatism, post-structuralism and analytic philosophy began to find common ground, paradoxically giving new impetus and depth to Hegelianism itself.[15] Hegel proposed a cosmic process to enable one to navigate through the conflicts that are inherent in the natural and social worlds. In modern science the human subject defines itself through its control of nature. There is an inherent contradiction in this relationship; when the self imposes itself on nature in order to be free of it, the self becomes involved even more deeply in nature. This conflict between the self and others manifests in a variety of dualisms, such as man and nature, thought and being, theory and practice, mind and body, individual and society, objectivity and subjectivity and freedom and necessity.

Hegel calls the cosmic principle, which enables one to navigate through the conflicts that emerge out of these dualisms, by names such as reason, ego, subjectivity, absolute and *Geist* (spirit). This principle is neither identical with the God of Christianity nor with the atheist denial of it.[16] Hegel believed that the finite world could only be understood as the expression of the infinite spirit. Perception is not the passive reception of sensory data because, for perception of the world to take place, the subject, who is involved in it, must interact with it. Purposive action or praxis moves the epistemological search into ontology.[17] Hegel's ontological vision provides a good introduction for Shaykh 'Abd al-Qādir 's interpretation of Heideggerian ontology to which we now turn.

Heideggerian Ontology

Hegel's ontological vision was born out of his efforts to transcend the dualities, made all the keener by modern science, of both nature and modern life. Shaykh 'Abd al-Qādir points out that Heidegger has not only provided us with a profound discourse on Being but "also opens the door on Nietzsche for us so that we can see in a clear light the profound and necessary illumination he brings to us about the problems of the modern age."[18] Nietzsche and Heidegger, like Hegel before them, saw that the greatest event to affect Western civilization was what they called the 'death of God' and its consequence, nihilism. To emphasize the importance of Heidegger, Shaykh 'Abd al-Qādir says that Heidegger's masterwork, *Sein und Zeit*, has towered over the philosophical scene and, along with his book on Nietzsche, has dominated Western thought in the present age.[19]

Before dealing with Heidegger's ontology it is necessary to investigate certain aspects of Nietzsche's philosophy. For Nietzsche, the statement 'God is dead' was a metaphor which stood for a major cultural event: namely, that the Christian idea of God had ceased to be a living force in Western society. Nietzsche said, in the words of Zarathustra, "'Whither is God?' ... 'I will tell you. We have killed him – you and I. All of us are his murderers...'"[20] The idea that God is dead points to the gradual demise of Christian theism as a major cultural force. This process was, and continues to be, brought about by many forces. Since Descartes, the philosophical traditions of the West have undermined Christian doctrines by positing science as an explanation of reality without reference to God. Other factors indicated by Nietzsche include industriousness as an end in itself, materialistic pursuits and democracy. With the loss of belief in God, and the collapse of the values that were built upon that belief, Nietzsche predicted the rise of nihilism, which he defined as a repudiation of value, meaning, knowledge, desirability, truth, virtue, philosophy and art.

Nietzsche called himself an 'immoralist' and objected to 'morality'. He felt it promoted a kind of person he referred to as a 'herd animal'. That is, one who negates greatness and merely seeks security and the absence of fear and suffering. His opposition to morality in its narrower sense was by no means the rejection of an ethical life. He made reference to what he calls 'noble morality' and 'higher moralities' and considered himself 'bound', 'pledged' and a human being 'of duty'. In his work, *Genealogy*, Nietzsche speaks of goodness among the politically superior classes in the ancient world, who called themselves 'the good'. He used the terms 'good' and 'virtue' as marks of distinction, which distinguish them from the commoners or slaves. He described the 'ruling class' as 'noble' because they were 'good' and 'virtuous' and the 'low-born' as 'bad'. The German word, *schlecht*, which he uses for 'low-born' and 'bad', etymologically means 'simple' or 'common'.

Nietzsche's use of 'bad' in this sense does not connote blame but simply that the person described is inferior. The nobles are superior but do not blame the common for being inferior or think that the inferior deserve punishment or that goodness should be rewarded. Inferiority is not judged as evil in moral terms. As the alternative to 'herd-animal' morality Nietzsche proposed his idea of the *Ubermensch* – the Overhuman or the Overman. Since God is dead, the time has come for humanity to rise and become higher kinds of beings by transcending their humanity. This idea was not intended to encourage human beings to throw off the constraints of morality but instead to combat the forces of barbarism and conformism by taking on more ethical tasks than those demanded by modernity.

Although there was agreement between Nietzsche and Heidegger on the existence of nihilism in modern society, Heidegger disagreed with Nietzsche about the way to overcome it. Whilst Nietzsche recommends that human beings become masters of the world and establish a new system of values, Heidegger believed that a completely different approach was needed. Heidegger explained that philosophical thinking in the West began with the thought of the post-Socratic[21] philosophers and had terminated with the nihilistic hegemony of technology, a technology that is sustained by scientific or instrumental rationality and which, in turn, underlies the industry, bureaucracy and other structures of modern society. The use of technology was initially seen as an instrument under the control of humanity whose aim was the subjugation of nature through human reasoning. Humankind, however, has not been liberated by the use of technology but has instead been subordinated by it, in its drive for world domination.

Heidegger's life was dedicated to correcting the misunderstandings about the nature of Being in general, and the nature of the human being in particular, in Western philosophy. He saw these two issues as inextricably linked since being human is to disclose and understand the Being of entities and, likewise, the Being of an entity is the meaning of that entity within human experience and knowledge. To understand the human being entails a proper understanding of the Being of everything else. Heidegger named the human being '*Dasein*', lit. 'being there', the entity whose being discloses and understands the Being of itself and that of other entities. Heidegger said that when Dasein discloses its own being it is called 'existence' to differentiate it from the Cartesian thinking substance. Dasein's being consists not in consciousness, subjectivity or rationality, but in understanding and concern for itself. Dasein, however, is not just related to itself, because existence occurs only as being-in-the-world, that is, maintaining an openness to other entities in the world. Self-disclosure of the human being makes possible the disclosure of other entities.

Heidegger described the structure of the human being as existing in three co-equal moments: becoming, alreadiness, and presence. As a unity, these three moments constitute what Heidegger calls 'temporality', that is, being meaningfully in the present by anticipating one's own death. Temporality, therefore, means being in the present by acknowledging what one already is. Being human, then, is a process of becoming oneself. Although human beings are always in the process of mortal becoming, we are usually so absorbed in the things that we encounter that we forget the becoming that makes encounters with those things possible. Heidegger refers to this as a state of 'fallenness'. Waking up to one's mortality can be an unusual kind of experience, more like a mood than a form of cognition. Heidegger says that during these special 'basic moods' such as 'dread', 'boredom' and 'call of conscience' we experience an awakening in which we encounter our finite nature.

What we experience, then, are not things but that which is not-a-thing or 'no-thing'. To attain 'authenticity' one has to heed this 'call of conscience' and acknowledge one's mortality and live accordingly. To ignore or refuse the 'call of conscience' does not mean one ceases being finite and mortal but, instead, it means to live according to an 'inauthentic' or 'fallen' self-understanding. The recovery and acknowledgement of one's finitude leads to the understanding that all forms of being are finite. As such, for Heidegger, the very meaning of being is time.

Shaykh 'Abd al-Qādir points out that, in Heidegger's understanding, the goal of modern society is liberation, which is to be achieved through the mastery of nature and scientific knowledge. What has been arrived at, however, is nihilism, a world technology system, fear of war and pollution of the ecosphere, the very ground of life on this planet. He says:

> To break through to a new situation Heidegger goes to the depths of the dynamic of our thinking and questions metaphysics and thinking itself. In his view, it is not enough to negate metaphysics but rather to confront its core and so be free of its overpowering grip on man. To do this Heidegger engaged in a lifelong discourse on the nature of the human being (Dasein), as a project directed entity, and Being itself.[22]

Shaykh 'Abd al-Qādir has argued that Heidegger was convinced that Being itself had a new destiny waiting for the West but that he was unable to work out what that new destiny would be. This is what is referred to below as the unfulfilled 'Heideggerian need'.

The Heideggerian Need

In his assessment of Heidegger's philosophy Shaykh 'Abd al-Qādir concludes that:

> It is our conviction that the only model which fits the Heideggerian need is Islam and that his own deeply moving and profound reflections of Being itself are nothing other than pure and exact delineations of what may be said about Allah.[23]

Reference to this 'Heideggerian need' raises several philosophical questions that will be addressed here. They relate to Heidegger's views on (a) the end of metaphysics, (b) the philosphical history of Being, and (c) religion. Without reviewing these aspects of Heidegger's thought, Shaykh 'Abd al-Qādir's profound insights into Western philosophy cannot be assessed.

(a) The End of Metaphysics

Heidegger believed that Plato (424/423 BC – 348/347 BC) distorted the meaning of Being as it was understood by the pre-Socratic philosophers, particularly Parmenides (b. 540 BC or 515 BC) and Heraclitus (535 BC – 475 BC), thereby initiating 'nihilism' in Western philosophical thinking. For Heidegger this meant the beginning, not only of metaphysics, but also of philosophy as we know it. He said:

> Therefore metaphysics begins with Plato's interpretation of 'Being' as idea. For all subsequent times, it shapes the essence of Western philosophy, whose history from Plato to Nietzsche is the history of metaphysics.[24]

This decline of philosophical thinking, starting with Plato and ending with Nietzsche, was caused by the abandonment of 'Being'. Plato interpreted the meaning of 'Being' as idea, value, production and even nothing. Heidegger's thinking was aimed at overcoming Plato's metaphysics and, as such, it signified a shift from metaphysics to ontology. The study of metaphysics focuses on beings whilst ontology focuses on the Being of beings. For Heidegger the task of philosophy was to bring metaphysics to an end and the overcoming of nihilism was dependent on bringing this end about. The following descriptive phrases give us some idea of Heidegger's understanding of nihilism: 'the flight of the gods', 'the darkening of the world', 'the destruction of the earth', 'the spiritual decline of the earth', 'the transformation of human beings into masses', 'hatred of freedom and creativity', 'calculative thinking', and 'the end of questioning'.[25] All of these are the result of the abandonment or forgetfulness of Being. Overcoming nihilism through the termination of metaphysics can be achieved through a radical rejection of the forgetfulness of Being.

Heidegger's philosophical position is a turning away from the metaphysics of essentialism to that of existentialism. Metaphysics is an enquiry into the essence of beings. When enquiring about the essence of something (a being), the question asked is, "What is it?"[26] This question however, cannot be applied to Being because in Heidegger's words:

> Being is what is emptiest and at the same time it is abundance, out of which all beings, known and experienced, or unknown and yet to be experienced, are endowed each with the essential form of its own individual Being. Being is most universal, encountered in every being, and is therefore most common: it has lost every distinction, or never possessed any. At the same time, Being is most singular, whose uniqueness cannot be attained by any being whatsoever.[27]

Heidegger was of the firm belief that, since Plato, Western philosophy has neglected the significance of Being as the being of all beings. This forgetfulness of Being gave rise to the technological age in which Being is taken to be a standing reserve, something of use value. He described this mode of metaphysics as nihilism. The way out of this nihilism, then, would be a turning away from the forgetfulness of Being and this itself would result in the full realization of Being. This would replace technological thinking, and its scientific and calculative discourse, with another mode of understanding that could enable human beings to arrive at their essences. The doctrine of the principality of Being shows that Being is not a mental concept but an objective reality not able to be apprehended or captured by rational thinking. On the other hand, essence is a mental phenomenon that exists in thought but does not exist by itself. Essence therefore, arises in thinking when a particular mode of Being is considered but it does not have its own ontological status.

Heidegger's critique of metaphysics leads to a new way of thinking. The old scientific, technological, calculative and rational way of thinking is blind to Being, or Truth, because, as Heidegger says, "Science does not think."[28] The scientific way of thinking turns the thing that needs to be thought away from the thinker.[29] For Heidegger the scientific way of thinking is none other than Platonic philosophy, metaphysics and rationalism. Essentialism enquires about the essence of Truth but not Truth itself, about being but not about Being. Heidegger talks of the trivialization of truth in modern philosophical language.[30] Access to truth has become a theory of correspondence between a proposition and what we understand of the entity.[31] Heidegger explained that, for post-Socratic philosophers, man had a detached relationship to truth which made him a 'logical maker of truth'. The term 'logic' is an abbreviated form of the Greek '*logike episteme*', the science of logos.

Logos means to make a statement about something and, consequently, the science of logos became the science of thinking.

Thinking in the form of statements entails thinking about 'something' and this 'something' is what can be thought and expressed through the science of logos. If logos cannot express 'something' it cannot be thought. Everything that cannot be apprehended by this way of thinking is therefore 'illogical'. Logic claims for itself a universal capacity to think everything. The upshot is that whatever cannot be thought logically is not true. Truth, through the science of logic, becomes a theory of correspondence. This means that if a statement is in accordance with an entity, then it is taken to be true. Whatever else that is related to the entity, which is not included in the statement is disregarded but the correctness of the statement is not affected. Vadillo argues that:

> When later philosophers (the Scholastics) discovered this fascinating way of thinking of the Greeks they applied it to 'knowledge' of God. God, inevitably, is reduced to 'something' (logical) in order to be thought. Yet, God is never thought, only the concept of God is thought. The problem here is that the result of logic's claim of universality is that 'everything' must become something, before it can be thought.[32]

Truth (*aletheia*) for the pre-Socratic philosophers, particularly Parmenides and Heraclitus, meant unconcealment, from the Greek '*a*', meaning not and '*leth*', to escape notice or to be concealed. The human being was understood as being 'the locus of the self-disclosure of Truth' and not a rational animal (a mistranslation of *zoon logon echon*). Heidegger redefined human beings as Dasein, which in German means 'being-there'. Dasein is the clearing for the disclosure of Being, that is, the locus where Being manifests. There is an abyss between thinking and science, between Being and being and between a human being as a rational animal and as a being who is the locus for the self-disclosure of Truth. Between these two modes there is no bridge. Heidegger stated:

> By way of a series of lectures, we are attempting to learn thinking.

> The way is long. We dare to take only a few steps. If all goes well, they will take us to the foot-hills of thought. But they will take us to places which we must explore to reach the point where only the leap will help further. The leap alone takes us into the neighbourhood where thinking resides. The leap will take us abruptly to where everything is different, so different that it strikes us as strange.[33]

Shaykh 'Abd al-Qādir asserts that Heidegger needed to make the leap himself but was never able to do so. Although Heidegger was a great admirer of Goethe (1749-1832)[34] he did not take the leap to Islam that Shaykh 'Abd al-Qādir claims Goethe did take, the leap needed to fill the need that he himself had so eloquently defined. Taking the leap into Islam for Heidegger would have required him to engage more profoundly with the philosophical issues that were raised by Goethe, Nietzsche and Ernst Jünger (1895-1998), whose writings he was so familiar with during his life.

(B) A PHILOSOPHICAL HISTORY OF BEING

Heidegger described the history of Western thought as a history of the forgetfulness of Being. Each epoch of the history of Being is characterized by the definitive metaphysical notion of that epoch and the philosopher that outlined that particular notion. Some examples are: '*idea*' for Plato, '*energeia*' for Aristotle, 'act' for Aquinas, 'cogito ergo sum' for Descartes, 'objectivity' for Kant, 'Absolute Spirit' for Hegel and 'will to power' for Nietzsche.

For Hegel the Absolute Spirit constituted the ground of history: firstly as the unity of consciousness throughout its historical development and secondly as the recognition of itself as the ground of knowledge. In this way Hegel attempted to bridge the abyss between freedom and determinism opened up by Kant's Third Antinomy, which states that we are free and at the same time our acts are predetermined. Hegel's philosophy acknowledged the political and spiritual nihilism of his day but nevertheless regarded the 'death of God' as the ground for reconciliation between the Divine and human. He attempted to establish a basis for reconciling nature and freedom, the aim of which was to resolve the contradictions that were apparent in the French Revolution, in English bourgeois society and in the spiritual life of the German people.

The first signs of the failure of his thought appeared with the split within the Hegelian school between the 'Right' and 'Left' or 'Young' Hegelians. The 'Right' Hegelians hoped that Hegel's reconciliation between human beings and God and his liberal political prescriptions would be embodied in a new reformed Germany. This was not to be. They turned instead towards Romantic[35] nationalism and a rapprochement with traditional Christianity and the Bismarckian state.[36] The 'Young' Hegelians on the other hand believed that Hegel had neglected the dialectical investigation of nature and history and they returned to the Enlightenment notion of progress, which in Hegel's view produced the French Revolution.

Karl Marx and Friedrich Engels (1820-1895) argued that the basis of history was class conflict produced by the dialectical development of the means of production and that the masses were the agents of historical change. This was an inversion of the Hegelian dialectic.[37] The Young Hegelians and the Right Hegelians abandoned Hegel's resolution of the Third Antinomy of Kant and appropriated his dialectical methodology. Both groups, however, failed to provide solutions to the political and spiritual contradictions that Hegel attempted to reconcile. The collapse of Hegelianism saw the unimpeded growth of the nihilism that is inherent in science and technology. Whilst science and technology appeared to improve the conditions of human life they failed to portray history as anything more than meaningless activity. Science and technology were not a means to an end, they were ends in themselves.

For Nietzsche God was dead and any appeals to Søren Kierkegaard's (1813-1855) transcendent God or Hegel's Absolute Spirit were out of the question. Instead of God or universal reason, Nietzsche asserted that it was the will to power that continually constituted and reconstituted itself in its confrontation with historical actuality and its efforts to explain the contradictions of the world. The ground of history, for Nietzsche, was eternal recurrence. He held that through will to power human beings could bring about the transvaluation of all values. For instance Nietzsche praises the virtues of justice and generosity but gives a new interpretation of them. The value of generosity lies not in selflessness but in the fact that it displays the richness and power of one's soul. Likewise justice is a great virtue not because it is impartial or obeys a higher law but because it is the rarest and highest desirable quality that one can master. Nietzsche claimed that qualities such as truthfulness, honesty, justice, generosity, malice, exuberance and laughter were all life affirming and saw in them positive elements which could be considered part of greatness.

In his new interpretations of old values Nietzsche aimed to push culture in new directions towards higher levels. It is at this high level that his philosophy becomes art.[38] It is an art that does not devalue knowledge but aims to complete it instead. He had set out a path in philosophy that he expected others to embark on. He wrote:

> It is for others that I wait here in these mountains and I will not lift my foot from here without them, for higher, stronger, more victorious, more joyful men, such as are square built in body and soul: laughing lions must come.[39]

The barbarity of World War One (1914-1918) shattered the comfortable illusions of Western civilization, that of the triumph of reason and science over faith and ignorance. It certainly was a victory for technology and capitalism but it signalled the beginning of the apotheosis of nihilism, the great contribution of Western philosophy to the world. World War One gave contemporary philosophical debate the urgency that it had previously lacked. Michael Allen Gillespie notes that:

> It seemed to many that a new beginning had to be made, that in some way the philosophical presuppositions of modernity, or perhaps even of the West itself, had been monstrously defective and that, consequently, a new way of thinking that went beyond modernity and the West was needed. This was the problem that impelled thinking in the years following the First World War, and it impelled no one's thought so completely and so powerfully as that of Heidegger.[40]

For Heidegger modernity was characterized by subjectivity, whereby modern man interprets himself as the ground and measure of truth. This subjectivity freed human beings from the theocentrism of traditional Christian society, and the authority of revelation was replaced by the perceptions, opinions, reflections and feelings of human beings. Subjectivity, whilst freeing humans from religious authority, created more terrible and universal forms of bondage, which culminated in a global totalitarianism of technology, will to power and nihilism. These negative consequences occurred because natural and rational law recognizes human beings as subjects, and subjectivity necessitates subjugation to an enforcing authority, which may take the form of a monarch, a dictator, a democracy, a party, a class, a state or a race.

Shaykh ʿAbd al-Qādir points out that "man manipulates nature to liberate himself in his supreme subjectivity and finds, by the objectification necessary for the control of nature, that he has enslaved himself."[41] Technological subordination, exploitation, production and consumption cause human beings to forget that it is their subjectivity and freedom themselves that alienate them and obliterate their place in the world and their humanity. As a reaction to this universal homelessness, humans objectify themselves and their tradition. This is the *Historie*, which is severed from *Geschichte* (history), that is the tradition itself and its involvement in making and remaking that tradition according to the necessities of power and technological development. Shaykh 'Abd al-Qādir states that for Heidegger it was *Historie* that:

> ... has delineated a view that brooks no critique of the ongoing world system. In that sense it becomes polemical and defensive and so turns into ideology. Ideology in its turn liquidates any genuine philosophical discourse, political renewal or artistic vision. ... The implication of the bleak scenario, in which we do most certainly live, is that to gain prosperity must imply to achieve the terrible and empty nihilism of masterful technology. If man destroys the earth (*humus*) then he destroys man himself (*humanus*).[42]

Heidegger described Americanism, Communism and Nazism as institutionalized nihilism and embodiments of subjectivity. They are qualitatively identical from the metaphysical point of view and are all characterized by the dictatorship of the public over the private and the dominance of natural science, technology, economics and public policy. The ideological forms of democracy and liberalism are not essential for Americanism. It is logical positivism[43] that subsumes all political, economic and social phenomena through the methodologies of psychology, psychoanalysis, sociology, cybernetics and mathematical physics. Americanism, like Europeanism, has submitted to the technological spirit of modernity, and philosophy has consequently become subordinated to science. Science facilitates the technological exploitation of nature and human beings through what Heidegger calls the 'industrial complex'. The industrial complex spreads its dominance through foreign aid and the development of a world market. Communism is merely another form of subjectivity and institutionalized nihilism.

Whilst Americanism distracts human beings from their true humanity with pleasure, prosperity and happiness, communism relies on indoctrination and coercion to do the same. It is in no way an answer to the underlying nihilism which characterizes modernity. Heidegger regards Marxism as the production of human beings as social beings and he says that this is the essence of subjectivity as technology. Marx interpreted Being as the process of production and believed that he overcame the subjectivism or idealism of the Hegelian dialectic and replaced it with scientific dialectical materialism.

Nazism, like Americanism and Communism, misconstrues human spirituality as calculative thinking in the service of the objectification and exploitation of human beings and nature. Nazism in Heidegger's understanding sets out to create a race of 'Overmen' who recognize a higher truth than reason – the truth of instinct. Subjectivity is absorbed in the will to power and appears as the Führer principle, in which the leaders establish the universal exploitation of nature and human beings through world domination. What Nazism fails to recognize is that the necessary complement to the 'Overman' is the 'Underman', that is, those who do not belong to the Nazi race and that there is no difference between the two. The super-rational 'Overman' and the sub-rational 'Underman' are the same. They are both beasts. The distinction between the two, according to Heidegger, is arbitrary and is only possible when subjectivity is unconditional in a form of nihilism in which anything and everything is permitted.

For Heidegger, modernity, with its promises of freedom and scientific certainty, ended up in institutionalized nihilism replete with its totalitarianism, world technology and total war. To reinterpret Being as history presupposes the liberation of thought, not only from subjectivity, but from metaphysics as a whole. This is a monumental task considering that it encompasses all realms of thought and life. The destruction of metaphysics entails, for Heidegger, the demonstration that metaphysics is nihilism. Heidegger explains that metaphysics is not intentionally nihilistic but, whilst metaphysics aims at overcoming nihilism, it fails to do so because it fails to grasp its own essence. The reason for this failure is that it leaves Being un-thought, so to speak, and, therefore, unperceived. In other words, metaphysics asks 'what is being?' without considering the Being of beings. It is the absence of Being, or the interpretation of Being in terms of being in Western metaphysics, that has led to nihilism. Being is always thought of as what lies behind beings, or what is other than beings, or prior to beings, or what is at their core. In this way the experience of Being is lost and human beings assume that Being is self evident. Being is thus neglected and forgotten, leading human beings to lose their humanity.

The human being is '*zoon logon echon*', 'life that has speech', and this speech asks the question 'what is being?' This reflection is the first step in the manifestation of Being to the human being because human beings (*Dasein*) are the place (*Da*) in which Being (*Sein*) reveals itself. The humanity of human beings lies in their relation to Being and not in their intellects or passions or in their social, economic and political interactions. At the heart of this inquiry into the meaning of Being lies the struggle with the different answers that come forth. Heidegger says that for the pre-Socratics this struggle was carried out in art and language (*Sprache*).

The art and language of the Greeks revealed how the question of Being (and its answers) determined the character and structure of their lives. The struggle with the question of Being was therefore a communal affair involving poets, architects, sculptors, thinkers and politicians, all of whom participated in establishing the customs, laws and institutions of their society. Living was an art as well as a science. The form of an activity was less important than the openness of it to the question of Being and the authenticity of the response to the answers arrived at. This question of Being engaged human beings in the effort to creatively uncover the ontological status of the world. Through the creation of a new ontology and new world, human beings become creative artists in the widest sense of the term. The creation of a new ontology, however, was not to be the destiny of Heidegger as Gillespie points out:

> ... Heidegger hoped to overcome the basic presuppositions of Western metaphysics that had, in his view, led to nihilism. He was unable to complete the project to his own satisfaction, however, and consequently never published the decisive second half of the work [*Being and Time*]. The failure was in part apparently the result of the Cartesian and Kantian presuppositions of his phenomenological methodology. As a result, the language of *Being and Time*, and consequently Heidegger's analysis, remained inextricably in subjectivity and subjectivistic metaphysics, which as Heidegger himself later argued, excluded even the possibility of raising the question of Being as such.[44]

Gillespie argued further that the completion of the project of *Being and Time* could have been achieved if Heidegger had abandoned phenomenology[45] and explicitly confronted the problem of subjectivity.[46] Although Heidegger failed in achieving the monumental task he had set for himself, his achievements and his thorough critique of modernity were nothing short of spectacular. Perhaps again a deeper reading into Goethe, Nietzsche and Jünger might have helped him achieve his goal and make the leap he had said was necessary for true thinking to take place.[47]

(c) Religion

Heidegger was born to Catholic parents and embarked on studies to become a priest. In 1911, after two years of theological studies at Freiburg University, he switched to mathematics and the natural sciences before finally beginning his doctorate in philosophy in 1913. Hoping to get an appointment to Freiburg's chair in Catholic philosophy, he wrote a dissertation in 1915 on "Die Kategorien – und Bedeutungslehre des Duns Scotus" (Duns Scotus' Doctrine of Categories and Meaning)[48] in 1916. Heidegger was a Thomist[49] at the time but became influenced by the phenomenology of Edmund Husserl (1859-1938) who had joined the Freiburg philosophy faculty in 1916. On his return from war service in 1919, Heidegger announced his break with Catholic philosophy, was appointed Husserl's assistant and began to lecture on his new approach to philosophy. Heidegger was clearly well versed in Christian philosophy and theology.

As we have seen, for Heidegger, forgetfulness of Being in the West began with Plato and he saw that the metaphysical dualisms of God and the world and mind and body had become embedded in its philosophical language. The second phase of the withdrawal of Being was ushered in via the translation of Greek ontological writings by the Romans and their consequent incorporation into Christian theology. The name of Being changed from *physis* (the shining forth) to *natura* (nature) and the experience of Being was no longer a sudden and inexplicable revelation but was taken to be a natural process of action and reaction and a chain of causes and effects. This new ontology reached its fullness in imperial Rome where human beings were understood to be *homo romanitas*, the embodiment of virtue. This virtue was attained by education (*humanitas*) which enables a rational animal to distinguish the ontological hierarchy. Within the Roman Empire, metaphysics lost touch with Being.

For the Christians, this absence of God came to depend upon scripture and dogmatism with its basis in metaphysics. When explaining the revelatory experience, the apostles John and Paul and later Augustine (354-430), Aquinas (1225-1274) and Luther

(1483-1586) became entangled in metaphysics.[50] The only ones who escaped such entanglement were mystics such as Meister Eckhart (1260-1328) who was, however, unable to articulate his experiences and hence unable to offer an alternative to dogmatic Christianity. This resulted in a new ontology and history which, whilst remaining within ancient Greek metaphysics, found its new centre in a transcendent God who created human beings and nature and revealed himself as Christ.

This conception impacted throughout the metaphysical framework of Christianity, which now held God to be the highest good and the underlying ground for existence. Action occurred through causality and God was the first cause. God was the Divine Artist who produced the universe and human beings perpetuated the creativity of God. Human beings were characterized by faith and the highest possibility for a human being was to be a priest or a saint. There was neither questioning nor knowledge because God was only comprehensible through scripture which was understood through Platonic metaphysics. It is this conception of Christianity that turned Heidegger away from it and turn away he did. His ideas nevertheless inspired a generation of Christian theologians such as Rudolf Bultman (1884-1976), Paul Tillich (1886-1965) and Karl Rahner (1904-1984).

Why Heidegger's Need Remained Unfulfilled

As we have seen, Shaykh 'Abd al-Qādir concluded that the only thing that would actually have fitted the Heideggerian need was Islam, because his deeply moving and profound reflections about the nature of Being are 'nothing other than pure and exact delineations' of what the Sufis say about God.[51] Heidegger understood that for him to arrive at Being, required what he called 'the leap' that would have taken him "to where everything is different, so different that it strikes us as strange."[52] The reason for his failure to take the leap to Islam was in Gillespie's opinion "the Cartesian and Kantian presuppositions of his phenomenological methodology."[53]

Heidegger, Husserl, Karl Jaspers (1883-1969) and Hans-Georg Gadamer (1900-2002) were, according to Ellis Dye, "Goethe's children", meaning that Goethe had a deep and lasting influence on their thinking.[54] Walter Kaufman pointed out that nineteenth century German philosophy "consisted to a considerable extent in a series of efforts to assimilate the phenomenon of Goethe."[55] In 1949, Heidegger wrote to Jaspers saying: "I admittedly still lack an adequate relationship to Goethe. That's a real shortcoming but only one of many."[56] Heidegger's studies of Goethe's writings were, nevertheless, instrumental in the development of his concept of Dasein. The word 'Sorge' or care, which Goethe uses in *Faust*, was for Heidegger an ontological term explaining the deep structures that underlie the ontic.[57] It refers to Dasein's integration in the world and its relation to other forms of Dasein.

The main theme of Goethe's *Faust* was access to transcendent knowledge, which the rational mind is incapable of attaining, and Heidegger explicitly discounts the five senses as a means of access to the ontological meaning of being. A physical thing, such as a lectern for example, is more than its material makeup and its dimensions. Its being includes its place and function and the Being of its being is not an entity or the property of an entity. In the case of human beings, the factor that determines their humanity is their activity. This activity is the means by which the human becomes the locus of the self-disclosure of Being. It was in Islam that Goethe found access to the knowledge that the rational mind is incapable of reaching. Goethe stated that:

> Stupid that everyone in his case is praising his particular opinion.

> If Islam means submission to God, we all live and die in Islam.[58]

Goethe also wrote:

> Whether the Koran is of eternity? I don't question that!
> That it is the book of books I believe out of a Muslim's duty.[59]

Nietzsche made similar statements about Islam. He refers to Muslims as manly warriors and Islam as a positive life-affirming faith of joy and celebration.[60]

According to Heidegger, Jünger described the major features of the rising technological age and he did so in terms of Nietzsche's thinking. Heidegger said that Jünger's *Der Arbeiter* was important because it was able to "communicate an experience of the entity and of how it is, in the light of Nietzsche's projection of the entity as will to power."[61] In 1932 Jünger saw the inescapable power of the phenomenon of technology. He recognized that technology did not represent a complex set of tools that were there for the use of human beings. He thought of technique or technology as a new power with its own inner logic which rendered human beings subservient. Jünger used the concept of *Gestalt*[62] to characterize the worker. Modern human beings are under the *Gestalt* of the worker each one of them defined within the all-embracing system of technique. Shaykh 'Abd al-Qādir points out: "It is in this sense that Heidegger declared Jünger to have defined nihilism for our time."[63]

The unstoppable movement of technology has ended in a world state, with the global power of technique forming an imperial unity. There are no classes because everyone is living under the domination of technique. Social identity is defined by the use of technology, such as electricity consumers, train users, television watchers, road users etc. The state that rules the infrastructure rules over the individual. All people have become slaves and they vote to install their slave drivers. There is no place on earth that will be able to resist this phenomenon "which from a long time ago has carried the seal of a great barbaric invasion."[64] This phenomenon has manifested itself through colonisation, exploration of deserts and forests, extermination of indigenous peoples, elimination of laws and religions and the destruction of social groups and nations.

This human being, the 'worker', this passive receptor of all technological procedures,[65] can, however, recover his or her deepest power. Jünger did not propose a withdrawal from technique. He calls on people to accept the vast wave of technology engulfing the time and prepare, not only for survival and escape, but ultimately for victory over it. The *Gestalt* of the worker can take on a new image argues Jünger. He says:

> Nothing may exist which cannot be conceived of as work. Work is the rhythm of the arm, of the thoughts, of the heart, the life of night and day, science, love, art, faith, ritual, war: work is the vibration of the atom and the force which moves the stars and the solar systems.[66]

Human beings are free once they accept that they are indeed the workers.

There are two types of individuals: one, the ordinary individual, the television watching single unit of the mass who votes away his or her freedom; the other, *der Einzelne*, the isolated one, who becomes the transformative force in existence. Once the limited nature of resources and technique is grasped, the transformation begins. Shaykh 'Abd al-Qādir says that in *Der Arbeiter* (*The Worker*), Jünger was taking on a very deep theme when he wrote: "It remains to destroy the legend that the essential quality of the worker is an economic quality."[67] Jünger argues that economics is an industrial process in itself and part of the total system that is technique. One of the consequences of this process is that, "Bourgeois society is condemned to death."[68] When a person is aware of his or her *Gestalt* that person becomes aware of other *Gestalts* and their relationships with one another. The *Gestalt* contains more than the sum of its parts. For example a human being is more than the sum of atoms, limbs, organs, and humours of which he or she is composed. Jünger explains:

> It is in the *Gestalt*, independent from every appreciation, that there resides innate value, immutable and imperishable, its existence the highest and most profound confirmation. The more we engage in movement, the more we become intimately persuaded that hidden behind it is a Calm Being, and that every acceleration of speed is only the translation of an original, imperishable language. ... The vision of the *Gestalt* is a revolutionary act in as much as it recognises a Being in the complete and unitary plenitude of his life.[69]

Jünger is suggesting here that the way of freedom lies in plunging into reality, taking it on, and, by a new *Gestalt*, going beyond it. The above quote implies the development of the Overman, who will achieve the transvaluation of all values through will to power, and that the self-disclosure of Being can come in the heroic actions of the here and now. He insists that the dissimilarity between the mechanical and organic worlds reveals the fantasy structure of political projections, and the *Gestalt* of the worker allows one to see beyond those projections. There is a stage that takes human beings beyond the 'Overman' to that of the *Waldganger* who can encounter a greater power. In Jünger's *Heliopolis* the hero of the novel Lucius says:

> The game [of technique] must have exhausted all its possibilities. Then only can one dare the impossible. We are searching for those who have escaped into the stratosphere. We approve of the doctrine of Zarathustra, according to which man must be surpassed by the Overman. We do not see a moral obligation but a historical necessity. The following stage will be the surpassing of the Overman. He will be broken on the human, which will draw from this encounter a superior power.[70]

Lucius is referring here to the *Waldganger*, an individual who acts in every situation. He or she does not need theories or laws "cooked up by party legalists."[71] These individuals know what is right through the purity within themselves. Jünger calls the encounter with a superior power 'the great experience of the Forest', which is "the encounter with one's own self, the invulnerable core, the essence, from which the temporal and individual phenomenon originates."[72]

Shaykh 'Abd al-Qādir explains that the central *Gestalt* of the mythology[73] created by Jünger is that of the one who goes into the Forest, which Jünger defines as the non-temporal, inner zone where the conscious break is made with the horrific reality of the contemporary social contract. The *Waldganger* is not an anarchist but he or she is free and sovereign. In *Eumeswil*, Jünger described the *Waldganger* as a weaker form of an *Anarch* who is a free human being living in private autonomy within society. When uncovered as a spiritual outsider he or she is forced to flee society to preserve his or her autonomy. The flight to the forest makes him or her a *Waldganger*. Jünger says in *Der Waldgang*, "Man sleeps in the forest. When he awakens and realizes his power, then order is reconstituted."[74] Although Jünger's hero was an Anarch and not an anarchist he never outlined the parameters of his behaviour within society.

On the occasion of the installation of Jünger as Doctor Honoris Causa of Literature in the University of Bilbao in 1989, Shaykh 'Abd al-Qādir presented a paper in Jünger's presence. Referring to Jünger's words "*Freiheit ist Existenz*" he said:

> *Freiheit ist Existenz*. Freedom is Existence. Which means that there can be no submission except to the Divine. This is called Islam.[75]

Shaykh 'Abd al-Qādir meant by this that human beings need to be in harmony with their *fiṭra*, their natural form, to ease the path to the unveiling of Being within themselves. As we saw earlier[76] Shaykh ʿAbd al-Qādir holds that human beings are imbued with *fiṭra*, defined as an inborn natural predisposition which cannot change and which exists at birth in all human beings. The destinies of all things in the universe, including human beings, are predetermined by their life form (*fiṭra/Gestalt*).[77] This way of defining human beings incorporates everything about them: their life-cycles, their habitat, their familial and social relations, their livelihoods and capacity for language. Whereas forms in the mineral, vegetal and animal kingdoms submit to their destinies unconsciously and involuntarily human beings are able to consciously choose to play their part in preserving the natural order and the balance of the universe.

This ability to choose is made possible by the human capacity for language. Language makes it possible for human beings to think and reflect on themselves and the part they play in maintaining the balance and order of the universe. It is via this capacity for language that God speaks to human beings. His speech comes in the form of *waḥy* (revelation/inspiration) and the recipients of *waḥy* are known as Prophets. God's revelation to the Prophet Muḥammad ﷺ took the form of the Qur'ān and it outlined what humans need to do in order to know Him. The term *fiṭra*, for Shaykh ʿAbd al-Qādir, also means the inborn natural predisposition in the human to know God. To know God requires that you first be in harmony with the destiny of your life form. In Qur'ānic terminology this harmonization is called service or worship. In other words in order to know God one has to submit to the Divine.

Descartes claimed that the essential quality of the being human was thinking and Kant went on to explain how the process of thinking works. Hegel challenged Kant's exposition indicating that the path to Truth must involve ontology and Nietzsche pointed out that theology, the path to Being prevalent in the Europe of his time, had ended in nihilism because of Western philosophy's reliance on Plato's metaphysics. Heidegger showed that the way to escape this nihilism was to reopen the 'question of Being' and Goethe's writings played an influential role in the development of Heidegger's concept of Dasein, which defines the human being as the locus for the self-disclosure of Being. Jünger used mythology to inspire people to take on the heroic struggle in the here and now, in order to open for themselves the possibility of the unveiling of Being. Shaykh 'Abd al-Qādir pointed out to Jünger that his hero, the *Waldganger*, needed to be in harmony with his *fiṭra*, to ease the path to the unveiling of Being within himself, and that this necessitated taking on the path of Islam, the path of submission to the Real. For Heidegger, taking the leap into Islam would have required a deeper engagement with the philosophical issues raised by Goethe, Nietzsche and Jünger.

So the philosophical discourse we have reviewed noted the movement away from epistemologies based on metaphysics to ones that are based on ontology. Thinking about Being however, is not the same as knowing Being. To know Being requires going beyond rationalism, empiricism, metaphysics, philosophy, theology and mythology. In Sufi terminology all these come under *'ilm al-'aql*, knowledge gained through the use of reason. The higher levels of knowledge beyond this are, as we saw earlier, *'ilm al-aḥwāl*, *'ilm al-asrār*, *fanā'* and *baqā'*. These higher kinds of knowledge are the inheritance of the people of *'amal ahl al-Madīna* and inaccessible to modernists with their dependence on empirical knowledge. To reach the "Calm Being" Jünger spoke of, he suggested plunging into reality, taking it on and achieving the transvaluation of all values through will to power. This self-disclosure of Being has to come through heroic actions in the present, which he called work, something Ibn al-ʿArabī called joy, Jalāl al-Dīn Rūmī (1207-1273) called love and Mālik ibn Anas called *ʿamal*.

However, when Shaykh ʿAbd al-Qādir says that the only model which fits the Heideggerian need – and we may add the Jüngerian – is Islam, he is not talking about an Islam which Jackson implies is the "Platonism for the masses."[78] Jackson says that the perception of itself that Islam has acquired can be attributed to a trans-historical utopian interpretation of certain key paradigms. The four key paradigms that make up what is called the 'Golden Age Paradigm' relate to the Qur'ān, the *sunna*, the Madinan state and the subsequent caliphal states. This trans-historical utopian vision of Islam is modernist, with codification, as we saw in the previous chapter, contributing to the modernization process.[79] The modern Islamic state bears no relation to the Prophetic state of Madīna with regards to its quintessential characteristics. The modern Islamic state, which is the brainchild of such men as Ruhollah Khomeini (1902-1989), Abū al-Ala Mawdudi (1903-1979), Hassan al-Banna (1906-1949), and Sayyid Quṭb (1906-1966) is capitalist and oligarchic, irrespective of whether its political system is democratic, monarchic or totalitarian. The Islam, advocated by Shaykh ʿAbd al-Qādir, that of traditional Sufism and the primal model of the *ʿamal ahl al-Madīna*, is a very different phenomenon.

Chapter 7

From Islamic Philosophy to Sufism: Intellect to Presence

Amongst the Greek founders of Western philosophy there was a close relationship between revelation and philosophy both in the thought and in the lives of the philosophers concerned. Their thinking and way of life present a complete contrast to the rationalism and empiricism of modern philosophy because, for the pre-Socratic philosophers such as Epimenides (7th or 6th century BC), Pythagoras (b. 570 BC), Parmenides (b. 540 BC) and Empedocles (b. 490 BC), there was, in fact, no separation between philosophy and revelation. Pythagoras, who is said to have invented the word philosophy, regarded himself as a prophet with extraordinary powers. Parmenides, sometimes characterized as a rationalist and logician, was however a visionary who could access states of consciousness other than those that people were generally familiar with. He regarded himself as a messenger from the Divine. Kingsley is of the opinion that the word 'prophet' best describes the kind of 'messenger' that Parmenides was. By 'prophet', he means "someone whose job it is to speak on behalf of a great power, of someone or something else."[1] Whilst Empedocles was a philosopher, physician, poet and political activist he also specialized in mystical states of consciousness.[2] Epimenides is said to have written on law and cosmogony as well as poetry. The laws that he outlined for people were the products of prophecy.

Western philosophy has been severed from its roots in ancient Greece and its focus, from the seventeenth century onwards, was determined by the rationalism and empiricism of modern science. This, as we saw in the previous chapter, was, in Heideggerian terms, the culmination of a long process of forgetfulness of Being which began with Plato. Modern philosophy has not yet found ways of resolving the paradoxes uncovered within it by Bertrand Russell, Kurt Gödel, Alan Turing and Antonio Damasio,[3] as Mehdi Ha'iri Yazdi points out when he says:

> Despite the prevalence of sundry epistemological considerations in the study of human knowledge, the fundamental pre-epistemic question regarding the relation between knowledge and the possessor of knowledge remains unresolved. Succinctly put, what beckons the attention of philosophical inquiry is the reason as to why and how a knowing subject, with or without knowing itself, becomes united with or otherwise related to an external object as the thing known.[4]

In his efforts to break out of the traditional Cartesian/Kantian philosophical position of the irreconcilable distinction between subject and object, Heidegger's work spells the end of metaphysics and consequently the end of modern philosophy. It was in philosophy, more than in any other area, that it could be said that modernity had come to an end. John Dewey (1859-1952), Heidegger, Wittgenstein and Richard Rorty (1931-2007) argued convincingly against the theory-centred style of philosophy that began with Descartes. Stephen Toulmin argues that philosophy has three options left: firstly it can continue to be the discredited research program of a purely theoretical modern philosophy; secondly it can develop less theoretical and more practical post-modern ways of working; or thirdly it can return to its pre-modern subjects which were obscured by Descartes.[5]

In this chapter we will deal with the Islamic philosophical and Sufi traditions' focus on ontology as a way of overcoming the subject/object and knower/known dichotomies encountered in the epistemology of modernism.

Knowledge by Presence

Epistemology and the means by which knowledge is acquired are central to Islamic philosophy. Among Islamic philosophers there is an ongoing discussion about demonstration or proof (*burhān*), which is related to reason, intellect (*al-ʿaql*),[6] and intuition or gnosis (*ʿirfān/maʿrifa*), which is related to the heart (*qalb*).[7] The words generally used for intuition are *ḥadas* and *firāsa* but terms such as *dhawq* (tasting), *ishrāq* (illumination), *mukāshafa* (unveiling), *baṣīra* (insight), *naẓar* (vision) and *badīha* (inspiration) also appear in philosophical, theological and Sufi literature.[8] These terms refer to forms of intuition that relate to the direct experience of truth as opposed to indirect knowledge based on mental concepts and ratiocination. In Islamic philosophy, the term *al-ʿilm al-ḥuḍūrī* (knowledge by presence) is also used for intuition of this kind and is contrasted with *al-ʿilm al-ḥuṣūlī* (representative knowledge). There have been rare exceptions of Islamic philosophers, for whom knowledge was confined to reason alone, but such thinkers have remained on the periphery and the Islamic intellectual tradition generally does not recognize any irreconcilable dichotomy between intellect and intuition.

The concept of knowledge by presence has been subjected to philosophical inquiry by many Islamic philosophers. Although Western and Islamic philosophy both derive from the Hellenist philosophical tradition, they understand Greek thought differently.

Ever since Plato and Aristotle, mainstream epistemology has been divided on the issue of intellectual knowledge. For Plato, it is the non-material abstract Forms of transcendental knowledge that have real and metaphysical existence.[9] These Forms are things or beings in themselves, which are independent of the human mind and the sensible objects of the physical world of becoming. "Without having had a 'vision' of this Form no one can act with wisdom, either in his own life or in matters pertaining to the state."[10] It is on this dualism between being and becoming that Plato based his notion of objective true reality. Opposite to this view was that of Aristotle, for whom no intelligible object could exist outside of human nature and spatio-temporal sensibility. That is to say that true objects of thought are apprehended through sensibility and are intellectualized in the mind through the process of abstraction. Aristotle stated that:

> Hence (1) no one can learn or understand anything in the absence of sense, and (2) when the mind is actively aware of anything, it is necessarily aware of it along with an image; for images are like sensuous contents except that they contain no matter.[11]

These divergent approaches of Plato and Aristotle have become so entrenched in the Western philosophical tradition that many modern philosophers believe that the two views are irreconcilable and antithetical. Whilst both the Platonic and Aristotelian philosophical traditions try to attain intellectual knowledge that is distinct from empiricism, their varied approaches have "obfuscated the search for the fundamental pre-epistemic foundation for human transcendent knowledge."[12] Islamic philosophy, on the other hand, has sought to unify the Platonic and Aristotelian systems of epistemology within a common philosophical framework, maintaining that the mind is able to function in different ways simultaneously. The mind is able to be perceptive of intelligible concepts on the one hand and speculate about sensory objects on the other. Islamic philosophy, however, goes well beyond a reconciliation of the Platonic and Aristotelian views by positing an ontological foundation for human awareness.

The ontological foundations for epistemology in Islamic Philosophy

Al-Kindī (801-873) is regarded as the first Muslim philosopher as well as the one who introduced Greek and Indian philosophical texts into the Muslim world. He defined *falsafa* (philosophy) as "the knowledge of the reality of things within man's possibility, because the philosopher's end in his theoretical knowledge is to gain truth and in his practical knowledge to behave in accordance with truth."[13] Al-Kindī is also known for bridging the gap between philosophy and theology through the application of rational processes to revealed texts. Whilst accepting many of the teachings of Aristotle, he departed from the Neoplatonists and Peripatetics on a number of major issues. He was of the view that the Muhammadan revelation could be demonstrated syllogistically, that revealed truth is superior to human knowledge and that prophetic science transcends human perception, that the world was created *ex nihilo*, that the body will be resurrected after death, that miracles are possible, and that the world originated from God and will be destroyed by Him.

Al-Kindī believed in different sources of human knowledge. The first was sense experience or the perception of external objects through the senses. The information received by the senses results in the formation of images by the representative faculty and these images are retained in one's memory. The second source of human knowledge is rational cognition, the object of which is universal and immaterial, as distinct from the particular and material with which sensation and representation are concerned. This broad division of the material and immaterial corresponds, for al-Kindī, to the twofold division of physics and metaphysics in philosophy. Al-Kindī referred to physics as the science of created things and metaphysics as the science of divine things. He did, however, say that there is a class of entities that fall midway between the two, which he describes as a conjunction between the immaterial and matter, an example of which is the soul. Al-Kindī's contribution to the development of philosophical terminology and the introduction of Greek philosophical ideas to the Muslim world was indeed great. He was able to achieve these by remaining committed to the tenets of Islamic belief as expressed in Mu'tazilite theology. He maintained that philosophy had to subordinate itself to revelation and surrender its claim to be the highest avenue to truth.

After al-Kindī the towering figure in Islamic philosophy is al-Fārābī (870-950). He was regarded as the Second Teacher after Aristotle by Ibn Sīnā (980-1037) and Ibn Rushd (1126-1198). It was in the tenth century that al-Fārābī revived the teaching of Plato and Aristotle and liberated Socratic philosophy from Christian theology. Among al-Fārābī's contributions to philosophy was the laying of the foundations of logic and metaphysics in the Muslim world, enunciating the metaphysical distinction between essence and existence, and describing the cosmological structure of the Intelligences in a systematic way.[14] The concept of God's Oneness (*tawḥīd*) is the central teaching of the Qur'ān and as such is of utmost importance to theologians, philosophers and Sufis. The Mu'tazilite theologians claimed that God was transcendent (*tanzīh*) with no possibility of contact with phenomenal reality. According to al-Fārābī, God communicated existence to other beings through emanation (*fayḍ*). Al-Fārābī referred to God as the First Being (*al-Awwal*) which corresponded explicitly with the God of revealed religion. He said:

> The genesis of that which comes into existence from it [God] takes place by way of an emanation, the existence of which is due to the existence of something else, so that the existence of something different from the First emanates from the First's existence.[15]

Other beings that have been given life by God through emanation are structured in hierarchical gradations in the cosmos. Emanation owes much to the Neoplatonic view of the cosmos, particularly to Plotinus' (204-270 CE) concept of cosmology. Emanation is also linked to the process of intellection, that is, how God understands Himself and how emanated beings understand God. From the First Being (God) emanates the existence of the Second and so on to the Eleventh Being. The system functions due to a dual process of emanation and intellection. Emanation descends from the First Being to the Eleventh Being or Tenth Intelligence and ascends from the Tenth Intelligence or Agent Intellect to the First Being. From the Second Being the First Heaven is produced through a "substantialisation of the specific essence."[16] Subsequent to the emanation of these Beings is the production of the sphere of fixed stars, the sphere of Jupiter, the sphere of Saturn, the sphere of Mars, the sphere of the Sun, the sphere of Venus, the sphere of Mercury, the sphere of the Moon, then the Sub-lunar world which contains the earth and human beings.

Like al-Fārābī, Ibn Sīnā's (980-1037) doctrine of Being was based on emanation. Before discussing his views on emanation, an introduction to his philosophy is necessary. He defined *ḥikma* (which literally means wisdom and is another word used for *falsafa*) as "the perfecting of the human soul through the conceptualization of things and the judgment of theoretical and practical truths to the measure of human capability."[17] Having mastered the purely rational and intellectual tradition of Hellenism, Ibn Sīnā discovered methods and arguments that sought to reformulate the tradition of Hellenism within the tradition of Islam. The originality of his methods and arguments made him unique, not only in the Muslim world but also in medieval Europe, where his ideas influenced Thomas Aquinas (1225-1274), Dominicus Gundissalinus (1110-1190), Albert the Great (1193-1280) and Roger Bacon (1214-1294). In the Muslim world he influenced prominent thinkers such as Nāṣir al-Dīn al-Ṭūsī (1201-1274), Shihāb al-Dīn Yaḥyā Suhrawardī (1154-1191), Quṭb al-Dīn al-Shīrāzī (1236-1311), Mīr Dāmād (d. 1631) and Ṣadr al-Dīn Shīrāzī, also known as Mulla Sadra, (1571-1640).

In Ibn Sīnā's theory of emanation, only the First Intelligence flows from God, the Necessary Existent, because for him, and according to Aristotle, from the One only one entity can emanate. From the First Intelligence arise two entities: the second actuality and the first sphere. This emanation process of duality continues until it reaches the Tenth Intelligence which governs the terrestrial world. Most Muslim philosophers refer to this Intelligence as the Angel Gabriel, because the Angel Gabriel informs the world of matter and the human intellect. Muslim philosophers resorted to the Neoplatonic theory of emanation in order to overcome the view of God formulated by Aristotle, according to whom multiplicity could not be derived from the One. They sought to reinterpret Greek thought in order to create a rational system which could be integrated into the tradition of Islam. Rahman very pointedly asked:

> But what about the Theory of Emanation itself? Would it not destroy the necessary and all important gulf between the Creator and the creation and lead to a downright pantheistic world-view – *tat tvam Asi* – against which Islam, like all higher religions, had warned so sternly? No doubt, this type of pantheism, being dynamic, is different from the absolutist and static forms of pantheism: yet it could lead to anthropomorphism, or by a reverse process of ascent to the re-absorption of the creature's being into the being of God. [18]

In order to avert this danger Ibn Sīnā proposed his doctrine of essence and existence. This theory was designed by him to satisfy both religious and rational needs. The meaning of the existence (*wujūd*) of something is derived by answering the question, 'Is it?' The meaning of the essence/quiddity (*māhiyya*) of something is derived by answering the question, 'What is it?'[19] For definitions to be made, the rules of logic require that there be genus and specific difference. It is not possible to define *wujūd* because *wujūd* is universally present and there is nothing else by which it can be defined. In Islamic philosophy the term *wujūd* has many meanings which are: Being, being, Existence and existence. Being refers to Absolute or Necessary Being, being is a universal concept encompassing the different levels of reality including Necessary Being. Existence refers to the first emanation from the Absolute Being and existence refers to all things except Necessary Being.[20]

For Ibn Sīnā there is an ontological poverty (*faqr*) in the universe because it is God who gives *wujūd* to all things. As he explained, "Everything except the One and Existent acquires existence from something else."[21] God is the eternal Reality and all else is finite. All else is brought into existence and must pass away. *Māhiyya* (quiddity) in its particular sense is information of what a thing is and in its general sense, it refers to the reality (*ḥaqīqa*) of a thing. The intellect is able to recognize the *māhiyya* of a particular object totally distinct from any form of *wujūd*. It does this in the container of the mind with no concern for its existence or nonexistence. *Māhiyya* as such is called 'natural universal' (*al-kullī al-ṭabīʿī*) by Ibn Sīnā. *Māhiyya* is not one of the constituent elements of *wujūd*. *Wujūd* is not a *muqawwim* of *māhiyya,* that is, *wujūd* is not the genus to which *māhiyya* belongs. As Seyyed Hossein Nasr points out:

> There is nothing in *mahiyyah* that would relate it to *wujūd* or necessitate the existence of that *mahiyyah*. The two concepts are

> totally distinct as are their causes. The causes of a *mahiyyah* are the elements that constitute its definition, namely, the genus and specific difference, while the causes of the *wujūd* of a particular existent are its efficient and final causes, as well as its substratum. For a *mahiyyah* to exist, therefore, *wujūd* must be 'added to it', that is, become wedded to it from outside itself.[22]

Ibn Sīnā has been criticized for regarding *wujūd* as an accident that happens to *māhiyya*.[23] If *wujūd* being an accident that happens to *māhiyya* is accepted as true then insurmountable problems arise. For example, what would the state of *māhiyya* have been before the accident of *wujūd* happened to it? If it had existed before then the accident of *wujūd* would have happened to it before and this argument would then go back ad infinitum. On the other hand if *māhiyya* were non-existent, then it would have no reality to which the accident of *wujūd* could occur. Nāṣir al-dīn al-Ṭūsī explained that 'accident' (*'araḍ*) was never used by Ibn Sīnā in the way the word is ordinarily meant. He wrote:

> Quiddity can never be independent of 'existence' except in the intellect. This, however, should not be taken as meaning that 'quiddity' in the intellect is separated from 'existence,' because 'being in the intellect' is itself a kind of 'existence,' namely 'mental existence' [*wujūd dhihnī*], just as 'being in the external world' is 'external existence' [*wujūd khārijī*].[24]

Ibn Sīnā believed there are two sources of knowledge, philosophical and mystical. He made a distinction between Peripatetic (*mashshā'ī*) Philosophy and Eastern Philosophy (*ḥikma mashriqiyya*) thereby expressing his dissatisfaction with discursive philosophy and his desire to transcend it. Whilst for most Islamic philosophers the abstract ideas that lie in the active intellect can be extracted from the world of experience, for Ibn Sīnā any correspondence between the ideas and phenomenal reality are entirely fortuitous. The acquisition of knowledge requires that one turn from the world and focus one's attention on what is beyond it. Ibn Sīnā differentiated between discursive thought and intuition. Discursive thought arrives at the knowledge of things or matters previously unknown through mediation whilst intuition apprehends the knowledge of things or matters previously unknown directly.

Attempts by Ibn Sīnā to assimilate emanation into Islam were inadequate in the view of Abū Ḥāmid Muḥammad al-Ghazālī (1058-1111), whose aim it was to harmonize philosophy, Sufism and law within one system. Whilst al-Ghazālī did criticize some twenty teachings of the Muslim philosophers, describing seventeen of them as blameworthy innovations (*bid'a*) and three of them as disbelief (*kufr*), claims that he was anti-philosophy are erroneous.[25] The three points that he regarded as contrary to the teachings of Islam were: the eternity of the world, meaning that the world does not have a beginning and is not created in time, an Aristotelian theory that excludes the creative activity of God; secondly, that God's knowledge is only of universal beings and does not include the particulars, specifically that God is unaware of individual beings and their circumstances; and, thirdly, the denial of the resurrection of the body after death. The consequences of al-Ghazālī's juristic opinions with regards to these three matters were very serious indeed because, in his view, anyone who actively propagated these teachings would be declared an apostate and would be subject to the death penalty. However, Campanini points out with regard to al-Ghazālī that...

> Despite his intention to refute the ideas of the philosophers, al-Ghazālī was anything but an 'irrationalist'. In the first place, he sought to oppose philosophy not with anathemas and theological dogma but with philosophical, dialectic and demonstrative tools – in other words, opposing philosophy with philosophy. Secondly, in expressing his own original ideas, he often makes use of terms, categories and concepts that are clearly derived from philosophy.[26]

What had occurred with al-Ghazālī was the absorption of philosophy into theology, a process similar to that of the Latin Middle Ages when philosophy and Christian theology became indistinguishable. Al-Ghazālī aimed at conveying to his readers, who may not have understood the intricacies of theology and philosophy, that whilst God was omnipotent there were benefits in pursuing the study of the natural sciences, medicine and psychology. In other words al-Ghazālī looked for ways of reconciling God's predetermination of events with the cosmological principle of creation through cause and effect. He believed that articulating such teachings to the general public could lead to confusion but, be that as it may, he made no distinction between 'exoteric' and 'esoteric' knowledge.[27]

According to Yazdi, al-Ghazālī uses the metaphorical Light Verse of the Qur'ān[28] to answer two questions: 1. "If epistemology should presuppose, or correspond, to ontology, what might the ontological features of our intelligible universal objects be and how and where do these universal objects exist?" And 2. "What is the nature of the being of these entities and how do they relate to our individual consciousness?"[29] Al-Ghazālī wrote:

> It is from this starting-point that Allah's gnostics rise from metaphors to realities, as one climbs from the lowlands to the mountains, and at the end of their ascent see, as with the direct sight of eye-witnesses, that there is nothing in existence save Allah alone and that "*everything perisheth except His Countenance, His Aspect* (*wajh*)" [Qur'ān 55: 24-25]; ... For everything has two aspects, an aspect to itself and an aspect to its Lord: in respect of the first, it is Not-being; but in respect of the God-aspect, it is Being. Therefore there is no Existent except God and the God-aspect, and therefore all things are perishing except the God-aspect from and to all eternity.[30]

Although al-Ghazālī's language here is not philosophical, his answer nevertheless deals directly with the correspondence of epistemology to ontology. It is an explanation for the ontological features of intelligible universal objects and the nature of the being of these entities and how they relate to individual consciousness, as Yazdi had argued.

Ibn Rushd's (1126-1198) *Incoherence of the Incoherence* was a rebuttal of al-Ghazālī's polemics against the philosophers. According to Majid Fakhry, Ibn Rushd is known as "the first and last great Aristotelian in Islam."[31] His legacy includes his commentaries on Aristotle, his reconciliation of philosophy and religion and his legal treatises. Besides the commentaries, his philosophical writings were directed towards pointing out how al-Fārābī's and Ibn Sīnā's works diverged from the teachings of Aristotle. Ibn Rushd demonstrated that the use of reason, i.e. rational thinking and philosophy, is not only permitted by the *sharīʿa* of Islam but is, in fact, obligatory – within legal limits.

In his *Kitāb faṣl al-maqāl*[32] he begins his argument by pointing out that the Qur'ān calls upon people to observe and reflect upon the phenomena of the natural universe in order to recognize how God manifests His power in it. This reflection must be conducted through demonstrative reasoning and a preliminary study of logic is required in order to master the art of demonstrative reasoning. Logic has to be learnt from the ancient masters even if they are not Muslims. Through analogical reasoning he compares the use of logic with other lawful practices such as the use of non-Muslim instruments. After logic one has to proceed to philosophy proper and this too must be learnt from the predecessors. For him, forbidding the study of ancient philosophy is wrong and any harm coming from this study is accidental.

Ibn Rushd argued that the nature and temperaments of people are different and that knowledge of God is available to all people in accordance with their nature and temperament. Religion communicates this knowledge by means of scripture that addresses people through demonstrative, dialectical and rhetorical means in accordance with their nature and temperament. The verses of the Qur'ān are divided into three categories, the overt, the allegorical and those whose classification is unclear. The verses of overt meaning are easily understood by all of the different classes (the demonstrative, dialectical and rhetorical minded) of people. They have to be taken literally and no allegorical interpretation is allowed with regards to them. The allegorical verses are to be taken in their apparent meaning by the majority but have to be interpreted allegorically by the demonstrative class of people. The majority of people are not permitted to interpret these verses allegorically and the demonstrative class of people are not permitted to take these verses literally. The classification of the third category of verses is unclear and Ibn Rushd says that one group of scholars attach them to the apparent verses saying that it is not permitted to interpret them allegorically, whereas others attach them to the allegorical verses saying that scholars are not permitted to take them in their apparent meanings. This divergence of opinions is due to the difficulty and ambiguity of this class of text. If the philosophers commit an error when interpreting these verses, they are to be excused.

Like Aristotle, Ibn Rushd advocated a distinction between the Active or Agent Intellect and the human intellect. He argued that the Agent Intellect is not a part of the human intellect and that the latter is designed to act through the process of unification with the former in the actualization of intellectual knowledge. Ibn Rushd maintained that the independent Agent Intellect unites with the human material intellect thereby existentially uniting immaterial form and matter.[33] During this state of awareness...

> ... knowledge is no longer an intentional or transcendental

> phenomenon of mind, rather it may be put forward as a kind of self-realization, transcending representational knowledge, "reaching" the self-awareness of the reality of the self. This process takes place by virtue of an existential unification and not by an intellectual or phenomenal act of knowing.[34]

The history of philosophy in Islam did not, as Goldziher claimed, come to an end with Ibn Rushd.[35] It continued in Persia with Shihāb al-Dīn Yaḥyā Suhrawardī (1154-1191) who had set out to develop the Eastern Philosophy (*ḥikma mashriqiyya*) that Ibn Sīnā had spoken of. Ibn Sīnā had mastered the two wisdoms – the experiential (*al-dhawqiyya*) and the discursive (*al-baḥthiyya*) – and had attained a high standing with regards the first.[36] Suhrawardī founded a new school of philosophy distinct from the Peripatetic school, called the Philosophy of Illumination (*ḥikmat al-ishrāq*). Illuminationist philosophy, also known as theosophy, is based on the metaphysics of light, which is immaterial and indefinable. The Light of lights (*nūr al-anwār*) is the absolute and infinite Light and the origin and source of all things (also called God, Necessary Light, Self-subsistent Light and Holy Light). It is above and beyond all the rays of light that emanate from it.

The entire universe is light and the different dimensions of reality are made up of different degrees and levels of light. From the Light of lights emanates a longitudinal/vertical hierarchy of lights that consists of the levels of universal existence. A latitudinal/horizontal order contains the archetypes of what appear as objects and entities in the universe and these lights are known as angels in religious terminology. These angels, given Islamic and Mazdaean names by Suhrawardī, play a central role in *Ishrāqī* cosmology. Despite the experiential elements of this philosophy, its cosmological and metaphysical groundwork is a further development of Ibn Sīnā's Neoplatonism with elements of Zoroastrianism incorporated into it.

Suhrawardī described how he acquired the basis of his Philosophy of Illumination as follows:

> I did not first obtain [the Philosophy of Illumination] through cogitation, but through something else, I only subsequently sought proofs for it.[37]

According to his commentators[38] this 'something else' was illuminationist vision (*al-mushāhada al-ishrāqiyya*), which is the foundation of true science (*al-ʿilm al-ṣaḥīḥ*). These in turn form the basis of his scientific methodology (*ṭarīq al-ʿulūm*), which is none other than knowledge by presence. The visionary experience takes place in the *ʿālam al-mithāl* (World of Analogies). This is an ontological realm independent of matter, although the beings of this realm possess the categorical attributes of time, place, relation, quality and quantity.

There are four stages in acquiring knowledge through the Philosophy of Illumination.[39] The first stage comprises of ascetic practices, such as a forty day retreat, not eating meat and doing exercises in preparation for witnessing and unveiling (*mushāhada wa mukāshafa*). The philosopher possesses the capacity to receive inspiration and vision and is able to accept/assimilate the reality of his or her intuition. In the second stage Divine Light is absorbed by the philosopher in the form of a series of apocalyptic lights (*al-anwār al-sanīḥa*) and through them he or she acquires the foundation of real sciences (*al-ʿulūm al-ḥaqīqiyya*). The third stage is accomplished when the experiences of witnessing and unveiling are demonstrated and validated by the discursive analysis of the philosopher. Suhrawardī explained that the "experience is put to the test, and the system of proof used is the Aristotelian demonstration (*burhān*) of the *Posterior Analytics*."[40] The fourth stage is the documentation of the visionary experience. Suhrawardī's writings give us access to this component.

Suhrawardī taught that there was a clear link between the religion of Islam and philosophy. He saw philosophy and spiritual realization as inner dimensions of the Qur'ānic revelation. He defined *ḥikma* (philosophy) as the "act of the soul's becoming imprinted by the spiritual truths and the intelligibles."[41] A philosopher, for Suhrawardī, was one who possessed both theoretical knowledge and spiritual vision and, from his time onwards, Islamic philosophy and spiritual realization came to be connected. Suhrawardī was a mystic and his Philosophy of Illumination aimed to create a bridge between the formal religious sciences and gnosis (*'irfān*). A fundamental principle of illuminationist philosophy is that in order to know something it is necessary to have an experience of it. The analysis of the experiential knowledge of things can be undertaken only after an immediate and intuitive grasp of them has been gained.

Suhrawardī's philosophy made a significant impact on the discipline of epistemology. Aristotle had indicated to him in a dream that the prelude of higher knowledge was self-knowledge and that this knowledge was both discursive and experiential.[42] The essential nature of Suhrawardī's self-knowledge was that self-awareness, and the entities and experiences of which the self is aware, are existentially the same. On the hypothesis of self-awareness Suhrawardī posited that...

> ... the self must be absolutely aware of itself without the interposition of a representation. Any representation of the self, empirical or transcendental, must necessarily render the hypothesis of self-awareness contradictory. It is, rather, by the very presence of the very reality of the self that the self is aware of itself in absolute terms. Consequently, the self and awareness of the self are individually and numerically a simple single entity. This train of thinking arrived directly, and inevitably, at the very notion of self-objectivity of knowledge by presence.[43]

It was Ṣadr al-Dīn Shīrāzī (1571-1640), also known as Mulla Sadra, who provided the most comprehensive and systematic exposition of ontology in Islamic philosophy. He sought to synthesize in his teachings the philosophy of Ibn Sīnā, *Ishrāqī* philosophy and Sufism. Mulla Sadra was in agreement with several of Ibn Sīnā's philosophical positions but differed with him with regards to certain others. Like Ibn Sīnā he believed that philosophy had two parts, the theoretical, which deals with things as they are, and the practical, which aims at perfecting the actions of human beings. Like Suhrawardī he believed in the unity of truth (*philosophia perennis*), as it was transmitted in an unbroken chain from Adam to Abraham and on to the Greeks, the Muslim philosophers and the Sufis. The two major differences between Mulla Sadra and Ibn Sīnā were their opposing views concerning the eternity of the world and the impossibility of bodily resurrection.

During the time that Mulla Sadra followed the metaphysics of Suhrawardī, he was an advocate for the doctrine of the principality of essence.[44] It was during this early period of Mulla Sadra's intellectual development that he studied Illuminationism, the writings of the Greek philosophers, the works of Muslim Neoplatonists, such as Ibn Sīnā and al-Fārābī, and the writings of the Andalusian philosophers Ibn Bājja (1095-1138), Ibn Ṭufayl (1105-1185), Ibn Rushd and Ibn al-ʿArabī. Mulla Sadra's study of this vast corpus of literature was instrumental in his decision to move away from postulating the primacy of essence to adopting the doctrine of the primacy of Being.[45]

Mulla Sadra outlined his existentialism in his *Kitāb al-asfār al-arbaʿa*, using the analogy of four journeys. The book is a deep meditation, critically analysing the philosophical ideas of his predecessors and contemporaries. Its contents are vast with regards to their depth and scope, covering the ideas of the pre-

Socratic thinkers, Plato, Aristotle, al-Kindī, al-Fārābī, Ibn Sīnā, Ibn Rushd, Ibn al-ʿArabī and Suhrawardī. He also makes reference to the Qur'ān, the *ḥadīth* and the sayings of the Shīʿī Imams. With regards to the influence of Sufism on Mulla Sadra, he has acknowledged his engagement with Ibn al-ʿArabī's writings, as is evident in his ontology and epistemology.[46] For Mulla Sadra, Being is the ontological foundation for knowing. For something to be known one has to begin with its existence. Explaining the meaning of this position Muḥammad Kamāl writes:

> Because Mulla Sadra's treatment of the problem of knowledge is so similar to Suhrawardī's, it is difficult to make a distinction between them. Nevertheless what is apprehended by Mulla Sadra is the reality of Being rather than essence. Being and knowledge are not two different things but are intertwined. Being, by revealing itself or being revealed, renders knowledge possible and knowledge makes the truth of Being comprehensible.[47]

Mulla Sadra advocated the belief that reality is best apprehended by intuition (*al-idrāk*) rather than discursive knowledge. *Al-idrāk* is the perception of something directly without mediation. It is the process by which the quiddity of things outside the human mind can be apprehended directly, thereby making them intelligible. This process does, however, include sense perception, which, for Mulla Sadra, is the lowest modality of intuition. The highest stage of cognition, for him, transcends rationalistic discourse and the power of reason. This, he maintains, is due to the fact that knowledge entails the transformation of existence as an external reality outside the human mind into mental existence, which is a form of Being. In this way Mulla Sadra overcomes the epistemological dichotomies between knower and known and between subject and object.

Mulla Sadra called his school of philosophy *al-ḥikmat al-mutaʿāliya* (metaphilosophy). This philosophy provided a meta-linguistic method by which the validity and soundness of philosophical issues could be made. The process of decision-making with regards to the validity and soundness of philosophical opinions depends on the univocal and primordial meaning that Mulla Sadra gave to the word existence. This concept of existence is able to absorb and accommodate all forms and degrees of reality, overcoming the Platonic separation of being and becoming. Using this meta-philosophy, one can make independent decisions with regards to the philosophical positions of Platonism, Aristotelianism, Neoplatonism, religion and mysticism, etc., without engaging in the particulars of each of these systems.[48] The word existence, for Mulla Sadra, was equivalent to the word reality and could be univocally applied to God as well as phenomenal objects. He saw no reason for separating the order of being from intelligence or from any other mode of knowledge.

In addition to this, Mulla Sadra held that mental existence transcended subjectivity by being connected to *ʿālam al-khayāl* (World of *Khayāl*).[49] *Khayāl* is a term derived from the technical language of Ibn al-ʿArabī which was used by Mulla Sadra when discussing the problems of cognition and Sufi ideas of knowledge. Sufism focuses on self-awareness and knowledge of the self. For Mulla Sadra, philosophy should do so too, because the metaphysical theory of human knowledge also requires systematic analysis of the relationship of self-objectivity to phenomenal knowledge. This is what Yazdi refers to as the "fundamental pre-epistemic foundation for human transcendent knowledge." As he has argued:

> The assertion: "I know something," certainly presupposes the fact that 'I' as the knowing subject is already, in one way or another, acquainted with itself. If such is the case, then it will become necessary to ascertain the nature of this acquaintance, and more specifically determine whether such an acquaintance is anything other than the very being of the self. In the light of this fundamental introvertive question, and

> by means of laws and principles of logic, the inquiry into the nature of the relation between knowledge and the knower can lead to the very foundation of human intellect where the word knowing does not mean anything other than being.[50]

With Mulla Sadra the connection between philosophy and Sufism became cemented since he had shown that it is in an ontological state of human consciousness that the constitutive dualism of the subject/object relationship is overcome and submerged into a unitary simplex. The discussion can now turn to the Sufi Science of Presence (*al-ʿilm al-ḥuḍūrī*) which outlines how such a state can be achieved and will also contextualize the Science of Presence within the parameters of Islamic epistemology.

Al-ʿilm al-ḥuḍūrī: The Science of Presence

The essential element of Sufi epistemology is unveiling (*kashf*) and the prototype for this unveiling is the ontological experience of the Prophet Muḥammad ﷺ. The revelation of the Qur'ān to the Prophet Muḥammad ﷺ is the result of an ontological experience, in which God reveals His Word by way of the Angel Gabriel and in which God reveals Himself directly to the Prophet ﷺ. The ultimate expression of these experiences is found in the Qur'ān and because of this the Qur'ānic revelation plays a major role in Sufi practice. Whilst philosophers may have differed as to the interpretation of its verses, Islamic philosophy is intrinsically related to the revelation received by the Prophet Muḥammad ﷺ. The Qur'ānic laws and moral teachings are the themes which offer themselves up for consideration in Islamic legal, ethical, economic and political philosophy. In addition to these, the Qur'ān deals with matters such as cosmogony, cosmology, the different levels of being and reality, eschatology, history, science, time, space and causality, all of which are of interest to philosophy.[51]

The philosophical discussions regarding these matters are

scattered over many traditional Islamic disciplines. These include *tafsīr* (Qur'ānic commentary), *uṣūl al-dīn* (science of the principles of religion), *uṣūl al-fiqh* (Islamic legal theory), *sīra* (biography of the Prophet Muḥammad ﷺ), *al-falsafa* (philosophy – meaning the attempts to form a worldview based on logical and scientific reasoning as manifest in the Peripatetic (*mashshā'ī*) and Illuminationist (*ishrāqī*) schools of philosophy), *al-ḥikmat al-ilāhiyya* (theosophy), *kalām* (theology), *tārīkh* (history, especially the philosophy of history), the natural and mathematical sciences, philology (science of literature and linguistics) and Sufism. Adding to this diversity of sources are the different dimensions of the Qur'ānic revelation commonly described as *al-islām* (law and practice), *al-īmān* (belief) and *al-iḥsān* (beautification of character) or, in Sufi terminology, *al-sharī'a* (the Law), *al-ṭarīqa* (the Path) and *al-ḥaqīqa* (the Reality).

Thinking about God (Being), however, is not the same as knowing Being. To know Being requires that one goes beyond empirical and rationalistic discourse and on to higher levels of knowledge. As we noted earlier, in Sufi terminology empirical and rationalistic discourse are categorized as *'ilm al-'aql* and the higher levels of knowledge are known as *'ilm al-aḥwāl*, *'ilm al-asrār*, *fanā'* and *baqā'*. Knowing Being requires that one ascend to these higher levels of knowledge and arrive at a state where the intellect and the intelligible are unified. This can be achieved through *fanā'*, the annihilation of the self. When the self, or individual being, is annihilated then Being manifests to the Sufi. This is known as the acquisition of knowledge by presence rather than knowledge by representation.

Shaykh 'Abd al-Qādir defines Sufism[52] as "taking the ancient way, the primordial path of direct experience of the Real [God]." Before the Sufi arrives at his or her goal of experiencing the Divine Presence, they must first embark on a path (*ṭarīqa*)[53] in a search for the realization of reality (*ḥaqīqa*).[54] On this path, the Sufi sets out to lift the veil of appearances in order to reveal the underlying reality of the cosmos[55] and this knowledge of reality is acquired by taste (*dhawq*) and state (*ḥāl*).[56] God lies beyond the realms of phenomenal existence, which means that God cannot be apprehended either through the discursive knowledge of the *nafs* (lower self) or the intuition and taste that is appropriate to the *rūḥ* (soul/spirit) and the *sirr* (innermost consciousness). The Divine Presence can only be experienced through *fanā'* because God is beyond the three worlds of *mulk* (phenomenal existence), *malakūt* (realms of the Unseen) and *jabarūt* (world of Divine Power), that is beyond space, time and all phenomena. As Ibn 'Ajība has noted[57] with regards to *fanā'*:

> If the poet tells you 'everything except Allah is false', or says, 'There is not anything in the cosmos other than You', you will not know that, nor will you grasp it by your intellect, though it is apparent. It is only grasped by the people of taste and penetrating inner sight, not by intellects tied to illusory imaginings. This matter is beyond the grasp of intellects and beyond recorded knowledge.[58]

The taste of *fanā'* is not anything like the taste that is experienced by the *rūḥ* and the *sirr*. Whilst the term 'taste' applied to it is the same, its reality is nevertheless fundamentally different.[59] The Sufi's goal is to reach God and his or her access to knowing Him is dependent on the annihilation of the self and its capacities. When the self is annihilated, all that remains is God consciousness. Whilst declaring that this experience is only grasped by the people of taste, Sufis have nevertheless tried to convey some sense of it in both poetry and prose. As noted earlier, al-Junayd[60] described the stages leading to the annihilation of the self and the vision of God. He said that obedience to God's laws leads to knowledge of Him. Knowledge of Him implies ascent toward Him and ultimately to reaching Him. From God's self-manifestation to the worshipper there follows bewilderment, the vision of God, and loss of individual identity and personal attributes. The knowledge that the Sufi attains during *fanā'* is in the vision or Divine Self-disclosure. Shaykh 'Abd al-Qādir says that *fanā'*...

> ... is the meaning death, based on the cessation of the attributes, even life itself. It is arrived at by the most fine process of withdrawal from the sensory by the means of the Supreme Name [Allah] until even the Name, the last contact with awareness disappears. From the depth of the Original Void the secrets and the lights emerge. The seeker will pass through the heavens, each with its own colour and meanings. Light upon light. Until the great *tajallī*[61] which unveils the secret and indicates Allah.[62]

The unique defining element of Sufism is the experience of *fanā'* followed by *baqā'*, the state that follows *fanā'*. The ultimate goal of the Sufi is attained when the self is annihilated and becomes the locus for the Self-manifestation of God. Shaykh 'Abd al-Qādir explains that *fanā'* is not a matter that can be covered by linguistics or epistemology because the science of the Sufis is the science of states that must be directly experienced.

Philosophical reflections on *fanā'*

The theoretical and philosophical exposition of Sufi modes of discernment and expression can be traced back to the school of al-Junayd.[63] An understanding of the metaphysical vision of the ultimate reality in Sufism can be attained when the unity of existence (*waḥdat al-wujūd*)[64] is experienced during *fanā'* and *baqā'*. This metaphysical vision comes from intuition, differentiating it from the statements and general conclusions of modern philosophy and science, which are based exclusively on discursive reason and sense experience. The view of reality as seen from the level of rationalism and empirical experience presents itself as one of variety and multiplicity in which cognition and volition is confined within the subject/object dichotomy. The Sufis call experience at this level the condition of separation (*farq*) or, more precisely, the first separation (*al-farq al-awwal*).[65] This is the condition of people in general (*'awāmm*) who, on the basis of reason and sense perception, see reality as consisting of a multiplicity of different phenomena with separate forms and identities.

An extension of this view is held by theologians, philosophers and scientists who see the world in this way. They see the things of the world as external things with substantial realities or quiddities that are the subjects of our knowledge. The existence of a thing is regarded as a property of its quiddity. Existence is seen, in philosophy, as an accident that happens to essence. Reality, when viewed through reason and sense perception and then investigated philosophically and scientifically, has tended to be attributed to the essences of things rather than to existence itself. Depending upon one's intellectual, religious and spiritual development, it is possible for this level of cognition to be transcended and to reveal to the Sufi the true nature of phenomena, which is the unity of all existence.

Returning to the world of phenomena after having transcended it and witnessed its underlying unity, the Sufi is said to be in a state of the second separation (*al-farq al-thānī*). The personal transformation of the Sufi involved in the process of transcending the first separation means that their existence is not, from then on, confined to the ordinary level of reason and sense experience. The first separation is a condition imposed on the human being by reason and sense perception, enabling the faculties of cognition and volition to perform their functions at the ordinary level. The terms first separation and second separation also imply that there was a condition of pre-separation prior to them, in which there was no separation.

This condition of pre-separation is described in the Qur'ān as being the soul's relationship to God prior to his or her arrival in the world.[66] Commenting on this phenomenon, which he called the covenant (*mīthāq*) between God and the souls of all human beings, al-Junayd said that God "spoke to them at a time when they did not exist, except in so far as they existed in Him."[67] This is a type of existence which only God knows and in which the souls are unaware of their future existence in the world but are, nevertheless, conscious of the distinction between themselves and God. Al-Junayd explained that in their timeless existence in God and in their state of unity with Him, the souls' consciousness of the distinction between themselves and God was a gracious gift from Him. God "gave them knowledge of Him when they were only concepts which He had conceived."[68]

Fanā' occurs both subjectively at the psychological level and objectively at the ontological level. Deep concentration on some matter, even at the empirical and phenomenal level, can cause one to become unaware of one's body. This gives us an indication, albeit in a limited sense, of the possibility of the passing away of subjective consciousness. The passing away of subjective consciousness also involves the passing away of the forms of the objects of multiplicity. This passing away of the forms is not only subjective because the multiplicity of forms is itself discontinuous and the forms are continuously perishing.[69] "Thus *fanā'* ... is a coincidence between the losing of the subjective consciousness, which entails the losing also of the objects of that consciousness, and the actual disappearance of the objects themselves."[70]

In this initial stage of *fanā'*, however, the subject is still aware of his or her self, which is able to witness the passing away of the forms of separate objects. What the self sees then is the gathering together (*jam'*) of the separate objects into a single unified Reality (*waḥda*). In the last phase of the experience of *fanā'* the Sufi also loses consciousness of his or her individual existence. Al-Attas notes:

> Ultimately when the human light is extinguished and the creaturely spirit passes away, there would not even be a trace of consciousness left in the ego of its passing away. The man has at this stage 'passed away from the passing away' (*fanā' al-fanā'*).[71]

In this state God imbues into the man or woman concerned, without incarnation (*ḥulūl*), a spiritual substance (*laṭīfah*) from His Essence (*dhāt*). God then reveals an aspect of Himself to that spiritual substance, which is named the Holy Spirit (*al-rūḥ al-qudus* or Active Intelligence). In this way God reveals Himself to Himself and the subject/object dichotomy ceases to exist.

In the second separation that follows the experience of *fanā'*, the Sufi does not make a distinction between essence and existence, knowing that such a distinction can only be posited in the mind and not in the extra mental reality itself. It is existence itself that is the reality of the essences of things and these mentally conceived essences or quiddities are not accidents that happen to existence, as the philosophers say. They have been made by God *bi'l-ḥaqq* (with truth) (Q. 10: 5). Knowledge is from God and has to be interpreted by the human being through his or her physical and spiritual faculties. At the stage of *fanā'*, prior to progressing on to *fanā' al-fanā'* and *baqā'*, many a Sufi has made the error of pantheism, monism, thinking that God is the world or that the world is God, or believing that the self is God or that God is the self.

As we saw earlier, the Sufis have described four categories of human beings depending on their perception of unity and multiplicity: *mahjūb*, *maghzūb*, *majdhūb* and *maḥbūb*.[72] A person who acknowledges only phenomenal existence is veiled and called *mahjūb*. One who identifies the phenomenal with God or regards the phenomenal as real is *maghzūb*, an illusionist. Someone who is enraptured and bewildered by the effect of Divine attraction is *majdhūb*, mad in God. The one who can clearly distinguish between the phenomenal and the Real and lives his or her life in accordance with that knowledge is *maḥbūb*, beloved of God.

The one who has attained *fanā' al-fanā'* is a friend of God (*walī'allāh*) and is known amongst the Sufis as one of the élite. The élite have realized that their existence is from God and that their relationship to God is one of ontological poverty. They have learnt by direct experience that entities other than God (*mā siwa'llah*) owe their existence entirely to God. In the language of the Qur'ān, "everything perishes except the Face of God",[73] and in the language of the *ḥadīth*, "God was and there was nothing with Him" on which, when it is was narrated in his presence, al-Junayd commented, "and He is as He was."[74] The elect of the élite have been granted *baqā'* after *fanā' al-fanā'*. In this condition the Sufi understands that nothing exists besides God and His existence is not static because "*everyday He is engaged in some affair*"[75] and "*everyone in the heavens and the earth requests His aid.*"[76]

For the elect of the élite, multiplicity has been gathered into Unity. When the Sufi returns to the world of phenomena, in the second separation after the final unveiling and after attaining *baqā'*, he or she witnesses...

> ... the inner articulations of the Unity, in which the Unity is neither joined to nor separate from the Multiplicity, and which goes on in continuous operation. This continuous operation of Unity articulating Itself into Multiplicity and back again into Unity, as witnessed by the spiritual adept, is called the 'gathering of the gathering' (*jam' al-jam'*).[77]

The experience of *fanā'* is encapsulated in the Qur'ān in the story of Mūsā (Moses). Shaykh 'Abd al-Qādir's views on that story have already been discussed[78] but here we want to look at the vital element that time plays in this experience. In the event of *fanā'* time is crucial. It occurs at the intersection of physical and spiritual time.[79] This intersection becomes possible during the spiritual journey and wayfaring (*safar*) of the Sufi. In *The Book of Safar*, Shaykh 'Abd al-Qādir describes how the Sufi is on an outward journey which is the catalyst for their inward journey into the Divine Presence (*fanā'*). He describes the Qur'ānic accounts of the Prophet Adam's journey from the Garden to the earth[80] and then the journey of the Prophet Yūnus (Jonah) in the water,[81] the Prophet Mūsā on the earth,[82] the Prophet Ibrahim (Abraham) in the fire[83] and the Prophet Muḥammad in the air.[84] All of these outward journeys culminated in *fanā'* for each of them. The journey itself is nothing other than the manifestation (*tajalliyāt*) of God from Unity to Multiplicity and from Multiplicity to Unity.[85] Existence itself is a journey, is in movement.

Everything in existence is alive, dynamic, moving and in action, including the actual atoms themselves.[86] Shaykh 'Abd al-Qādir calls physical time 'natural time' and the name he gives to spiritual time is 'time of destiny'. The movement of a thing or the journeying of a person is called their destiny. Natural time is fixed by God as part of His governance of the universe (*rubūbiyyah*), for example planetary movements, weather changes and the DNA in biological entities. Explaining the time of destiny, Shaykh 'Abd al-Qādir says that there is another set of times that are fixed by God and lie between the decree of God (*qadr*) and the execution of His decree (*qaḍā*). In these times of destiny, God, without interfering with the universal laws, manifests, at the moment He has decreed for it, the *tajalliyāt*[87] of His light.[88]

The time of destiny is appointed by God and is part of His decree. The relationship between the two times, natural time and the time of destiny, is referred to in the following verse of the

Qur'ān: "*We set aside thirty nights for Mūsā and then completed them with ten, so the appointed time of his Lord was forty nights in all.*"[91] Shaykh 'Abd al-Qādir points out that God has divided this 'set aside' time into two, the last ten nights and the earlier thirty nights and says:

> [In] that sense we see that the last ten represent the hidden time of *ma'rifa* [gnosis]. [In the first thirty nights] you could say it is the meeting with the Act [of God] and the *ṣifāt* (Attributes of God) and the final ten nights represent the encounter with the *dhāt* (the Essence of God), the *tajalliyāt al-dhāt* [Self-disclosure of the Essence of God] and the *fanā'* [annihilation] of existence, which comes as the amazing explanation of Allah's showing Himself to the mountain.[92]

Between natural time and the time of destiny there is a *barzakh*, an interspace or dimension between two realities that both separates and links them. We saw above that the event of *fanā'*, at the intersection of physical and spiritual time, is made possible by travelling. Shaykh 'Abd al-Qādir points out that the root verb, from which the word travelling is derived, is *yusfiru* (he unveils). In the context of Sufism, therefore, travelling, in this sense, is Divine Self-unveiling to the one who has submitted to his or her destiny, which, in turn, is the literal meaning of the word *muslim*. The Muslim, then, is one who has annihilated his or her *nafs* (self) in God, and this is what all human beings naturally aspire to consciously or unconsciously.[93] This is the first of al-Junayd's five rules by which Sufis acquire unveiling.[94]

In his description of *fanā'*, Shaykh 'Abd al-Qādir has woven together Ash'arī theology, Mālikī legal methodology and Junaydī Sufism, all of which are incorporated in the dictum: "God is One in His essence, attributes and actions."[95] The acts and attributes of God can be contemplated but whilst His essence is unthinkable it can nevertheless be known through *fanā'*.

Praxis, *Himma* and *Maḥabba*

Shaykh 'Abd al-Qādir explains that it is very often said that *fanā'* means a state of annihilation. It is as if this linguistic statement somehow answers the question, 'What is *fanā'*?' He emphasizes that *fanā'* is not a matter of linguistics or epistemology. It is a state that is only known to those who experience it, just as the taste of honey is only known to a person who has tasted it.[96] Shaykh 'Abd al-Qādir insists that the knowledge and experience of *fanā'* comes from a specific praxis: adherence to the *sunna* of the Prophet Muḥammad ﷺ.[97]

Ibn al-'Arabī also emphasized the necessary connection between the law and unveiling. The three groups of people that Ibn al-'Arabī calls the men of God, are all obedient to the laws of God: the worshippers (*'ubbād*) who occupy themselves with renunciation, constant devotion and outwardly praiseworthy acts; the Sufis who see all acts as belonging to God and who possess earnestness, piety, renunciation, trust in God and other virtues, and have knowledge of states, stations and unveilings; and the third group is made up of people who follow in the footsteps of Abū Bakr.

This last group performs the five prayers and the supererogatory exercises, they visit the markets and mingle with people, but their special distinction is that their hearts are entirely preoccupied with God. The friends of God (*awliyā'-Allāh*) can therefore be ranked hierarchically, with the Prophet Muḥammad ﷺ being the closest to Him, followed by his Companions, then the Sufis and finally the worshippers (*'ubbād*). Whilst insisting on the need to follow the *sharī'a*, Ibn al-'Arabī was nevertheless scathing in his criticisms of the jurists (*fuqahā'*) of his time. There are several criticisms directed at the *fuqahā'* scattered throughout the *Futūḥāt*, the purpose of which is summed up concisely by James Morris:

> The essential motivation of Ibn al-ʿArabī's criticism of the assumptions underlying the religious paradigm of the *fuqahā'*, however, is not any sort of 'liberation' from religious (or legal) constraints, but rather his consistent stress on the individual's inalienable responsibility in realizing the spiritual intentions of revelation, along with the freedom which is the prerequisite of that responsibility and the diversity and openness that are its inevitable consequences.[98]

Ibn al-ʿArabī spoke out against the inability of the *fuqahā'* to delve into the deeper and wider meanings of the Qur'ān and *ḥadīth*, against their attacks on the Sufis, their ignorance of the inspired spiritual insights of the *awliyā'* (Sufi saints), and the masking of their (the *fuqahā'*s) arbitrary personal opinions in the name of *qiyās* (juristic analogical deductions). However, there were jurists who possessed the qualities that Ibn al-ʿArabī found admirable and he was personally familiar with them. This accords with Shaykh ʿAbd al-Qādir's position on Sufism which is that *ʿamal* (action/behaviour) elevates people spiritually and initiates unveiling for them. Shaykh ʿAbd al-Qādir calls this

> ... a protected *taṣawwuf* because it is not accessible, touchable, visible or speakable. It is buried in the hearts of great men of knowledge of *kitab wa sunna* [the Qur'ān and normative practice of the Prophet]. And if we take this path, there is no need for anything visible on the face of the earth that you can call Sufism.[99]

The *silsila* shows that the originator of Sufism, and first in the link in the Qādiriyya-Shādhiliyya-Darqawiyya *ṭarīqa*, is the Prophet Muḥammad ﷺ.[100] *Maʿrifa* (acquired through *ʿilm al-aḥwāl* and *ʿilm al-asrār*), *fanā'* and *baqā'* have always been firmly grounded in the Prophetic *sunna*. The Prophet's ﷺ Night Journey and Ascension were, respectively, his *maʿrifa* and *fanā'*.[101] The ultimate goal of Sufism is to experience the self-manifestation of God during the annihilation of the self, that is, one's very being. When the mind is confronted with the ultimate paradox[102] it becomes bewildered (*ḥayra*) causing it to stop, at which point the self is annihilated and becomes the locus for the self-manifestation of God.[103]

For Shaykh ʿAbd al-Qādir, and for Sufis in general, God's actions and attributes can be known but His essence is unthinkable. It is something which cannot be known intellectually.[104] This is, theologically speaking, the Ashʿarī position but, for the Sufis, the fact that God's essence is unthinkable does not mean that it is unknowable. Shaykh ʿAbd al-Qādir says that it is possible to go beyond the Ashʿarī position without negating it.[105] To know the essence of God requires, in the language of Sufism, *himma*. This refers to spiritual aspiration and the highest energy impulse in a human to discover reality.[106] Shaykh ʿAbd al-Qādir's says of *himma*:

> In the beginning it is the aspiration to acquire the sciences. In the middle it is aspiration to arrive at direct experience. In the end it is aspiration to be granted further gnosis in witnessing and absorption in the vision of the Lord.[107]

God unveils His essence to the one who yearns for Him.[108] Shaykh ʿAbd al-Qādir explains that this yearning is born out of Divine love (*maḥabba*) and to illustrate this he makes references to Sufi poetry. The theme of *fanāʾ* and *baqāʾ* recurs regularly in the writings of Sufi poets and Shaykh ʿAbd al-Qādir has commented extensively on the poetry of Rūmī, al-Ḥallāj, Ibn al-Fāriḍ (1181-1235) and Ibn al-ʿArabī, in addition to that of his masters Ibn al-Ḥabīb and al-Faytūrī. Poetry brings out clearly the difference between worshipping God out of duty and worshipping God out of love. The latter is the path of delight and ecstasy as is evident in the life and works of Shaykh ʿAbd al-Qādir.[109]

From this we have seen that in the Greek founders of Western philosophy there was a close relationship between revelation and philosophy both in respect of their thought and lives, placing them in stark contrast to the rationalism and empiricism of modern philosophy. Islamic philosophy, however, goes well beyond a reconciliation of the Platonic and Aristotelian views on existence by focusing on the fundamental pre-epistemic question regarding the relation between knowledge and the possessor of knowledge. It answers the question of how a knowing subject becomes united with, or is related to, an external object by positing an ontological foundation for human awareness. From the beginnings of Islamic philosophy, the Qur'ān was seen as the record of the ontological experiences of the Prophet ﷺ in which God manifests His Word and His Presence to him.

Al-Kindī maintained that philosophy had to subordinate itself to revelation and surrender its claims to be the highest avenue to truth. Al-Fārābī referred to God as the First Being which corresponds explicitly to the God of revealed religion. For Ibn Sīnā there is an ontological poverty in the universe because it is God who gives existence to all things. He made a distinction between Peripatetic Philosophy and Eastern Philosophy, thereby expressing his dissatisfaction with merely discursive philosophy and showing his desire to transcend it. Al-Ghazālī sought to harmonize philosophy, Sufism and law within one system. His writings dealt directly with the correspondence of epistemology to ontology, endeavouring to explain the ontological features of intelligible universal objects and the nature of the being of these entities and how they related to individual consciousness.

Ibn Rushd demonstrated that the use of reason, rational thinking and philosophy was not only permitted by the *sharīʿa* of Islam but obligatory within its legal limits. Like Aristotle, Ibn Rushd advocated a distinction between the Active or Agent Intellect and the human intellect. He argued that the Agent Intellect was not a part of the human intellect and that the latter is designed to act through the process of unification with the former in the actualization of intellectual knowledge. Suhrawardī said that he did not base his Philosophy of Illumination on cogitation, but on something else. According to his commentators this 'something else' was illuminationist vision which was the foundation of true science.

Mulla Sadra advocated the belief that reality was best apprehended by intuition. Intuition, he believed, was the perception of something directly without mediation, the process by which the quiddity of things outside the human mind can be apprehended directly, thereby making them intelligible. For him, knowledge entailed the transformation of existence as an external reality outside the human mind into mental existence, which is a form of Being. It is in this ontological state of human consciousness that the constitutive dualism of the subject-object relationship is overcome and submerged into a unitary simplex. Philosophizing about Being is not the same as knowing Being. To know Being requires that one go beyond empirical and rationalistic discourse to higher levels of knowledge. In Sufi terminology empirical and rationalistic discourse are categorized as *'ilm al-'aql*; the higher levels of knowledge referred to are *'ilm al-aḥwāl*, *'ilm al-asrār*, *fanā'* and *baqā'*.

Knowing Being requires that one ascends to these higher levels of knowledge and arrives at unity of the intellect and the intelligible, which can be achieved through *fanā'*. When the self is forgotten, and natural time and the time of destiny intersect, then God manifests Himself to the Sufi. The knowledge that the Sufi attains during *fanā'* is in the vision of God or, in the expression of Ibn al-'Arabī, Divine Self-disclosure. The unique defining element of Sufism is that it is a science by means of which *fanā'* and *baqā'* can be experienced. Shaykh 'Abd al-Qādir indicates that the knowledge and experience of *fanā'* comes from a specific praxis, the life pattern, the behavioural mode, the *sunna* of the Prophet Muḥammad ﷺ. To know the Essence of God requires, in the language of Sufism, *himma*, which means spiritual aspiration. God unveils Himself to those who yearn for Him. Shaykh ʿAbd al-Qādir explains that this yearning is born out of Divine love.

Chapter 8

The Sufi Path of Social Cohesion: Calling Things by Their Names

Shaykh 'Abd al-Qādir's socio-economic and political critique of contemporary society is naturally based on the epistemology of Sufism. In Shaykh 'Abd al-Qādir's view, an epistemology grounded on such an approach protects the balance between the *sharīʿa* and the *ḥaqīqa*, between the outer law and the inner reality, which as we have seen is an essential element of classical Sufism, and, in this case, inhibits the separation of "man from his idea and the political and economic from the elements of personality."[1] When this split between the inner and outer dimensions of the human personality occurs, as it does in modern society, human beings lose contact with reality (*ḥaqīqa*). In modern terminology this state of being – loss of contact with reality – is called psychosis. The mass psychosis of modern society, as understood by Shaykh 'Abd al-Qādir, is not caused simply by people's acceptance of the media's fictional and propagandist versions of democracy and capitalism, which, as is daily demonstrated, are very different from the reality of what is actually happening in the world we live in. That is a secondary issue. The primary cause of the psychosis is their belief in what lies at the core of the capitalist system, its motor force, the money supply itself, which, as has also been made painfully clear by recent events, far from being a store of value is in reality essentially valueless.

According to Shaykh 'Abd al-Qādir, modern societies are oligarchies – even if believed by the people within them to be either democracies or totalitarian states – and the source of oligarchic wealth is not, as is commonly supposed, commerce and trading – generally going by the name of either capitalism or state-capitalism/communism[2] – but is in reality usury (*ribā*). Capitalism is totally reliant on credit creation, and the mechanism for the creation of money as credit is, in fact, usury, taking the various forms of fractional reserve banking, simple and compound interest, speculation, derivatives, futures trading, and other such things. The assumption underlying credit creation is clearly that there can be infinite growth in a finite world. This is a completely irrational belief and, since capitalism is constructed on this belief, Shaykh 'Abd al-Qādir says that it is not the system it claims to be but is in fact a psychosis – an estrangement from, and loss of contact with, reality.

It would not have been possible for usury to become an acceptable social and economic practice without the complete transformation of the pre-modern worldview about it. The condemnation of usury in pre-modern times was almost universal, coming from Divine revelation, Greek and Roman philosophers and both Christians and Muslims, and this condemnation continued well into the modern period.[3] It is only with the arrival of the secularist mindset that the practice of usury became seen as possible and acceptable and then eventually essential. Modern socio-economic systems, be they democracies, monarchic dictatorships or one-party totalitarianisms, are all de facto capitalist and every other aspect of society is subsumed under the capitalist hegemony. In most parts of the world the much-vaunted system of representative democracy in reality functions merely as a public relations interface for the capitalist system[4] which underpins and sustains it.

What is clearly observable in the modern period is an historical progression from the rise of secularism to usury-based capitalism and democracy and finally to oligarchy, and in this chapter we will look at Shaykh 'Abd al-Qādir's analysis of the way that politics in the modern world has become in real terms oligarchic and of how usury is indeed the motor force of capitalism. This discussion will lay the foundations for understanding Shaykh 'Abd al-Qādir's proposal for an alternative to capitalism based on Sufi epistemology. The four areas covered will be: secularism, a critique of political economy, democracy and oligarchy, and finally the new nomos. By 'new nomos' is meant a new ordering of the external reality of the world and the internal experience of the individual in order for there to be true social cohesion.

Secularism

Shaykh 'Abd al-Qādir is of the view that the cause of the crisis of modern civilization is "lack of recognition of the Divine."[5] Prior to the modern age the basic worldview of Europe was founded on scholasticism, a harmonization between Christian theological thinking and the classical philosophical tradition of ancient Greece.[6] This religious worldview was supplanted over a period of time by a modern worldview. The exact chronology of this process is the subject of some historical dispute but it is clear that the transition from the medieval to modern modes of thought and practice was supported by rationalist methodology being applied during this period in all fields of inquiry and, before long, empiricism and rationalism became the primary sources for the acquisition of knowledge. Rationalism is the belief that phenomena are best understood through logic and reason and empiricism is the belief that knowledge is based on sense experience. Modernist epistemology led to the philosophies of mechanism and materialism and the methodology of structuralism. The underlying assumptions of modernity were secularism, individualism and a commitment to progress through science and technology. Development was defined as the control of nature for the benefit of human beings according to the principle of liberal market forces, and modernity led to the establishment of nationalism, capitalism and democracy.

Much of the modernization process outlined above was made possible through the development of science, and the world-view fostered by science came into direct conflict with that of religion. In order to make "science possible, religion's claim to hegemony over the mind had to be broken."[7] Challenging the hegemony of the Church, both Catholic and Protestant, was fraught with danger. The leaders of the Reformation, in particular Martin Luther (1483-1546) and John Calvin (1509-1564), whilst dissenting with the Catholic Church on many issues, were, nevertheless, no champions of freedom and liberalism, and the Counter Reformation, which began in the 1540's, lasted a hundred years and brought about millions of deaths, was an attempt to re-establish the authority of the Catholic Church throughout Europe.

It was in this environment that the champions of science insisted that the scientific method was merely an objective endeavour, using rationalism and empirical measurements to test hypotheses. Scientific methodology involved experimentation, observation, reasoning and review and its success was evaluated in terms of the application of scientific discoveries to technology. However, the universe as understood by science turned out to be radically different from the universe as understood by Christianity. Science thrived in circumstances of doubt, scepticism and revision. Such ideas were anathema to Christian theological orthodoxy and culminated in the Church burning many scientists at the stake. But thinkers such as Galileo Galilei, René Descartes, Francis Bacon, Marin Mersenne (1588-1648) and Pierre Gassendi (1592-1655) gradually created an inexorable split between science and religion, claiming that religion dealt with spiritual matters and science dealt with the material world.

This attitude opened up a debate about the relation of religion to science, which resulted in the ultimate triumph of the scientific attitude over religious belief as the final arbiter over thought and action. It was, in essence, a victory of atheism over religion. Once the power of God over natural processes is denied this inevitably extends itself to individual thought and social action. When that happens religion ceases to be a dynamic and activating factor in human life and becomes, at best, nothing more than a personal belief system with no real social or political impact. In other words, as expressed in the philosophy of Nietzsche, God dies. It is in this sense that Shaykh 'Abd al-Qādir argues:

> At the centre of this ruined world is the lack of recognition of the Divine. The age is both atheist and bankrupt. Man has been reduced to being a debtor when the world is rich and full. The atheist is at the core of the disaster, having mistaken the idea of god for Divinity. Rightly he rejects theism. So too, do the Muslims. The reality of man is that he has a dynamic opening to the Divine.[8]

It must be understood that modernity and secularism are closely related. Religious practice, even where it exists, has been relegated to purely personal matters and individual belief preferences, and all socio-economic and political affairs are now determined by capitalism, either of the laissez-faire or state variety, no matter whether the nations concerned are called liberal democracies, dictatorships or one party totalitarianisms.

Critique of Political Economy

In his analysis of modern society, Shaykh 'Abd al-Qādir points out that one of the major outcomes stemming from the lack of adherence to Divine law has been "the embracing of usury as no longer forbidden, but necessary. In a limited but finite world modern men declared that increase in the exchange was not only permitted but theoretically without limits."[9] The critical historical event that determined the acceptance of usury in Europe was the Reformation, the religious revolution which transformed the Western church in the sixteenth century. In reaction to the Anabaptist movement[10] in 1521 and the Peasants' War of 1525[11] Martin Luther turned against Divine legislation, declaring that to "the extent that I take hold of Christ by faith, therefore to that extent the Law has been abrogated for me."[12] John Calvin promoted the revival of natural law, arguing for Christian assimilation into the world, and joined the civil revolt against the prohibition of usury.

Within just three decades the condemnation of usury, which until that time had been universal, came to be regarded as non-modern and medieval. Previously the Prophets Moses, Jesus and Muḥammad had prohibited it, while others who condemned it included Socrates, Plato, Aristotle, Aristophanes and Plutarch amongst the Greeks; Seneca, Cicero and Cato amongst the Romans; Gregorius Nysennas, Juan Chrisostomos, Augustinus, Thomas Aquinas, Duns Scotus, and the majority of Popes and Councils amongst the Christians; Christian Kings such as Alfonso the Wise and Alfonso XII; and the founders of all the schools of Islamic law and all the caliphs amongst the Muslims.[13] Yet, despite this, Calvin and other leaders of the Reformation sanctioned usury as legitimate business practice and, for the first time, permitted the lending and borrowing of money at interest.

After Protestantism arrived in England, Henry VIII and Elizabeth

I allowed usury at a fixed rate. Whilst previously the terms usury and interest had been synonymous, under the new science of political economy they were given different meanings. Usury was now defined as excessive interest, whereas a 'fair rate' of interest, which until then had also been called usury, was now justified for the use of money borrowed. From universal condemnation usurious transactions and practices became themselves universal and eventually the money supply itself became infected with usury. Shaykh 'Abd al-Qādir notes that:

> The monetarist[14] society is one based on usury. It is a society of usurers. That means, alas, all of us within the financial system now globally established.[15]

To understand how the modern economy functions it is necessary to take a closer look at money "the venous system of the present world society ... The life-blood which activates every organ, limb and sinew of human life on our planet."[16] The role of money in the economy has been glossed over by the majority of political theorists. What has been emphasized is the relationship between the state and the economy and this has defined political opinion for the past two hundred years. On one side there are those who argue for minimal state intervention and autonomy within the economy for private ownership. On the other side are the socialists who highlight the problems associated with private ownership in the market economy.[17] There is in fact something else that is rarely examined, something absolutely fundamental to both of these positions, and that is the currency itself.

Currencies are the life-blood of all economies. They are essential to all economic activity and without them economies could not function. The legitimacy and integrity of currencies should take precedence over the question of whether the means of production, distribution and exchange are owned privately or by the state.

Neither the right nor left side of this debate give this issue the weight it deserves. For Muslims, just as the production, distribution and exchange of goods and services are governed by Islamic law, so too are the currencies which are used in transactions. There is a vast corpus of Islamic literature dealing with currencies and money substitutes. For example, al-Qurṭubī in his legal commentary of the Qur'ān regarded the minting of gold dinars and silver dirhams as one of the seven most important aspects of Islam.[18] Ibn Khaldūn deals extensively with the minting of currencies in his *al-Muqaddima*. Referring to the dinar and dirham currencies he said:

> The Revelation undertook to mention them and attached many judgments to them, for example, *zakāt*, marriage, and *ḥudūd* [legal boundaries] etc., therefore within the Revelation they have to have a reality and a specific measure for assessment (of *zakāt* etc.) upon which its judgments may be based rather than on the non-shar'ī currencies that have become common.[19]

The fundamental question in any economic system is, "What is money?" Mālik ibn Anas, the founder of the Mālikī school of law, described money as any commodity that is commonly accepted as a means of exchange.[20] There are three basic concepts in this description: money is a commodity, it is communally accepted and it serves as a means of exchange. A commodity must possess the "quality of being a property and being of value"[21] and must be ready to be exchanged in a transaction. There is a difference between the value of a thing and its utility. Utility is what we deem useful therefore it is what connects us to the world. Value refers to the interchange of utilities and commodities and is "identical to the price established under conditions of equity, in other words when there is freedom of trade and justice in transactions."[22] There are two types of commodities, those that can be used and those that can be consumed.[23] The commodities of use (non-fungible) are rentable and those of consumption (fungible) are not rentable. It has been understood for centuries that money, "whose normal utility is to serve as a means of exchange, is consumed when it is exchanged and for this reason is a commodity of consumption or a non-rentable commodity."[24]

Money, however, can be loaned or invested in business. In respect of the lending of money 'Abdullāh ibn 'Umar, a Companion of the Prophet Muḥammad ﷺ, said:

> A dinar [gold coin of specific weight and value] for a dinar and a dirham [silver coin of specific weight and value] for a dirham. There is no increase between them. This is the command of the Prophet to us and our advice to you.[25]

It is permissible to receive a profit on investments in business but no profit can be taken from a loan of money. The repayment of the loan must be exactly equal to the amount loaned since no business risk was taken by the lender and no work was contributed by the lender. All unjustified increase is prohibited in Islamic law and called *ribā*, usury.[26] According to Prophetic traditions there are seventy different types of usury and everyone involved in any usurious transaction is condemned, including those who take it, pay it, witness it and record it.[27] Any transaction in which there is an unjustified increase between the value of the goods received and the price of the goods paid for them is usury. Unjustified increase is the result of inequity in the market, examples of which are: monopolies and monopsonies, enforced minimum and maximum prices, enforced use of one particular commodity as money, the renting of money or other fungible commodities, lotteries and gambling.

In order to understand how circumstances changed so dramatically from the almost universal condemnation of usury to viewing it with approbation, it is necessary to examine some aspects of the history of money. In ancient times the exchange of goods took place without the use of money; rather goods were exchanged for other goods using the barter system. For practical considerations a medium of exchange was adopted, because people's needs frequently failed to coincide. For example, a corn farmer who needed a coat would not always find a tailor who needed corn. Furthermore, there was the question of what quantity of a particular product, for example potatoes, would correspond to a given quantity of another product, for example oil.

It, therefore, became necessary to find one thing that would correspond to defined values of all other things and because of this gold was frequently chosen as a general equivalent in which the value of all goods could be expressed. Silver was also selected but was recognized to have a lower value than gold because it was more available and less durable.[28] Gold and silver were, therefore, minted into coins as a means of exchange and rulers were responsible for standardizing them, guarding them against falsification or clipping, and guaranteeing their weight and quality.

In Europe, where the current financial system evolved, people with large quantities of gold and silver coins would often deposit them for safekeeping with gold and silversmiths because, owing to the nature of their businesses in precious metals and bullion, the gold and silversmiths had secure strong-rooms in which these deposits could be kept safe. As acknowledgement for the deposit the gold or silversmith would issue a receipt against it and charge a fee for the service he was providing. People holding these receipts started to find it more convenient to exchange them in their business transactions rather than actually going to the silver and goldsmiths and withdrawing the coins to make payments.

In this way privately issued notes – these receipts for deposited gold and silver – came into circulation as a form of paper money.

They were originally exactly equivalent to the amount of gold and silver held by the goldsmiths but in due course the goldsmiths started to issue receipts against the bullion they held over and above the actual amounts of gold and silver deposited with them. People could use these receipts to buy goods and even cash them in if they so desired. The goldsmiths used these receipts to pay for things for themselves and to provide loans which people would pay back in gold coinage with interest.

This, properly speaking, constituted the origin of paper notes that are today all the money we know. The important thing to realise is that a considerable number of these notes were in reality entirely fictitious; they were not backed up by any gold at all. Money had, in effect, been conjured out of thin air.[29]

Shaykh 'Abd al-Qādir states that at this point the process involves two elements that are prohibited in Islamic law, the issuing of receipts over and above the value of deposits held and the lending out of those receipts at interest. Both of these practices constitute unjustified increase, that is, the *ribā* of Islamic law.[30] The paper money created in this way is technically a promissory note, a promise to pay a debt and, once again, this practice is prohibited by Islamic law, which stipulates that a debt cannot be paid by means of another debt. In other words both the transactions involved and also the money itself are usurious and therefore prohibited by Islamic law. The next stage was when the goldsmiths took on new functions such as processing bills of exchange and the negotiation of loans and by doing this became what is now known as bankers.[31]

The turning point for banking and the money system was the French Revolution and the Napoleonic state.[32] No comprehension of modern money is possible without understanding what happened during that time. Shaykh 'Abd al-Qādir points out that "the primal model is to be found in the Napoleonic state. The event of the

Revolution could not have been accomplished without the creation of the *assignats*, the paper money printed by the Revolutionary State and devoid of collateral. One of the key institutions Napoleon founded was the Banque de France."[33] The three stages in the evolution of paper money, as outlined by Vadillo,[34] were clearly manifest during the French Revolution of 1789. They are: "A promissory note backed by gold or silver, a process of unilateral devaluation leading to a complete revocation of the contractual agreement, and a piece of paper not backed by any specie, whose legal value is determined by the compulsion of the State Law."

With regards to Vadillo's first point, using the French Republic as the model, paper money and public banking were necessitated by the financial crisis experienced by the French state[35] at that time. The purpose of issuing paper *assignats* in large and small notes was to relieve that financial crisis. In the eyes of the revolutionary government, these *assignats*, not in fact backed by gold or silver but rather by expropriated land[36] formerly owned by the Church, "would soon be considered better than the coin now hoarded, and will bring it out again into circulation,"[37] and in April 1790 they issued four hundred million livres in paper money, using the confiscated property of the Church as security. White wrote that:

> No irredeemable currency has ever claimed a more scientific and practical guarantee for its goodness and for its proper action on public finances. On the one hand, it had what the world recognized as a most practical security – a mortgage on productive real estate of vastly greater value than the issue. On the other hand, as the notes bore interest, there seemed cogent reason for their being withdrawn from circulation whenever they became redundant.[38]

With regards to Vadillo's second point, of devaluation, the French government continued to issue paper money, firstly on an annual and then on a monthly basis. This was due to the fact that within five months of the first issue the government had spent all the paper money they had issued and was in difficulties again. The effects of these issues were inevitably inflation, depreciation and, finally, economic ruin.[39] The third point raised by Vadillo is that the legal value of paper money "is determined by the compulsion of the State Law." In revolutionary France the full force of the law was used to ensure that the *assignats* were a success. Anyone who sold the *assignats* for less than their nominal value would be imprisoned in chains for twenty years and those making investments in foreign countries would face the death sentence. The Reign of Terror of the French Revolution extended even into trade and commerce.[40]

This attempt at public banking was a complete failure and the government destroyed the machinery for printing *assignats* on February 18, 1796. The engraving apparatus for the *mandats*, a new currency issued to rescue the government, was also destroyed in accordance to the decrees and orders of February 4 and 14, 1797. The riots in Paris in April and May 1795, largely caused by this financial chaos, opened the way for the rise of Napoleon. Having witnessed the failure of public banking and the issuing of paper money – the *assignats*, *livres* and *mandats* – by the government, Napoleon decided that the control of the money supply by private banking was better for financial stability. He established La Banque de France in 1800.[41]

From this it is clear that central or reserve banking, the foundation upon which the modern state is built, was based entirely on the issuing of paper money and this has now been superseded by plastic and electronic currencies issued in exactly the same way. Public and private banking, based on the paper money issued during the French Revolution, vividly illustrate the processes generally involved in banking both past and contemporary. The system of banking that existed during the French Revolution is fundamentally exactly the same as today's global banking system which governs the economic life of every country in the world.

Due to the enormous profitability inherent in their money lending and money creating activities, banks started to appear everywhere and networks of banks developed within every country. They loaned money to monarchs, governments and commercial enterprises. Through advertising, these commercial banking enterprises nurtured people's desires for goods and property and encouraged them to go into debt in order to satisfy these desires. The banks made it easy for people to borrow money through mortgages, hire purchase, home loans, point of sale cash access, credit cards and automatic teller machines.

In the Eleventh Fiqh Conference in Cape Town, 2008 organized by Shaykh 'Abd al-Qādir, the CEO of E-Dinar, Dr. Zeno Dahinden, began his paper by describing fiat money, which is the currency of modern states and is imposed on the populace by government regulation or law. Dahinden explained why the two parties, the government on the one hand and the privately owned banking cartels such as Central Banks and the Federal Reserve System on the other, work together. He noted that the benefits to the two parties are:

> 1) It allows governments to create an unlimited amount of money out of nothing without having to burden the taxpayer with direct taxes (they prefer to take our money indirectly through inflation).
>
> 2) The banking cartel is able to create a perpetual flow of unearned wealth in the form of interest on money made out of nothing.[42]

Peter White explains how, in the case of the Federal Reserve Bank of New York, money is created out of nothing. He says that each morning the bank buys U.S. Treasury bills, which are promissory notes, from securities dealers who keep stocks of them to trade with the public. If the Federal Reserve Bank buys a hundred million dollars in Treasury bills from the securities dealers and pays for them, a hundred million dollars are added to the countries money supply. White then asks:

> But where did the Fed get that hundred million dollars? 'We created it,' a Fed official tells me. He means that anytime the central bank writes a check, so to speak, it creates money. 'It's money that didn't exist before,' he says. Is there no limit on that? 'No limit. Only the good judgement and the conscience of the Federal Reserve people.' And where did they get this vast authority? It was delegated to them in the Federal Reserve Act of 1913, based on the Constitution, Article I, Section 8.[43]

Peter White goes on to say that the hundred million dollars injected by the Federal Reserve into the commercial banking system could theoretically stimulate the appearance of 900 million dollars in new cheque book money. All of this money never existed before. The introduction of other financial instruments and products, also based on *ribā*, make the creation of fiat money described above appear paltry by comparison. These financial instruments include currency speculation and all types of derivatives and leveraging. Describing the present economic system and its descent into uncontrollability Shaykh 'Abd al-Qādir says:

> The very frame, structure, pattern of society, which had until now seemed actual, solid, founded on material itself, has now begun to fragment, disintegrate and collapse. As it does so, a further condition is revealed, simply that that very frame was in itself illusory, a simulation of stuff, a non-existent presence, sustained by a mathematic of ever multiplying dementia so that, where before it had a decimal connection to things, that in turn had so increased that from hundreds to thousands it had hurtled into being millions. In the final phase of its enmeshing power it had turned into billions and ultimately, trillions.[44]

Industrial capitalism has transformed into finance capitalism, which makes wealth through debt leveraging and interest extraction rather than by new investment in businesses and employment. This type of so-called wealth creation does not produce a large enough surplus to service its debts. It permits creditors to foreclose allowing for the concentration of property in their hands, whilst imposing financial and fiscal austerity on the population at large. This in turn causes the economy to shrink, be debt-strapped and burdened by heavy taxes. Hudson says that this strategy "contains the seeds of its own destruction, because it builds up financial claims on the assets pledged as collateral – without creating new means of production."[45]

There is no evidence to demonstrate that this strategy will be reversed in order to avert a catastrophic outcome. Everything points to the use of political power being exercised by the financial sector to take debt and financial policy away from elected government representatives and steer economic planning and tax policy towards supranational central banks which are controlled by private bankers. This is exactly how it is has been for some time and, according to Shaykh 'Abd al-Qādir's reckoning, we have, during the whole of that time, been living in a global oligarchic state.

Democracy and oligarchy

Shaykh 'Abd al-Qādir explains that there has been a gradual progression in the development of the concept of the modern state leading from monarchy to democracy to oligarchy. The foundations of the current social paradigm lie with the ancient Greeks. The complex and ritual patterns of their life first revolved around patricide, matricide, fratricide and sororicide. The ancient Greeks then turned themselves to examining human social issues in a systematic manner. "That system was philosophy"[47] but the ideal states of Plato (*Republic*) and Aristotle (*Politics*) were never realized in practice. It not until the eighteenth century, beginning with the French Revolution, that the modern political state, with its dialectical parliamentary democracy, came into existence and the full implementation of structuralism and systematic thinking, which had its origins in ancient Greek philosophy, became a reality.

The modern political state has always needed to dehumanize its enemies, as was apparent in the Terror that followed the French Revolution. Shaykh 'Abd al-Qādir notes that there has always been an integral connection between structural government, and murder and genocide. Statism inevitability entails civil war, concentration camps, executions, genocide and dictatorship. Shaykh 'Abd al-Qādir argues that statism also ensures that the structural state, as an instrument of power, will be placed in the hands of inferior human beings, for example Churchill, Hitler, Stalin, Reagan, Napoleon, Clinton, etc. He points out that democracy "is the civic instrument of the enslavement and the oppression of the masses. The current structuralist state is the perfect copy of the slave camps of the Hitler/Stalin pact, only today the city is the concentration camp and the gulag."[48]

What emerges from Shaykh 'Abd al-Qādir's critique is that modernity has subverted human nature and the social, political and economic institutions that were established up until the modern period. The entire world has been incorporated into the global capitalist system, irrespective of the political systems existing within the various national states, whether they be democracy, monarchy, dictatorship or one party totalitarianism. He has given succinct definitions of economics and politics and the relations between the two. He maintains firstly that capitalism is not free enterprise, as is claimed, secondly that liberal democracy is not the expression of the will of the people, as is claimed, and thirdly that liberal democracy is in fact subsumed under capitalism and actually serves as the public relations apparatus for it.

The 19th century witnessed the great expansion and evolution on the world stage of banking and the bankers took advantage of the great technological advances that were taking place around them. Banks evolved from being usurious clearinghouses of currencies into powerful institutions of technological project investment. They acted as middlemen between governments and these technological projects. As we saw earlier, governments gave privately owned Central Banks control over the money supply on the condition that they guaranteed government expenditure. At that point the power nexus of nations moved from the political to the economic.

In the West, the operational model of political economy became oligarchy, with liberal democracy acting as the public relations interface for it. The national state and its institutions, both executive and judiciary, have no access to or control over the financial system. In order to receive a loan, the recipient country must adhere to the political programs designed for it by the IMF and the World Bank, the financial oligarchs. The financial élite works closely with the commodities and media élites to sustain the current status quo for their mutual benefit. Shaykh ʿAbd al-Qādir explains that such a view as described above is not a conspiracy theory.[49] Rather it is the repetition of a continuously existing historical paradigm. He quotes the introduction to *The Roman Revolution* in which Ronald Syme says:

> In all ages, whatever the form and name of government, be it monarchy, republic, democracy, an oligarchy lurks behind the façade[50] ... As an oligarchy is not a figment of political theory, a specious fraud, or a mere term of abuse, but very precisely a collection of individuals, its shape and character, so far from fading away on close scrutiny, at once stands out, solid and manifest. In any age of the history of Republican Rome about twenty or thirty men, drawn from a dozen dominant families, hold a monopoly of office and power.[51]

Shaykh ʿAbd al-Qādir speaks of the inability of the general population to identify the motor forces of the social reality in which they live. He points out that in 1913 the U.S. Supreme Court Judge, Louis

Brandeis (1864-1941) said that the "dominant element in our financial oligarchy is the investment banker,"[52] and notes that from 1947 onwards the new oligarchy introduced a set of complex instruments and techniques, which for over half a century were adopted globally, encompassing world markets. Detailed studies were published with regard to instruments such as securitization, high yield debt, arbitrage trading, derivatives, credit default swaps and interest rate swaps. Research around financial concepts, structures and theories produced the Black-Scholes model, deregulation doctrines and efficient market hypothesis. It is these things, not anything that politicians may or may not do, that are in truth the motor forces dictating the day-to-day reality of the world we live in.

In the last decade of the twentieth century the financial élite exercised very significant influence over politicians, winning for the banks extended powers and banking deregulation. In the US the Riegle-Neal Act of 1974 removed restrictions on interstate banking. The Gramm-Leach-Bliley Act of 1999 demolished remaining barriers between commercial and investment banking and the Commodity Futures Modernization Act of 2000 prohibited Federal regulation of over-the-counter (O.T.C.) derivatives. One of those who introduced the Gramm-Leach-Bliley Act of 1999 for legislation to the U.S. Senate was Senator Phil Gramm who became Vice-Chairman of the Investment Bank Division of UBS AG after retiring from the Senate.

Shaykh 'Abd al-Qādir records that in the Spring of 2009 the following C.E.O.'s of thirteen of America's leading banks met with the U.S. President: Ken Chenault of American Express, Ken Lewis of the Bank of America, Robert Kelly of the Bank of New York Mellon, Vikram Pandit from Citigroup, John Koskinen of Freddie Mac, Lloyd Blankfein of Goldman Sachs, Jamie Dimon from JPMorgan Chase, John Mack of Morgan Stanley, Rick Waddell from Northern

Trust, James Rohr of PNC, Ronald Logue from State Street, Richard Davis of the US Bank and John Stumpf from Wells Fargo. Shaykh 'Abd al-Qādir says about this:

> The important thing to recognize is that these names would have remained completely hidden and unknown to the masses. It was only the financial collapse of 2008 that forced the oligarchic chiefs into the open. It must also be taken into account that they were responsible for the loss of billions of dollars.[53]

He continues his analysis by arguing that the result of the financial crisis of 2008 was to reduce the number of mega-banks and increase their wealth substantially. The people were shocked that their governments had bailed out the financial system with funds intended for health, education and infrastructure projects. The Greek national economy was irretrievably damaged and Italy, Spain, Portugal and the USA descended into poverty, causing the abolition of many social services. With the withdrawal of medical care, the shortage of homes, the radical dismantling of the universities and a population deep in unemployment, future social order would become largely a matter of crowd control. The police would become uniquely responsible for the state's stability. In short, civil war would become the future norm.[54] Shaykh 'Abd al-Qādir holds the oligarchs responsible for poisoning the oceans, polluting the air, stripping the oxygen-producing forests bare and supplying the poorest peasants with genetically modified seeds from which the following year's crop cannot be sown, forcing them to buy new seeds from multinational corporations owned and controlled by them.

The New Nomos

Shaykh 'Abd al-Qādir's investigation into atheism, secularism, usury, capitalism, democracy and oligarchy led him to ask: "What manner of man – and note the absence of woman – is capable of dragging millions of people into this black hole?"[55] Shaykh 'Abd al-Qādir has indicated that the existential crisis of modern society was mirrored by Roman history. The importance of what happened in ancient Rome was not related to the events or even the individual actors. What actually happened was that an inner dislocation of the people gradually took place over a period of about half a century, starting at the time of the primal dictator Lucius Cornelius Sulla (138 B.C. – 78 B.C.) and ending with that of the absolute dictator Augustus (63 B.C. – 14 A.D.). During that time the free Roman citizen gradually became enslaved "but it was not the gladiator's enslavement. Spartacus could rebel, the citizen could not. This was a new achievement, the forging of an obedient slave, to all accounts free, enjoying the circus and the spectacle. Here our contemporary species was born."[56]

Shaykh 'Abd al-Qādir argues that a devolutionary process had been set in motion and was instrumental in producing a different kind of human being. He points out that Roman society devolved from being a naturally functioning polity to one which adopted a metaphysical pseudo-reality and then sank into a metaphysical fantasy. It is a process that begins in the real world then turns to self-delusion and ends up in complete fantasy. On a political level it is a progression that starts with monarchy, becomes democracy and capitalism, and ends in oligarchy. The second stage of metaphysical pseudo-reality, in other words estrangement from the real nature of what is actually happening, takes the form of democracy and capitalism. For the oligarchic stage to come into existence a further metamorphosis is necessary, when the general population take democracy and capitalism as a religion and the oligarchs as gods. This is the stage of metaphysical fantasy.

He goes on to show how the British Empire and the contemporary

American Empire have followed exactly the same pattern as the one which unfolded itself in ancient Rome. Shaykh 'Abd al-Qādir puts it this way:

> The unfolding of this ultimate nihilism, in which not only is nothing (the oligarchy) and nobody (the Emperor) what it presents itself as, also requires that people (the Empire) believe that the charade and the actors are genuine, while also aware that all is false. Accepting the pretences (oligarchy, Empire, Emperor) as the real world demands a dislocation between nature and event, which implies that survival depends on transforming a psychosis into a reality. Thus the fully evolved post-Claudian Empire makes men complicit in a madness that demands total collaboration from the Legion, the magistrates, the Senate, the Emperors themselves and the citizens.[57]

Shaykh 'Abd al-Qādir points out that the mathematical inevitability of the collapse of the capitalist system and its public relations apparatus of liberal democracy was sealed in 1945 and that the two hundred year old religion of modernity actually came to an end in 2008 with the global financial crisis. The collapse of the structure will gather momentum with the passage of time. Shaykh 'Abd al-Qādir argues that by the mid-twentieth century "only a quartet of intellectuals stood apart from the mass ethos, insisting not just that the whole social system was, in Malaparte's diagnosis, 'Kaputt', but that the time was moving towards an utterly renewed world order."[58] The four intellectuals he refers to are Werner Heisenberg (1901–1976), Ernst Jünger (1895-1998), Martin Heidegger (1889-1976) and Carl Schmitt (1888–1985).

Shaykh 'Abd al-Qādir makes it clear that, although Sufis accept the validity of the ideas of such people as Descartes and Newton in as far as they apply in a limited way to the physical world, Heisenberg's discoveries, even at the empirical level, pointed to a universe that is very different to the Newtonian model and far more in tune with the cosmological view of classical Sufism.

What Heisenberg did was to demonstrate that "the Kantian world of categorical imperatives and fixed terms bounded by logical processes had given way to paradox, and precision had yielded to models of 'fuzzy' mathematics."[59]

The Heideggerian critique of modernity opened the way beyond modernist modes of conceptualization. Shaykh 'Abd al-Qādir says that:

> Heidegger opened up for the future nothing less than the phenomenology of freedom, which by implication, laid bare the mechanisms of slavery which made peace look like war, made legislated liberty produce slave camps, abstract research produce nuclear weaponry and psychotherapy produce passive consumers.[60]

Heidegger, in later life, set out on the path of aesthetics and poetry, a path well known to the Sufis.

With regards to the third thinker in the quartet Shaykh 'Abd al-Qādir points out that Jünger went beyond the Marxist analysis by defining the worker as subsumed under the process of technique. Jünger asserted that the figure of the worker is dependent on, submitted to, and a participant in, the technological project. Technology and technical processes do not serve human beings. On the contrary we serve them and therefore we are all workers, enslaved by them and working for them. He saw bourgeois society (the Gestalt of the worker) with its all-encompassing technological systems as "condemned to death."[61] Jünger showed that Marx failed to see not only that all humans are workers (not just the proletarians) but that logical technology and technical processes are sustained by an irrational economic system (fractional reserve banking and interest).

Schmitt, the political theorist of the quartet, said as early as 1963 that the modern state had lost substantive power. In his words: "the model of political unity, which embodied the monopoly of political decision, the State, this work of art, made in a European mould and with Western rationalism, is dethroned."[62] Schmitt saw the establishment of a new nomos as the way to end the worldwide civil war. Shaykh 'Abd al-Qādir argues that nihilism, suicide and terrorism are synonyms. They are not political doctrines but the failure of politics. They indicate an endgame and after it must come a new beginning, a "new Nomos."[63]

In a world that has lost its moral and Divine imperatives, Shaykh 'Abd al-Qādir sees that it is the task of the Muslims to replace materialism, consumerism and nihilism with the natural nomos (*dīn al-fiṭra*), with respect for women, safety for children, protection of human beings by the rule of law, and defence of the ecosphere from destruction, pollution and over-exploitation. For him the new nomos is none other than the *'amal ahl al-madīna*, the Practice of the People of Madīna, the Mālikī existential methodology. In his seminal text, *Root Islamic Education*, Shaykh 'Abd al-Qādir indicates that the prime example of a society in which the inward and outward sciences were unified was early Madīna. He notes that:

> The Madinah of the Salafi community [early generations of Muslims] was neither a primitive nor a formative society but a complete blueprint from then on. It is clear that in Madinah at the time of the Salafi communities man was at his greatest and the social contract at its healthiest and most balanced.[64]

According to Shaykh 'Abd al-Qādir, *'amal* (action/behaviour), which characterizes the teaching of Mālik ibn Anas, is the vehicle for the highest spiritual stations and states. Furthermore, he states that *'amal* in Islam is raised to a higher level than mankind has ever known by becoming transformed into *birr* (action that is truly just) and *birr* functions at three different levels namely; *futuwwa* (the individual functioning at the level of community), *jamā'a* (the community functioning within the context of broader society), and *umma* (the whole Muslim community as one entity functioning within the world).[65]

Referring to the present, Shaykh ʿAbd al-Qādir argues that in Ibn Khaldūn's philosophy of history the first stage of social change is Bedouinism (people becoming estranged from mainstream society). The Bedouins (those estranged from mainstream society) are cut off from the social project and they do not identify with the social system within which they live. They are the oppressed, exploited, stateless, homeless and poverty-stricken people of the world. The second stage happens when when the Bedouins coalesce into a group, united by kinship (*ʿaṣabiyya*). The third stage is when the Bedouins adopt kingship by swearing allegiance to a leader. This new force then overthrows the old regime and establishes itself in power. Shaykh ʿAbd al-Qādir says of the present time "this is clearly that moment when a new *ʿaṣabiyya* must inevitably arise in response to the identified nihilism which is the immediate present."[66]

For Shaykh ʿAbd al-Qādir, the new nomos will be established on the model of the *ʿamal ahl al-madīna* by the people who are estranged from contemporary society. In his eyes the Madīna of the Prophet Muḥammad ﷺ was established as the primary model for humankind, and the principle of governance for the Madinan "state",[67] as laid down in the Qur'ān, was justice.[68] Since the act of governing is primarily associated with the production, distribution and consumption of resources, the Islamic state had to guarantee justice and equity in the financial affairs of its citizens. The central function of governance in the Islamic state was to facilitate the movement of wealth to all sections of the community and this circulation of wealth is guaranteed by the *sharīʿa*. In economic terms Islam demands equity, freedom and justice in trade and commerce.

By forbidding usury in any form, Islamic law promotes the free circulation of wealth and inhibits its stagnation, thereby impeding the development of oligarchy,[69] which depends on wealth being gathered into the hands of the few.

The proper application of legal modalities of the *sharīʿa*, therefore, results in general prosperity for society as a whole. The Islamic state established by the Prophet in Madīna was a law-governed society, a nomocracy,[70] in which free trade and the movement of wealth to all sections of the community were central to the establishment of justice. The institutions that developed from this Madinan model and became implemented throughout Islamic history were the caliphate, the *wazirate* (vizierate), the judiciary, the *bayt al-māl* (the treasury), *ḥisba* (administration of the city), the mint, the *sūq* (market), the *awqāf* (charitable endowments), the *aṣnāf* (guilds), the *shurṭa* (*police*) and the army (*jaysh*). These institutions, regulated by Islamic law, provided the means by which Muslim societies functioned.[71]

The so-called Islamic states of today, like the fundamentalists of Saudi Arabia and Iran and the modernists of Egypt and Tunisia, bear no resemblance to the Madinan state of the Prophet Muḥammad ﷺ, either in their spirit or in their institutions. These fundamentalists and modernists have, to use an expression of Greek historian and Athenian general Thucydides (460 B.C. – 395 B.C.), re-defined their moral evaluations and actions in a completely opposite way.[72] Or as senator and historian of the Roman Empire Tacitus (56-117) said: "The name of liberty was a lying pretext in the mouths of men who, base in private, dangerous in public life, had nothing to hope except from civil discord. ...The truth is we have long since lost the true names of things."[73]

About the true names of things Shaykh ʿAbd al-Qādir says that God taught the prophets the names of all things.[74] Naming is the link between the creature and creation. It is the differentiating faculty in humans that indicates thresholds and limits. The name of a thing is the primal signal of language and by language the human social group is able to give both order and meaning to lived existence. Human beings have a dynamic opening to the Divine through language itself. Humans are designed for language and it lies embedded in the tongue, glottis, throat and vocal chords. Speech is the door to wisdom because God speaks to human beings through language.

Shaykh 'Abd al-Qādir states that knowledge begins with the phrase, "There is no god but Allah. From this follow the obligations of Divine worship. The Divine is named. It has no thingness. With this situation, however, comes the initiation which is naming itself."[75] Shaykh 'Abd al-Qādir points out that God's revelation also contains the words 'Muḥammad is the Messenger of Allah' and from this "follow the rules of trust-based trade and the abolition of usury, even to a blade of grass. The capitalist investment economy is replaced by an exchange economy."[76] In this way he shows how the inward – the worship of the Divine – and the outward – economic transactions between people are brought together in the Prophet Muḥammad ﷺ and found their highest expression in the prophetically guided early community in Madīna. The new nomos entails the re-generation of that primal model in the context of the 21st century in which we live today and this is the true task of Sufism in this time.

To further the goals of establishing the new nomos Shaykh 'Abd al-Qādir founded the Murābiṭūn Da'wa Movement with communities in twenty countries. The principal pillars of this movement include *bay'a* (allegiance) to an *amīr* (leader), the restoration of the *zakāt* tax and the establishment of the *'amal ahl al-Madīna* within each of those communities. He has set about establishing the institutions on which Islam has always been based, such as local governance, markets, *ḥisba* (market administration), charitable endowments, guilds and the minting of gold and silver currencies based on the Madinan model. He has also established schools, colleges and mosques in the cities which have Murābiṭūn communities.

At the same time he has a busy and vibrant *zāwiya* in Cape Town and, in order to supplement the processes described by Mālik ibn Anas, following the pattern of all the Sufi masters who preceded him, Shaykh ʿAbd al-Qādir holds weekly gatherings of *dhikr* (invocation of Allah), in which the Qurʾān and *wird* (recitation of a litany of *dhikr*) are recited. Poems from the *dīwāns* (collections of poems), including al-Buṣayrī's *Burda* (Poem of the Cloak), are sung, the *ʿimāra* (a form of *dhikr* involving the movement of the limbs) is done, and discourses are given. And moussems (festivals of *dhikr*), which are attended by his disciples from around the world, are held on an annual basis.

All of this is underpinned by that basic pattern of Sufi epistemology, which, as we have seen, has always lain at the heart of every true manifestation of Sufism throughout the Islamic history: the progression from *ʿilm al-ʿaql* to *ʿilm al-aḥwāl* to *ʿilm al-asrār* and, finally through the experience of *fanāʾ* to *baqāʾ* the goal of Sufism – to live in this world with complete awareness of the Divine Presence at every moment.

Postface

This has been a book on Sufi epistemology and its encounter with modernity in the *ṭarīqa* of Shaykh ʿAbd al-Qādir. It is based on an analysis of his writings, an interview with him and interviews with scholars who have researched his work. In addition to this I spent time in Cape Town in South Africa where I recorded my observations at the institutions established by him and the Murābiṭūn community. At the *zāwiya*, mosque, and market established by him there and at Dallas College, which he also founded, I met many of his followers and was able to gain an insight into the daily lives and work of community members. This book is what resulted from all of this research and my direct exposure to the Shaykh and his teaching in the existential situation of its unfolding in the present time. The material covered in it has been extensive and it seemed appropriate to me that I should end it with a general summary of its contents.

Sufi Epistemology

The essential element of Sufi epistemology is unveiling and the prototype for this unveiling is the ontological experience of the Prophet Muḥammad ﷺ. The revelation of the Qur'ān to the Prophet Muḥammad ﷺ is the result of an ontological experience in which God revealed His Word and Himself directly to the Prophet ﷺ. The text of the Qur'ān is the primary source of knowledge for all epistemological endeavours in Islam. The Qur'ānic text and how it was acted upon by the Prophet ﷺ and his Companions have been approached very differently by jurists, exegetes, linguists, grammarians, theologians, philosophers, theosophers and Sufis in the history of Islam. The Sufis have derived from it a cosmology in which there are three realms of existence, namely *mulk*, *malakūt* and *jabarūt*. The *nafs* inhabits the *mulk* and the means by which it perceives its realm of existence is through *ʿilm al-ʿaql*. The *rūḥ* inhabits the *malakūt* and the means of perceiving its realm is *ʿilm al-aḥwāl* and the *sirr* inhabits the *jabarūt* and perceives its realm by means of *ʿilm al-asrār*.

Beyond the *mulk*, *malakūt* and *jabarūt*, that is, beyond space, time and phenomena, is God. The Sufi's goal is to have a direct experience of God's presence. In Sufi terminology empiricism and rationalism are categorized as *ʿilm al-ʿaql* and to reach God requires that one go beyond empirical and rationalistic discourse and on to higher levels of knowledge. The higher levels of knowledge referred to are *ʿilm al-aḥwāl*, *ʿilm al-asrār*, *fanā'* and *baqā'*. The knowledge and experience of the *rūḥ* and the *sirr* are acquired by taste (*dhawq*) and states (*aḥwāl*). The Divine Presence of God however, is experienced only through *fanā'* because God is beyond the three worlds of Sufi cosmology, that is, beyond all phenomenal existence. The taste of *fanā'* is not anything like the taste that is experienced by the *rūḥ* and the *sirr*. Whilst the term taste applied to it is the same, its reality is nevertheless fundamentally different. Arrival at God is dependent on the annihilation of the self and its capacities. Annihilation in the context of Sufism is understood to involve the cessation of the Sufi's personal actions, attributes and essence. When the self is annihilated all that remains is God consciousness. This means that in *fanā'* God discloses Himself to the Sufi so that he or she has the vision of the Divine Presence.

The experience of *fanā'* is intuitive thereby differentiating it from the statements and general conclusions of modern philosophy and science, which are based on discursive reason and sense experience. *Fanā'* occurs within the synergy between the loss of subjective consciousness and the disappearance of entities themselves. In the state of *fanā'* God puts into the human being, without incarnation, a spiritual substance (*laṭīfa*) from His Essence and reveals an aspect of Himself to that spiritual substance. In this way God reveals Himself to Himself and at this stage the subject/object dichotomy ceases to exist. *Baqā'* pertains to the subsistence of the Sufi in God after he or she has returned from the experience of *fanā'*. After *fanā'* the Sufi is able to speak about God with firm knowledge which was granted through the Divine Self-disclosure experienced in it. It follows from this that for the Sufi, also, *fanā'* is an ontological experience in which God reveals His Word and Himself directly to him or her. Shaykh 'Abd al-Qādir has indicated that the knowledge and experience of *fanā'* comes from praxis, *himma*, *maḥabba* and the intersection of natural time and the time of destiny.

Based on the Qur'ānic revelation, Shaykh 'Abd al-Qādir is of the view that God has created the world as a stable and secure home with ample provision for all human beings. God has also imbued human beings with *fiṭra*, an inborn natural predisposition to fulfil their destinies which are predetermined by their life-forms. In Qur'ānic terminology, to act in harmony with one's *fiṭra* is called service or worship. All beliefs and behaviour for the Sufi exist within this context or framework of understanding. In pre-modern Islamic society this background understanding allowed believers to function in a way in which there was no distinction between experience and its construed meaning. The natural world displayed order, design, divine purpose and action. The existence of God and His direct involvement in the cosmos were apparent.

The Qur'ān outlined what humans need to do in order to attain direct knowledge of God. The Prophet Muḥammad ﷺ delivered the Qur'ānic message from God, which contained laws by which human societies could function harmoniously both amongst themselves and with their environment. Madīna al-Munawwara – the Illuminated City – was established by the Prophet ﷺ and set up as a model community for future generations. Its socio/spiritual fabric was based on an ethos wherein the inward and outward sciences were unified. This Madinan phenomenon was recorded by Mālik ibn Anas in his book *al-Muwaṭṭa'*. Madinan society was a law-governed society and the legal judgements of the Prophet ﷺ were based upon the Qur'ānic revelations and came to constitute Islamic law. The law guaranteed the movement of wealth among all sections of the society implying the end of the oligarchy that had prevailed in Arabia until that time.

Epistemologies of Modernity

Shaykh 'Abd al-Qādir has pointed out that all people, including modern Muslims, have taken on a materialistic, technological way of thinking, devoid of inwardness and spirituality, a way of thinking that has its underpinnings in Kantian and Cartesian philosophy, Newtonian physics, Darwinian biology, Freudian psychology, Smith's capitalist free market economics and Hobbes' political theories, amongst others in a similar vein. It is upon these epistemological building blocks that the whole edifice of modern civilization has been constructed. Modern politics, law, education, economics, medicine and psychology were built on these philosophical and scientific foundations.

In their search for answers, for the 'truth', philosophers applied themselves to the study of epistemology and metaphysics. Descartes claimed that the essential quality of the human being was thinking and Kant explained how the process of thinking worked. Hegel challenged Kant's exposition indicating that the path to Truth must involve ontology and Nietzsche pointed out that theology, the path to Being prevalent in the Europe of his time, had ended in nihilism because of Western philosophy's reliance on Plato's metaphysics. For Heidegger, modernity was characterized by subjectivity, whereby modern man interprets himself as the ground and measure of truth. This subjectivity freed human beings from the theocentrism of traditional Christian society, but the authority of revelation was replaced by the subjective perceptions, opinions, reflections and feelings of human beings. Subjectivity, whilst freeing humans from religious authority, created more terrible and universal forms of bondage, which culminated in a global totalitarianism of technology, will to power and total war.

Although famous philosophers such as David Hume, John Stuart Mill, Bertrand Russell, Alfred Jules Ayer and a host of others have made contributions to the philosophical study of epistemology, there are still numerous questions that remain unanswered. These questions relate to the nature of reason, the nature of truth, the justification of induction and deduction, observation, perception, experiment and evidence. Fearing reprisal from the Catholic Church, modernist thinkers found ways of separating science and religion, implying that religion dealt with spiritual matters and science dealt with the material world. This attitude opened up the debate about the relation of religion to science and the scientific attitude ultimately triumphed over religious belief as the final arbiter of thought and action.

Although this can be seen merely as the arrival of secularism, it was effectively the victory of atheism over religion because, once the power of God over individual thought and action is denied, religion ceases to be a vital factor in human life, even though some individual belief in God may remain. It is in this sense that

Nietzsche stated 'God is dead.' With the loss of belief in God and the collapse of the values that were built upon that belief, Nietzsche predicted the rise of nihilism, which he defined as a repudiation of value, meaning, knowledge, truth, virtue, philosophy and art.

Shaykh 'Abd al-Qādir believes that modernity, through its rationalist and empiricist epistemologies, has subverted human nature and the social, political and economic institutions that were established prior to the modern period. In his analysis of modern society, Shaykh 'Abd al-Qādir points out that the major outcome of the lack of adherence to Divine law was the permitting of usury and this made it possible for bankers to accrue enormous wealth. The banks generated their wealth through usurious transactions such as fractional reserve banking, interest, speculation, derivatives, leveraging, futures trading, etc. Governments gave privately owned Central Banks control over the money supply on condition that they guaranteed government expenditure.

When that happened, the power nexus of states moved from the political to the economic. The entire world was incorporated into the global capitalist system irrespective of the political system espoused by the various national states, be it democracy, monarchy, dictatorship or one-party-totalitarianism. Shaykh 'Abd al-Qādir explains that in the political sphere there was a gradual progression from monarchy to democracy to oligarchy. The operational model of political economy in modern society became oligarchy. In the West, liberal democracy simply acts as the public relations interface for it. The national state and its institutions, both executive and judiciary, have no access to or control over the financial system. The financial élite works closely with the commodities and media élites to sustain their global political and economic domination for their mutual benefit.

Shaykh 'Abd al-Qādir holds the oligarchs responsible for

poisoning the oceans, polluting the air, stripping the forests bare, the pandemic of poverty and worldwide civil war. He points out, however, that the collapse of the capitalist system and its public relations apparatus of liberal democracy began in 1945 and the two hundred year old religion of modernity came to an end in 2008 with the global financial crisis. The collapse of the structure will gather momentum with the passage of time.

The Search for New Epistemologies

Philosophers and scientists have been addressing the paradoxes and contradictions that they have encountered in the course of their work. We find these paradoxes and contradictions, for example, in Heidegger's and Russel's philosophy, Gödel's mathematics, Turing's artificial intelligence and Damasio's neuroscience. From the beginning of the twentieth century physicists have been dealing with the paradoxical nature of matter. Based upon research on these paradoxes, an outline of what is known as 'complexity theory' or 'nonlinear dynamics' is becoming apparent. Whereas science and mathematics are only now beginning to develop a unified approach to overcome the paradoxes that they have encountered, Shaykh 'Abd al-Qādir, like the Sufis before him, sees the need to join the two paradoxically opposing perspectives, as Sufis have always done in the face of the apparent incompatibility of *tanzīh* and *tashbīh*.

There has been a dichotomy in the modern social sciences, since the Enlightenment, between objective social scientific knowledge and the influence that subjective historical and cultural factors have on that knowledge, that is, between the positivist and interpretive approaches. The abiding conundrum faced by the social sciences is to find a way of resolving the dichotomy between rationalism and subjectivism. Whilst classical social theories dealt with macro-level issues such as capitalism, the national state, globalism, order, inequality, freedom and change, they have not been able to resolve the dualities between reason and emotion and between the objective and the subjective. The epistemological poverty of the modern social sciences can be traced back to the paradigm of the mechanical sciences, which was generally adopted as the model for all aspects of social organization.

Amongst the Greek founders of Western philosophy there was a close relationship between revelation and philosophy in both their thought and lives. Their thought and their ways of life are in complete contrast to the rationalism and empiricism of modern philosophy. Muslim philosophers advocated the belief that reality is best apprehended by intuition rather than discursive knowledge. Intuition is the perception of something directly without mediation. It is the process by which the quiddity of things outside the human mind can be apprehended directly thereby making them intelligible. This process does include sense perception, which is the lowest modality of intuition, but the highest stage of cognition transcends rationalistic discourse and the power of reason.

For Muslim philosophers (such as Mulla Sadra) it is in an ontological state of human consciousness that the constitutive dualism of the subject/object relationship is overcome and submerged into a unitary simplex. The ontological foundation for epistemology is a major theme in Islamic philosophy, which focuses on the fundamental pre-epistemic question regarding the relation between knowledge and the possessor of knowledge. It answers the question of how a knowing subject becomes united with, or is related to, an external object by positing an ontological foundation for human awareness.

Shaykh ʿAbd al-Qādir's Contributions to Epistemology

One of the questions I have addressed is that of whether the epistemologies of modernity and Sufism are in conflict with each other. The question is a good point of departure for a discussion of different types of epistemology but, at a deeper level, the question itself is flawed if, by it, we regard them as mutually exclusive categories, in the way that science and religion are regarded in popular usage. From a Sufi perspective, although rationalism and empiricism, the sources of modernist epistemology, also constitute epistemic sources in Sufism, modern epistemologies based on rationalism and empiricism are limited in the sense that they have no way of reconciling the paradoxes that we encounter in philosophy, the natural sciences and the social sciences. Sufism, however, does provide the means by which they can be reconciled.

Shaykh 'Abd al-Qādir has shown that the means for resolving the key questions of social science, philosophy and theory can be found in the writings of Mālik ibn Anas. The unification of the inward (spiritual) and outward (socio-political and economic) aspects of human beings was integral to Mālik's teaching of the *'amal ahl al-Madīna*. For Mālik, practice or behaviour is evidence of knowledge, or to put it differently, the *'amal ahl al-Madīna* guarantees that theory and practice are inseparable. Religion in Mālik's view was not something people thought but something they did and the truth of religion was acquired through practical action, which in turn led to the discovery of deeper levels of being.

Shaykh 'Abd al-Qādir is of the view that this is clearly the moment when a new *'aṣabiyya* will arise in response to the nihilism of the age we are in. In a world that has lost its moral and Divine imperatives, Shaykh 'Abd al-Qādir sees the Muslims as people who can replace materialism, consumerism and nihilism with a new nomos or with the *dīn al-fiṭra* (the religion of one's innate disposition) with respect for everyone irrespective of gender, safety for children, protection of human beings by the rule of law, and defending the ecosphere from destruction, pollution and over-exploitation. For Shaykh 'Abd al-Qādir the new nomos will be established by the people who are estranged from contemporary society (the New Bedouins), on the basis of the *'amal ahl al-madīna.*

Whilst Sufi masters guide their disciples to direct experience of God they also perform an important social function by their broad participation in society. Shaykh 'Abd al-Qādir has taken the rules of al-Junayd and applied them within a contemporary social and historical context. To further the goals of establishing the new nomos, Shaykh 'Abd al-Qādir has founded the Murābiṭūn Da'wa Movement with communities in twenty countries. The principle objectives of this movement include *bay'a* (allegiance) to an *amīr* (leader), the restoration of the *zakāt* tax and the establishment of the *'amal ahl al-Madīna.* At the same time he has a busy and vibrant *zāwiya* and in order to supplement the processes described by Mālik ibn Anas, Shaykh 'Abd al-Qādir holds weekly gatherings of *dhikr* and annual moussems.

The legacy of Shaykh 'Abd al-Qādir lies in his identification of a devolutionary process that has produced a different kind of human being. He has pointed out that the existential crisis of modern society is mirrored in Roman history. Roman society devolved from being a naturally functioning society to adopting a metaphysical pseudo-reality and then sinking into a metaphysical fantasy. It is a process that begins in nature then turns to fantasy and ends up in metaphysics. The process starts with monarchy, becomes democracy and ends in oligarchy. He has also shown how the British Empire and the contemporary American Empire have repeated the exact same pattern. It is now a global reality and humankind requires an antidote to wake itself up from the metaphysical pseudo-reality and metaphysical fantasy that it is transfixed by. Shaykh 'Abd al-Qādir has provided the key to enable just that to happen.

Notes

Introduction

1 Muḥyī al-Dīn ibn al-'Arabī, *al-Futūḥāt al-Makkiyya*, (section on 'The Mysteries of Bearing Witness to the Oneness of God and Prophethood of Muḥammad') tr. Aisha Bewley, *Great Books of the Islamic World*, Chicago, 2002. p. 2

2 The Caliph 'Umar reported that "He (the angel Gabriel) said, then tell me about *iḥsān*. He (the Prophet Muḥammad) said: It is to worship God as though you are seeing Him for while you do not see Him, He sees you." (*Ṣaḥīḥ Muslim* Collection)

3 Alvin Plantinga, "Religion and Science", *Stanford Encyclopaedia of Philosophy*, First published Mar 12, 2007; substantive revision Apr 27, 2010, http://plato.stanford.edu/entries/religion-science/

4 Adi Setia, "Al-Attas' Philosophy of Science: An Extended Outline", Islam and Science, Dec. 2003

5 Ibn Rushd, *Faṣl al-maqāl*, tr. George F. Hourani in *Averroes: On the Harmony of Religion and Philosophy*, Luzac, London, 1976

6 Alvin Plantinga, "Religion and Science", *Stanford Encyclopaedia of Philosophy*, First published Mar 12, 2007; substantive revision Apr 27, 2010, http://plato.stanford.edu/entries/religion-science/

7 Joseph Lumbard, "The Decline of Knowledge and the Rise of Ideology in the Modern World", *Islam, Fundamentalism, and the Betrayal of Tradition: Essays by Western Muslim Scholars*, World Wisdom Inc., Bloomington, 2004, p. 68

11 Reported statements of the Prophet Muḥammad

12 Sari Nuseibeh, "Epistemology," *History of Islamic Philosophy*, ed. Seyyed Hossein Nasr and Oliver Leaman, Routledge, 1996, p. 826

13 Abū Ḥāmid al-Ghazālī, cited in Alexander Knysh, *Islamic Mysticism: A Short History*, Brill, 1999, p. 313

Chapter 1 – The Chain of Masters

1 This diagram is taken from *The Meaning of Man* by 'Alī al-Jamal, Diwan Press, Norwich, 1977, p. 443

2 Qur'ān 10:26

3 Reported speech of the Prophet Muḥammad in answer to questions from the Archangel Gabriel

4 *Ṣaḥīḥ Muslim*

5 Mālik ibn Anas, in Abdalhaqq Bewley, *Islam: Its Basic Practices and Beliefs*, Ta-Ha Publishers Ltd., London 2008, p. 228-9

6 Qur'ān 7: 143. All translations of the Qur'ān are taken from Aisha and Abdalhaqq Bewley's translation entitled *The Noble Qur'ān – A New Rendering of its Meaning in English*, Bookwork, Norwich, 1999. The numbering is according to the Warsh reading.

7 It is obligatory because it is spoken of in the Qur'ān 7: 143

8 Abū Bakr al-Kalābādhī, *The Doctrine of the Sufis*, tr. A.J. Arberry, Cambridge University Press, Cambridge, 1935, p. 24

9 Plural of hadith, reported speech of the Prophet Muḥammad

10 The Prophet said, "Verily ye shall see your Lord as ye see the moon on the night of its fullness, without confusion in the vision of Him." Abū Bakr al-Kalābādhī, *The Doctrine of the Sufis*, p.25

11 Qur'ān 6: 104

12 'Abd al-Qādir al-Sufi, *The Book of Tawḥīd*, Madina Press, Cape Town, 2006, p.119

13 'Abd al-Qādir al-Sufi, *The Book of Tawḥīd*, p.120

14 Qur'ān 17: 1

15 Qāḍī 'Iyāḍ ibn Mūsā al-Yaḥṣubī, *Muhammad, Messenger of Allah, translation of Ash-Shifā of Qāḍī 'Iyāḍ*, Madinah Press, Granada, 1991, p. 91

16 Qur'ān 53: 1-12

17 'Abd al-Qādir al-Sufi, *The Book of Safar*, Madina Press, Cape Town, 2009, p.30

18 Majid 'Alī Khan, *The Pious Caliphs*, Islamic Book Publishers, Kuwait, 1982, p. 224

19 Majid 'Alī Khan, *The Pious Caliphs*, p. 222

20 Abū al-Ḥasan al-Hujwīrī, *Kashf al-Maḥjūb of al-Hujwīrī*, tr. RA Nicholson, Luzac & Co. Ltd., London, 1976, p. 20

21 Abū al-Ḥasan al-Hujwīrī, *Kashf al-Maḥjūb of al-Hujwīrī*, p. 45

22 'Abd al-Qādir al-Sufi, A., *The Hundred Steps*, Madinah Press, Kuala Lumpur, 1998, p. 1

23 H. Ritter, "Ḥasan al-Baṣrī", EI2

24 Ibn 'Abd Rabbihi, *Al-'Iqd al-Farīd*, Bk. I, pp.25-26 tr. J.A. Williams in *Themes of Islamic Civilization*, University of California Press, Berkeley, 1971, p. 70

25 Abū Nu'aym al-Isfahānī, *Tadhkirat al-Awliyā'*, tr. GH Haddad, Bk. VI, pp. 149-155 at http://www.sunnah.org/history/Scholars/story_of_habib_the_persian.htm

26 A retreat where a Sufi master instructs his disciples

27 Abū Nu'aym al-Isfahānī, *Tadhkirat al-Awliyā'*, tr. GH Haddad, Bk. VI, pp. 149-155

28 Abū al-Ḥasan al-Hujwīrī, A., *Kashf al-Maḥjūb of al-Hujwīrī*, p. 74

29 Abū al-Ḥasan al-Hujwīrī, A., *Kashf al-Maḥjūb of al-Hujwīrī*, p. 89

30 Generation following the Prophet and his companions

31 Abū al-Ḥasan al-Hujwīrī, A., *Kashf al-Maḥjūb of al-Hujwīrī*, p. 109

32 Ibn al-Jawzī, *Ṣifat al-Ṣafwa*, tr. G.H. Haddad at http://www.sunnah.org/history/Scholars/Dāwūd_al-Tai.pdf

33 Ibn al-Jawzī, *Ṣifat al-Ṣafwa*, tr. G.H. Haddad at http://www.sunnah.org/history/Scholars/Dāwūd_al-Tai.pdf

34 Abū al-Ḥasan al-Hujwīrī, A., *Kashf al-Maḥjūb of al-Hujwīrī*, p. 110

35 'Abd al-Karīm al-Qushayrī, A., *Risāla*, http://privat.bahnhof.se/wb042294/Texter/bionotes/bio_ma3ruf_karkhi.html

36 Abū Bakr al-Baghdādī, *Iqtidā' al-'ilm al-'amal*, article 123, http://islamicemirate.com/resources/ islamic-quotes/232

37 Fariduddin 'Aṭṭār, *Tadhkirat al-Awliyā'*, tr A.J Arberry, Omphaloskepsis, Ames, Iowa, 2000, p. 213

38 Abū Ṭālib al-Makkī, *Qūt al-qulūb*, v. 4, p. 61, tr. AH Abdel-Kader, *The Life, Personality and Writings of Al-Junayd*, Luzac & Co. Ltd., London, 1976. p. 15

39 Abū Ṭālib al-Makkī, *Qūt al-qulūb*, v. 3, p. 82, tr. AH Abdel-Kader, *The Life, Personality and Writings of Al-Junayd*, p. 15

40 Ibn Khallikan, *Wafāyāt al-a'yān*, http://www.spiritualfoundation.net/sufisshaykhs2.htm#111141853

41 Abū al-Ḥasan al-Hujwīrī, *Kashf al-Maḥjūb of al-Hujwīrī*, p. 110

42 Abū al-Qāsim al-Qushayrī, *Risāla*, tr. AH Abdel-Kader, *The Life, Personality and Writings of Al-Junayd*, Luzac & Co. Ltd., London, 1976, p. 10

43 Abū al-Ḥasan al-Hujwīrī, *Kashf al-Maḥjūb of al-Hujwīrī*, p. 128

44 Tāj al-Dīn al-Subkī, *Ṭabaqāt*, v. 2, p. 36, tr. AH Abdel-Kader, *The Life, Personality and Writings of Al-Junayd*, p. 2

45 Abū al-Ḥasan al-Hujwīrī, *Kashf al-Maḥjūb of al-Hujwīrī*, p. 130

46 Abū al-Qāsim al-Junayd, *Al-Rasā'il*, p.172

47 Qur'ān 7: 172

48 Abū al-Qāsim al-Junayd, *al-Rasā'il*, p. 76

49 A more detailed discussion of al-Junayd's views on *fanā'* will be undertaken in p.46

50 Abū al-Qāsim al-Junayd, *al-Rasā'il*, p. 172

51 Ahmet T. Karamustafa, *Sufism: The Formative Period*, Edinburgh University Press, Edinburgh, 2007, p. 18

52 Abū al-Qāsim al-Junayd, *Al-Rasā'il*, p. 142

53 Abū al-Qāsim al-Junayd, *Al-Rasā'il*, p. 143

54 Abū al-Qāsim al-Junayd, *Al-Rasā'il*, p. 142

55 Ahmet T. Karamustafa, *Sufism: The Formative Period*, p. 18

56 Qāḍī 'Iyāḍ ibn Mūsā al-Yaḥṣubī, *Tartīb al-Madārik*, http://bewley.virtualave.net/madarikcont.html

57 Qāḍī 'Iyāḍ ibn Mūsā al-Yaḥṣubī, *Tartīb al-Madārik*, http://bewley.virtualave.net/madarikcont.html

58 Qāḍī 'Iyāḍ ibn Mūsā al-Yaḥṣubī, *Tartīb al-Madārik*, http://bewley.virtualave

59 Abū al-Ḥasan al-Hujwīrī, *Kashf al-Maḥjūb of al-Hujwīrī*, p. 330

60 Manṣūr al-Ḥallāj (858-922) who was executed on the orders of the Abbasid Caliph al-Muqtadir for blasphemy.

61 See page 13

62 'Abd al-Qādir al-Sufi, *The Book of 'Amal*, pp. 69-70

63 'Abd al-Qādir al-Sufi, *The Book of 'Amal*, Madinah Press, Cape Town, 2007, p. 95

64 Qur'ān 9: 128

65 'Abd al-Qādir al-Sufi, *The Book of 'Amal*, pp. 71-72

66 'Abd al-Qādir al-Sufi, *The Book of 'Amal*, p. 44

67 'Abd al-Qādir al-Sufi, *The Book of 'Amal*, pp. 49-50

68 'Abd al-Qādir al-Sufi, *The Book of 'Amal*, p. 49

69 Qur'ān 51: 56 "*I have created jinn and man to worship Me.*"

70 'Abd al-Qādir al-Sufi, *Root Islamic Education*, Madinah Press, London, 1993, p. 113

71 Qur'ān. 13: 12

72 'Abd al-Qādir al-Sufi, *Root Islamic Education*, p.3

73 Yasin Dutton, *The Origins of Islamic Law: The Qur'ān, the Muwaṭṭa' and Madīnan 'Amal*, Curzon Press, Richmond, 1999, p. 3

74 Abdalhaqq Bewley, *Madhhabs Today*, BTBIL, Gabarone, 2009, p. 45

75 "He who practises *tasawwuf* without learning *fiqh* corrupts his faith, while he who learns *fiqh* without practising *tasawwuf* corrupts himself. Only he who

combines the two proves true." Mālik ibn Anas, cited in Aisha Bewley, *Islam: The Empowering of Women*, Ta-Ha Publishers, London, 1999, p. 48

76 Qāḍī 'Iyāḍ ibn Mūsā al-Yaḥṣubī, *Tartīb al-Madārik*, cited in 'Abd al-Qādir al-Sufi, *Root Islamic Education*, 1993, pp. 123-125

77 'Abd al-Qādir al-Sufi, *Root Islamic Education*, 1993, p. 125

78 'Abd al-Qādir al-Sufi, *Root Islamic Education*, 1993, p. 113

79 Qur'ān 40: 64

80 "A star has no option but to behave the way it does. The planets have no choice as to their orbit. The same applies in the mineral, vegetable and animal worlds on the earth's surface. A daffodil cannot become a rose. A donkey cannot change into a horse." Abdalhaqq Bewley, *Islam: Its Basic Practices and Beliefs*, Ta-Ha, London, 2008, p. 8

81 'Abd al-Qādir al-Sufi (written under his family name Ian Dallas), "The Gestalt of Freedom", *Collected Works*, Budgate Press, Erasmia, 2005, p. 824

82 "A human being is as prepared by his form for talking as a bird is for flying or a fish for swimming. Modern research has shown that language is not something acquired but rather that linguistic capacity is genetically inherent in a child and emerges gradually." Abdalhaqq Bewley, *Islam: Its Basic Practices and Beliefs*, p.9

83 Muḥammad Iqbal, *The Reconstruction of Religious Thought in Islam*, Muḥammad Ashraf, Lahore, 1977, p. 125

84 Qur'ān 33:21

85 Qur'ān 2: 142

86 'Abd al-Qādir al-Sufi, *The Book of 'Amal*, p. 120

87 Here he is referring to Qur'ān 103: 1-3 which says "*By the Late Afternoon, truly man is in loss – except for those who believe and do right actions and urge each other to the truth and urge each other to patience.*"

88 'Abd al-Qādir al-Sufi, *The Book of 'Amal*, p. 97

89 Qur'ān 90: 12-18

Chapter 2 – Sufi Epistemology: the Sources of Sufi Knowledge

1 Qur'ān 2: 268

2 Ibn Mājah, *Muqaddima*, 17

3 "I seek refuge in God from knowledge which has no benefit." said the Prophet Muḥammad. This hadith is found in the collection of Muslim, *Kitāb al-dhikr*, 73. The benefit referred to here is for this world (*dunyā*) and the Hereafter (*ākhira*).

4 Referred to in ʻUthmān dan Fodio, *Handbook on Islām, Īmān and Iḥsān*, Diwan Press, Norwich, 1978, p. 8

5 Qur'ān 16: 89

6 Francis Edward Peters, "The Greek and Syriac Background", *History of Islamic Philosophy*, ed. S.H. Nasr & O. Leaman, Routledge, London, 1996, p. 40

7 Sari Nuseibeh, "Epistemology", *History of Islamic Philosophy*, p. 454

8 Roxanne D. Marcotte, "Reason (*ʻaql*) and Direct Intuition (*mushāhada*) in the works of Shihāb al-Dīn al-Suhrawardī (d. 587/1191)", *Reason and Inspiration in Islam: Theology, Philosophy and Mysticism in Muslim Thought*, ed. Todd Lawson, IB Tauris, London, 2005, pp. 228-229

9 Hossein Ziai, "Shihāb al-Dīn al-Suhrawardī: founder of the Illuminationist school", *History of Islamic Philosophy*, p. 829

10 Alexander Knysh, *Islamic Mysticism: A Short History*, Brill, Leiden, 2000, p. 311

11 Mentioned by Alexander Knysh, *Islamic Mysticism: A Short History*, p. 312

12 Qur'ān 50: 22

13 Aisha Bewley, *Glossary of Islamic Terms*, Ta-Ha Publishers, London, 1998, p. 213

14 Abū al-Qāsim al-Qushayrī cited by Alexander Knysh, *Islamic Mysticism: A Short History*, p.311

15 Abū Ḥāmid al-Ghazālī cited in Alexander Knysh, *Islamic Mysticism: A Short History*, pp. 313-314

16 Louis Gardet, "Kalb", EI2

17 Muḥammad Waziri, quoted by Leonard Lewisohn in "The Spiritual Journey in Kubrawi Sufism", *Reason and Inspiration in Islam: Theology, Philosophy and Mysticism in Muslim Thought*, p. 368

18 Close companion of the Prophet Muḥammad ﷺ.

19 Muḥyī al-Dīn ibn al-ʻArabī, M., *al-Futūḥāt al-Makkiyya*, quoted by Richard J.A. Mcgregor, "Notes on the Transmission of Mystical Philosophy, *Reason and Inspiration in Islam: Theology, Philosophy and Mysticism in Muslim Thought*, pp. 385-386

20 Muḥyī al-Dīn ibn al-ʻArabī, M., *al-Futūḥāt al-Makkiyya*, quoted by Richard J.A. McGregor, "Notes on the Transmission of Mystical Philosophy, *Reason and Inspiration in Islam: Theology, Philosophy and Mysticism in Muslim Thought*, p. 383

21 ʻAbd al-Qādir al-Sufi, A., *Root Islamic Education*, 1993, p. 125

22 Aḥmad ibn ʻAjība's commentary on Ibn al-Banna's *al-Futūḥāt al-ilāhiyya fī sharḥ al-mabāḥith al-aṣliyya* published as, *The Basic Research*, Madinah Press,

Cape Town, 1998, p. 20

23 'Abd al-Qādir al-Sufi, *The Hundred Steps*, p. 7

24 'Abd al-Qādir al-Sufi, *The Hundred Steps*, p. 7

25 'Abd al-Qādir al-Sufi, *The Hundred Steps*, p. 2

26 'Abd al-Qādir al-Sufi, *The Hundred Steps*, p. 3

27 'Abd al-Qādir al-Sufi, *The Hundred Steps*, p. 4

28 Aḥmad ibn 'Ajība, *The Basic Research*, p. 20

29 A collection of poetry

30 'Abd al-Qādir al-Sufi, *The Hundred Steps*, p.52

31 'Abd al-Qādir al-Sufi, A., *The Hundred Steps*, p. 27

32 Fritjof Capra, quoted by 'Abd al-Qādir al-Sufi, *The Way of Muḥammad*, Madinah Press, London, 1995, pp. 211-212

33 'Abd al-Qādir al-Sufi, *The Hundred Steps*, p. 24

34 'Abd al-Qādir al-Sufi, *The Hundred Steps*, p. 24

35 'Abd al-Qādir al-Sufi, *The Hundred Steps*, p. 25

36 *Sidrat al-muntahā* is a Qur'ānic term representing "a lote tree above the seventh heaven near the Paradise, denoting the limit of Being and the cessation of form itself; the place where the knowledge of every creature, even the angels close to Allah, stops." Aisha Bewley, *Glossary of Islamic Terms*, Ta- Ha, London, 1998, p. 64

37 *Mawāzīn* are the scales set up to weigh the actions of people on the Day of Judgment.

38 *'Arsh* is "the ceiling of all creatures and the greatest of them. The Throne contains immense expanses, height and resplendent beauty but it is beyond the power of any human being to describe it or imagine its form. ... The throne has bearers who carry it and Allah Almighty is settled on it, in a way that is beyond definition or concept." Aisha Bewley, *Glossary of Islamic Terms*, p. 64

39 'Abd al-Qādir al-Sufi, *The Hundred Steps*, p. 28

40 the pure maidens of Paradise

41 'Abd al-'Azīz al-Dabbāgh cited by Aḥmad ibn al-Mubārak al-Lamaṭī, *Al-Dhabab al-Ibrīz min Kalām Sayyidī 'Abd al-'Azīz al-Dabbāgh*, tr. John O'Kane and Bernd Radtke, Brill, Leiden, 2007, pp. 131-132

42 "Spiritual aspiration, yearning to be free of illusion; highest energy impulse in a human to reconnect with reality." Aisha Bewley, *Glossary of Islamic Terms*, Ta-Ha, London, 1998, p. 210

43 'Abd al-Qādir al-Sufi, *The Hundred Steps*, p. 26

44 'Abd al-Qādir al-Sufi, *The Hundred Steps*, p. 26

45 'Abd al-Qādir al-Sufi, *The Hundred Steps*, p. 29

46 One example is the verse: *"He is the First and the Last. The Outward and the Inward."* (Qur'ān 57: 3)

47 Abū al-Qāsim al-Junayd, *Al-Rasā'il*, tr. A.H. Abdel-Kader in *The Life, Personality and Writings of al-Junayd*, Luzac, London, 1976, p. 172

48 Aḥmad Ibn 'Ajība, A., *The Basic Research*, p. 26

49 "Self-manifestation, presencing, self-disclosing, the unveiling of a spiritual reality in the realm of vision, a showing forth of the secrets of the One in existence." Aisha Bewley, *Glossary of Islamic Terms*, p. 224

50 'Abd al-Qādir al-Sufi, *The Hundred Steps*, p. 78. Italics are the author's own.

51 Muḥammad ibn al-Ḥabīb, *The Diwan of Shaykh Muḥammad ibn al-Ḥabīb*, Madinah Press, Cape Town, 2001, p. 75

52 Muḥammad ibn al-Ḥabīb, *The Diwan of Shaykh Muḥammad ibn al-Ḥabīb*, p. 87

53 Manṣūr al-Ḥallāj, *Ṭawāsīn al-Ḥallāj*, tr. A. Bewley, Taj Company, Delhi, 1982, p. 46

54 Manṣūr al-Ḥallāj, *Ṭawāsīn al-Ḥallāj*, p. 25

55 'Abd al-Qādir al-Sufi, Introduction to *Ṭawāsīn al-Ḥallāj*, p. 25

56 Muḥyī al-Dīn ibn al-'Arabī, cited in Mir Valliuddin, *Qur'ānic Sufism*, Motilal Banarsidass, Delhi, p. 46

57 Qur'ān 57: 3

58 Muḥyī al-Dīn ibn al-'Arabī, cited in Mir Valliuddin, *Qur'ānic Sufism*, p. 71

59 Abū al-Qāsim al-Junayd, *al-Rasā'il*, p.172

60 Abū Bakr al-Kalābādhī, *The Doctrine of the Sufis*, p. 3

61 Muḥyī al-Dīn ibn al-'Arabī, M., *al-Futūḥāt al-Makkiyya*, section on 'The Mysteries of Bearing Witness to the Oneness of God and Prophethood of Muḥammad', p. 26

62 'Abd al-Qādir al-Sufi, *The Hundred Steps*, p. 80

Chapter 3 – Sufi Epistemology and Cosmology

1 Alexander Knysh, *Ibn 'Arabī in the Later Islamic Tradition: The Making of a Polemical Image in Medieval Islam*, SUNY Press, Albany, 1999, p.1

2 Alexander Knysh, *Ibn 'Arabī in the Later Islamic Tradition: The Making of a Polemical Image in Medieval Islam*, p.1

3 Words of God reported by the Prophet Muḥammad that are not part of the Qur'ān

4 Mulla 'Alī al-Qārī [the renowned Ḥanafī hadith scholar] said that the meaning of this statement is authentic and for the Qur'ānic commentator Mujāhid the knowing referred to is *ma'rifa*, the gnostic knowledge of God.

5 Aisha Bewley, *Glossary of Islamic Terms*, Ta-Ha Publishers, London, 1998, p. 180

6 It has to be noted however, that much of Ibn al-ʿArabī's cosmology resembles that of al-Fārābī (870- 950) and Ibn Sīnā (980-1037). According to al-Fārābī, God communicates existence to other beings through emanation (*fayḍ*). Emanation owes much to the Neoplatonic view of the cosmos, particularly to Plotinus' (204-270 C.E.) concept of cosmology.

7 Refer to William Chittick, *Ibn al-ʿArabī's Metaphysics of Imagination: The Sufi Path of Knowledge*, SUNY Press, Albany, 1989, p. 226

8 Beyond ordinary time

9 See Qur'ān 17: 1 and 53: 1-12

10 Qur'ān 18: 9-26

11 Muḥyī al-Dīn ibn al-ʿArabī, *al-Futūḥāt al-Makkiyya*, tr. by Mohamed Haj Yousef in *Ibn ʿArabī – Time and Cosmology*, Routledge, Oxon, 2008, p. 46

12 Islamic theological school founded by Abū al-Ḥasan al-Ashʿarī in the tenth century

13 Qur'ān 55: 27

14 Mohamed Haj Yousef, *Ibn ʿArabī – Time and Cosmology*, p. 50

15 Al-Muttaqī al-Hindī, *Kanz al-ʿUmmāl*, cited in Mohamed Haj Yousef, *Ibn ʿArabī – Time and Cosmology*, p. 70

16 Qur'ān 36: 81

17 Mohamed Haj Yousef, *Ibn ʿArabī – Time and Cosmology*, p. 96

18 Qur'ān 37: 180

19 Qur'ān 2: 114

20 Muḥyī al-Dīn ibn al-ʿArabī, cited in Samer Akkach, "The World of Imagination in Ibn ʿArabī's Ontology," British Journal of Middle Eastern Studies (1997), 24(1), p. 98

21 Samer Akkach, "The World of Imagination in Ibn ʿArabī's Ontology," p. 98

22 "*Have taqwā of Allah and Allah will give you knowledge. Allah has knowledge of all things.*" Qur'ān 2: 281

23 Muḥyī al-Dīn ibn al-ʿArabī, *al-Futūḥāt al-Makkiyya*, in Chittick, W.C., *Ibn al-ʿArabī's Metaphysics of Imagination: The Sufi Path of Knowledge*, p. 75

24 Qur'ān 42: 11

25 ʿAbd al-Qādir al-Sufi, *The Way of Muḥammad*, Madinah Press, London, 1995, p. 189

26 Martin Heidegger, *Being and Time*, tr. John Macquarrie & Edward Robinson, Blackwell Publishing Ltd., London, 2000, p. 22.

27 Gregory Chaitin, "Computers, Paradoxes and the Foundations of

Mathematics," American Scientist, v. 90, p. 164

28 Gregory Chaitin, "The Limits of Reason," Scientific American, March 2006, p.76

29 Gregory Chaitin, "Computers, Paradoxes and the Foundations of Mathematics," American Scientist, Volume 90, 2000, p. 168

30 Antonio Damasio, *Descartes' Error*, G.P. Putnam's Sons, New York, 1994, p. 252

31 'Abd al-Qādir al-Sufi, *The Way of Muḥammad*, pp. 211-212

32 Fritjof Capra, *The Hidden Connections*, Doubleday, New York, 2002, p. 261

33 The Merciful is one of the attributes or Names of God.

34 Qur'ān 36: 81

35 'Abd al-Qādir al-Sufi, *The Way of Muḥammad*, p. 210

36 Heisenberg's quantum mechanical uncertainty principle for position and momentum states that the more precisely the position of a particle is given, the less precisely can one say what its momentum is. When measuring one magnitude of a particle such as its mass or its velocity or its position the other magnitudes become blurred. This is not due to technological deficiencies but to the fundamental property of nature itself. Quantum mechanics is regarded as the theory that best describes the physical world. The conceptual framework of this theory differs radically from that of classical physics.

37 Fritjof Capra cited in 'Abd al-Qādir al-Sufi, *The Way of Muḥammad*, pp. 210-211

38 Mohamed Haj Yousef, *Ibn 'Arabī – Time and Cosmology*, p. 180

39 Muḥyī al-Dīn ibn al-'Arabī, *Fuṣūṣ al-Ḥikam*, cited in 'Abd al-Qādir al-Sufi, *The Way of Muḥammad*, pp. 219

40 'Abd al-Qādir al-Sufi, *The Way of Muḥammad*, p. 210

41 Earth, water, air, and fire

42 Fritjof Capra in 'Abd al-Qādir al-Sufi, A., *The Way of Muḥammad*, p. 217

Chapter 4 – Sufi Epistemology and the Science of Unveiling

1 Compared to Radke's list mine is more condensed. He has split the categories as follows: 1. Ritual purity; 2. Spiritual withdrawal; 3. Fasting; 4. Silence; 5. Recollection of God; 6. Rejecting stray thoughts; 7. Binding the heart to the shaykh; 8. surrender to God and the master. Bernd Radke, "The Eight Rules of Junayd," *Reason and Inspiration in Islam: Theology, Philosophy and Mysticism in Muslim Thought*, p. 494

2 'Abd al-Qādir al-Sufi, *The Way of Muḥammad*, Madinah Press, London, 1995, p. xiii

3 'Abd al-Qādir al-Sufi, *The Way of Muḥammad*, p. 21

4 *Muwaṭṭa'*

5 'Abd al-Qādir al-Sufi, *The Book of 'Amal*, Madinah Press, Cape Town, 2008, p. 36

6 'Abd al-Qādir al-Sufi, *The Way of Muḥammad*, p. 22

7 Qāḍī 'Iyāḍ, ibn Mūsā al-Yaḥṣubī, *Kitāb al-shifā bi ta'rīf ḥuqūq al-Muṣṭafā*, trans. as *Muḥammad, Messenger of Allah* by Aisha Bewley, Madinah Press, Granada, 1991, p. 59

8 Qāḍī 'Iyāḍ, ibn Mūsā al-Yaḥṣubī, *Kitāb al-shifā bi ta'rīf ḥuqūq al-Muṣṭafā*, p. 56

9 'Abd al-Qādir al-Sufi, *The Way of Muḥammad*, p. 80

10 'Abd al-Qādir al-Sufi, *The Way of Muḥammad*, p. 82

11 'Abd al-Qādir al-Sufi, *The Way of Muḥammad*, p. 84

12 'Abd al-Qādir al-Sufi, *The Way of Muḥammad*, p. 84

13 Literally means ignorance but is also taken to refer to the Time of Ignorance before the coming of Islam

14 'Abd al-Qādir al-Sufi, *The Way of Muḥammad*, p. 84

15 Other categories of shaykhs are teaching shaykhs, directing shaykhs, shaykhs of states and shaykhs of blessing. See Arthur Buehler, *Sufi Heirs of the Prophet*, University of South Carolina Press, Columbia, 1998, p.29

16 'Abd al-Qādir al-Sufi, *The Way of Muḥammad*, pp. 37-38

17 Aḥmad ibn 'Ajība, *The Basic Research*, p. 83

18 Aḥmad ibn 'Ajība, *The Basic Research*, p. 84

19 Abūl Ḥasan al-Shādhilī, cited in Aḥmad ibn 'Ajība, *The Basic Research*, p. 88

20 Abū al-'Abbās al-Mursī, cited in Aḥmad ibn 'Ajība, *The Basic Research*, p. 88

21 Quoted in Aḥmad ibn 'Ajība, *The Basic Research*, pp. 103-104

22 Qur'ān 18: 24

23 Qur'ān 33: 41-42

24 Qur'ān 13: 29

25 'Abd al-Qādir al-Sufi, *The Way of Muḥammad*, pp. 120-121

26 Abū al-Qāsim al-Qushayrī, cited in Arthur John Arberry, *Sufism: An Account of the Mystics of Islam*, George Allen & Unwin Ltd., London, 1950, p. 75

27 'Abd al-Qādir al-Sufi, *The Way of Muḥammad*, p. 111

28 'Abd al-Qādir al-Sufi, *The Way of Muḥammad*, p. 118

29 'Abd al-Qādir al-Sufi, *The Way of Muḥammad*, p. 132

30 'Abd al-Qādir al-Sufi, *The Hundred Steps*, p. 87

31 The *ṭarīqa* of Muḥammad al-'Arabī al-Darqāwī (1760-1823)

32 'Abd al-Qādir al-Sufi, *The Hundred Steps*, p. 67

33 Muḥammad al-'Arabī al-Darqāwī, *The Darqāwī Way*, Diwan Press, Norwich, 1979, p. 315

34 Muḥammad al-'Arabī al-Darqāwī, *The Darqāwī Way*, p. 315

35 Nile Green, *Indian Sufism since the Seventeenth Century: Saints, books and empires in the Muslim Deccan*, Routledge, Oxon, 2006, p. xiii

36 Nile Green, *Indian Sufism since the Seventeenth Century: Saints, books and empires in the Muslim Deccan*, p. xiv

37 Nile Green, *Indian Sufism since the Seventeenth Century: Saints, books and empires in the Muslim Deccan*, p. xiv

38 Nile Green, *Indian Sufism since the Seventeenth Century: Saints, books and empires in the Muslim Deccan*, p. 158

39 Richard Eaton, "Sufis as Warriors", in *Sufism: Critical Concepts in Islamic Studies*, ed. Lloyd Ridgeon, Routledge, London, 2008

40 Mohammad Umar, *Islam in Northern India During the Eighteenth Century*, Munshiram Manoharial Publishers, New Delhi, 1993

41 A north-Indian tribe

42 Vincent Cornell. *Realm of the Saint: Power and Authority in Moroccan Sufism*, University of Texas Press, Austin, 1998, p. 272

43 Max Weber, *Charisma and Institution Building*, ed. S.N. Eisenstadt, University of Chicago, Chicago,

1968. See also Barnes, D., "Charisma and Religious Leadership: An Historical Analysis", Journal for the Scientific Study of Religion, 1978, Vol. 17, Issue 1, pp.1-18

44 Shmuel N. Eisenstadt, *Comparative Civilizations and Multiple Modernities*, Brill, Leiden ; Boston, 2003, pp. 12-13

45 Shmuel N. Eisenstadt, *Comparative Civilizations and Multiple Modernities*, p. 13

46 Shmuel N. Eisenstadt, *Comparative Civilizations and Multiple Modernities*, p. 15

47 Shmuel N. Eisenstadt, *Comparative Civilizations and Multiple Modernities*, p.p. 15-16

48 Vincent Cornell, *Realm of the Saint: Power and Authority in Moroccan Sufism*, p. xxvi

49 Vincent Cornell, *Realm of the Saint: Power and Authority in Moroccan Sufism*, pp. 272-273

50 Vincent Cornell, *Realm of the Saint: Power and Authority in Moroccan Sufism*, p. 273

51 Vincent Cornell, *Realm of the Saint: Power and Authority in Moroccan Sufism*, p. 273

52 Ernest Gellner, *Postmodernism, Reason and Religion*, Routledge, London, 1992

53 Ernest Gellner, *Postmodernism, Reason and Religion*, pp. vii-viii

54 Madawi al-Rasheed, *A History of Saudi Arabia*, Cambridge University Press, Cambridge, 2002

55 Daniel Crecelius, "The Course of Secularization in Modern Egypt", *Islam and Development*, (ed.) John L. Esposito, Syracruse University Press, New York, 1982

56 Nikki R. Keddie, *An Islamic Response to Imperialism*, University of California Press, Berkeley, 1983

57 Elie Kedourie, *Afghānī and 'Abduh – An Essay on Religious Unbelief and Political Activism in Modern Islam*, Frank Cass and Co. Ltd., London, 1966

58 Nazih N. Ayubi, "Islamic State", *The Oxford Encyclopedia of the Modern Islamic World*, Oxford University Press, Oxford, 1995

59 Bassam Tibi, "Authority and Legitimation", *The Oxford Encyclopedia of the Modern Islamic World*, Oxford, 1995

60 Aharon Layish, "The Contribution of the Modernists to the Secularization of Islamic Law", *Islamic Law and Legal Theory*, edited by Ian Edge, Dartmouth, Aldershot, 1996

61 See p. 6

62 'Abd al-Qādir al-Sufi, *The Way of Muḥammad*, pp. 207-208

63 Abdelwahab M. Elmessiri, *Epistemological Bias in the Physical and Social Sciences*, The International Institute of Islamic Thought, London, 2006, p. xi

64 Michel Chodkiewicz, *The Spiritual Writings of Amir 'Abd al-Kader*, SUNY Press, New York, 1995, p.

65 Paul Hardy, "Epistemology and Divine Discourse", *The Cambridge Companion to Classical Islamic Theology*, ed. Tim Winter, Cambridge University Press, Cambridge, 2008, p. 300

66 Aisha Bewley, *Islam: The Empowering of Women*, Ta-Ha Publishers, London, 1999, p. 57

67 Suleman Dangor, *Shaykh Yusuf*, Iqra Research Centre, Mobeni, 1982

68 Umar E. Vadillo, *The Esoteric Deviation in Islam*, Madinah Press, Cape Town, 2003, p. 377

69 'Alī al-Jamal, *The Meaning of Man*, Diwan Press, Norwich, 1977, p. 246

70 www.ammanmessage.com

71 www.ammanmessage.com

72 "*Arm yourself against them with all the firepower and cavalry* (*ribāt*) *you can muster.*" Qur'ān 8: 60

73 "The *ribāt* of a day and a night in the way of God is better than fasting and praying at night for a month." *Ṣaḥīḥ Muslim*

74 All of them have a corresponding feminine form as well.

75 Al-Andalus was an area covering parts of Spain, Gibraltar, Portugal and France that was ruled by the Murābiṭūn.

76 Aisha Bewley, A., Qāḍī Abū Bakr ibn al-'Arabī, http://bewley.virtualave.net/QadiAbūBakr.html

77 J.F.P. Hopkins, EI2, "Ibn Tumart"

78 Aisha Bewley, "Qāḍī Abū Bakr ibn al-'Arabī", http://bewley.virtualave.net/QadiAbūBakr.html

79 Ibn Farḥūn, *Dibāj al-Dhahab*, tr. Aisha Bewley in *Muhammad, Messenger of Allah, translation of Ash-Shifā of Qāḍī 'Iyāḍ*, Madinah Press, Granada, 1991, p. 510

80 Mohamed Talbi, EI2, "'Iyad b. Musa b. 'Iyad b. Amrun al-Mahsubi al-Sabti al-Kadi"

81 'Abd al-Qādir al-Sufi, *Root Islamic Education*, p. 4

82 'Abd al-Qādir al-Sufi, *Root Islamic Education*, p. 16

83 'Abd al-Qādir al-Sufi, *Root Islamic Education*, 1993, p. 125

84 Mohamed Talbi, EI2, "Ṣaḥnūn Abū Sa'īd 'Abd al-Salām Sa'īd b. Ḥabīb b. Ḥasan b. Hilāl b. Bakkār b. Rabī'a al-Tanūkhī"

85 Qāḍī 'Iyāḍ ibn Mūsā al-Yaḥṣubī, *Tartīb al-Madārik*, http://bewley.virtualave.net/madı.html

Chapter 5 – The Sufi Deconstruction of Modern Science

1 Charles Taylor, *A Secular Age*, Harvard University Press, Cambridge, Mass., 2007, p. 3

2 Charles Taylor, *A Secular Age*, p. 13

3 The idea that consciousness and will are entirely due to material movements and modifications. Similar processes as it occurred in science and philosophy are not dealt with in this chapter. Issues relating to rational/emotional and subjective/objective dichotomies in Islamic philosophy are discussed in Chapter Eight.

4 The idea that complex systems are nothing more than the interaction of their parts

5 'Abd al-Qādir al-Sufi, *Root Islamic Education*, Madinah Press, London, 1993, p. 155

6 Yasin Dutton, *Origins of Islamic Law: the Qur'ān, Muwaṭṭa', and Madīnan 'Amal*, Curzon, Richmond, Surrey, 1999, p. 1

7 The *Muwaṭṭa'*, the first book on hadith and Islamic law, was written by Mālik ibn Anas

8 Yasin Dutton, *Origins of Islamic Law: the Qur'ān, Muwaṭṭa', and Madīnan 'Amal*, p. 2

9 Yasin Dutton, *Origins of Islamic Law: the Qur'ān, Muwaṭṭa', and Madīnan 'Amal*, p. 3

10 The Mālikī *madhhab* grew out of the texts compiled by students of Mālik's legal decisions like the *Mudawwana* of Abū Sa'īd Saḥnūn (776-854)

11 The natural and unchangeable predisposition that exists from birth in all human beings. Refer to pages 31-32 for further explanation of this term.

12 Taylor, C., *A Secular Age*, pp. 1-2

13 Whilst many studies have been made investigating the rise of modernity (e.g. Max Weber, Richard Tawney, Maxime Rodinson, Anthony Giddens, Ernest Gellner and Shmuel Eisenstadt), Taylor's analysis is from a philosophical perspective and more relevant to epistemology

14 Taylor, C., *A Secular Age*, p. 290

15 Taylor C., *A Secular Age*, p. 291

16 Taylor C., *A Secular Age*, p. 291

17 John Carroll, *The Wreck of Western Culture – Humanism Revisited*, Scribe, Melbourne, 2004

18 Ted Benton and Ian Craib, *Philosophy of Social Science: the philosophical foundations of social thought*, Palgrave Macmillan, New York, 2011, p. 232

19 Anthony Thomson, *The Making of Social Theory: order, reason and desire*, Oxford University Press Canada, Don Mills, Ont. c2010, p. xii

20 Robert Wolker (1998). "Enlightenment, Continental." In E. Craig (Ed.), *Routledge Encyclopedia of Philosophy*. London: Routledge. http://www.rep.routledge.com/article/DB025

21 Hicham Djait, *Europe and Islam: Cultures and Modernity*, University of California Press, Berkeley, 1985, p. 166

22 Friedrich Nietzsche, *The Gay Science; with a Prelude in Rhymes and an Appendix of Songs* (tr. Walter Kaufmann), Random House, New York, 1974, Section 125, "The Madman"

23 John Ralston Saul, *The Collapse of Globalism and the Reinvention of the World*, Viking, Australia, 2005

24 Francis Fukuyama, *The End of History and the Last Man*, Penguin, London, 1992, p. 4

25 Glyn Davies, *A History of Money: From Ancient Times to the Present Day*, University of Wales Press, Cardiff, 2002

26 Masoud Kamali, *Multiple Modernities, Civil Society and Islam: the case of Iran and Turkey*, Liverpool University Press, Liverpool, c2006, p. 23

27 Niall Ferguson, *The Ascent of Money: a financial history of the world*, Penguin, London, 2008

28 Peter T. White, The Power of Money, National Geographic, January, 1993

29 Mike Whitney, http://www.globalresearch.ca/index.php?aid=16517&context=va

30 Ted Benton and Ian Craib, *Philosophy of Social Science*, p. 107

31 Ted Benton. and Ian Craib, *Philosophy of Social Science*, p. 232

32 Roy Bhaskar, http://dica-lab.org/rab/contributions/abstracts/bhaskar2

33 Ted Benton.and Ian Craib, I., *Philosophy of Social Science*, p. 232

34 Anthony Thomson, *The Making of Social Theory*, pp. 398-399

35 Shaykh 'Abd al-Qādir (written under his family name of Ian Dallas), *Oedipus and Dionysus*, Freiburg, Granada, 1992, pp. 9-10

36 Mālik ibn Anas, *Muwaṭṭa'*, 46.1. 3

37 'Abd al-Qādir al-Sufi, *Jihad – a groundplan*, Diwan Press, Norwich, 1978, p. 9

38 'Abd al-Qādir al-Sufi, *Jihad – a groundplan*, p. 10

39 'Abd al-Qādir al-Sufi, *Jihad – a groundplan*, pp. 10-11

40 'Abd al-Qādir al-Sufi, *Jihad – a groundplan*, p. 11

41 Pharaohs were the political and religious leaders in ancient Egypt.

42 'Abd al-Qādir al-Sufi, *Jihad – a groundplan*, pp. 41-42

43 'Abd al-Qādir al-Sufi, *Jihad – a groundplan*, p. 42

44 'Abd al-Qādir al-Sufi, *Jihad – a groundplan*, p. 18

Chapter 6 – Sufi Deconstruction of Modern Philosophy

1 Immanuel Kant (1724-1804)

2 'Abd al-Qādir al-Sufi, A., *For the Coming Man*, Murabitun Press, Norwich, 1988, p. 81

3 René Descartes, *Principles of Philosophy*, Part 1, Article vii, tr. by John Veitch, http://cat.lib.unimelb.edu.au:80/record=b3987012~S30

4 He agreed with Locke that secondary qualities like taste, colour, sound and smell are not present in the object itself but are produced by us in our minds. He, however, criticized Locke for saying that primary qualities are intrinsically present in the object because he believed that primary qualities are just as subjective as secondary qualities.

5 Albert Einstein (1879-1955) said: "God does not play dice with the universe."

6 Named after Galileo Galilei (1564-1642) the Italian mathematician, physicist and astronomer

7 The inscription reads: "Two things fill the mind with ever new and increasing admiration and awe, the oftener and more steadily we reflect on them: the starry heavens above me, and the moral law within me." David Bell, 'Kant', *A Blackwell Companion to Philosophy*, eds. Nicoholas Bunnin and E.P. Tsui-James, Blackwell Publishing, Oxford, 2002, p. 726

8 Immanuel Kant, *Critique of Pure Reason*, tr. N. Kemp Smith, Macmillan, London, 1929, p. xvi

9 Immanuel Kant, *Critique of Pure Reason*, B 131-B 132

10 Immanuel Kant, *Critique of Pure Reason*, B 276

11 Edward Craig, "Ontology" in E. Craig (Ed.), *Routledge Encyclopedia of Philosophy*. London, Routledge, http://www.rep.routledge.com/article/N039SECT3

12 Thomas Hofweber, *Stanford Encyclopedia of Philosophy*, http://plato.stanford.edu/entries/logic- ontology/

13 Rolf-Peter Horstmann, "Hegel, Georg Wilhelm Friedrich" in E. Craig (Ed.), *Routledge Encyclopedia of Philosophy*. London: Routledge. http://www.rep.routledge.com/article/DC036

14 Hegelianism is the intellectual tradition that deals with the reception and influence of Hegel's philosophy.

15 Robert Stern and Nicolas Walker, "Hegelianism" in E. Craig (Ed.), *Routledge Encyclopedia of Philosophy*. London: Routledge. http://www.rep.routledge.com/article/DC037

16 Charles Taylor, *Hegel*, Cambridge University Press, Cambridge, 1975

17 Kenneth L.Schmitz, "Embodiment and Situation: Charles Taylor's Hegel", The Journal of Philosophy, Vol. 73, No. 19 (Nov. 4, 1976), p. 719

18 'Abd al-Qādir al-Sufi, *For the Coming Man*, Murabitun Press, Norwich, 1988, p. 27

19 'Abd al-Qādir Al-Sufi, *For the Coming Man*, p. 80

20 Friedrich Nietzsche, *The Gay Science*, tr. with commentary by Walter Kaufmann ,Vintage Books, New York, 1974

21 Greek philosophers after Socrates (469 BC – 399BC)

22 'Abd al-Qādir al-Sufi, *For the Coming Man*, pp. 85-86

23 'Abd al-Qādir al-Sufi, *For the Coming Man*, p. 88

24 Martin Heidegger, *Nietzsche IV*, tr. F.A. Capuzzi, ed. D.F. Krell, Harper and Row, San Francisco, 1982, p. 164

25 Muḥammad Kamāl, *From Essence to Being: The Philosophy of Mulla Sadra and Martin Heidegger*, ICAS Press, London, 2010, p. 66

26 "According to ancient doctrine, the essence of a thing is considered to be 'what' the thing is." Martin Heidegger, *Question Concerning Technology and Other Essays*, tr. William Lovitt, Harper and Row, New York, 1977, p. 4

27 Martin Heidegger, *Being and Time*, tr. John Macquarrie & Edward Robinson, Blackwell Publishing Ltd., London, 2000, p. 22.

28 "This situation is grounded in the fact that science itself does not think, and cannot think – which is its good fortune, here meaning the assurance of its own pointed course. Science does not think. This is a shocking statement. Let the statement be shocking, even though we immediately add the supplementary statement that science always and in its own fashion has to do with thinking. That fashion, however, is genuine and consequently fruitful only after the gulf has become visible that lies between thinking and science, lies there unbridgeably. There is no bridge – only the leap. Here there is nothing but mischief ties and asses' bridges by which men today would set up a comfortable commerce between thinking and science." Martin Heidegger, *What is Called Thinking*, Harper and Row Publishers, New York, 1968, p. 8

29 "What must be thought about, turns away from man. It withdraws from him. But how can we have the least knowledge of something that withdraws from the beginning, how can we give it a name? Whatever withdraws refuses arrival." Martin Heidegger, *What is Called Thinking*, pp. 8-9

30 "Language is not true to itself, insofar as it has not yet succeeded in giving up the absurd intention of being 'science' and 'research'." Martin Heidegger, *Introduction to Metaphysics*, Yale University Press, 2000

31 "What do we ordinarily understand by truth? This elevated yet at the same time worn and almost dull word 'truth' means what makes a true thing true. What is a true thing? ... However, we call true not only an actual joy, genuine gold, and all beings of such kind, but also and above all we call true or false our statements about beings, which can themselves be genuine or not with regard to their kind, which can be thus or otherwise in their actuality. A statement is true if what it means and says is in accordance with the matter about which the statement is made. Here too we say, 'It is in accord.' Now, though, it is not the matter that is in accord but rather the proposition." Martin Heidegger, "On the Essence of Truth", *Pathmarks*, Cambridge University Press, Cambridge, 1998, pp. 137-138

32 Umar E. Vadillo, "Heidegger for Muslims" at http://asadullahali.wordpress.com/2012/05/02/heidegger-for-muslims/, p. 17

33 Martin Heidegger, *What is Called Thinking*, p. 12

34 Paul Neumarkt, "Martin Heidegger: the philosopher of psychological confusion", Journal of Evolutionary Psychology, March 2003, p.36

35 Romanticism was a literary, intellectual and artistic movement that originated in Europe in the eighteenth and early nineteenth century as a reaction to the Industrial Revolution. It was a movement against the social and political norms of the Age of Enlightenment and a reaction against the scientific rationalization of nature.

36 The state led by Otto von Bismarck, first Chancellor of the German Empire (1871-1890)

37 "After Marx, first Engels (in Ludwig Feuerbach and Anti-Dühring) and then Lenin affirm that the Hegelian dialectic is acceptable only if 'put back on its feet'." Louis Althusser, http://www.marxists.org/reference/ archive/ althusser/ 1953/onmarx/on-marxism.htm

38 M.L. Clark, "Nietzsche, Friedrich", in E. Craig (Ed.), *Routledge Encyclopedia of Philosophy*. London: Routledge. http://www.rep.routledge.com/article/ DC057SECT12

39 Friedrich Nietzsche, *Thus Spoke Zarathustra*, cited in Al-Sufi, A., *For the Coming Man*, p. 74

40 Michael Allen Gillespie, *Hegel, Heidegger and the Ground of History*, The University of Chicago Press, Chicago, 1984, pp. 122-123

41 'Abd al-Qādir al-Sufi, *For the Coming Man*, p. 82

42 'Abd al-Qādir al-Sufi, *For the Coming Man*, pp. 84-85

43 The view that there is no factual knowledge except scientific knowledge

44 Michael Allen Gillespie, *Hegel, Heidegger and the Ground of History*, p. 124

45 The study of conscious experience from the subjective point of view

46 Michael Allen Gillespie, *Hegel, Heidegger and the Ground of History*, p. 124

47 See discussion below

48 Duns Scotus (1256-1308) was a very influential Catholic theologian and philosopher.

49 Thomism is the philosophical school that developed as a legacy to Saint Thomas Aquinas (1225- 1274), the Catholic theologian and philosopher.

50 "A 'Christian philosophy' is a round square and a misunderstanding. There is, to be sure, a thinking and questioning elaboration of the world of Christian experience, i.e, of faith. That is theology. Only epochs which no longer fully believe in the true greatness of the task of theology arrive at the disastrous notion that philosophy can help provide a refurbished theology if not a substitute for theology, which will satisfy the needs of the time. For the original Christian

faith philosophy is foolishness. To philosophise is to ask 'why are there beings rather than nothing?' Really to ask the question signifies: a daring attempt to fathom this unfathomable question by disclosing what it summons us to ask, to push our questioning to the very end. Where such an attempt occurs there is philosophy." Martin Heidegger, An *Introduction to Metaphysics*, tr. R. Manheim, Yale University Press, New Haven, 1959, pp. 7-8)

51 'Abd al-Qādir al-Sufi, *For the Coming Man*, p. 88

52 Martin Heidegger, *What is Called Thinking*, p. 12

53 Michael Allen Gillespie, *Hegel, Heidegger and the Ground of History*, p. 124

54 Ellis Dye, "Sorge in Heidegger and in Goethe's Faust", *Goethe Yearbook*, Vol. 16, 2009, p. 207

55 Walter Kaufman, cited by Ellis Dye, in "Sorge in Heidegger and in Goethe's Faust", p. 207

56 Martin Heidegger, cited by Ellis Dye, in "Sorge in Heidegger and in Goethe's Faust", p. 207

57 Ontic relates to the physical existence of a thing

58 Johann Wolfgang von Goethe, cited by 'Abd al-Qādir al-Sufi, *Fatwa on the Acceptance of Goethe Being a Muslim*, Weimer Institute, Weimer, 1995, p. 9

59 Johann Wolfgang von Goethe, cited in 'Abd al-Qādir al-Sufi, *Fatwa on the Acceptance of Goethe Being a Muslim*, p. 6

60 "Christianity destroyed for us the whole harvest of ancient civilization, and later it also destroyed for us the whole harvest of Mohammedan civilization. The wonderful culture of the Moors in Spain, which was fundamentally nearer to us and appealed more to our senses and tastes than that of Rome and Greece, was trampled down (—I do not say by what sort of feet—) Why? Because it had to thank noble and manly instincts for its origin—because it said yes to life, even to the rare and refined luxuriousness of Moorish life! ... Intrinsically there should be no more choice between Islam and Christianity than there is between an Arab and a Jew. The decision is already reached; nobody remains at liberty to choose here. Either a man is a Chandala or he is not.... "War to the knife with Rome! Peace and friendship with Islam!": this was the feeling, this was the act, of that great free spirit, that genius among German emperors, Frederick II. What! must a German first be a genius, a free spirit, before he can feel decently? I can't make out how a German could ever feel Christian...." Friedrich Nietzsche, *The Antichrist*, Chapter 60, http://www.lexido.com/EBOOK_TEXTS/THE_ANTICHRIST_.aspx?S=60

61 Michael E. Zimmerman, *The Development of Heidegger's Nietzsche Interpretation*, p. 10 http://www.colorado.edu/ArtsSciences/CHA/profiles/

zimmpdf/The%20Development%20of%20Heidegger.pdf

62 "What is the Gestalt?" Heidegger, in his famous reply to Jünger's text *Uber die Linie* said: 'For you, Jünger, the Gestalt, stands for what is only accessible in a seeing, to be found in this seeing, which among the Greeks is called *Idein* – a word which Plato employed for a look which considered not the changing of sense perception, but the immutable, the being, the idea. You also characterise the Gestalt as the Calm Being. The Gestalt is certainly not an idea, in the sense of the meaning of modern philosophy, any more than it is by consequence a regulative representation in the sense of Kant. ... It had undertaken to make possible an experience of being and of the way in which it is, in the light of the Nietzschean project of being and will to power.' Despite this impressive Heideggerian definition, one must take into account Jünger's own view. In conversation with me he categorically refuted the idea that the Gestalt was Platonic. He pointed out, 'You cannot SEE a Platonic idea.' Rather, he referred the matter to the great discussion which took place between Schiller and Goethe. There, Goethe made exactly this point, when Schiller defined the Goethean description of the metamorphosis of plants as being merely the Platonic idea. Goethe's concern went much deeper – he was trying to move the modern imagination into a new way of seeing biological phenomena as entities moving through time and thus taking their meaning from their full realisation in nature, from seed to decay." 'Abd al-Qādir al-Sufi, "The Gestalt of Freedom", *Ian Dallas: Collected Works*, Budgate Press, 2005, Erasmia, South Africa, pp. 824-825

63 'Abd al-Qādir al-Sufi, "The Gestalt of Freedom", *Ian Dallas: Collected Works*, p. 826

64 Ernst Jünger, cited by 'Abd al-Qādir al-Sufi, "The Gestalt of Freedom", *Ian Dallas: Collected Works*, p. 831

65 'Abd al-Qādir al-Sufi, "The Gestalt of Freedom", *Ian Dallas: Collected Works*, p. 830

66 Ernst Jünger, cited by Al-Sufi, "The Gestalt of Freedom", *Ian Dallas: Collected Works*, p. 830

67 Ernst Jünger cited by Al-Sufi, "The Gestalt of Freedom", *Ian Dallas: Collected Works*, p. 824

68 Ernst Jünger, cited by Al-Sufi, "The Gestalt of Freedom", *Ian Dallas: Collected Works*, p. 826

69 Ernst Jünger, cited by 'Abd al-Qādir al-Sufi, "The Gestalt of Freedom", *Ian Dallas: Collected Works*, p. 828

70 Ernst Jünger, cited by 'Abd al-Qādir al-Sufi, "The Gestalt of Freedom", *Ian*

Dallas: Collected Works, p. 835

71 Ernst Jünger, cited by 'Abd al-Qādir al-Sufi, "The Gestalt of Freedom", *Ian Dallas: Collected Works*, p. 836

72 Ernst Jünger, cited by 'Abd al-Qādir al-Sufi, "The Gestalt of Freedom", *Ian Dallas: Collected Works*, p. 836

73 According to Armstrong logos and mythos were two ways of thinking, speaking and acquiring knowledge. "Logos ('reason') was the pragmatic mode of thought that enabled people to function effectively in the world. ... Logos was essential to the survival of our species. But it had its limitations: it could not assuage human grief or find ultimate meaning in life's struggles. For that people turned to *mythos* or 'myth'. ... But a myth would not be effective if people simply 'believed' in it. It was essentially a programme of action. It could be put into correct spiritual and psychological posture but it was up to you to take the next step and make the 'truth' of the myth a reality in your own life. The only way to access the value and truth of any myth was to act upon it. The myth of the hero, for example, which takes the same form in nearly all cultural traditions, taught people how to unlock their own heroic potential." (Karen Armstrong, *The Case for God*, The Bodly Head, London, 2009, p. 3)

74 Ernst Jünger, http://www.ernst-juenger.org/2009/10/anarch-and-waldganger-1.html

75 'Abd al-Qādir al-Sufi, "The Gestalt of Freedom", *Ian Dallas: Collected Works*, p. 837

76 Refer to pages 31-32

77 'Abd al-Qādir al-Sufi explains that Goethe's Gestalt: "tried to move the modern imagination into a new way of seeing biological phenomena as entities moving through time and thus taking their meaning from their full realization in nature, from seed to decay." ("The Gestalt of Freedom", *Ian Dallas: Collected Works*, Budgate Press, Erasmia, 2005, p. 824)

78 "For Nietzsche the problem of Christianity is that it was 'Platonism for the masses', yet this accusation can also be made against the way Islam is starting to present itself to the world and to itself. Islam is killing its own God and, as a consequence, will be forced to either remain an enemy to secularisation, leading to greater fundamentalism, or will be 'secularised' so that it ceases to have any identity or life enhancing philosophy of its own." (Roy Jackson, *Nietzsche and Islam*, Routledge, Abington, Oxon, 2007, p. 146)

79 See Postface for discussion on oligarchy

Chapter 7 – From Islamic Philosophy to Sufism: Intellect to Presence

1 Peter Kingsley, cited in Seyyed Hossein Nasr, *Islamic Philosophy from its Origin to the Present*, State University of New York Press, c2006, p. 4

2 Peter Kingsley, *Ancient Philosophy, Mystery and Magic*, Clarendon Press, Oxford, 1995, p. 228

3 See p. 62

4 Mehdi Ha'iri Yazdi, *The Principles of Epistemology in Islamic Philosophy: Knowledge by Presence*, State University of New York Press, Albany, 1992, p. 1

5 Stephen Toulmin, *Cosmopolis: The Hidden Agenda of Modernity*, Free Press, New York, c1990

6 *Al-ʿaql* has two meanings for Islamic philosophers, the first which relates to its Arabic root, meaning to bind, therefore *al-ʿaql* is the intellectual faculty which binds human beings to God, the Truth. The other meaning relates to reason, which is intellectual reflection at the level of material existence.

7 See p. 39 for discussion on *qalb*

8 Seyyed Hossein Nasr, *Islamic Philosophy from its Origin to the Present*, State University of New York Press, Albany, c2006, p. 95

9 Plato, *Republic*, Book III, 402-403(W)

10 Plato, *Republic*, Vol.7, p. 513 (Y)

11 Aristotle, *De Anima*, Book 3, B. 427-429 (Y)

12 Mehdi Ha'iri Yazdi, *The Principles of Epistemology in Islamic Philosophy: Knowledge by Presence*, p. 8

13 Al-Kindī, cited by Seyyed Hossein Nasr, *Islamic Philosophy from its Origin to the Present*, pp. 35- 36

14 Massimo Campanini, *An Introduction to Islamic Philosophy*, tr. Caroline Higgitt, Edinburgh University Press, Edinburgh, 2008, p. 10

15 Abū Naṣr al-Fārābī, *Al-Madīna al-fāḍila*, tr. R. Walzer, Clarendon Press, Oxford, 1985, 1 1.2: 95

16 "This phrase is not entirely clear but appears to mean that the production of bodies and celestial spheres is not the result of a 'physical' act but of a 'metaphysical' act." Massimo Campanini, *An Introduction to Islamic Philosophy*, p. 97

17 Ibn Sīnā, cited by Seyyed Hossein Nasr, *Islamic Philosophy from its Origin to the Present*, p. 34

18 Fazlur Rahman, "Ibn Sīnā", *History of Muslim Philosophy*, ed. M.M. Sharif, Otto Harrassowitz, Wiesbaden, 1963, p. 482

19 Seyyed Hossein Nasr, *Islamic Philosophy from its Origin to the Present*, p. 65

20 Seyyed Hossein Nasr, *Islamic Philosophy from its Origin to the Present*, p. 66

21 Ibn Sīnā, cited by Fazlur Rahman, in "Ibn Sīnā", *History of Muslim Philosophy*, pp. 483-484

22 Seyyed Hossein Nasr, *Islamic Philosophy from its Origin to the Present*, p. 68

23 By Fakhr al-Dīn al-Razi (1149-1209) for example

24 Nāṣir al-Dīn al-Ṭūsī, *Sharḥ al-ishārāt*, cited in Seyyed Hossein Nasr, *Islamic Philosophy from its Origin to the Present*, p. 70

25 There has been a widespread misconception that al-Ghazālī was anti-philosophy and that his attacks on certain aspects of Islamic philosophy in general and Ibn Sīnā's philosophy in particular, in his Incoherence of the Philosophers, dealt the deathblow to philosophy in the Muslim world. (Refer to TJ de Boer, Solomon Munk, Ernest Renan, Ignaz Goldzihher and WM Watt.) For example, Ignaz Goldziher said that whilst there had been opposition to philosophy and the rationalist sciences among Muslim theologians prior to the eleventh century, it had become much more forceful after that, with some of them even considering the study of logic prohibited (*ḥarām*). He claimed that the history of philosophy in Islam came to an end with Ibn Rushd (1126-1198). Ignaz Goldziher, *Die islamische und die judische Philosophie des Mittelalters*, cited in Frank Griffel, *Al-Ghazali's Philosophical Theology*, Oxford University Press, Oxford, 2009, p. 4

26 Massimo Campanini, *An Introduction to Islamic Philosophy*, p. 19

27 Frank Griffel, *Al-Ghazālī's Philosophical Theology*, p. 286

28 Qur'ān 24: 35

29 Mehdi Ha'iri Yazdi, *The Principles of Epistemology in Islamic Philosophy: Knowledge by Presence*, p. 16

30 Al-Ghazali, *Mishkāt al-Anwār*, tr. W.H.T. Gairdner, http://www.ghazali.org/books/mishkat/index.html

31 Majid Fakhry, "Ibn Rushd and the Defense of Aristotelianism", A *History of Islamic Philosophy*, Columbia University Press, New York, 1980, p. 302

32 Ibn Rushd, *Kitāb faṣl al-maqāl fī mā bayn al-sharī'ati wal-ḥikmati min al-ittiṣāl* (*The Decisive Treatise, Determining the Nature of the Connection Between Religion and Philosophy*), tr. Hourani, G.F., in *Averroes – On the Harmony of Religion and Philosophy*, Luzac, London, 1976

33 Ibn Rushd, *Kitāb tafsīr mā ba'd al-ṭabī'a, The Long Commentary*, ed. Maurice Bouyges, tr. Mehdi Ha'iri Yazdi in *The Principles of Epistemology in Islamic Philosophy: Knowledge by Presence*, pp. 18- 19

34 Mehdi Ha'iri Yazdi, *The Principles of Epistemology in Islamic Philosophy:*

Knowledge by Presence, p. 20

35 See note 26. Refer to pages 176 and 177

36 Shams al-Dīn al-Shahrazuri, cited in Majid Fakhry, "Al-Suhrawardī", A *History of Islamic Philosophy*, p. 327

37 Shihāb al-Dīn Suhrawardī, cited in Hossein Ziai, "Shihāb al-Dīn Suhrawardī: founder of the Illuminationist school", *History of Islamic Philosophy*, ed. Seyyed Hossein Nasr and Oliver Leaman, Routledge, London, 1996, p. 451

38 Shams al-Dīn Shahrazuri (d. after 1288) and Quṭb al-Dīn al-Shīrāzī

39 Shihāb al-Dīn Suhrawardī, *Opera II*, 248 discussed by Hossein Ziai, "Shihāb al-Dīn Suhrawardī: founder of the Illuminationist school", *History of Islamic Philosophy*, p. 450

40 Hossein Ziai, "Shihāb al-Dīn Suhrawardī: founder of the Illuminationist school", *History of Islamic Philosophy*, p. 450

41 Shihāb al-Dīn Suhrawardī, cited by Seyyed Hossein Nasr, in *Islamic Philosophy from its Origin to the Present*, p. 34

42 Aristotle said to Suhrawardi: "Think of yourself before thinking of anything else. If you do so, you will then find that the very selfhood of yourself helps you solve your problem." Shihāb al-Dīn Suhrawardī, *Kitāb al-talwīḥāt*, cited in Mehdi Ha'iri Yazdi, *The Principles of Epistemology in Islamic Philosophy: Knowledge by Presence*, p. 24

43 Mehdi Ha'iri Yazdi, *The Principles of Epistemology in Islamic Philosophy: Knowledge by Presence*, pp. 24-25

44 Muḥammad Kamāl, *Mulla Sadra's Transcendent Philosophy*, Asgate, Aldershot, 2006, p. 31

45 "In the past, I used to be firm on the defence of the principality of essence a [mentally dependent] abstract entity, until my God guided me and showed me his proof. It became clear to me that the issue is opposite of what has been conceived and determined. ... Existences are genuine [determinate] realities and essences are the eternal 'thisnesses' which have never inhaled the perfume of real existence at all. These existences are merely the rays of reflected lights of The True Light and of the Eternal Existence. Exalted be His Sublimity! However, each of them has essential predicates and contain intelligible concepts called essences." Mulla Sadra, *al-Mashā'ir*, cited in Muḥammad Kamāl, *Mulla Sadra's Transcendent Philosophy*, pp. 33-34

46 Mulla Sadra, *Ṭarḥ al-kawnayn*, refer to Muḥammad Kamāl, *Mulla Sadra's Transcendent Philosophy*, p. 23

47 Muḥammad Kamāl, *Mulla Sadra's Transcendent Philosophy*, p. 88

48 Mehdi Ha'iri Yazdi, *The Principles of Epistemology in Islamic Philosophy:*

Knowledge by Presence, p. 25

49 See p. 60 for a detailed discussion on the four different levels of *khayāl*

50 Mehdi Ha'iri Yazdi, *The Principles of Epistemology in Islamic Philosophy: Knowledge by Presence*, p. 1 (italics are in the original)

51 See Aḥmad Dallal, "Science in the Qur'ān", *Encyclopaedia of the Qur'ān*. General Editor: Jane Dammen McAuliffe, Georgetown University, Washington DC, Brill Online, 2012

52 Refer to pages 1 and 2.

53 Refer to page 2.

54 Aḥmad ibn 'Ajība, *The Basic Research*, p. 20

55 Aḥmad ibn 'Ajība, *The Basic Research*, p. 20

56 Aḥmad ibn 'Ajība, *The Basic Research*, p. 20

57 See also p. 57

58 Aḥmad ibn 'Ajība, *The Basic Research*, p. 26

59 Sayyidī 'Abd al-'Azīz al-Dabbāgh gave us a rare insight into the *dhawq* experienced by the *rūḥ* and *sirr*: He said: "Three days after the death of Sayyidī 'Umar I experienced illumination - praise be to God. ... Things began to reveal themselves to me and they appeared as if they were right in front of me. I saw all the towns and cities and small villages. I saw everything that's on the land. ... I saw all the seas and I saw all the seven earths and all the beasts of burden and the creatures found on them. I saw the sky and it was as if I was above it looking at what it contains. Then behold there was a great light like sudden lightning that came from every direction. The light appeared above me and below me, on my right and on my left and from behind. ... And when I lay down I perceived that my body was all eyes. My eye saw, my head saw, my leg saw, and all my limbs saw. I looked at the clothes I had on and found that they didn't hinder the sight which was spread throughout my body. I realized that lying face down or standing up made no difference."Aḥmad ibn al-Mubārak al-Lamaṭī, *Al-Dhabab al-Ibrīz min Kalām Sayyidī 'Abd al-'Azīz al-Dabbāgh*, tr. John O'Kane and Bernd Radtke, Brill, 2007, pp. 131-132

60 Abū al-Qāsim al-Junayd, *al-Rasā'il*, tr. A.H. Abdel-Kader in *The Life, Personality and Writings of al-Junayd*, pp. 171-172

61 "Self-manifestation, presencing, self-disclosing, the unveiling of a spiritual reality in the realm of vision, a showing forth of the secrets of the One in existence." Aisha Bewley, *Glossary of Islamic Terms*, p. 224

62 'Abd al-Qādir al-Sufi, *The Hundred Steps*, p. 78 Italics are the author's own.

63 "They [adherents of the school of al-Junayd] affirmed the transcendent unity of existence (*waḥdat al-wujūd*). Among the notable early representatives

of this school after al-Junayd were Abū Nasr al-Sarrāj, 'Alī al-Hujwīrī, Abū al-Qāsim al-Qushayrī and 'Abd Allāh al-Anṣārī. To this school also belonged al-Ghazālī. But their chief exponent was Ibn 'Arabī, who first formulated what was originally given in the intuition of existence into an integrated metaphysics expressed in rational and intellectual terms. Among his erudite commentators were Ṣadr al-Dīn al-Qunyawī, 'Abd al-Razzāq al-Qāshānī, Dāwūd al-Qayṣarī, 'Abd al-Raḥmān al-Jami; and his doctrine of the Perfect Man (*al-Insān al-Kāmil*) was developed by 'Abd al-Karīm al-Jili. The philosophical expression of the transcendent unity of existence was formulated by Ṣadr al-Dīn al-Shīrāzī, called Mulla Sadra, whose metaphysics bears marked traces of the thoughts of ibn Sīnā, al-Ghazālī, ibn 'Arabī and al-Suhrawardī." Syed Muḥammad Naquib al-Attas, *Prolegomena to the Metaphysics of Islam*, Suhail Academy, Lahore, 2001, pp. 214- 215

64 Ian Netton says that for Ibn al-'Arabī, "the doctrine of *waḥdat al-wujūd* precluded 'union' with the Deity in the usual various senses in which the term has been peddled. This was because the logic of Ibn al-'Arabī's position meant that the mystic could not, in some way, unite with that with which he was already one. Such a term as 'union' for the partisan of a doctrine of unity of being could only be used metaphorically; for him the mystic already was, not becoming, the Object of his striving. In other words, the language, under the alchemy of Ibn al-'Arabī's key doctrine of *waḥdat al-wujūd*, was once again transmuted so that Arabic words indicating 'union' like *ittiḥād* and *jam'* took on meanings more akin to 'realization' or 'discovery' of the meaning and actuality of a oneness with God that already existed and the 'detection' of His various manifestations." Ian Netton, "*Ishrāq* and *Waḥda*," in *Sufism: Critical Concepts in Islamic Studies*, ed. Lloyd Ridgeon, Routledge, London, 2008, p. 164

65 Syed Muḥammad Naquib al-Attas, *Prolegomena to the Metaphysics of Islam*, p. 178

66 "*When your Lord took out all their descendents from the loins of the children of Adam and made them testify against themselves 'Am I not your Lord?' they said, 'We testify that indeed You are!'*" Qur'ān 7; 172

67 Abū al-Qāsim al-Junayd, *Risāla*, tr. 'Alī Ḥasan AbdelKader, in *The Life, Personality and Writings of Al-Junayd*, p. 76

68 Abū al-Qāsim al-Junayd, *Risāla*, tr. 'Alī Ḥasan AbdelKader, in *The Life, Personality and Writings of Al-Junayd*, pp. 160-161

69 This refers to the second law of thermodynamics in entropy which describes the 'heat death" of the universe. see Paul Davis, *God and the New Physics*, Penguin, London, 1990, p.11

70 Syed Muḥammad Naquib al-Attas, *Prolegomena to the Metaphysics of Islam*, pp. 184-185

71 Syed Muḥammad Naquib al-Attas, *Prolegomena to the Metaphysics of Islam*, p. 186

72 See p. 52 for a detailed discussion on these categories

73 See *"All things are passing except His Face,"* Qur'ān 28: 88 and, *"Everyone on it will pass away; but the Face of your Lord will remain, Master of Majesty and Generosity"* 55: 24-25.

74 *Ṣaḥīḥ al-Bukhārī*, Chapter *Al-Tawḥīd*

75 Qur'ān 55: 27

76 Qur'ān 55: 27

77 Syed Muḥammad Naquib al-Attas, *Prolegomena to the Metaphysics of Islam*, p. 192

78 Refer to page 10.

79 For Ibn al-'Arabī's discussion on time see p. 56.

80 Qur'ān 2:35-39

81 Qur'ān 37: 139-148

82 Qur'ān 28: 29

83 Qur'ān 21:68

84 Qur'ān 17: 1

85 *"We belong to Allah and to Him we will return."* Qur'ān 2: 155

86 'Abd al-Qādir al-Sufi, *The Book of Safar*, p. 31

87 "Self-manifestation, presencing, self-disclosing, the unveiling of a reality in the realm of vision, a showing forth of the secrets of the One in existence." Aisha Bewley, *Glossary of Islamic Terms*, p. 224

88 'Abd al-Qādir al-Sufi, *The Book of Safar*, p. 31

89 Qur'ān 20: 82

90 Jalāl al-Dīn al-Maḥallī and Jalāl al-Dīn al-Suyūṭī, *Tafsīr al-Jalālayn*, Dar al-Taqwa, London, 2007, p.676

91 Qur'ān 7: 142

92 'Abd al-Qādir al-Sufi, *The Book of Safar*, p. 43

93 See discussion of *fiṭra* in p. 31

94 Conformity with the *sharī'a* as revealed by God in the Qur'ān and as practised by the Prophet Muḥammad.

95 'Uthmān Dan Fodio, *Handbook on Islam, Iman, Ihsan*, Diwan Press, Norwich, 1978, p. 29

96 'Abd al-Qādir al-Sufi, introduction to the translation of *The Ṭawāsīn of Ḥusayn ibn Manṣūr al-Ḥallāj*, Taj Co., Dehli, 1982, p. 16

97 "Sufism is totally dependent on a life pattern, a behavioural mode, a total anthropology one might say, for all one's life-transactions from birth up to death must be in approximation to the wisdom- method of the sunna which the Messenger laid down for mankind and which is the Sufi's whole reason for existing. The climax and gift of living this way is the gnosis and spiritual experience that the pseudo-Sufis suggest one can gain in some kind of mental vacuum devoid of any spiritual transformation of action and life-style." 'Abd al-Qādir al-Sufi, introduction to the translation of *The Ṭawāsīn of Ḥusayn ibn Manṣūr al-Ḥallāj*, p. 4

98 James W. Morris, Ibn 'Arabī's "Esotericism," in *Islamic Philosophy and Theology: Critical Concepts in Islamic Thought*, ed. Ian Richard Netton, Routledge, London. 2007, p. 174. Italics appear in the original.

99 'Abd al-Qādir al-Sufi, *Root Islamic Education*, p. 125

100 See p. 7

101 See pp. 11-12

102 There are many paradoxical verses in the Qur'ān. Refer to Chapter 4 with our discussion of *tashbīh* and *tanzīh* and the apparently contradictory statements in the Qur'ān

103 *Ḥayra* is a term used by Ibn al-'Arabī, which means "bewilderment, confusion, continual amazement, perplexity, in which every intellectual channel is blocked; this results in an intensity which allows for illumination, because only finite things can be expressed in words and there is no way to articulate the infinite and ineffable, either mentally or vocally. Al-Shiblī said, 'Real gnosis is the inability to achieve gnosis.' How can the temporal grasp the Timeless, the finite the Infinite, the limited the Limitless? Out of confusion comes fusion." Bewley, A., *Glossary of Islamic Terms*, Ta Ha Publishers, London, 1998, pp. 209-210

104 'Abd al-Qādir al-Sufi, *The Book of Tawḥīd*, p. 67

105 'Abd al-Qādir al-Sufi, *The Book of Tawḥīd*, p. 130

106 Aisha Bewley, *Glossary of Islamic Terms*, p. 210

107 'Abd al-Qādir al-Sufi, *The Hundred Steps*, p. 23

108 'Abd al-Qādir al-Sufi, *The Book of Ḥubb*, p. 38

109 In his review of *The Book of Strangers* Alan Watts says of al-Sufi: "He has – as is very rare with mystical writers – given a vision of God that, instead of summoning with duty, allures with delight."

'Abd al-Qādir al-Sufi, *The Book of Strangers*, State University of New York Press, New York, 1988

Chapter 8 – The Sufi Path of Social Cohesion: Calling Things by Their Names

1 'Abd al-Qādir al-Sufi (published under his family name Ian Dallas), *Oedipus and Dionysus*, Freiburg, Granada, 1992, pp. 9-10

2 As practised, for example, in China.

3 'Umar Vadillo, *The End of Economics*, pp. 13-15

4 'Abd al-Qādir al-Sufi, "The Epoch of the Young Ottomans", *First Annual International Conference on Islamic Thought*, Istanbul, March 15&16, 1996

5 'Abd al-Qādir al-Sufi (published under his family name Ian Dallas), *The Engines of the Broken World: Discourses on Tacitus and Lucan*, Budgate Press, Cape Town, 2012, p. 166

6 Norman Kretzmann and Elononore Stump, "Aquinas, Thomas", in E. Craig (Ed.), *Routledge Encyclopedia of Philosophy*. London: Routledge. http://www.rep.routledge.com/article/B007

7 A.C. Grayling, *Towards the Light: The Story of the Struggles for Liberty and Rights that Made the Modern West*, Bloomsbury, London, 2007, p. 59

8 'Abd al-Qādir al-Sufi (published under his family name Ian Dallas), *The Engines of the Broken World: Discourses on Tacitus and Lucan*, Budgate Press, Cape Town, 2012, p. 166

9 'Abd al-Qādir al-Sufi, "The Collapse of the Monetarist Society: Part Three", *Financial Crisis*, BTBIL, Gaberone, 2008, p. 65

10 "The Anabaptists were so called because they did not accept infant baptism, arguing that people could only properly become Christian by mature choice and self-dedication, and baptism must therefore take place in adulthood." A.C. Grayling, *Towards the Light: The Story of the Struggles for Liberty and Rights that Made the Modern West*, p. 36

11 "The Peasants' War was a mass insurgency that broke out in the Southern German states of Thuringia, Swabia and Franconia in 1524; some estimates say that as many as 300,000 people rose in revolt against their temporal princes and Catholic clergy." A.C. Grayling, *Towards the Light: The Story of the Struggles for Liberty and Rights that Made the Modern West*, p. 37

12 Martin Luther, cited by 'Umar Vadillo, *The Esoteric Deviation in Islam*, Madinah Press, Cape Town, 2003, p. 201

13 'Umar Vadillo, *The End of Economics*, pp. 13-15

14 Monetarism is an economic theory that focuses on the macroeconomic effects of the supply of money and central banking. It emphasizes the role of governments in controlling the amount of money in circulation.

15 'Abd al-Qādir al-Sufi, "The Collapse of the Monetarist Society: Part Three", *Financial Crisis*, p. 65

16 'Abd al-Qādir al-Sufi, "The Collapse of the Monetarist Society: Part One", *Financial Crisis*, p. 55

17 C. Pierson, *The Modern State*, Routledge, London, 1996, pp. 78-79

18 Al-Qurṭubī, "Obey the Sultan with respect to seven things: the minting of the dinar and the dirham, fixing weights and measures, legal judgments, Hajj, Jumu'ah, the two Eids and Jihad." Cited in Vadillo, U.A., *The Return of the Gold Dinar*, Madinah Press, Cape Town, 1996, p. v

19 Ibn Khaldūn, *al-Muqaddima*, cited in Vadillo, U.A., *The Return of the Gold Dinar*, p. 91

20 Mālik ibn Anas, *Al-Muwaṭṭa'*, tr. Aisha Bewley and Ya'qub Johnson, Diwan Press, Norwich, 1982, chapter 31 " "Book of Business Transactions", pp. 283-308

21 'Umar Vadillo, *The End of Economics*, Madinah Press, Granada, 1991, p. 76

22 'Umar Vadillo, *The End of Economics*, p. 77

23 "1. Commodities of use or those commodities whose normal utility can be divided into other utilities of partial use ; like for example, a car, a horse, a plot of land, a house etc., these things are called non-fungible quantities. 2. Commodities of consumption or those commodities whose normal utilities cannot be divided into other utilities of partial use; like for example an apple, meat, gold, silver, raw materials in general, etc., these things are ... called fungible commodities." 'Umar Vadillo, *The End of Economics*, p. 78

24 'Umar Vadillo, *The End of Economics*, p. 79

25 Mālik ibn Anas, *Al-Muwaṭṭa'*, tr. Aisha Bewley and Ya'qub Johnson, chapter 31.31, p. 291

26 *"Allah has permitted trade and forbidden usury ribā."* Qur'ān 2: 274

27 Al-Qurṭubī, *Tafsīr al-Qurṭubī*, tr, Aisha Bewley, Dar al-Taqwa, London. 2003, p. 725

28 Yassine Essid, *Critique of the Origins of Islamic Economic Thought*, E.J. Brill, Leiden, 1995, p. 95

29 Abdalhaqq Bewley, "Islam and the World Financial System", BTBIL, Gaberone, 2009, pp. 6-7

30 See 'Umar Vadillo, "Fatwa on Banking", http://www.shaykhabdalqadir.com/content/index.html

31 "Bankers were a tribe that had risen and grown up in Cromwell's time and never even been heard of before the late troubles [referring to the English Civil War], till when the whole trade of money had passed through the hands of the scriveners [the people who wrote contracts and negotiated loans];

these bankers were for the most part goldsmiths." Edward Hyde (the Earl of Clarendon – English Chancellor of the Exchequer between 1643 and 1646 and Lord Chancellor between 1658 to 1667), cited in Abdalhaqq Bewley, "Islam and the World Financial System", p. 7

32 J-P Hirsch, "Revolutionary France, Cradle of Free Enterprise", American Historical Review 94 (1989): 1281

33 'Abd al-Qādir Al-Sufi, A., *Technique of the Coup De Banque*, Kutubia Mayurqa, Palma De Mallorca, 2000, p. 68

34 'Umar Vadillio, "Fatwa on Banking", http://www.shaykhabdalqadir.com/content/index.html

35 It "would give the treasury something to pay out immediately, and relieve the national necessities; that having been put into circulation, this paper money would stimulate business; that it would give to all capitalists, large or small, the means for buying from the nation the ecclesiastical real estate, and from the proceeds of this real estate, the nation would pay its debts and also obtain new funds for new necessities ... "35 A.D. White, *Fiat Money Inflation in France*, D. Appleton-Century Company, New York, 1933, pp. 1-2

36 Land, which like gold and silver possesses intrinsic value, was accepted as collateral upon which currency can be issued.

37 A.D. White, *Fiat Money Inflation in France*, pp. 8-9

38 A.D. White, *Fiat Money Inflation in France*, pp. 7-8

39 G. Davies, *A History of Money: From Ancient Times to the Present Day*, pp. 557-558

40 A.D. White, *Fiat Money Inflation in France*, pp. 42-43

41 J. Jonker, "Competing in tandem: Securities markets and commercial banking patterns in Europe during the nineteenth century", *The Origins of National Financial Systems* (ed. Douglas J. Forsyth and Daniel Verdier), Routledge, London, 3003, p. 75

42 Zeno Dahinden, "Deconstruction of the World Financial System," *A Crisis for Usury Capitalism*, BTBIL, Gaberone, 2008, p. 18

43 P.T. White, "The Power of Money", *National Geographic*, January 1993, p. 83

44 http://www.shaykhabdalqadir.com/content/articles/The%20Psychosis%20of%20Systems-Society.php

45 Michael Hudson, ISLET; eBook Edition edition (4 Oct 2012)

46 A.C. Grayling, *Towards the Light: The Story of the Struggles for Liberty and Rights that Made the Modern West*, Bloomsbury, London, 2007, p. 1

47 'Abd al-Qādir al-Sufi, *Technique of the Coup De Banque*, Editorial Kutubia Mayurqa, Palma De Mallorca, 2000

48 http://www.shaykhabdalqadir.com/content/Conference/2009/ShaykhAbdalqadir_Day2.mp3

49 "The term 'conspiracy theory' implies both a fantastical view of history coupled with a psychiatric condition of imbalance bordering on or plainly located in paranoia." 'Abd al-Qādir al-Sufi, *For the Coming Man*, p. 14

50 Ronald Syme, cited in 'Abd al-Qādir al-Sufi (published under his family name Ian Dallas), *The Engines of the Broken World: Discourses on Tacitus and Lucan*, Budgate Press, Cape Town, 2012, p. 21

51 'Abd al-Qādir al-Sufi, *The Engines of the Broken World: Discourses on Tacitus and Lucan*, p. 23

52 'Abd al-Qādir al-Sufi, *The Engines of the Broken World: Discourses on Tacitus and Lucan*, p. 104

53 'Abd al-Qādir al-Sufi, *The Engines of the Broken World: Discourses on Tacitus and Lucan*, pp. 111- 112

54 'Abd al-Qādir al-Sufi, *The Engines of the Broken World: Discourses on Tacitus and Lucan*, pp. 112- 113

55 'Abd al-Qādir al-Sufi, *The Engines of the Broken World: Discourses on Tacitus and Lucan*, p. 112

56 'Abd al-Qādir al-Sufi, *The Engines of the Broken World: Discourses on Tacitus and Lucan*, p. 31

57 'Abd al-Qādir al-Sufi, *The Engines of the Broken World: Discourses on Tacitus and Lucan*, p. 41

58 'Abd al-Qādir al-Sufi (published under his family name Ian Dallas), *The Time of the Bedouin*, Budgate Press, Cape Town, 2006, p. 278

59 'Abd al-Qādir al-Sufi, *The Time of the Bedouin*, p. 279

60 'Abd al-Qādir al-Sufi, *The Time of the Bedouin*, p. 280

61 'Abd al-Qādir al-Sufi, *The Time of the Bedouin*, p. 283

62 'Abd al-Qādir al-Sufi, *The Time of the Bedouin*, p. 284

63 'Abd al-Qādir al-Sufi, *The Time of the Bedouin*, p. 263

64 'Abd al-Qādir al-Sufi, *Root Islamic Education*, p. 3

65 Refer to pages 26 to 34 for al-Sufi's discussion on *futuwwa*, *jamā'a* and *umma*

66 'Abd al-Qādir al-Sufi, *The Time of the Bedouin*, p. 266

67 The word "state" is used as a convenience because without it the modern mind struggles to envisage governance

68 Qur'ān 5: 42

69 Qur'ān 59: 6,7

70 Abū al-Ḥasan al-Mawardī, *al-Aḥkām as-Sulṭāniyya*,. tr. A. Yate, Ta-Ha

Publishers Ltd., London, 1996

71 G. Baer, "Guilds in Middle Eastern History", Studies in the Economic History of the Middle East, (ed.) M.A. Cook, Oxford University Press, Oxford, 1970; D.A. Breebart, "The Futuvvet-name-i kebir. A Manual on Turkish Guilds", Journal of Economic and Social History of the Orient, Vol. 15, No. 1/2. (June, 1972), pp. 203-215; M. Cizakca, "Cash Waqfs of Bursa 1555-1823", Journal of Economic and Social History of the Orient, 38, 3: 313, Richmond Surrey, 1999; Y. Essid, *A Critique of the Origins of Islamic Economic Thought*, E.J. Brill, Leiden, 1995; S.D. Goitein, *A Mediterranean Society: An Abridgement in One Volume*, revised and edited by Jacob Lassner, University of California Press, Berkeley, 1999; M. Hoexter, "Waqf Studies in the Twentieth Century: The State of the Art", Journal of the Economic and Social History of the Orient, Vol. 41, No. 4. (1998); T. Kuran, "The Provision of Public Goods Under Islamic Law: Origins, Impact, and Limitations of the Waqf System", Law and Society Review, Vol. 35, No. 4. (2001); B. Lewis, "The Islamic Guilds", The Economic History Review, Vol. 8, No. 1. (Nov., 1937), pp. 20-34; M. Maksudoğlu, "Waqf", *Sultaniyya*, Madinah Press, Cape Town, 2002; and A-K. Rafeq, "Craft Organization, Work Ethics, and the Strains of Change in Ottoman Syria", Journal of the American Oriental Society, Vol. III, No. 3 (Jul. Sep., 1991) pp. 495-511

72 "They reversed the usual evaluative force of words to suit their own assessment of actions." Thucydides, cited by 'Abd al-Qādir al-Sufi in *The Engines of the Broken World: Discourses on Tacitus and Lucan*, p. 158

73 Tacitus, cited by"Abd al-Qādir al-Sufi in *The Engines of the Broken World: Discourses on Tacitus and Lucan*, pp. 160-161

74 Refer to Qur'ān 2: 29-32

75 'Abd al-Qādir al-Sufi, *The Engines of the Broken World: Discourses on Tacitus and Lucan*, pp. 116- 167

76 'Abd al-Qādir al-Sufi, *The Engines of the Broken World: Discourses on Tacitus and Lucan*, pp. 169

Glossary

abdāl – the Substitutes

af'āl – one's acts being the actions of God

akhlāq – behaviour that is characterized by good character

'alam al-mithāl – World of Analogies

al-'amā' – the Great Mist or Cloud, which has been described as the primordial non-spatiality in non-time or abstract space

al-anwār al-sanīha – apocalyptic lights

al-'aql al-kullī – the Universal Intellect or, in Qur'ānic terminology, the Highest Pen (*al-qalam al-a'lā*)

al-a'rāḍ – the accidental forms

al-'arsh – the Throne on which God established His authority

'amal – behaviour/action

'amal ahl al-Madīna – the practice of the first three generations of Muslims in Madīna, the city in which Islam was first established

amīr – governor/leader

amr – command

'aqīda also 'ilm al-kalām – creed/theology

'araḍ – accident

arbāb al-tawḥīd – members *of* the Sufi school of Baghdad, or the Iraqi school, who were renowned for being the masters of unification

'ārifīn – gnostics

aṣnāf – guilds

awqāf – charitable endowments

awtād – the Pillars

ʿawāmm – people in general

B

badīha – inspiration

al-bahthiyya – *discursive* (*wisdom*)

balāʾ – trials which purify the Sufi in his or her new situation and adjust the lens of his or her new vision

baqāʾ – subsistence in God, when the Sufi returns to mankind after annihilation in God

barzakh – the interspace between the visible and the invisible

basṭ – expansion

bāṭinī – inward (knowledge)

bayʿa – allegiance

bayt al-māl – the treasury

bidʿa – innovations

birr – regard for others, just behaviour

burāq – is a celestial being, described by the Prophet as a white animal taller than a donkey but smaller than a mule and whose step covered a distance equal to the range of its vision

burhān – demonstration or proof

D

al-dahr – the age or time/space

dawrī – cyclical or periodic

dhāt – essence of God

dhawq – taste

al-dhawqiyya – experiential (wisdom)

dhikr – remembrance or invocation of God

F

falak al-aṭlas – the Isotropic Orb, which is so described because it has no distinguishing features and is homogeneous in all directions

falak al-burūj – the sphere of the constellations

al-falak al-mukawkab – the sphere of the stars

al-falsafa – philosophy

fanā' also *fanā' fi'llāh* – annihilation in God, the cessation of personal actions, attributes and essence

fanā' al-fanā' – passing away from the passing away

faqr – poverty

faqīh – jurist (pl. *fuqahā'*)

faqīr – literally a poor person, also used to mean a Sufi (pl. *fuqara*)

farq – separation

al-farq al-awwal – the first separation

al-farq al-thānī – the second separation

fayḍ – emanation

fiqh – the science for the application of the *sharī'a*

firāsa – intuitive knowledge of human nature

fiṭra – the inborn natural predisposition in the human being

futuwwa – connotes high morality, fraternity, chivalry, altruism, honour and virtue

G

ghurba – exile

H

ḥadas – intuition

ḥadīth – reported saying of the Prophet Muhammad ﷺ

ḥadīth qudsī – the words of God as reported by the Prophet Muhammad ﷺ which are not part of the Qur'ān

ḥāl – state (pl. *aḥwāl*)

ḥaqīqa – means "reality" and refers to the inward illuminations of knowledge which flood the heart of the seeker on the Path. The highest levels of *ḥaqīqa* are *fanā'* and *baqā'*

al-hayūlā al-ūlā – Prime Matter

ḥikma – wisdom

al-ḥikmat al-ilahiyya – theosophy

ḥikmat al-ishrāq – Philosophy of Illumination

ḥikma mashshā'ī – Peripatetic Philosophy

ḥikma mashriqiyya – Eastern Philosophy

al-ḥikmat al-muta'āliya – metaphilosophy

ḥilm – state of calm serenity, which is not overcome by anger from within or threats of violence from without. Its opposite is another Qur'ānic term *jāhiliyya* which is: "... the energy force of the unbridled *nafs*, utterly flamboyant and expressed, ruthless in its infantile determination to experience gratification whether of appetite or violence." (See text for reference)

himma – spiritual aspiration

ḥiss – sensory

ḥubb – love

ḥulūl – incarnation

I

'ibāda – worship

idhn – authorization

al-idrak – intuition

iḥsān – Prophetic terminology for Sufism

ijtihād – personal judgements in legal matters

ikhlāṣ – pure, unadulterated sincerity

'ilm al-aḥwāl – science of states

'ilm al-'aql – science of the intellect

'ilm al-asrār – science of the innermost consciousness

al-ʿilm al-huduri – knowledge by presence
al-ʿilm al-husuli – representative knowledge
ʿilm al-kalām – creed/theology
ʿilm al-muʿāmala – the science of behaviour
ʿilm al-mukāshafa – the science of unveiling
al-ʿilm al-sahih – true science
Imam – leader
īmān – faith/belief/creed
al-insān al-kāmil – the perfect man
irāda – stripping away of self will and accepting what God wills
ishrāq – illumination
Islam – religion established by the Prophet Muhammad ﷺ
islām – outward practice
isnād – chains of authority
Isrāʾ – Night-journey of the Prophet
ittiḥād – union

J

jabarūt – the domain of Divine power

jadhb – attraction to God. A *sālik* is one whose attraction to God has not driven him to madness-in-God thereby becoming *majdhūb*. To be *sālik/majdhūb* is to be outwardly sober and inwardly drunk.

jamʿ – gatheredness
jamʿ al-jamʿ – gatheredness of gatheredness
jamāʿa – the community
al-jawhar al-fard – the unique non-divisible Single Essence
al-jawhar al-ṣuwarī – the formable essence
jaysh – army
al-jinān – the Seven Gardens
al-jism al-kull – Universal Body

K

kamāl – perfection

kashf – stripping away, unveiling

khalwa – seclusion, meaning withdrawal from the world in the concentration of invocation of the *al-ism al-aʿẓam* (the Supreme Name – i.e. Allah) under the supervision of an authorized master

khawf – fear of God

khayāl – understood by the Sufis "as the creative source of manifestation, the very cause of our existence, and the powerful intermediary that enables us to remain in constant contact with the Infinite and the Absolute." (See text for reference)

al-khayāl al-muṭlaq – the first manifestation of the universe; it is the *ʿamāʾ* (the Great Mist), the energy that contains all the forms but is as yet undifferentiated

al-khayāl al-muḥaqqaq – the level which contains the knowledge that there are two ways of perceiving reality: that of *sharīʿa* and that of *ḥaqīqa*

al-khayāl al-munfaṣil – the way by which the universe is ordered into different forms and kingdoms, such as the mineral kingdom, animal kingdom, jinn etc.

al-hayāl al-muttaṣil – the *khayāl* that enables one to create pictures in the mind. It separates reality from fantasy and things as they are from things as they can be

khuṭba – Friday sermon

kufr – disbelief

al-kursī – the Pedestal whose dimensions, compared to the Throne, are described by Ibn al-ʿArabī as a tiny ring in a vast desert

L

lāhūt – this is when God's Lordship over existence in its inward aspect is defined *laṭīfah* – spiritual substance

layl – night

lawā'iḥ – first flashes of awareness of lights/ *lawāmiʿ* – gleams of genuine lights that come to the longing heart/ *ṭawāliʿ* – Shaykh ʿAbd al-Qādir explains that the *lawā'iḥ* lights are like meteors, the *lawāmiʿ* lights are like the Milky Way through clouds and the *ṭawāliʿ* lights are like the full view of the Northern Lights that fill the whole night sky

lisān – audition

M

madhhab – school of law

maghzūb – one who identifies the phenomenal with God or regards the phenomenal as real is *maghzūb*, an illusionist

maḥabba – love

maḥbūb – one who can clearly distinguish between the phenomenal and the Real and lives his life in accordance with that knowledge is *maḥbūb*, one favoured and loved by God

māhiyya – essence/quiddity

mahjūb – a person who acknowledges only phenomena is veiled and is called *mahjūb*

maḥq – annihilation in His source

majdhūb – someone who is enraptured and bewildered by the effect of Divine attraction is *majdhūb*

majlis al-dhikr – a gathering of *dhikr*

majnūn – mad

al-makān – place

malakūt – the domain of unseen forms

maqām – station on the Sufi's journey (pl. *maqāmāt*)

maʿrifa – gnosis, the direct awareness of the Divine Reality in the heart, the organ in the human being with the capacity to perceive spiritual realities that the intellect cannot grasp

martaba al-ṭabīʿa – Level of Nature

mawlā – client

miʿrāj – ascension of the Prophet Muhammad ﷺ

Mīthāq – the Primordial Covenant

muḥāḍara – is the positioning of the Sufi in his relation to God. At this stage, while he is still veiled, he aligns himself to God through demonstrative reasoning (*burhān*) and the workings of the intellect (*ʿaql*).

muḥtasib – city administrator

muhsinin – people of *iḥsān* i.e. Sufis

mukāshafa – is when the veil is partly lifted. At this stage the Sufi transcends discursive reasoning; that is to say, he sees beyond God's signs (*āyāt*) and observes His attributes (*ṣifāt*).

mulk – the domain of solid forms

muqaddam – representative of the Shaykh

murābiṭūn – people of the *ribāṭ*

murāqaba – watching

murid – disciple

murshid – Sufi master

mushāhada – contemplation of God during which the Sufi experiences the Presence of the Reality (*al-ḥaqīqa*)

al-mushāhada al-ishrāqiyya – illuminationist vision

N

nāfila – voluntary worship (*pl. nawāfil*)

nafs – the experiencing self, i.e. the body and psyche of the human being

al-nafs al-kulliyya – the Universal Intellect is aware of its ontic 'shadow' which is called the Universal Soul (or the Qur'ānic Preserved Tablet (*al-lawḥ al-maḥfūẓ*)

al-Nafas al-Raḥmānī – the Breath of the Merciful
nahār – daytime
nāsūt – man/womanhood
nazar – vision
nuqabā' – the Chieftains
nūri-muḥammadiyya – Light of Muḥammad ﷺ

Q

qabḍ – constriction
qāḍī – judges
qaṣīda – poem
qiyās – analogical extrapolation in law
qurb – nearness
quṭb – the 'Axis' of the spiritual universe – who is at the apex of the hierarchy of the *awliyā'* (friends of God/saints)

R

raḥamūt – when the gnosis of the Real replaces the concept of essence
rajā' – hope in God
rasm – form of *faqr* as opposed to its essence (*ḥaqīqa*)
ribā – usury
ribāṭ – a fortress where soldiers were garrisoned for the purpose of defending the territory of the Muslims and repelling enemy attacks, but it was also a place of learning and intensive worship
riḍā – contentment
al-rūḥ al-qudus – the Holy Spirit (or Active Intelligence)
rūḥānī – spiritual

S

al-sabt – Saturday, but in the context cited in the text it means the cosmic Saturday which is considered to be the 'day of eternity' (*yawm al-abad*) and all the cosmic days of the cosmic week are actually occurring on the cosmic Saturday

ṣabr – patience

ṣafwa min al-ʿibād – the elect of the élite, the most excellent of the believers and the pure ones (*khulāṣa min al-khalq*)

ṣāḥib al-waqt – the master of time. The *quṭb* is called the master of time because he witnesses space and time in their totality.

sālik – one who is journeying on the Sufi path to God

ṣaḥwa – sobriety

ṣāʿiqa – annihilation in the Divine manifestation

shȧn – matter, concern, business, situation and event

shaykh al-tarbiya – Sufi Master of Instruction

shawq – desire, the hearts longing to meet the Beloved

sharīʿa – literally means "road" but also refers to the legal parameters of Islam and the science of the outward

shukr – thankfulness

shūrā – consultative body

shurṭa – police

ṣidq – truthfulness

ṣifāt – the attributes of God

silsila – the chain of authoritative spiritual transmission from one master to another, going back to and originating with the Prophet ﷺ

simsima – gnosis that is too fine to express

sīra – biography of the Prophet Muḥammad ﷺ

sukr – drunkenness

sulṭān – political ruler

sulūk – the Sufi path to God

sunna- normative practice of the Prophet Muḥammad ﷺ

T

tābiʿīn – the generation of Muslims after the Prophet ﷺ and his Companions in Madīna; the *tābiʿī at-tābiʿīn were the* generation after them

tafrīd – isolation

takhallī – revelation of the treasure-chests of one's inwardness

talwīn – change

tamkīn – fixity

tanzīh muṭlaq – absolutely transcendent

tajalliyāt – Divine manifestations

tajrīd – stripping away

talaqqī – receiving

taqwā – being aware and in awe of God

taraqqī – rising

tārīkh – history, especially the philosophy of history

ṭarīq al-ʿulūm – scientific methodology

ṭarīqa – Sufi Order. *Ṭarīqa* means "path" or "way" and refers to travelling on the Path to God under the guidance of a Sufi master

taṣawwuf – Sufism

tashbīh – immanence

tawba – turning away from wrong actions

tawhid – unification, the doctrine of Divine Unity

tawakkul – reliance on God

tekkes – centres for Sufi gatherings (also called *takiyas*)

U

ʿubbād – worshippers

ʿubūdiyya – recognition that one is a slave of God, to be in harmony with one's innate nature

ʿulamāʾ – scholars (s. *ʿālim*)

umma – the world Muslim community

umm al-madhāhib – legal school of Madīna, which is also known as *'amal ahl al-Madīna*

uṣūl al-dīn – science of the principles of religion

uṣūl al-fiqh – Islamic legal methodology, sources of the law

'uzla – retirement in order to fix in the heart the meanings and secrets attained in the *khalwa*

W

waḥdat al-wujūd – oneness of existence

wahm – illusion

waḥy – revelation/inspiration

wajd – the first degree of ecstasy, finding oneself

walī-Allāh – saint, friend of God (pl. *awliyā-Allāh*)

wara' – scrupulousness

wazīr – minister of the *sulṭān*

wilāya – sainthood, friendship with God

wijdān – the second degree of ecstasy, when the sweetness of witnessing lasts

wird or *waẓīfa* – to be recited regularly by the disciples of a Shaykh within a Sufi Order. A *wird* is a collection of Qur'ānic verses, prayers from the *ḥadīth* and the writings of the great masters (pl. *award*)

wujūd – existence

wujūd dhihnī – mental existence

wujūd khārijī – external existence

Y

yawm – day

yawm al-shȧn – the day of the event

Z

ẓāhir – outward

zakāt – wealth tax
zamān – time
zamān fawq ṭabīʿī – para-natural time
zamān ṭabīʿī – natural or physical time
zāwiya – the place where the Sufi Shaykh teaches
zuhd – doing-without (*zāhid* – ascetic, one who chooses to go without)

Bibliography

'Aṭṭār, F., *Tadhkirat al-Awliyā'*, tr. A.J Arberry, Omphaloskepsis, Ames, Iowa, 2000

Al-Attas, S.M.N., *Prolegomena to the Metaphysics of Islam*, Suhail Academy, Lahore, 2001

Al-Jamal, A., *The Meaning of Man*, Diwan Press, Norwich, 1977

Akkach, S., "The World of Imagination in Ibn 'Arabī's Ontology", British Journal of Middle Eastern Studies (1997), 24(1)

Alvares, C., *Science, Development, and Violence: The Revolt Against Modernity*, Oxford University Press, New York, 1992

Arberry, A.J., *Sufism: An Account of the Mystics of Islam*, George Allen & Unwin Ltd., London, 1950

Armstrong, K., *The Case for God*, The Bodley Head, London, 2009

Ayubi, N.N., "Islamic State", *The Oxford Encyclopedia of the Modern Islamic World*, Oxford University Press, Oxford, 1995

Baer, G., "Guilds in Middle Eastern History", Studies in the Economic History of the Middle East, (ed.) M.A. Cook, Oxford University Press, Oxford, 1970

Barnes, D., "Charisma and Religious Leadership: An Historical Analysis", Journal for the Scientific Study of Religion, 1978, Vol. 17, Iss. 1

Bashir, Z., *Sunshine at Madina*, The Islamic Foundation, Leicester, 1990

Bell, D., "Kant," A Blackwell Companion to Philosophy, eds. Nicoholas Bunnin and E.P. Tsui-James, Blackwell Publishing, Oxford, 2002

Benton, T. and Craib, I., *Philosophy of Social Science: the philosophical foundations of social thought*, Palgrave Macmillan, New York, 2011

Buehler, A., *Sufi Heirs of the Prophet*, University of South Carolina Press, Columbia, 1998

Bewley, Aisha and Abdalhaqq, *The Noble Qur'ān – A New Rendering of its Meaning in English*, Bookwork, Norwich, 1999

Bewley, Abdalhaqq, *Islam: Its Basic Practices and Beliefs*, Ta-Ha, London, 2008

Bewley, A. and Abdalhakim-Douglas, A., *Zakat: Raising a Fallen Pillar*, Blackstone Press, Norwich, 2001

Bewley, Aisha, *Glossary of Islamic Terms*, Ta-Ha Publishers, London, 1998

Bewley, Aisha, *Islam: The Empowering of Women*, Ta-Ha Publishers, London, 1999

Bober, S., *Marx and the Meaning of Capitalism: Introduction and Analyses*, Palgrave Macmillan, New York, 2008

Breebart, D.A., "The *Futuvvet-name-i kebir.* A Manual on Turkish Guilds", Journal of Economic and Social History of the Orient, Vol. 15, No. 1/2. (June, 1972), pp. 203-215

Campanini, M., *An Introduction to Islamic Philosophy*, tr. Caroline Higgitt, Edinburgh University Press, Edinburgh, 2008

Capra, F., *The Tao of Physics*, Bantam Books, New York, 1983

_______, The Hidden Connections, Doubleday, New York, 2002

Carroll, J., *The Wreck of Western Culture - Humanism Revisited*, Scribe, Melbourne, 2004

Cizakca, M., "Cash Waqfs of Bursa 1555-1823", Journal of Economic and Social History of the Orient, 38, 3: 313

Chaitin, G., "The Limits of Reason," Scientific American, March 2006

________, "Computers, Paradoxes and the Foundations of Mathematics," American Scientist, Volume 90, 2000

Chittick, W., *Ibn al-'Arabī's Metaphysics of Imagination: The Sufi Path of Knowledge*, SUNY Press, Albany, 1989

Chodkiewicz, M., *The Spiritual Writings of Amir 'Abd al-Kader*, SUNY Press, New York, 1995

Choudry, M.A., *The Principles of Islamic Political Economy*, St. Martin's Press, New York, 1992

Commins, D., "Modernism", *The Oxford Encyclopedia of the Modern Islamic World*, Oxford University Press, Oxford, 1995

Cornell. V., *Realm of the Saint: Power and Authority in Moroccan Sufism*, University of Texas Press, Austin, 1998

Crecelius, D., "The Course of Secularization in Modern Egypt", *Islam and Development*, (ed.) John L. Esposito, Syracruse University Press, New York, 1982

Crone, P., *Medieval Islamic Political Thought*, Edinburgh University Press, Edinburgh, 2004

Dahinden, Z., "Deconstruction of the World Financial System," A Crisis for Usury Capitalism, Botswana Translation Bureau of Islamic Literature, Gaberone, 2008

Dallas, I., *The Book of Strangers*, State University of New York Press, Albany, 1988

_______, *The Ten Symphonies of Gorka König*, Kegan Paul International, London, 1989

_______, *The New Wagnerian*, Freiburg Books, Granada, 1990

_______, *Oedipus and Dionysus*, Freiburg Books, Granada, 1992

_______, *Collected Works*, Budgate Press, Cape Town, 2005

_______, *The Time of the Bedouin: on the politics of power*, Budgate Press, Cape Town, 2006

_______, *Political Renewal*, Budgate Press, Cape Town, 2009
_______, *The Interim is Mine*, Budgate Press, Cape Town, 2010
_______, *The Engines of the Broken World: Discourses on Tacitus and Lucan*, Budgate Press, Cape Town, 2012
Damasio, A., *Descartes' Error*, G.P. Putnam's Sons, New York, 1994
Dan Fodio, U., *Handbook on Islām, Īmān and Iḥsān*, Diwan Press, Norwich, 1978
Dangor, S., *Shaykh Yūsuf*, Iqra Research Centre, Mobeni, 1982
Al-Darqāwī, M., *The Darqāwī Way*, Diwan Press, Norwich, 1979
Davies, G, *A History of Money: From Ancient Times to the Present Day*, University of Wales Press, Cardiff, 2002
De Tocqueville, A., *Democracy in America* (with an introduction by Alan Ryan), Knopf, New York, c1994
Djait, H., *Europe and Islam: Cultures and Modernity*, University of California Press, Berkeley, 1985
Dutton, Y., "Sunna, Hadith and Madīnan 'Amal", Journal of Islamic Studies 4: 1 (1993)
_______, *The Origins of Islamic Law: The Qur'ān, the Muwaṭṭa' and Madīnan 'Amal*, Curzon, Richmond, Surrey, 1999
Dye, E., "Sorge in Heidegger and in Goethe's Faust," Goethe Yearbook, Vol. 16, 2009
Eaton, R., "Sufis as Warriors," in *Sufism: Critical Concepts in Islamic Studies*, ed. Lloyd Ridgeon, Routledge, London, 2008
Eisenstadt, S.N., *Comparative Civilizations and Multiple Modernities*, Brill, Leiden ; Boston, 2003
Eccles, J.C., *The Self and Its Brain: An Argument for Interactionism*, Routledge and Kegan Paul, London, 1983
Elmessiri, A.M., *Epistemological Bias in the Physical and Social Sciences*, The International Institute of Islamic Thought, London, 2006
Essid, Y., *A Critique of the Origins of Islamic Economic Thought*, E.J. Brill, Leiden, 1995

Fakhry, M., *History of Islamic Philosophy*, Columbia University Press, New York, 1983

Al-Fārābī, A., *Al-Madīna al-fāḍila*, tr. R. Walzer, Clarendon Press, Oxford, 1985

Faroqhi, S., *The Ottoman Empire and the World Around It*, I.B. Tauris, London, 2006

Ferguson, N., *The Ascent of Money: a financial history of the world*, Penguin, London, 2008

Fukuyama, F., *The End of History and the Last Man*, Penguin, London, 1992

Gellner, E., *Postmodernism, Reason and Religion*, Routledge, London, 1992

Gillespie, M.A., *Hegel, Heidegger and the Ground of History*, The University of Chicago Press, Chicago, 1984

Gleick, J., *Isaac Newton*, Pantheon Books, New York, 2003

Goitein, S.D., *A Mediterranean Society: An Abridgement in One Volume*, revised and edited by Jacob Lassner, University of California Press, Berkeley, 1999

Grayling, A.C., *Towards the Light: The Story of the Struggles for Liberty and Rights that Made the Modern West*, Bloomsbury, London, 2007

Green, N., *Indian Sufism since the Seventeenth Century: Saints, books and empires in the Muslim Deccan*, Routledge, Oxon, 2006

Griffel, F., *Al-Ghazali's Philosophical Theology*, Oxford University Press, Oxford, 2009

Guyer, P., *The Cambridge Companion to Kant and Modern Philosophy*, Cambridge University Press, Cambridge, 2006

Grof, S., *Ancient Wisdom and Modern Science*, State University of New York Press, Albany, c1984

Al-Ḥallāj, M., *Ṭawāsīn al-Ḥallāj*, tr. A. Bewley, Taj Company, Delhi, 1982

Hardy, P., "Epistemology and Divine Discourse," *The Cambridge Companion to Classical Islamic Theology* (ed. Tim Winter), Cambridge University Press, Cambridge, 2008

Heidegger, M., *Question Concerning Technology and Other Essays*, tr. William Lovitt, Harper and Row, New York, 1977

________, *Being and Time*, tr. John Macquarrie & Edward Robinson, Blackwell Publishing Ltd., London, 2000

________, *What is Called Thinking*, Harper and Row Publishers, New York, 1968

________, *Introduction to Metaphysics*, tr. R. Manheim, Yale University Press, New Haven, 1959

Heisenberg, W., *Physics and Philosophy*: The Revolution in Modern Science, Harper & Row, New York, 1958

Hirsch, J-P, "Revolutionary France, Cradle of Free Enterprise", American Historical Review 94 (1989)

Hobbes, T., *Leviathan* (ed. Richard Tuck), Cambridge University Press, Cambridge, 1996

Hodge, M.J.S., *Before and After Darwin: Origins, Species, Cosmogonies, and Ontologies*, Ashgate, Aldershot, c2008

Hodgson, M.G.S., *The Venture of Islam: Conscience and History in a World Civilization*, University of Chicago Press, Chicago, 1974

Hoexter, M., "Waqf Studies in the Twentieth Century: The State of the Art", Journal of the Economic and Social History of the Orient, Vol. 41, No. 4. (1998)

Hourani, G.F., *Averroes – On the Harmony of Religion and Philosophy*, Luzac, London, 1976

Al-Hujwīrī, A., *Kashf al-Maḥjūb of al-Hujwīrī*, tr. R.A. Nicholson, Luzac & Co. Ltd., London, 1976

Ibn Anas, M., *Al-Muwaṭṭa'*, tr. Aisha Bewley and Ya'qub Johnson, Diwan Press, Norwich, 1982

Ibn 'Ajība, A., *Commentary on Ibn al-Banna's al-Futūḥāt al-*

ilāhiyya fī sharḥ al-mabāḥith al-aṣliyya published as, *The Basic Research*, Madinah Press, Cape Town, 1998

Ibn al-'Arabī, M., *Al-Futūḥāt al-Makkiyya*, (section on 'The Mysteries of Bearing Witness to the Oneness of God and Prophethood of Muhammad') tr. Aisha Bewley, Great Books of the Islamic World, Chicago, 2002

Ibn al-Ḥabīb, M., *The Diwan of Shaykh Muhammad ibn al-Habib*, Madinah Press, Cape Town, 2001

Ibn Isḥāq, *Sīrat Rasūl Allāh* tr. as *The Life of Muhammad* by A. Guillaume, Oxford University Press, Oxford, 1978

Ibn al-Mubārak al-Lamaṭī, A., *al-Dhabab al-Ibrīz min Kalām Sayyidī 'Abd al-'Azīz al-Dabbāgh*, tr. John O'Kane and Bernd Radtke, Brill, Leiden, 2007

Ibn Rushd, *Faṣl al-maqāl*, tr. George F. Hourani in *Averroes: On the Harmony of Religion and Philosophy*, Luzac, London, 1976

Ibrahim, M., *Merchant Capital and Islam*, University of Texas, Austin, 1990

Illich, I., *Deschooling Society*, Harper & Row, New York, 1971

Inalcık, H. and Donald Quataert (eds.), *An Economic and Social History of the Ottoman Empire, 1300-1914*, Cambridge University Press, Cambridge, 1994

Iqbal, M., *The Reconstruction of Religious Thought in Islam*, Sh. Muhammad Ashraf, Lahore, 1977

'Iyāḍ, ibn Mūsā al-Yaḥṣūbī, *Muhammad, Messenger of Allah, translation of ash-Shifā of Qāḍī 'Iyāḍ*, Madinah Press, Granada, 1991

Jackson, R., *Nietzsche and Islam*, Routledge, Abington, Oxon, 2007

Kamal, M., *From Essence to Being: The Philosophy of Mulla Sadra and Martin Heidegger*, ICAS Press, London, 2010

_______, *Mulla Sadra's Transcendent Philosophy*, Asgate, Aldershot, 2006

Kamali, M., *Multiple Modernities, Civil Society and Islam: the case of Iran and Turkey*, Liverpool University Press, Liverpool, c2006

Kingsley, P., *Ancient Philosophy, Mystery and Magic*, Clarendon Press, Oxford, 1995

Al-Kalābādhī, A., *The Doctrine of the Sufis*, tr. A.J. Arberry, Cambridge, Cambridge University Press, 1935

Kant, I., *Critique of Pure Reason*, tr. N. Kemp Smith, Macmillan, London, 1929

Karamustafa, A.T., *Sufism: The Formative Period*, Edinburgh University Press, Edinburgh, 2007

Keddie, N.R., *An Islamic Response to Imperialism*, University of California Press, Berkeley, 1983

Kedourie, E., *Afghānī and 'Abduh – An Essay on Religious Unbelief and Political Activism in Modern Islam*, Frank Cass and Co. Ltd., London, 1966

Khan, M.A., *The Pious Caliphs*, Islamic Book Publishers, Kuwait, 1982

Knysh, A., *Islamic Mysticism: A Short History*, Brill, Leiden, 2000

_____, *Ibn 'Arabī in the Later Islamic Tradition: The Making of a Polemical Image in Medieval Islam*, SUNY Press, Albany, 1999

Kuhn, T., *The Structure of Scientific Revolutions*, University of Chicago Press, Chicago, 1970

Kuran, T., "The Provision of Public Goods Under Islamic Law: Origins, Impact, and Limitations of the Waqf System", Law and Society Review, Vol. 35, No. 4. (2001)

Layish, A., "The Contribution of the Modernists to the Secularization of Islamic Law", *Islamic Law and Legal Theory*, edited by Ian Edge, Dartmouth, Aldershot, 1996

Lewis, B., *What Went Wrong?: The Clash Between Islam and Modernity in the Middle East*, Perennial, New York, 2002

_______, "The Islamic Guilds", The Economic History Review, Vol. 8, No. 1. (Nov., 1937), pp. 20-34

Lewontin, R.C., *Biology as Ideology: The Doctrine of DNA*, Harper and Collins, New York, 1992

Longino, H.E., *Science as Social Knowledge: Values and Objectivity in Scientific Inquiry*, Princeton University Press, Princeton, 1990

Lumbard, J., "The Decline of Knowledge and the Rise of Ideology in the Modern World," *Islam, Fundamentalism, and the Betrayal of Tradition: Essays by Western Muslim Scholars*, World Wisdom Inc., Bloomington, 2004

Al-Maḥallī, J. and al-Suyūṭī, J., *Tafsīr al-Jalālayn* (tr. Aisha Bewley), Dar al-Taqwa, London, 2007

Muhammad Khalid Masud, Armando Salvatore, and Martin van Bruinessen (eds), *Islam and Modernity: Key Issues and Debates*, Edinburgh, Edinburgh University Press, c2009 (page 293)

Mcgregor, R.J.A., "Notes on the Transmission of Mystical Philosophy, *Reason and Inspiration in Islam: Theology, Philosophy and Mysticism in Muslim Thought*, ed. Todd Lawson, IB Tauris, London, 2005

Maksudoğlu, M., "Waqf", *Sultaniyya*, Madinah Press, Cape Town, 2002

Marcotte, R.D., "Reason (*'aql*) and Direct Intuition (*mushahada*) in the works of Shihāb al-Dīn al-Suhrawardī (d. 587/1191)", *Reason and Inspiration in Islam: Theology, Philosophy and Mysticism in Muslim Thought*, ed. Todd Lawson, IB Tauris, London, 2005

Al-Mawardī, Abu'l Ḥasan, *al-Ahkam as-Sultaniyyah* (tr. A. Yate), Ta-Ha Publishers Ltd., London, 1996

McMurtry, J., *The Cancer Stage of Capitalism*, Pluto Press, London, 1999

McNeese, T., *Galileo: Renaissance Scientist and Astronomer*, Chelsea House Publishers, Philadelphia, 2005

Medawar, P.B., *Induction and Intuition in Scientific Thought*, London, Methuen, 1969

Mermer, Y. and Ameur, R., "Beyond the Modern: Sa'id al-Nursi's View of Science," Islam and Science (2004):119-60

Montgomery, R.E., *The Visionary D.H. Lawrence: Beyond Philosophy and Art*, Cambridge University Press, Cambridge, 1994

Morris, J.W., "Ibn 'Arabī's 'Esotericism,'" in *Islamic Philosophy and Theology: Critical Concepts in Islamic Thought*, ed. Ian Richard Netton, Routledge, London. 2007

Netton, I., "*Ishrāq* and *Waḥda*," in *Sufism: Critical Concepts in Islamic Studies*, ed. Lloyd Ridgeon, Routledge, London, 2008

Neumarkt, P., "Martin Heidegger: the philosopher of psychological confusion", Journal of Evolutionary Psychology, March 2003

Nietzsche, F., *The Gay Science* (tr. Walter Kaufmann), Vintage Books, New York, 1974

Nuseibeh, S., "Epistemology", *History of Islamic Philosophy* (ed. by Seyyed Hossein Nasr and Oliver Leaman): Routledge, London, 1996

Ojembarrena, A., "*Bildung* and *Bildunsroman*: From Goethe's *Wihelm Meister's Apprenticeship* to Ian Dallas' *Book of Strangers*", conference paper delivered at the 4th International Islamic Political Economy Conference: Asia Europe Muslim Partnership organized by the Universiti Sains Malaysia in 2000. On file with the researcher.

Pamuk, S., *The Ottoman Empire and European Capitalism*, Cambridge University Press, Cambridge, 1987

Peters, F.E., "The Greek and Syriac Background", in *History of Islamic Philosophy*, ed. S.H. Nasr & O. Leaman, Routledge, London, 1996

Alvin Plantinga, "Religion and Science", *Stanford Encyclopaedia of Philosophy*, http://plato.stanford.edu/entries/religion-science/

Polyani, M., *Personal Knowledge: Towards a Post Critical Philosophy*, Routledge, London, 1998

Popper, K., *Knowledge and the Body-Mind Problem: In Defence of Interaction*, (ed. M.A. Notturno, Routledge, London, 1994

Pound, E., *Cantos*, Faber, London, 1954

Quinodoz, J-M. (tr. David Alcorn), *Reading Freud: A Chronological Exploration of Freud's Writings*, Routledge, New York, 2005

Al-Qurṭubī, A., *Tafsīr al-Qurṭubī* (tr, Aisha Bewley), Dar al-Taqwa, London. 2003

Radke, B., "The Eight Rules of Junayd", in *Reason and Inspiration in Islam: Theology, Philosophy and Mysticism in Muslim Thought*, ed. Todd Lawson, IB Tauris, London, 2005

Rafeq, A-K., "Craft Organization, Work Ethics, and the Strains of Change in Ottoman Syria", Journal of the American Oriental Society, Vol. III, No. 3 (Jul. Sep., 1991) pp. 495-511

Rahman, F., "Ibn Sina," *History of Muslim Philosophy*, ed. M.M. Sharif, Otto Harrassowitz, Wiesbaden, 1963

Al-Rasheed, M., *A History of Saudi Arabia*, Cambridge University Press, Cambridge, 2002

Resnik, D.B., *The Ethics of Science: An Introduction*, Routledge, London, 1998

Robinson, N., "Ibn al-'Arabī, Muḥyi al-Dīn (1164-1240)" at http://www.muslimphilosophy.com/ip/rep/H022)

Ibn Rushd, *Bidāyat al-Mujtahid* (tr. I.A.K. Nyazee), Garnet Publishing Limited, Reading, 1996

Saul, J.R., *The Collapse of Globalism and the Reinvention of the World*, Viking, Camberwell, Vic., 2005

Schmaltz, T.M., *Descartes on Causation*, Oxford University Press, New York, c2008

Schmitz, K.L., "Embodiment and Situation: Charles Taylor's Hegel," The Journal of Philosophy, Vol. 73, No. 19 (Nov. 4, 1976)

Setia, A, "Al-Attas' Philosophy of Science: An Extended Outline", Islam and Science, Dec. 2003

Shaban, M.A., *Islamic History: A New Interpretation* 1, Cambridge University Press, Cambridge, 1971

Shariati, A., *Marxism and Other Western Fallacies* (tr. R. Campbell), Mizan Press, 1980

Sorrel, T., *Scientism: Philosophy and the Infatuation with Science*, Routledge, London, 1991

Smith, A., *An Inquiry into the Nature and Causes of the Wealth of Nations*: a selected edition ed. Kathryn Sutherland, Oxford University Press, Oxford, 1998

Shaykh 'Abd al-Qādir, *The Hundred Steps*, Madinah Press, Kuala Lumpur, 1998

________, *The Return of the Khalifate*, Madinah Press, Cape Town, 1996

________, *Technique of the Coup De Banque*, Editorial Kutubia Mayurqa, Palma De Mallorca, 2000

________, *Root Islamic Education*, Madinah Press, London, 1993

________, *The Way of Muhammad*, Diwan Press, London, 1975

________, *The Muslim Prince*, Madinah Press, Cape Town, 2009

________, *Sultaniyya*, Madinah Press, Cape Town, 2002

________, *Letter to an Arab Muslim*, Editorial Kutubia Mayurqa, Palma De Mallorca, 2000

________, *Qur'ānic Tawḥīd*, Diwan Press, Norwich, 1981

________, *Kufr: An Islamic Critique*, Diwan Press, Norwich, 1982

________, *The Sign of the Sword*, Murabitun publications, Norwich, 1984

________, *Jihad a Groundplan*, Diwan Press, Norwich, 1978

________, *The Book of Tawḥīd*, Madinah Press, Cape Town, 2006

________, *The Book of 'Amal*, Madinah Press, Cape Town, 2008

________, *The Book of Safar*, Madinah Press, Cape Town, 2008

________, *The Book of Ḥubb*, Madinah Press, Cape Town, 2007

Taylor, C., *The Ethics of Authenticity*, Harvard University Press, Cambridge, Mass., c1991

________, *A Secular Age*, Harvard University Press, Cambridge, Mass., 2007

________, *Hegel*, Cambridge University Press, Cambridge, 1975

Thomson, A., *The Making of Social Theory: order, reason and desire*, Oxford University Press Canada, Don Mills, Ont. c2010

Tibi, B., "Authority and Legitimation", *The Oxford Encyclopedia of the Modern Islamic World*, Oxford, 1995

Toulmin, S., *Cosmopolis: The Hidden Agenda of Modernity*, Free Press, New York, c1990

Umar, M., *Islam in Northern India During the Eighteenth Century*, Munshiram Manoharial Publishers, New Delhi, 1993

Vadillo, U. I., *The Esoteric Deviation in Islam*, Madinah Press, Cape Town, 2003

________, *The Return of the Gold Dinar*, Madinah Press, Cape Town, 1996

________, http://www.shaykhabdalqadir.com/content/index.html, "Fatwa on Banking", accessed 6 March, 2008

________, *Fatwa on Paper-Money*, Madinah Press, Granada, 1991

________, *The End of Economics*, Madinah Press, Granada, 1991

Valliuddin, M., *Qur'ānic Sufism*, Motilal Banarsidass, Delhi, 1977

Van Bruinessen, M. and Howell, J.D., *Sufism and the Modern in Islam*, I.B. Taurus, London, 2007

Vogel, F.E., *Islamic Law and Legal System: Studies of Saudi Arabia*, Brill, Leiden, 2000

Wallernstein, I., Decdeli, H., and Kasaba, R., "Incorporation of the Ottoman Empire and the World Economy", *The Ottoman Empire and the World-Economy*, Islamoglu-Inan, (ed). Cambridge, Cambridge University Press, 1987

Waugh, P., *Postmodernism – A Reader*, E. Arnold, London, 1992

Weber, M., *Charisma and Institution Building*, ed. S.N. Eisenstadt, University of Chicago, Chicago, 1968

White, A D, *Fiat Money Inflation in France*, D. Appleton-Century Company, New York, 1933

White, P.T., "The Power of Money", National Geographic, January 1993

Williams, J.A. (ed.), *Themes of Islamic Civilization*, University of California Press, Berkeley, 1971

Yate, A., *Ibn Rushd – Mujtahid of Europe*, Turmverlag, 1999

Yazdi, M.H., *The Principles of Epistemology in Islamic Philosophy: Knowledge by Presence*, State University of New York Press, Albany, 1992

Yousef, M.H., *Ibn 'Arabī – Time and Cosmology*, Routledge, Oxon, 2008

Hossein Ziai, "Shihāb al-Dīn Suhrawardī: founder of the Illuminationist school" in *History of Islamic Philosophy*, ed. S.H. Nasr & O. Leaman, Routledge, London, 1996

Index

A

Abbasid 19, 23
abdāl 87
'Abd al-Malik ibn Ḥabīb 97, 98
'Abd al-Malik ibn Marwān 14
'Abd al-Muṭṭalib 12
'Abd al-Qādir al-Jazā'irī 89
'Abd al-Wāḥid Yaḥyā 92
Abdelwahhab Elmesseri 88
'Abdullāh ibn 'Umar 210
King Abdullah II of Jordan 92
abolition of the *ṭarīqas* 90
abolition of usury 228
Abraham 183
Absolute Being 61
absolute dictator 222
Absolute non-Being 61
Absolute or Necessary Being 174
Absolute Spirit 148, 149
the absolute 137
absorption in the vision of the Lord 198
abstract forms 169
Abū al-'Abbās Muḥammad 99
Abū Bakr al-Ṣiddīq 14, 39, 104, 196
Abū Dāwūd 105
Abū Ḥafṣ 26
Abū Ḥanīfa 16
Abū Hurayra 104
Abū Khālid al-Aḥmar 16
Abū Nu'aym al-Isfahānī 15
Abū Sa'īd Ṣaḥnūn 98
Abū Ṭālib 12
Abū Ṭālib al-Makkī 17
Abū Thawr 19
Abū 'Alī al-Ṣadafī 96
Abū 'Amr al-Ḥārith ibn Miskīn 98
Abū 'Imrān 23, 24
'act' 148
Active or Agent Intellect 172, 179, 199
acts and attributes of God 195
Adam 183
Theodor Adorno 117
adultery 71
aesthesis 133
aesthetics 224
Africa 89, 113
after death state 79
af'āl (acts) 78
Age of Enlightenment 113
Aghlabid 99

Aḥmad ibn 'Āshir 85
Aḥmad ibn 'Aṭā' 23
aḥwāl (states) 18, 68, 77, 231
al-'Ajamī 15
akhlāq (good character) 39, 69
'ālam al-khayāl (World of *Khayāl*) 185
'ālam al-mithāl (World of Analogies) 181
Albert the Great 173
alcohol 71
aletheia 147
Alexandria 23
Alfonso XII the Wise 207
Algeria 89, 94
'Alī al-Jamal 92
'Alī ibn Abī Ṭālib 12, 13, 14, 16
'Alī ibn Mūsā al-Riḍā 17
'Alī ibn Ziyād 99
allegorical [verses] 179
Almoravids (Murābiṭūn) 93
alreadiness 142
Qādirī-Shādhilī-Darqāwī 2, 6, 8
alternative to capitalism 204
'amal (action/behaviour) 25, 28, 40, 85, 105, 106, 164, 197, 225
'amal ahl al-madīna (the Practice of the People of Madīna) 25, 28, 29, 30, 33, 97, 98, 100, 106, 120, 164, 165, 225, 226, 228, 238, 239
'amā' 61
America 113, 138
American Empire 223, 239
American Express 220
Americanism 152
amīr (leader) 96, 97, 228, 239
amīrs (leaders) 83, 98
Amman Declaration/Message 92, 93
ample provision 232
amr (command) 58, 97, 105
Anabaptist movement 207
ana'l-ḥaqq 48
analogical reasoning 178
analytic philosophy 138
Anarch 162
anarchist 162
anarchy 15
Anas ibn Mālik 69
Anatolian frontier 82
ancient Greece 167, 204
ancient Greeks 217
ancient masters 178
ancient Rome 222, 223
Ancient World 107
al-Andalus 94, 95, 96, 97, 99
Andalusian philosophers 183
Angel Gabriel 173, 186
angels 180
anger 75
annihilation of the self 73, 189, 231
anthropocentrism 113
anthropomorphism 173
anti-Hegelian movements 138
al-anwār al-sanīḥa (apocalyptic lights) 181
anxiety about provision 75
apostate 176
apostles John and Paul 156
approbation of usury 210
'aqīda 86, 103
al-'aql al-kullī 54
al-'aql 38, 168
Thomas Aquinas 148, 156, 173, 207
Arabic 14
Arab Islam 84

ʿaraḍ (accident) 175
Arbaʿīniyyat (collections of forty hadith) 105
Der Arbeiter (The Worker) 159, 160
arbitrage trading 220
Archangel Gabriel 11
archetypes 180
ʿārifīn (gnostics) 87
Aristophanes 207
Aristotelian demonstration 181
Aristotelianism 185
Aristotelian theory 176
Aristotelian view 170
Aristotle 37, 127, 148, 169, 170, 171, 173, 178, 179, 182, 184, 199, 207
Aristotle's *Politics* 217
arithmetic 131, 132
arrival 45
artificial intelligence 236
artisans 83
ʿaṣabiyya (united by kinship) 226, 238
new *ʿaṣabiyya* 238
Asad ibn al-Furāt 99
Ascending Steps 33
Ascension 197
ascetic practices 181
Ashʿarites 60
Ashʿarī position 198
Ashʿarī theology 195
Asia 113
aṣnāf (guilds) 227
assignats 213, 214
atheism 103, 114, 206, 221
atoms 194
al-Attas 192
Augustine 156
Augustinus 207
Augustus 222
Aurangabad 82
authenticity 143, 154
automatic teller machines 215
autonomy of private ownership 208
ʿawāmm (people in general) 190
awliyāʾ-Allāh (friends of God) 57, 196, 197
awqāf (charitable endowments) 227, 229
Awrangzeb 82
awtād (Pillars) 87
al-Awwal (the First) 171
āyāt 38
Ayatollah Sistānī 92
Alfred Jules Ayer 129, 234
Ayubi 86
al-aʿrāḍ (accidents) 56

B

background 103
Francis Bacon 114, 206
Roger Bacon 173
badīha (inspiration) 168
Badr 14
Baghdad 18, 19, 23
al-baḥthiyya (discursive wisdom) 180
bail-out 221
Balance 44
balāʾ (trials which purify the Sufi... 79
bankers 212, 235
banking cartel 215
Bank of America 220
Bank of New York Mellon 220
banks 235
Hassan al-Banna 165

La Banque de France 213, 214
baqā' (subsistence in God) 3, 11, 12, 20, 22, 27, 40, 47, 50, 51, 67, 79, 101, 164, 187, 189, 192, 193, 197, 198, 200, 229, 231, 232
barter system 211
barzakh (an interspace or dimension between two realities) 46, 51, 121, 195
Bashkar 119
basic moods 143
baṣīra (insight) 168
Basra 14, 15
basṭ (expansion) 78
bāṭinī (inner) 27
bāṭin (internal visage) 85
Jean Baudrillard 118
Bāyazīd al-Bisṭāmī 48
bayt al-māl (the treasury) 94, 227
bay'a (allegiance) 100, 228, 239
BBC 2
becoming 142
Bedouinism (people becoming estranged from mainstream society) 226
Bedouins (those estranged from mainstream society) 226
Being 62, 139, 142, 143, 144, 146, 147, 153, 154, 157, 161, 164, 174, 184, 234
Being and Time 155
being in the intellect 175
being-in-the-world 142
Being of beings 145
being of God 173
beings 145, 154
being-there (*Dasein*) 142, 147
Alfred Bel 84, 85
Benghazi 93
Jeremy Bentham 109
Berber superstition 84
George Berkeley 129
Beton and Crabb 119
Abdalhaqq Bewley 29
Aisha Bewley 95
Roy Bhaskar 118
bid'a (blameworthy innovations) 176
Bijapur plateau 82
bills of exchange 212
birr (action that is truly just) 25, 27, 28, 30, 33, 225
Bishr ibn al-Ḥārith 18
Bismarckian state 149
Black-Scholes model 220
Lloyd Blankfein 220
blueprint pattern for Islamic societies 225
body/mind dichotomy 127
Book of Allah 120
Book of Safar 194
boredom 143
bourgeois society 224
Boyle 4
Louis Brandeis 220
Breath of the Merciful 63
Britain 138
British Empire 223, 239
British occupation 90
the British 5, 89
al-Buhlūl ibn Rāshid 99
al-Bukhārī 104, 105
bullion 212
Rudolf Bultman 157
Burāq 11
burhān (demonstration or proof) 38, 168, 182

burning scientists at the stake 206
al-Buṣayrī's *Burda* (Poem of the Cloak) 229

C

calculative thinking 145
caliphal states 165
caliphate 227
caliphs 106, 207
call of conscience 143
Calm Being 164
calm serenity 71
John Calvin 4, 205, 207
Campanini 176
Cape Town 2, 215, 229, 230
capitalism 91, 93, 113, 115, 116, 120, 150, 203, 205, 218, 222, 236
capitalist economic system 114
capitalist free market economics 124
capitalist hegemony 204
capitalist investment economy 228
capitalist system 203, 236
Fritjof Capra 42, 62, 65
care for the young and old 70
Cartesian and Kantian presuppositions 157
Cartesian/Kantian philosophical position 167
Cartesian philosophy 124, 233
Cartesian thinking substance 142
categorical imperatives 111, 224
categories 133
Catholic Church 112, 205, 234
Catholic philosophy 155
Cato 207
the Caucasus 89
causality 131, 134, 157
causation 132
cause and effect 177
central banks 215, 216, 219
central or reserve banking 214
Ceuta 96
change 120, 130
charisma 83
charismatic authority 84
Ken Chenault 220
China 98
Chinese authorities 89
the Chinese 89
Juan Chrisostomos 207
Christian Councils 207
Christian doctrines 140
Christian idea of God 140
Christianity 111, 137, 205
Christian Kings 207
Christian philosophy 156
Christian society 151
Christian theism 140
Christian theologians 157
Christian theological orthodoxy 206
Christian theological thinking 107
Christian theology 156, 171, 177
Winston Churchill 218
Cicero 207
circulation of wealth 226
Citigroup 220
civil war 218, 221
class conflict 149
classical philosophical tradition 107
classical social theories 236
Bill Clinton 218
clipping coins 211
codex 103
cogito ergo sum 112, 127, 148
cognition 237

coins 211
Cold War 115
collapse of the capitalist system 223
colleges 229
colonialism 96
colonial period 88
colonisation 160
colonisers 5
commentaries on Aristotle 178
commentary on the Qur'ān 209
commerce 203
commercial banking system 216
commodities and media élites 235
commodities élites 219
Commodity Futures Modernization Act 220
commodity of consumption 210
Communism 114, 152
communist economy 114
communist era 89
communities 239
community 83, 134
Companions 14, 40, 104, 196, 210, 231
Companions of the Cave 57
Companions of the Right 33
Complexity Theory 62, 236
compulsion of State Law 214
Auguste Comte 116
concentration camps 218
condemnation of usury 203, 207
condition of pre-separation 191
confiscated property of the Church 213
conspiracy theory 219
constant devotion 196
constitutional law 111
the Constitution 216
consumerism 225, 238
consumption 151
contemporary social and historical context 239
context of understanding 102
control of nature 139
Copernicus 4, 54
Vincent Cornell 83, 84, 85, 86
cosmogony 53, 54, 65, 130, 167, 186
cosmology 53, 54, 65, 87, 130, 172, 186, 231
courtesy 70
craftsmen 83
creation ex nihilo 170
creation of fiat money 216
Crecelius 86
credit cards 215
credit creation 203
credit default swaps 220
Critical Realism 118, 119
critique of modernity 224
Critique of Pure Reason 112, 133
crowd control 221
currencies 208, 209
non-shar'ī currencies 209
currency speculation 216
current social paradigm 217
cybernetics 152

D

Abd al-'Azīz al-Dabbāgh 44
Zeno Dahinden 215
al-dahr 58
Dallas College 230
Ian Dallas 2
Mīr Dāmād 173
Antonio Damasio 62, 66, 167, 236
the darkening of the world 145

Muḥammad al-ʿArabī al-Darqāwī 80
Charles Darwin 112
Darwinian biology 124, 233
Dasein 142, 143, 147, 154, 158, 164
Richard Davis 221
dawrī (cyclical or periodic time) 59
death of God 126, 139, 148
debt leveraging 216
debtor 206
deconstruction 118
deduction 129, 234
deeper levels of being 238
defending the ecosphere 225, 238
definitions 174
Deism 108, 110, 111
democracy 91, 140, 151, 152, 203, 204, 205, 217, 218, 219, 222, 235, 239
democratic government 92
democratization 93
demonstrative reasoning 178
denial of the resurrection 176
depreciation 214
deregulation doctrines 220
derivatives 203, 216, 220
Jacques Derrida 118
Descartes' Error 62
René Descartes 112, 126, 127, 128, 131, 135, 140, 148, 163, 167, 168, 206, 223, 233
design 232
destruction 238
destruction of metaphysics 153
destruction of social groups and nations 160
the destruction of the earth 145
determinacy 134
determinism 130, 148
devaluation 213
development 122, 123
devolutionary process 239
John Dewey 167
dhāt (the Essence of God) 49, 78, 192, 195
al-dhawqiyya (experiential wisdom) 180
dhawq (taste) 4, 38, 41, 44, 67, 78, 168, 188, 231
dhikr (invocation of Allah) 68, 76, 77, 80, 229, 239
dhikr of the heart 76
dhikr of the *sirr* 76
dhikr of the tongue 76
Dhū al-Nūn al-Miṣrī 26
dialectical parliamentary democracy 217
Dialogue Concerning the Two World Systems 112
dictatorship 151, 152, 218, 235
dictatorships 91, 206
Jamie Dimon 220
dīn 69
dīn al-fiṭra (the religion of one's innate disposition, natural nomos) 225, 238
dinar [gold coin of specific weight and value] 210
Ḍirār al-Asadī 13
direct experience 198
direct experience of God 239
direct experience of God's presence 231
direct knowledge of God 8, 233
dirham [silver coin of specific weight and value] 210
disappearance of entities 232

discursive knowledge 188, 237
discursive philosophy 175, 199
distinction between subject and object 167
Divine Artist 157
Divine Attributes 59, 65
Divine Command 63
Divine imperatives 225
Divine law 235
Divine legislation 207
Divine Light 181
Divine love 63, 201
Divine Names 54, 65
Divine Presence 8, 14, 80, 188, 229, 231
Divine purpose 232
Divine revelation 203
Divine Self-disclosure 11, 21, 50, 189, 200, 232
the Divine 163, 166, 206, 228
Divine union 81
Divine worship 228
Divinity 206
dīwāns (collections of poems) 229
the Diwan 41
Hicham Djait 113
DNA 194
Doctor Honoris Causa of Literature 162
doctrine of Being 172
doctrine of essence and existence 174
The Doctrine of the Sufis (*Kitab al-ta'arruf li-madhhab ahl al-tasawwuf*) 9
doing without 74
doubt 205
dread 143
dualism between being and becoming 169
dualisms 139
Émile Durkheim 115, 118
Dutch colonialism 90
Yasin Dutton 29, 105, 106
Ellis Dye 158
dyeing 79

E

early Madīna 225
earnestness 196
the earth 172
Eastern Europe 138
Eastern Philosophy 180, 199
Richard Eaton 82
Meister Eckhart 156
economic ruin 214
economics 152, 218, 233
ecstasy 51, 75
E-Dinar 215
education 221, 233
efficient market hypothesis 220
ego 139
The Ego and the Id 112
Egypt 5, 90, 116, 227
der Einzelne (the isolated one) 160
Shmuel Noah Eisenstadt 84
elect of the élite 87, 193
Eleventh Being 172
Eleventh Fiqh Conference 215
elimination of laws and religions 160
élite 87
Elizabeth I 207
Abdelwahhab Elmesseri 88
emanation 172, 176
emancipation 118
embracing usury 207

emotion 120, 237
emotional 120
Empedocles 166
empirical and phenomenal level 191
empirical experience 190
empirical measurements 205
empirical scientific method 116
empiricism 1, 3, 32, 37, 38, 42, 44, 52, 102, 113, 127, 128, 131, 164, 166, 167, 198, 204, 205, 231, 237, 238
empiricists 119
Encyclopedia of the Philosophical Sciences 138
end of history 115
the end of metaphysics 144, 167
the end of modern philosophy 167
the end of questioning 145
energeia 148
enforced minimum and maximum prices 210
enforced use of one particular commodity as money 210
Friedrich Engels 149
English bourgeois society 149
Enlightenment 111, 114, 116, 119, 130, 131, 149, 236
Enlightenment rationalism 86
enslavement and oppression 218
Epimenides 166, 167
epistemological endeavours 231
epistemological poverty 237
epistemologies of modernity 233, 237
epistemology 37, 128, 129, 135, 168, 169, 177, 178, 182, 184, 189, 196, 199, 202, 233, 237, 238
epistemology of Sufism 202
equity 227
Recep Tayyip Erdoğan 227
eschatology 187
esotericisation of *taṣawwuf* 91
esotericists 91
esoteric knowledge 177
essence and existence 192
Essence of God 121, 201
the essence 146, 184
essentialism 145, 146
establishment of the *'amal ahl al-Madīna* 239
eternal recurrence 150
eternity of the world 176
ethical norms 111
ethics 128, 131
Eumeswil 162
Euphrates 15
Europe 90, 98, 107, 108, 113, 205, 211, 234
European culture 115
Europeanism 152
European Middle Ages 112, 114
evidence 129, 234
evolutionary theory 112
exchange economy 228
executions 218
exegetes 231
Existence 134, 174, 175, 185
existence of God 232
existential crisis 222, 239
existentialism 138, 145, 183
existentialist 2
exoteric knowledge 177
experience 128
experiment 128, 129, 234
experimentation 205
exploitation 151
exploited 226

exploration 160
expropriated land 213
extermination of indigenous peoples 160
external object 199

F

façade 219
'fair rate' of interest 208
faith 150
Majid Fakhry 178
al-falak al-aṭlas 55
al-falak al-burūj 55
al-falak al-mukawkab 55
fallenness 143
fall of the USSR 114
falsafa (philosophy) 172, 187
falsification 211
fanā' (annihilation) 12, 20, 21, 22, 25, 27, 40, 44, 46, 47, 48, 49, 50, 51, 79, 100, 164, 187, 188, 189, 191, 192, 194, 195, 196, 197, 198, 200, 229, 231, 232
fanā' al-fanā' (passing away from the passing away) 192, 193
fantasy 239
faqīh 29, 96
faqīr 13, 41, 92
faqr (ontological poverty) 174
faqr (poverty 13, 78
al-Fārābī 171, 178, 183, 184, 199
farq (separation) 78, 190
al-farq al-awwal (first separation) 190
al-farq al-thānī (second separation) 190
fasting 74
Fāṭima, the daughter of the Prophet 12
fatwās 92
Faust 158
Shaykh Muḥammad al-Faytūrī Ḥamūda 2, 93, 198
fear of creation 75
Federal Reserve Act of 1913 216
Federal Reserve Bank of New York 215
Federal Reserve System 215
the Federal Reserve 216
feelings 234
female infanticide 71
Niall Ferguson 116
Fes 93
feudal authority 84
fiat money 215, 216
finance capitalism 216
financial and fiscal austerity 217
financial collapse of 2008 221
financial crisis 213
financial élite 219, 220, 235
financial instruments 216
financial oligarchs 219
financial oligarchy 220
financial system 211, 221, 235
fiqh 9, 14, 16, 106
First Being 172, 199
first cause 157
first emanation 174
First Heaven 172
First Intelligence 173
first separation 191
first sphere 173
First World War 151
fiṭra (an inborn natural predisposition to fulfil their destinies)

31, 32, 107, 162, 164, 232
five prayers 196
the flight of the gods 145
a Follower 104
the Forest 162
forgetfulness of Being 145, 146, 148, 156, 167
fornication 71
forty day retreat 181
Michel Foucault 118
founders of the schools of Islamic law 207
fractional reserve banking 203, 224, 235
France 138
Frankfurt School 117
fratricide 217
Freddie Mac 220
free circulation of wealth 227
freedom 120, 227, 237
freedom and necessity 139
freedom from domination 118
freedom of religion 92
freedom of trade 209
freedom of will/determinism 130
free enterprise 218
freeing of slaves 71
free trade 227
free will 130
Freiburg philosophy faculty 156
Freiburg University 155
Freiheit ist Existenz 162
French colonialists 89
French government 213
French Republic 213
French Revolution 112, 149, 212, 213, 214, 217, 218
French state 213
the French 5, 89
Freudian psychology 124, 233
Sigmund Freud 112
Führer principle 153
Francis Fukuyama 115
full realization of Being 146
fundamentalists 227
fundamental pre-epistemic question 199, 237
fungible commodities (those of consumption) 210
fuqahā' (jurists) 23, 69, 97, 98, 196, 197
al-Futūḥāt al-Makkiyya 39
futures trading 203, 235
futuwwa (the individual functioning at the level of community) 26, 27, 39, 78, 225
fuzzy mathematics 77, 224

G

Hans-Georg Gadamer 117, 158
Galilean worldview 131
Galileo Galilei 4, 112, 119, 206
gambling 71, 210
Louis Gardet 39
Pierre Gassendi 206
Gawrath ibn al-Ḥārith 70
Geist (spirit) 139
Ernest Gellner 86
Genealogy of Morals 140
generals of the army 83
generosity 150
genetically modified seeds 221
genocide 218
genus 175
geometry 131, 132

Geschichte 151
Gestalt 159, 162
Gestalt of the worker 224
Abū Ḥāmid Muḥammad al-Ghazālī 25, 38, 95, 176, 177, 178, 199
ghurba (exile) 78
Michael Allen Gillespie 151, 155, 157
global capitalism 90, 115
global capitalist system 218, 235
global financial crisis of 2008 116, 223, 236
globalism 120, 236
globalization 114
global oligarchic state 217
global political and economic domination 235
global totalitarianism of technology 151, 234
global world state 115
gnostic knowledge 86
gnostics 177
God discloses Himself 231
Kurt Gödel 62, 66, 167, 236
"God is dead" 114, 140, 141, 235
God of Christianity 139
God of revealed religion 199
God's caliph 28
God's knowledge only of universal beings 176
God's presence 231
Johann Wolfgang von Goethe 31, 148, 155, 158, 164
gold 211
Golden Age Paradigm 165
Goldman Sachs 220
goldsmiths 212
goldsmiths and silversmiths 211
Goldziher 180
good citizenship 92
governance 97, 98
government expenditure 219
governors 106
grammarians 96, 231
Gramm-Leach-Bliley Act 220
Senator Phil Gramm 220
Granada 96
grave 79
Greek 147
Greek and Roman philosophers 203
Greek founders of Western philosophy 166, 198, 237
Greek historian 227
Greek metaphysics 157
Greek national economy 221
Greek ontological writings 156
Greek philosophers 183
Greek philosophical ideas 171
Greek philosophy 218
Greeks 147, 183, 207
Greek thought 173
Nile Green 81, 82
gross national product 122, 123
growth 123
René Guenon 91
guilds 108, 229
Guinea 89
gulag 218
Dominicus Gundissalinus 173

H

Jurgen Habermas 117
Ḥabīb al-ʿAjamī 15, 16
ḥadas 168
ḥadīth 14, 19, 23, 27, 40, 49, 54, 56, 60, 77, 94, 96, 104, 105, 106,

184, 197
al-dīn al-mu'āmalah 32
Be one who does without in this world and Allah will love you. 74
Do not curse *al-dahr* because Allah is *al-dahr* 58
God was and there was nothing with Him. 193
I am the city of knowledge and 'Ali is its gate 13
I was only sent to perfect noble qualities of character 69
Religion is behaviour (*al-dīn al-mu'āmalah*). 35
seeking knowledge is an obligation for every Muslim 35
The Messenger of God did not store up anything for the next day 69
Ḥadīth Jibrīl 9
ḥadīth qudsī
If the main occupation of My slave is to be occupied with Me, I make his yearning and his sweetness in remembering Me. 75
I was a hidden treasure and I loved to be known. So I created the Universe in order to be known. 54
The son of Adam hurts me, he curses *al-dahr* and I am *al-dahr* 58
Hadron Bootstrap Model 65, 66
hadrons 65
ḥāfiẓ 29
Ḥafṣa bint 'Umar ibn al-Khaṭṭāb 104
al-Ḥājj 'Umar Tal 89
Manṣūr al-Ḥallāj 14, 48, 198
ḥāl (state) 41, 56, 77, 188
Hammām ibn Munabbih 104
Ḥanafī 16, 106
Ḥanbalī 16, 106
al-ḥaqīqa (the Reality) 3, 13, 38, 40, 41, 51, 61, 74, 92, 100, 121, 122, 124, 174, 187, 188, 202
al-Ḥaqq (the Real) 86, 121
al-Ḥārith ibn Miskīn Muḥammad ibn Yūsuf 98
al-Ḥasan al-Baṣrī 13, 14
Hāshim 12
hatred of freedom and creativity 145
ḥayra (bewilderment) 198
al-hayūlā al-ūlā (Prime Matter) 55
health 221
Georg Wilhelm Friedrich Hegel 109, 115, 118, 126, 129, 135, 136, 137, 138, 139, 148, 149, 163, 234
Hegelian dialectic 149, 153
Hegelianism 138
Hegelian school 149
Young Hegelians 149
hegemony of the Church 205
Heidegger 66, 102, 103, 139, 140, 141, 142, 143, 144, 145, 146, 147, 148, 151, 152, 153, 154, 155, 156, 157, 158, 159, 164, 167, 224, 234, 236
Heideggerian need 143, 144, 157, 165
Heideggerian ontology 139
Martin Heidegger 62, 126, 127, 223
Heidegger's ontology 140
Werner Heisenberg 223, 224
heliocentrism 54, 66, 112
Heliopolis 161

Hellenism 172, 173
Hellenist philosophical tradition 168
Henry VIII 207
Heraclitus 144, 147
herd-animal 141
higher moralities 140
Highest Pen 54
high yield debt 220
Hijra 106
ḥikma (wisdom/philosophy) 71, 172, 182
ḥikma mashriqiyya (Eastern Philosophy) 175, 180
al-ḥikmat al-ilāhiyya (theosophy) 187
ḥikmat al-ishrāq (Philosophy of Illumination) 37, 180
al-ḥikmat al-muta'āliya (metaphilosophy) 185
ḥilm 71
himma 45, 198, 201, 232
hire purchase 215
ḥisba (administration of the city/market) 227, 229
His Essence 232
ḥiss (the senses) 42
historian 96
Historie (science of history) 151, 152
history 187
history of money 211
Adolf Hitler 218
Hitler/Stalin pact 218
hoarding 71
Hobbes' political theories 233
Thomas Hobbes 112, 124
Holy Light 180
homeless 226
home loans 215
homo romanitas 156
homosexuality 71
Honorary Doctorate of Literature 2
Max Horkheimer 117
houris 44
Michael Hudson 217
ḥudūd [legal boundaries] 209
Hui Muslims 89
al-Hujwīrī 13, 14, 19, 20, 24
ḥulūl (incarnation) 49, 192
human being 142
human intellect 173, 179, 199
Humanism 32, 108, 111, 114, 116
humanitas 156
human reasoning 142
human rights 92
humanus (man himself) 152
Friedrich Wilhelm von Humboldt 109
David Hume 129, 130, 234
humus (the earth) 152
The Hundred Steps 78
Edmund Husserl 156, 158
hypotheses 205

I

Iberian Peninsula 93
Ibn al-Fāriḍ 46, 198
Ibn al-Ḥabīb 198
Shaykh Muḥammad ibn al-Ḥabīb 2
ibn al-Jawzī 16
Ibn al-Qāsim 99
Ibn al-'Arabī 11, 21, 39, 46, 47, 49, 53, 54, 55, 56, 57, 58, 59, 60, 61, 63, 64, 66, 77, 89, 164, 183, 184, 185, 196, 197, 198, 200
Qāḍī Abū Bakr ibn al-'Arabī 94, 95, 96

Ibn Ash'ath 14
Ibn Bājja (Avempace) 183
Ibn Ḥamdīn 96
Ibn Khaldūn 209, 226
Ibn Mājah 105
Ibn Rushd (Averroes) 4, 36, 171, 178, 179, 183, 184, 199
Ibn Sīnā (Avicenna) 37, 60, 171, 172, 173, 174, 175, 176, 178, 180, 181, 183, 184, 199
Ibn Sīrīn 15
Ibn Ṭufayl 183
Ibn 'Ajība 47, 74, 188
Ibn 'Āshir 85
idea 144, 148
idealism 131
idea of god 206
identity 130
identity across time 130
ideology 152
idhn (authorisation) 2, 50, 93
al-idrāk (intuition) 184
al-iḥsān (beautification of character) 3, 8, 40, 51, 72, 187
Iḥyā' 'Ulūm al-Dīn 95
ijtihād 36, 105
ikhlāṣ 78
illogical 147
Illuminationism 183
Illuminationist 187
Illuminationist philosophy 180, 182
illuminationist vision 200
'ilm (knowledge) 85
'ilm al-aḥwāl 12, 27, 40, 41, 42, 45, 51, 164, 187, 197, 200, 229, 231
'ilm al-asrār 12, 27, 40, 42, 51, 164, 187, 197, 200, 229, 231
al-'ilm al-ḥuḍūrī (Sufi Science of Presence) 168, 186
al-'ilm al-ḥuṣūlī (representative knowledge) 168
'ilm al-kalām 103
al-'Ilm al-ladunī 80
'ilm al-mukāshafa 25, 38
'ilm al-mu'āmala 25
al-'ilm al-ṣaḥīḥ (true science) 181
'ilm al-'aql 27, 40, 41, 42, 44, 51, 52, 67, 164, 187, 200, 229, 231
imām 20
Imam Mālik 98
Imams 87
imams of mosques 83
al-īmān (belief/creed) 3, 9, 40, 51, 72, 75, 187
'imāra (a form of *dhikr* involving the movement of the limbs) 229
IMF (International Monetary Fund) 90, 115, 219
impatience 75
inauthentic self-understanding 143
Incoherence of the Incoherence 178
increase in the exchange 207
independence 73
India 82, 98
Indian Sufism 81
individual and society 139
individualism 91, 110, 205
Indonesia 90
induction 129, 234
inductive reasoning 4
Industrial capitalism 216
industrial complex 152
industrialism 127
industrialized labour 113
Industrial Revolution 113
industriousness 140

industry 113
inequality 120, 237
inequity in the market 210
inflation 214, 215
influence 73
infrastructure projects 221
inner reality 202
inner state 121
al-insān al-kāmil 55, 64, 65, 70, 87
instinct 153
institutionalized nihilism 152
institution building 84
instrumental stance 111
instrumental stance towards the world 108
intellect 175
intellection 172
intelligible universal objects 177
interest 224, 235
interest extraction 216
interest rate swaps 220
Internal Regulations for the Sufi Orders 90
interpretive approach 117, 119, 236
interview 230
interviews with scholars 230
intuition 37, 128, 133, 134, 168, 176, 188, 200, 237
invocation 80
inward 88, 120
Muḥammad Iqbal 31
irāda (will) 78
Iran 116, 227
Iraq 14, 95
'irfān (gnosis) 168, 182
irrational economic system 224
irrationalist 176
irredeemable currency 213
ishāra (indication) 89
Ishrāqī cosmology 180
ishrāqī (Illuminationist) 187
ishrāq (illumination) 38, 168
Ishrāqī philosophy 183
Islamic epistemology 186
Islamic governance 12
Islamic law 105, 106, 212, 227, 233
Islamic materialism 103
Islamic philosophers 175
Islamic philosophy 168, 169, 199, 237
Islamic state 227
Islamic Studies 85
al-islām (law and practice) 3, 9, 40, 51, 72, 187
Islam of the Companions 70
al-ism al-a'ẓam 22, 68, 80
isnād 23
isolation 73
Isotropic Orb 55
Isrā (Night Journey) 11, 57
Italians 5, 89
Italy 138, 221
ittiḥād 49

J

jabarūt (the domain of Divine power) 4, 11, 41, 42, 46, 51, 72, 188, 231
Roy Jackson 165
jadhb (attraction to the Divine) 41, 78
jāhiliyya (the Age of Ignorance) 71
jamā'a (the community functioning within the context of broader society) 28, 226
Jāmi' 104
jam' (gathering together) 51, 78, 92,

192
jam' al-jam' (gathering of the gathering) 78, 193
Karl Jaspers 158
Jats 83
al-jawhar al-fard (the atom) 57
al-jawhar al-ṣuwarī 56
jaysh (army) 227
Amīr 'Abd al-Qādir al-Jazā'irī 89
Jesus 111, 207
al-jinān (the Gardens) 55
al-jism al-kull 55
Jonah (Yūnus) 123
Jordan 92
joy 164
JPMorgan 220
JPMorgan Chase 220
Judeo/Christian tradition 126
judiciary 227
al-Junayd 20, 21, 22, 24, 47, 48, 50, 67, 68, 80, 81, 86, 87, 100, 101, 189, 191, 195, 239
Junaydī Sufism 93, 195
Ernst Jünger 148, 155, 159, 160, 161, 162, 164, 223, 224
Jüngerian need 165
juristic opinions 176
jurists 231
justice 150, 227
justice and equity 226
justice in transactions 209
Juz' 104

K

al-Kalābādhī 9, 10, 27, 50
kalām (theology) 187
Masoud Kamali 115
Muḥammad Kamāl 184
kamāl (perfection) 79
Kantian philosophy 124, 155, 233
Kantians 119
Kantian world 224
Immanuel Kant 112, 127, 129, 131, 132, 133, 135, 148, 163, 233
Kant's Third Antinomy 148
karāmāt (miracles) 82
Ma'rūf al-Karkhī 17
kashf (unveiling) 38, 39, 67, 100, 186
Walter Kaufman 158
Nickie R. Keddie 86
Elie Kedourie 86
Robert Kelly 220
Johannes Kepler 4
khalq (creation) 69
khalwa (isolation) 2, 22, 68, 78, 80
khawf (fear) 78
khayāl 60, 185
al-khayāl al-muḥaqqaq 60
al-khayāl al-munfaṣil 60
al-khayāl al-muṭlaq 60
al-khayāl al-muttaṣil 60
Ruhollah Khomeini 165
khulāṣa min al-khalq (the pure ones) 22
khuṭba (the Friday sermon) 94
Søren Kierkegaard 149
al-Kindī 170, 171, 184, 199
kindness 70
kingship 226
Peter Kingsley 166
Kitāb al-asfār al-arba'a 183
Kitāb al-Mawāqif 89
Kitāb al-shifā 69
Kitāb faṣl al-maqāl 178
kitāb wa sunna 30, 197

knower/known dichotomy 168
knowing about God 103
knowing Being 187, 200
knowing oneself 70
knowing subject 199
knowledge by presence 168, 181, 183
knowledge of God 103, 179
A. Knysh 37
John Koskinen 220
kufr (disbelief) 176
al-kullī al-ṭabīʿī (natural universal) 174
al-kursī (the Pedestal) 55

L

lack of recognition of the Divine 206
lāhūt (God's Lordship over existence in its inward aspect) 79
laissez-faire 91, 206
language 163, 228
laṭīfa (spiritual substance) 192, 232
Latin Middle Ages 177
latitudinal/horizontal order of lights 180
laughing lions 150
law 167, 233
lawāmiʿ (gleams of genuine lights that come to the longing heart) 78
lawāqiḥ (flashes) 38
lawā'iḥ (first flashes of awareness of lights) 78
law-governed society 233
al-lawḥ al-maḥfūẓ (Preserved Tablet) 54
Aharon Layish 86
layl (night) 56
the leap 157
Leben (Life) 138
legal authority 84
the Legion 223
legislated liberty 224
legitimate *jihād* 92
Gottfried Wilhelm Leibniz 128
Level of Nature 55
levels of being and reality 186
leveraging 216, 235
Leviathan 112
Ken Lewis 220
liberal democracies 206
liberal democracy 91, 114, 218, 219, 223, 235, 236
liberalism 152
Libya 89, 93
  Benghazi 2
Light of Muḥammad 87
Light Verse 177
limitation 134
linguist 96
linguistics 189, 196
linguists 231
lisān (audition) 79
local governance 229
local government 108
John Locke 109, 128, 129
locus of the self-disclosure of Truth 147
logic 36, 118, 128, 130, 131, 138, 146, 147, 174, 178, 205
logical maker of truth 146
logical positivism 152
logical technology and technical processes 224
logike episteme 146
logocentrism 118

logos 118, 133, 146, 147
Ronald Logue 221
longitudinal/vertical hierarchy of lights 180
loss of subjective consciousness 232
Lote-tree 44
lotteries 210
love 164
love of God 18
Martin Luther 156, 205, 207
Jean-Franciose Lyotard 118

M

John Mack 221
macro-level issues 236
madhhab 106
al-Madīna al-Munawwara (the Illuminated City) 12, 28, 30, 97, 98, 106, 226, 227, 228, 233
Madinan Islam 95
Madinan paradigm 96
Madinan society 233
Madinan state 165, 226
Maghrib 83, 93, 95, 99
maghzūb (an illusionist) 193
magistrates 223
maḥabba (Divine love) 79, 198, 232
maḥbūb (beloved of Allah) 50, 193
Mahdī of Sudan 89
māhiyya (essence/quiddity) 174, 175
mahjūb (veiled) 50, 193
maḥq (annihilation in His source) 79
Ma Hualong 89
majdhūb (mad in Allah) 41, 50, 193
majlis al-dhikr (assembly of *dhikr*) 76
majnūn (mad) 44
al-makān (place) 56
malakūt (realms of the Unseen) 4, 11, 41, 42, 44, 45, 46, 51, 72, 188, 231
Curzio Malaparte 223
Mali 89
Mālik ibn Anas 9, 12, 23, 28, 30, 97, 98, 99, 100, 104, 105, 106, 107, 120, 121, 164, 209, 225, 229, 233, 238, 239
Mālikī existential methodology 225
Mālikī *faqīh* 96
Mālikī law 94, 99
Mālikī legal methodology 195
Mālikī *madhhab* 93, 94, 96, 106
Mālikī scholar 96
Mālikī school of law 93, 97, 209
management and choice 75
man and nature 139
mandats (a currency) 214
maqām (station) 77
maqamāt (stations) 18, 68, 77, 80
Herbert Marcuse 117
market 230
market economy 208
market forces 205
markets 196, 229
Marrakesh 94
marriage 209
Marxism 138, 153
Marxist analysis 224
Karl Marx 109, 113, 114, 115, 118, 149, 153, 224
Mashāriq al-anwār ʿalā ṣiḥāḥ al-athār 97
mashshāʾī (Peripatetic) philosophy 175, 187
mā siwaʾllāh (entities other than God) 193

al-Masjid al-Aqṣā (the Distant Mosque in Jerusalem) 11
al-Masjid al-Ḥarām (Sacred Mosque in Makka) 11
mass psychosis of modern society 202
masterful technology 152
material 88
materialism 91, 205, 225, 238
materialistic pursuits 140
materialistic, technological way of thinking 233
material world 206, 234
mathematical inevitability 223
mathematical physics 152
mathematics 130, 155, 236
matricide 217
matter 130
Mauritania 89
Abū al-Ala Mawdudi 165
mawlā (client) 17
maximization of utility, happiness, welfare and well-being 108
Mazdaean names 180
Mā' al-'Aynayn al-Qalqamī 89
ma'rifa (gnosis) 10, 20, 27, 33, 38, 39, 50, 67, 72, 78, 82, 100, 168, 195, 197
Alisdair McIntyre 117
meaning 72
means of production 208
Mecca 71, 92
mechanical sciences 119, 124, 237
mechanism 91, 205
media élites 219
medicine 177, 233
medieval Europe 173
medium of exchange 211
mega-banks 221
Meknes 93
mental existence 175
Mercury 59
Marin Mersenne 206
the Messenger 98
meta-linguistic method 185
meta-narrative of modernity 115, 116
meta-narratives 117
meta-ontology 136
metaphors 177
metaphysical fantasy 239
metaphysical pseudo-reality 239
metaphysics 4, 128, 129, 130, 132, 133, 143, 144, 145, 153, 154, 164, 171, 183, 233, 239
metaphysics of light 180
meta-Reality 119
methodology of structuralism 205
Middle East 98
John Stuart Mill 129, 234
mind 130
mind and body 139
minimal state intervention 208
mint 227
minting of currencies 209
minting of gold and silver currencies 229
minting of gold dinars and silver dirhams 209
miracles 170
mīthāq (covenant) 20, 21, 191
Mi'rāj (Ascension) 11, 57
model community 233
moderation 70
modern economy 208
modern Islamic state 165
modernism 82, 107, 168

modernist epistemology 91, 205, 238
modernist institutions 91
modernist paradigm 112, 113
modernists 227
modernist science 116
modernist thinkers 234
modernity 1, 82, 88, 91, 113, 120, 127, 141, 151, 152, 153, 155, 167, 205, 206, 218, 223, 230, 234, 235, 236
modern money 212
modern period 113, 235
modern philosophy 190, 198
modern politics 233
modern science 139, 167
modern social sciences 237
modern society 239
a monarch 151
monarchic political system 165
monarchy 217, 218, 219, 222, 235, 239
monetarist society 208
money 208
money, a non-rentable commodity 210
money creation 215
money is a commodity 209
money is a means of exchange 209
money is communally accepted 209
money lending 215
creating money out of nothing 215
role of money 208
money substitutes 209
money supply 203, 219, 235
monism 192
monism of reason 137
monopolies 210
monopoly of office and power 219
monopsonies 210
moral and Divine imperatives 238
moral character 98
Morgan Stanley 221
Moroccan Sufism 83, 84, 92
Morocco 83, 89, 93, 94
  Fes 2
James Morris 196
mortality 143
mortgages 215
Moses (Mūsā) 10, 123, 207
mosque 230
mosques 229
motor forces 219
moussems (festivals of *dhikr*) 229, 239
movement of wealth 233
al-Mudawwana 99
Mughal India 82
the Mughals 82
muḥāḍara (the positioning of the Sufi in his relation to God) 38
Muḥammad 123, 207
Muḥammadan revelation 170
Muḥammad ibn al-Ḥabīb 48, 93
Muḥammad Sayyid Ṭanṭāwī 92
al-Ḥārith al-Muḥāsibī 20
muḥsinīn (those who do good) 8
muḥtasib (the official who oversaw the markets and matters of public order) 83, 94
mukāshafa (unveiling) 25, 38, 40, 67, 168
mulk (phenomenal existence, the domain of solid forms) 3, 41, 42, 46, 51, 72, 188, 231
Mulla Sadra (Ṣadr al-Dīn Shīrāzī) 173, 184, 186, 200, 237
multinational corporations 221

multiple competing paradigms 120
multiple modernities 115, 116
multiplicity 173, 190, 193
muqaddam (representative of a shaykh) 2
al-Muqaddima 209
murābiṭ (term for a saint) 94
Murābiṭūn 2, 93, 94, 95, 96, 97, 100
Murābiṭūn communities 229
Murābiṭūn community 230
Murābiṭūn Da'wa Movement 100, 228, 239
murāqaba (watching) 46, 79
murder 218
murīd (disciple) 17, 80
Abū al-'Abbās al-Mursī 75
Mūsā (Moses) 194
Muṣannaf (large collection of ḥadīth) 104
Muṣḥaf 'Uthmānī 104
al-mushāhada al-ishrāqiyya (illuminationist vision) 181
mushāhada wa mukāshafa (witnessing and unveiling) 181
mushāhada (witnessing) 24, 38, 67, 79
Mushāwarūn (counsellors or advisors) 97
Muslim 105
Muslim fundamentalists 86
Muslim modernists 5
Muslim Neoplatonists 183
Muslim philosophers 173, 176, 183, 237
Muslim West 96
Musnad (ḥadīth collection arranged by chain of transmission) 105
Mustadrak 105
Mustakhraj 105
Mu'tazilites 60, 171
Mu'tazilite theology 171
al-Muwaffaq (Abbasid Caliph) 23
al-Muwaṭṭa' 12, 23, 28, 97, 104, 105, 106, 233
Mu'jam 105
mystical states of consciousness 167
mysticism 185
mythology 162, 164

N

al-Nafas al-Raḥmānī 63, 64
al-nafs al-kulliyya (Universal Soul) 54
nafs (lower self) 39, 41, 42, 46, 51, 67, 71, 72, 188, 195, 231
nahār (daytime) 56
name of liberty 227
naming 228
Napoleon Bonaparte 213, 214, 218
Napoleonic state 113, 212
Naqshabandī 89
Naqshabandī *ṭarīqa* 90
Naqshbandī Sufi Master 89
al-Nasā'ī 105
Seyyed Hossein Nasr 174
Khayr al-Nassāj 23
nāsūt (man/womanhood) 79
nationalism 91, 205
national state 120, 235, 236
natural and mathematical sciences 187
Natural Law 111
natural religion 137
natural science 130, 152
natural sciences 116, 117, 155, 177, 238

natural time (physical time) 194, 195, 200, 232
natura (nature) 156
nature 111
nature of reason 234
nature of truth 234
naẓar (vision) 168
Nazism 152, 153
Necessary Being 39
Necessary Existent 173
Necessary Light 180
necessity 130, 134
negation 134
negotiation of loans 212
neo-colonial period 88, 90
neo-colonial regimes 5
Neo-Kantianism 138
Neoplatonic theory 173
Neoplatonic view 172
Neoplatonism 181, 185
Neoplatonists 170
neuroscience 236
New Bedouins (people who are estranged from contemporary society) 239
new investment 216
new nomos 204, 221, 225, 228, 238, 239
new ontology 157
Newtonian model 223
Newtonian physics 124, 233
Isaac Newton 4, 112, 119, 223
Friedrich Nietzsche 114, 126, 139, 140, 141, 144, 148, 149, 150, 155, 159, 163, 206, 234, 235
Nietzsche's philosophy 140
Nihawand 23
nihilism 126, 139, 140, 141, 143, 144, 145, 148, 149, 150, 151, 152, 153, 154, 155, 159, 163, 164, 223, 225, 226, 234, 235, 238
nihilistic hegemony of technology 141
Niẓām al-Dīn of Aurangabad 82
Noah (Nūḥ) 123
noble morality 140
nomocracy (law-governed society) 12, 227
non-duality 119
non-fungible (commodities of use) 209
nonlinear dynamics 62, 236
North Africa 83, 93, 94, 96, 98
North American culture 115
northern Europe 138
Northern Trust 221
no-thing 143
nuqabā' (Chieftains) 87
nūr al-anwār (Light of lights) 180
nūri-muḥammadiyya 87
Gregorius Nysennas 207

O

obedience to God's laws 189
objective social scientific knowledge 119, 236
the objective 120, 237
objectivity 119, 134, 148
objectivity and subjectivity 139
obscurity 73
observation 128, 129, 205, 234
oligarchic chiefs 221
the oligarchic modern Islamic state 165
oligarchic wealth 203

oligarchies 203
oligarchs 221, 235
oligarchy 204, 217, 219, 222, 223, 227, 233, 235, 239
oneness of existence 55
one-party totalitarianism 206, 218, 235
the One 173
one world government 115
On the Origin of Species 112
the ontic 158
ontological experiences 77, 186, 230, 232
ontological experiences of the Prophet 199
ontological foundation 170, 237
ontological foundation for human awareness 199
ontological level 191
ontological monism 137
ontological poverty 193, 199
ontological questions 136
ontological realm 181
ontological state 237
ontology 129, 135, 136, 139, 140, 145, 155, 156, 163, 164, 168, 177, 178, 183, 184, 199, 234
opinions 234
opium of the masses 114
the oppressed 226
order 120, 232, 237
Organization of the Islamic Conference 92
Original Void 47
origin of paper notes 212
O.T.C. (over-the-counter derivatives) 220
outer law 121, 202
outward 88, 120
outwardly praiseworthy acts 196
over-exploitation 238
Overmen 153, 161
overt [verses] 179

P

pandemic of poverty 236
Vikram Pandit 220
pantheism 192
pantheistic world-view 173
paper money 211, 213, 214
Paradise 71
paradox 224
paradoxes 167
paradoxical nature of matter 236
paralysis 122
paranormal 85
parish 108
Parmenides 144, 147, 166
party 151
path to Being 234
patricide 217
Peasants' War 207
Pedestal (*kursī*) 55, 57
perception 129, 133, 139, 234
Perfect Man 55, 65
Peripatetic (*mashshā'ī*) Philosophy 175, 187, 199
Peripatetics 37, 170
Peripatetic school 180
permanence 134
permitting of usury 235
personal aspect of Sufism 88
petro-dollars 91
Pharaonic model 122, 123
phenomenological methodology 155,

157
phenomenology 155, 156
phenomenology of freedom 224
The Phenomenology of Spirit 138
philology (science of literature and linguistics) 187
philosophers 60, 190, 231, 233
philosophia perennis (unity of truth) 183
philosophical history of Being 148
philosophical terminology 171
philosophizing about Being 200
philosophy 1, 36, 117, 155, 164, 177, 198, 237, 238
  epistemology 1
Philosophy of Illumination 180, 181, 182, 200
philosophy of meta-Reality 117, 118
the philosphical history of Being 144
photocentricism 118
physical science 131
physician 167
physics 131, 132, 171
physis (the shining forth) 156
piety 196
pilgrimage 75
Pillars (*awtād*) 87
planetary movements 194
planets 54
Plato 127, 144, 145, 148, 156, 167, 169, 171, 184, 199, 207, 217, 234
Platonic metaphysics 157
Platonic philosophy 146
Platonic view 170
Platonism 185
Plato's metaphysics 164, 234
Plato's *Republic* 217
Plotinus 172
Plurality 134
Plutarch 207
PNC 221
poet 96, 167
poetry 167, 224
point of sale cash access 215
poisoning the oceans 221, 236
Karl Polanyi 103
police 221
political activist 167
political economy 204, 208
politics 6, 204, 218
polluting the air 221, 236
pollution 238
pollution of the ecosphere 143
Popes 207
popular Sufism 85
Portugal 221
positive religion 137
positivism 116, 117, 236
positivist approach 119
Possibility 134
Possible Being 39
post-Claudian Empire 223
Posterior Analytics 182
Postface 282
post-modernism 86, 117, 118
Post-modernism, Reason and Religion 86
post-Shāfiʿī scholars 105
post-Socratic philosophers 141, 146
post-structuralism 117, 118, 138
poverty-stricken 226
power nexus 219
power nexus of states 235
power of reason 237
practice of the People of Madīna 97, 225

pragmatism 138
praxis 196, 200, 232
prayer 74
pre-modern 82
pre-modern Europe 107
pre-modern European state 108
pre-modern Islamic society 103, 232
pre-modern period 113
pre-modern worldview 102, 107, 203
preoccupied with God 196
pre-ontology 102
presence 142
presence of God 103, 107
Presence of the Lord of the Universe 75
Preserved Tablet 54
pre-Socratic philosophers 144, 147, 166
pre-Socratics 154
pre-Socratic thinkers 184
priest 157
primacy of Being 183
Prime Matter 55
principality of essence 183
Principia Mathematica 112
Principles of Philosophy 112
private bankers 217
privately owned Central Banks 235
probability 130
process of production 153
process of technique 224
production 151
production process 122
productive real estate 213
progress 91, 149, 205
prohibition of usury 207
proletarians 224
promissory notes 212, 213, 215
prophecy 167
the Prophet Adam 194
the Prophet Ibrāhīm (Abraham) 194
prophetic science 170
Prophetic state of Madīna 165
Prophetic traditions 210
Prophet Muḥammad 8, 12, 26, 28, 31, 32, 35, 40, 54, 56, 58, 68, 69, 87, 92, 97, 104, 120, 163, 186, 194, 196, 197, 201, 210, 226, 227, 228, 230, 233
Prophet Mūsā 194
Prophets 163
Prophet's Night Journey 197
Prophet Yūnus (Jonah) 194
the Prophet 6, 9, 10, 11, 21, 32, 36, 68, 70, 71, 74, 97, 104, 231, 233
Protestant Church 205
Protestantism 207
psychoanalysis 152
psychological level 191
psychology 152, 177, 233
psychosis 202, 203, 223
psychotherapy 224
public banking 213, 214
public education 137
public policy 152
pure mathematics 128
Puritan Reformers 110
Pythagoras 166

Q

qabḍ (constriction) 78
qaḍā (execution of the decree) 194
qāḍī (judge) 95, 99
qāḍī of Granada 96
Qādirī-Shādhilī-Darqāwī *ṭarīqa* 33,

93, 197
Qādiriyya *ṭarīqa* 89
qāḍīs (judges) 83
Qāḍī 'Iyāḍ ibn Mūsā al-Yaḥṣubī 69, 94, 96, 97
qadr (decree of God) 194
al-qalam al-a'lā 54
qalb (heart) 168
Shaykh Yūsuf al-Qarḍāwī 92
qaṣīda 48
al-Qawtham 68, 70
Qayrawān 98, 99
qiyās (juristic analogical deductions) 197
quantum mechanics 62
quantum theory 63
question of Being 154, 155, 164
quiddities 190
quiddity 175, 184, 200, 237
Willard van Orman Quine 136
qurb (nearness) 79
al-Qurṭubī 209
Qur'ān 5, 14, 20, 27, 29, 40, 46, 51, 54, 56, 67, 68, 75, 77, 89, 94, 97, 98, 103, 104, 105, 106, 120, 163, 165, 171, 177, 178, 179, 184, 186, 191, 197, 199, 226, 229, 230, 233
  2:142
    In this way We have made you a middlemost community (umma)... 32
  7:142
    We set aside thirty nights for Mūsā and then completed them with ten, so the appointed time of his Lord was forty nights in all 195
  7:143
    When Mūsā [Moses] came to Our appointed time and his Lord spoke to him, he said, 'My Lord, show me Yourself so that I may look at You!'... 10
  9:128-9
    A Messenger has come to you from among yourselves. 26
  10:26
    Those who do good (aḥsan) will have the best (al-ḥusnā) and more. 8
  13:12
    Allah never changes a people's state until they change what is in themselves 28
  13:29
    Only in the remembrance of Allah (dhikrillāh) can the heart find peace 76
  18:24
    Remember (udhkur) your Lord when you forget 76
  33:21
    You have an excellent model (uswatun ḥasana) in the Messenger of God. 31
  33:41-42
    You who believe! Remember (udhkurū) Allah much and glorify Him in the morning and the evening 76
  55:24-25
    everything perisheth except His Countenance, His Aspect (wajh). 177
  55:27
    everyday He is engaged in some

affair 193
everyone in the heavens and the earth requests His aid 193, 194
55:27
Every day (yawm) He is engaged in some affair (sha'n). 57
57:3
He is the First and the Last, the Outward and the Inward. 49
7:172
When your Lord took out all their descendents from the loins of the children of Adam 21
Sūrat al-Isrā' 11
Qur'ān and Sunna 98
Qur'ānic revelation 182, 187, 232
Qur'ānic text 231
Qur'ānic verses 77
al-Qushayrī 77
Sayyid Qutb 165
quṭb (the 'Axis' of the spiritual universe) 57, 87

R

race 151
radio station 77
raḥamūt 79
Fazlur Rahman 173
Karl Rahner 157
rajā' (hope) 78
raqā'iq (subtle affinities) 40
Rasā'il (collections of *ḥadīth*) 104
Madawi al-Rasheed 86
rasm (form) 13
rational animal 147
rational authority 84
rational cognition 170
rational demonstration 37
rationalism 1, 3, 32, 37, 38, 42, 44, 52, 102, 113, 114, 116, 120, 127, 128, 131, 164, 166, 167, 190, 198, 204, 205, 231, 236, 237, 238
rationalist and empiricist epistemologies 235
rationalist approach 117
rationalistic discourse 237
rationalist methodology 204
rationalists 119
rationality 118
rational principles 111
the rational 120
rational thinking 178, 199
Ronald Reagan 218
Reality 122, 134
Realm of the Saint: Power and Authority in Moroccan Sufism 83, 84
reason 39, 103, 108, 110, 111, 120, 128, 135, 136, 137, 139, 150, 168, 199, 205, 237
reasoning 205
receipts 211, 212
reconciliation of philosophy and religion 178
reductionism 104
reductionist theoretical models 83
reflections 234
Reform 108, 111
Reformation 205, 207
Reign of Terror 112, 214
relation of religion to science 234
relativism 86
religion 144, 155, 179, 185, 205, 206, 234, 238
religious authority 151, 234

religious epistemic sources 102
religious fundamentalism 86
Renaissance 114
renting of fungible commodities 210
renting of money 210
renunciation 196
representational knowledge 180
representative democracy 204
representative faculty 170
representative knowledge 168
republic 219
Republican Rome 219
Republic of Turkey 90
reputation 73
respect 70
respect for women 225
restoration of the zakāh 228, 239
resurrection 170
retreat 80
revealed truth 170
revelation 151, 171, 198, 199, 209, 237
revelation and philosophy 166
revelation of the Qur'ān 186, 230
review 205
revision 205
revival of natural law 207
revolutionary France 214
Revolutionary State 213
ribāṭ (fortress) 93, 94, 99
ribāṭ of Qaṣr Ziyād 99
ribā (usury) 203, 210, 212, 216
riḍā (contentment) 13, 78
Riegle-Neal Act 220
Right Hegelians 149
a *Risāla* (collection of *ḥadīth*) 104
Risāla of Abū al-Qāsim al-Qushayri 38
James Rohr 221
Roman Empire 83, 156, 227
Roman history 239
The Roman Revolution 219
Romans 207
Roman society 222, 239
Romantic nationalism 149
Root Islamic Education 29, 97, 98, 120, 225
Richard Rorty 167
Jean-Jaques Rousseau 109
Royal Academy of Dramatic Arts 2
rubūbiyyah (governance of the universe) 194
al-rūḥ al-qudus (Holy Spirit or Active Intelligence) 192
rūḥānī (spiritual) 25
rūḥ (soul/spirit) 41, 42, 44, 46, 51, 57, 67, 188, 231
rule of law 225, 238
rulers responsible for minting 211
rules of purification 74
Jalāl al-Dīn Rumi 164, 198
Bertrand Russell 62, 66, 129, 167, 234, 236
Russia 98

S

ṣabr (patience/steadfastness) 17, 78
al-sabt (Saturday) 59
Mulla Sadra (Ṣadr al-Dīn Shīrāzī) 185
safar (wayfaring) 194
safety for children 225
ṣafwa min al-ʿibād (most excellent of the believers) 22
ṣāḥib al-waqt (the master of time) 57
Ṣaḥīfa (collection of ḥadīth written by a Companion or Follower)

104
Ṣaḥīḥ Muslim 105
Abū Saʿīd Ṣaḥnūn 29, 98, 99
saḥq (the disappearance of your structure under the force of God) 79
ṣaḥwa (sobriety) 78
saint 157
sainthood 83, 85
salafī 30
Salafī community [early generations of Muslims] 225
sālik (wayfarer) 41
samāʿ (the singing of the Diwan and the dance) 41
Sanūsī *ṭarīqa* 89
Sarī al-Saqaṭī 18, 19
Sassanid empire 83
Saudi Arabia 5, 90, 91, 227
Kingdom of Saudi Arabia 91
Saudis 91
John Ralston Saul 114
ṣāʿiqa (annihilation in the Divine manifestation) 79
scepticism 129, 205
schlecht (low-born) 141
Carl Schmitt 223, 224, 225
scholars 106
scholasticism 107, 204
Scholastics 147
the school of Madīna 99
schools 229
Alfred Schutz 117
science 91, 116, 150, 187, 190, 234, 238
science and technology 149, 205
Science of Logic 138
science of logos 146, 147
Science of the Experience of Consciousness 138
science of thinking 146
sciences 198
scientific and calculative discourse 146
scientific dialectical materialism 153
scientific discoveries 205
scientific method 114, 205
scientific revolution 131
scientists 190
Scotland 2
Duns Scotus 156, 207
Duns Scotus' Doctrine of Categories and Meaning 156
scribes 104
scripture 157, 179
scripture and dogmatism 156
seclusion 80
second actuality 173
second separation 191, 193
Second Teacher after Aristotle 171
secularisation 108
secularism 88, 91, 111, 204, 205, 206, 221, 234
secularization 93, 124
secularization of religion 91
secularization of time 108, 110, 111
secure strong-rooms 211
securities dealers 215
securitization 220
Sein (Being) 138, 154
self-awareness 185
self-complacence 74
self-consciousness 134
self-disclosure of Being 161, 164
self-knowledge 182
self-knowledge of cognition 137
Self-manifestation of God 189, 197

self-realization 180
self-satisfied fatalism 85
Self-subsistent Light 180
the Senate 223
Seneca 207
Senegal 89
sensations 133, 134
sense experience 205
sense perception 128, 237
sensory 72
separation 92
service 232
service debts 217
Seven Gardens 55
seven levels of being 119
seventy different types of usury 210
Seville 94
Abū al-Ḥasan al-Shādhilī 75, 80
the Shāfiʿī *madhhab* 106
Shah Musafir 82
Shah Nur 82
Shah Palangposh 82
Shāh Waliyullāh 82
Imam Shāmil 89
al-sharīʿa (the Law) 3, 6, 9, 12, 16, 17, 18, 19, 21, 27, 28, 33, 39, 40, 41, 51, 61, 68, 72, 74, 75, 83, 91, 92, 95, 97, 100, 121, 122, 124, 125, 178, 187, 196, 199, 202, 226, 227
shawq (longing) 78
Shaykh al-Akbar 53
Shaykh al-Azhar 92
shaykh (master) of instruction 21
shaykh of instruction 72, 73, 76
sha'n (an affair) 57
al-Shiblī 8, 23
al-Shifā' bi-taʿrīf ḥuqūq al-Muṣṭafā 96
Quṭb al-Dīn al-Shīrāzī 173
Ṣadr al-Dīn Shīrāzī (Mulla Sadra) 173, 183
shirk (assigning power to entities other than Allah) 73
shukr (thankfulness) 78
shūrā (the ruler's consultative body) 96, 97
ṣidq (truthfulness) 21, 78
ṣifāt (Attributes of God) 38, 78, 195
Signs of God 11
silsila (chain of transmission) 6, 8, 33, 197
silver 211
simple and compound interest 203
simplicity 70
simsima (gnosis that is too fine to express) 79
sincerity 9
Single Essence 57
sīra (biography of the Prophet Muḥammad) 187
sirr (innermost consciousness) 41, 42, 44, 45, 46, 51, 57, 67, 188, 231
sitr al-maqām (curtain of the station) 40
slave camps 218, 224
Adam Smith 112, 124, 233
Adam Smith's capitalist free market economics 233
sobriety 51
so-called wealth creation 216
social cohesion 202
social contract 112
social evolution 122
socialism 115
socialists 208

social science 112, 113, 118, 120, 238
social sciences 113, 117, 119, 124, 236, 238
social science theory 116
sociology 152
Socrates 19, 207
Socratic philosophy 171
solar system 55
Sorge (care) 158
sororicide 217
soteriological doctrines 111
soul 171
South Africa 90, 230
space and causality 187
Spain 95, 221
Spartacus 222
spectacle 222
speculation 235
Herbert Spencer 115, 117
sphere of fixed stars 172
sphere of Jupiter 172
sphere of Mars 172
sphere of Mercury 172
sphere of Saturn 172
sphere of the Moon 172
sphere of the Sun 172
sphere of Venus 172
Benedict Spinoza 128
the spiritual decline of the earth 145
spiritual life of the German people 149
spiritual matters 206, 234
spiritual realization 182
spiritual vision 182
split between science and religion 206
Sprache (language) 154
Stalin 218
standing reserve 145
stars 54
stasis 122
state 151
state capitalism 114, 206
state-capitalism/communism 203
State Law 213
stateless 226
states 75, 77, 79, 196, 225
State Street 221
station of *iḥsān* 72
station of *īmān* 72
station of *islām* 72
stations 75, 77, 79, 196, 225
statism 218
store of value 203
stray thoughts 21
String Theory 64, 66
stripping the forests bare 236
structural government 218
structuralism 91, 205, 217
John Stumpf 221
sub-atomic physics 64, 65
subjective consciousness 191
subjective historical and cultural factors 119, 236
subjective perceptions 234
the subjective 120, 237
subjectivism 116, 120, 236
subjectivity 139, 151, 152, 155, 234
subject/object dichotomy 168, 190, 192, 232
subject/object relationship 237
the subject 139
subjugation of nature 141
sub-lunar world 172
Substance 134
Substitutes (*Abdāl*) 87

Sufi cosmology 231
Sufi epistemology 35, 186, 204, 229, 230
Sufi poetry 198
Sufis 13
Sufis as Warriors 82
Sufi school of Baghdad 19
Sufi shrines 81
Sufism, definition of 188
Shihāb al-Dīn Yaḥyā Suhrawardī 37, 173, 180, 181, 182, 183, 184, 200
suicide 225
sukr (drunkenness) 78
Lucius Cornelius Sulla 222
Sultan Awrangzeb 82
the *sulṭān* 83
sulūk (travelling on the Path) 23, 33, 39, 40, 41, 44, 46, 51, 72, 75, 100
Muḥammad ʿAbdallāh al-Ṣūmālī 89
Sunan 105
Sunna (normative practice of the Prophet Muhammad) 5, 20, 27, 29, 74, 75, 95, 97, 98, 104, 105, 106, 120, 165, 196, 197, 201
supererogatory exercises 196
supernatural 111
supranational central banks 217
Supreme Name [Allah] 80, 189
sūq (market) 227
swearing allegiance 226
Ronald Syme 219
synthesis 134
synthetic a priori knowledge 132
systematic thinking 217

T

tābiʿīn (the Followers of the Companions) 16, 30
tābiʿī at-tābiʿīn (the Followers of the Followers) 30
tabula rasa 128
Tacitus 227
tafrīd (isolation) 78
tafsīr (Qurʾānic commentary) 96, 187
taḥqīq (verification) 38
tajallī (Self-disclosure) 47, 48, 79, 189
tajalliyāt al-dhāt (Self-disclosure of the Essence of God) 195
tajalliyāt (manifestations) 41, 194
tajrīd (detachment from the world) 14, 79
takhallī (revelation of the treasure-chests of one's inwardness) 79
takiyas (another name for *tekkes*) 90
talaqqī (receiving) 79
talwīn (change) 79
tamkīn (fixity) 79
tanzīh (transcendence) 60, 61, 63, 66, 171, 236
tanzīh muṭlaq tanzīh (absolute transcendence) 49
taraqqī (rising) 79
tarbiya (instruction) 2, 68, 72
tārīkh (history, especially the philosophy of history) 187
ṭarīq al-ʿulūm (scientific methodology) 181
al-ṭarīqa (the Path) 3, 19, 23, 25, 27, 28, 40, 41, 51, 67, 74, 75, 80, 81, 83, 93, 100, 187-8, 230
ṭarīqa of Shaykh ʿAbd al-Qādir 100
ṭarīqas 89, 90
Tartīb al-Madārik wa taqrīb al-masālik bi-maʿrifat aʿlām

madhhab Mālik 97
taṣawwuf 8, 9, 30, 197
tashbīh (Immanence) 49, 60, 61, 63, 66, 236
tawakkul (reliance on God) 78
ṭawāli' (lights) 78
Ṭawāsīn 48
tawba (turning away from wrong actions) 78
tawḥīd (God's Oneness) 20, 61, 78, 124, 171
Charles Taylor 102, 108, 110, 111
Dāwūd al-Ṭā'ī 16
technique 159, 160
technological age 145
technological exploitation 152
technological procedures 160
technological project 224
technological subordination 151
technological thinking 146
technology 91, 113, 141, 142, 150, 152, 153, 159, 205
technology and technical processes 224
tekkes 90
closing the *tekkes* 90
teleology 4, 110
temporality 142
tenets of the faith 88
Tenth Intelligence 172, 173
terrestrial world 173
terrorism 225
the Terror 218
textual codex 103
Sufyān al-Thawrī 16, 19
theism 206
theocentrism 151, 234
theologians 190, 231
theological studies 155
theology 36, 103, 111, 163, 164, 177, 234
theoretical knowledge 182
theory and practice 139
theory of correspondence 147
theory of emanation 173
theosophers 36, 231
theosophy 180, 187
things-in-themselves 135
thinking 143, 163
Third Antinomy of Kant 149
Thomas Aquinas 4
Thomist 156
Anthony Thomson 120
thought and being 139
Three Points of the Amman Message 92
three realms of existence 231
Throne (*'Arsh*) 44, 55, 57
Thucydides 227
Bassam Tibi 86
Tigris 23
Tījānī ṭarīqa 89
Paul Tillich 157
time 187
time of destiny (spiritual time) 194, 195, 200, 232
al-Tirmidhī 104, 105
Abadin Tadia Tjoessoep 90
totalitarianism 91, 114, 153, 218
the totalitarian model 122, 165
totalitarian states 203
Totality 134
total war 153, 234
Stephen Toulmin 167
trade and commerce 227
trading 203

traditional authority 84
traditional Christianity 149
traditional Christian society 234
traditional Islamic disciplines 187
transcendence 60
Transcendental Aesthetic 133
Transcendental Analytic 133
Transcendental Dialectic 133
Transcendental Logic 133
transcendent God 111, 149
the transformation of human beings into masses 145
transvaluation of all values 150, 161, 164
travelling 195
the treasury 69
trust in God 196
Tsarist Russians 89
Tunisia 99, 227
Alan Turing 62, 66, 167, 236
Turkey 5, 90, 116, 227
Turkoman 82
Turkoman Sufis 82
Nāṣir al-Dīn al-Ṭūsī 173, 175
twentieth century 138
two bow-lengths 11

U

ʿubbād (worshippers) 39, 196
Ubermensch (the Overhuman or the Overman) 141
UBS AG 220
ʿubūdiyya (obedience, service and devotion to God) 78, 123
ʿulamāʾ (scholars) 83
al-ʿulūm al-ḥaqīqiyya (real sciences) 181
ʿUmar al-Mukhtār 89
ʿUmar ibn al-Khaṭṭāb 14, 104
ʿUmar ibn ʿAbd al-ʿAzīz 15
Mohammad Umar 82
Umayyad 15
umm al-madhāhib (mother of the *madhhabs*) 106
umma (the whole Muslim community as one entity functioning within the world) 30, 33, 226
uncertainty principle 63
unconcealment 147
the Underman 153
unemployment 221
unfulfilled 'Heideggerian need' 143
unification of actions 72
unification of Attributes 72
unification of the Essence 72
unified theory of reality 136
unilateral devaluation 213
Unitarianism 108, 110, 111
unitary simplex 237
United Nations Organization 90, 93, 115
United Nations Organization. 93
United States of America 90
Unity 134, 193
unity of all existence 190
Universal Body 55
universal condemnation of usury 210
Universal Intellect 54
universality 119
universal reason 149
Universal Soul 54
Universiti Sains Malaysia 2
University of Bilbao 162
University of London 2
unjustified increase 210, 212

unjust trading practices 71
UNO 115
unseen 79
unveiling 79, 195
unveiling of Being 162
unveilings 196
USA 221
US Bank 221
US dollar 115
U.S. Senate 220
USSR 89
U.S. Supreme Court Judge 219
U.S. Treasury bills 215
uṣūl al-dīn (science of the principles of religion) 187
uṣūl al-fiqh (Islamic legal theory) 8, 25, 28, 34, 187
usurious clearinghouses 219
usurious transactions 235
usury 71, 222, 227
usury as legitimate business practice 207
usury-based capitalism 204
usury redefined as excessive interest 208
'Uthmān ibn 'Affān 14, 104
Utilitarianism 108, 109, 110
Utilitarian principle 111
utility 209
'uzla (retirement) 78

V

'Umar Vadillo 91, 92, 147, 213, 214
value 209
[verses] whose classification is unclear 179
victory of atheism over religion 234
vision 44
visionary experience 181, 182
vision of God 10, 189, 200
vision of the Divine Presence 231
visualising the letters of the Name 80
Voyages of Discovery 113

W

Rick Waddell 221
waḥda (single unified Reality) 192
waḥdat al-wujūd (unity of existence) 55, 189
Wahhabism 91
wahm (illusion) 42, 56
waḥy (revelation/inspiration) 26, 31, 163
wajd (the first degree of ecstasy, finding oneself) 78
walāya (sainthood) 85
Der Waldgang 162
Waldganger 161, 162, 164
al-walī al-kāmil 40
walī'allāh (friend of God) 193
wara' (scrupulousness) 18, 21, 78
waẓīfa (a wird) 77
wazirate (vizierate) 227
Muḥammad Waziri 39
wazīr (minister) 95
wazīrs (ministers) 83
wealth 71
The Wealth of Nations 112
weather changes 194
Max Weber 83, 84, 115, 117, 118
Wells Fargo 221
West Africa 93, 94
Western church 207
Western civilization 126, 139

Western liberal democracy 115
Western metaphysics 154, 155
Western philosophy 142, 144, 145, 150, 163, 166, 167, 234, 237
Western rationalism 225
Western thought 148
What is money? 209
Peter T. White 116, 215, 216
Mike Whitney 116
wijdān (the second degree of ecstasy) 78
wilāya (saintship) 20, 74, 79, 85
will of the people 218
will to power 148, 150, 151, 159, 161, 164, 234
Peter Winch 117
wird (recitation of a litany of *dhikr*) 77, 229
Withdrawal into the Perception of the Essence 48
withdrawal of Being 156
witnessing 198
Wittgenstein 102, 167
women's rights 92
work 160, 164
the 'worker' 160
World Bank 90, 115, 219
world domination 142, 153
world markets 220
world of matter 173
world of spirits 79
world state 159
world technology 153
world technology system 143
World Trade Organization 90, 115
worldview 187
World War One 150
worldwide civil war 225, 236
worship 232
worshipping God out of duty 198
worshipping God out of love 198
wujūd dhihnī (mental existence) 175
wujūd (existence) 78, 174, 175
wujūd khārijī (external existence) 175

Y

Yaḥyā ibn Yaḥyā 97
yaqīn (certainty) 20
yawm al-abad (day of eternity) 59
yawm al-sha'n (the day of the event) 58
yawm (day) 56
Mehdi Ha'iri Yazdi 167, 177, 178, 185
Mohamed Haj Yousef 58, 59, 64
yusfiru (he unveils) 195

Z

zāhid (ascetic) 29
ẓāhir (outward visage) 85
zakat 74, 94, 209
zamān fawq ṭabīʿī (para-natural time) 57
zamān ṭabīʿī (natural time) 57
zamān (time) 56
Zarathustra 140, 161
Aḥmad Zarrūq 9, 85
zāwiyas 2, 15, 81, 94, 100, 229, 230, 239
Zodiac 59
zoon logon echon (mistranslated as 'rational animal') 147, 154
Zoroastrianism 181
zuhd (doing-without) 78

www.ingramcontent.com/pod-product-compliance
Lightning Source LLC
Chambersburg PA
CBHW032017230426
43671CB00005B/111

* 9 7 8 0 9 9 5 3 8 8 4 0 6 *